BUILT BY SARGON II.
The architecture was of a more solid order than in the palace of his son Sennacherib at Kouyunjik; nevertheless, with its pilasters, battlements, and buttress-towers, it was by no means gross or ill-proportioned. The formation of the great tower is shown in full.

MINOR PROPHETS

BIBLE STUDY TEXTBOOK SERIES

MINOR PROPHETS

A Study of Micah Through Malachi

by

Clinton R. Gill

College Press, Joplin, Missouri

Copyright 1971
College Press

THE PROPHETS AND THEIR NEIGHBORS

PROPHET	CONTEMPORARY HISTORIC EVENT	DATE (B.C.)
Elijah	—Judah received tribute from Philistines and Arabians	c. 869
	—Israel wars with Syria, is victorious. Ahab makes alliance with defeated enemy Ben-Hadad II	
	—Judah in alliance with Ahab	
	—Israel furnishes troops to Syria against Assyria under Salmaneser III	c. 854
	—Judah invaded by Moabites, Ammonites and Edomites	c. 853
Elisha	—Moab attacked by kings of Israel, Judah and Edom	c. 852
	—Ben-Hadad II lays siege to Samaria	c. 846
	—Athaliah usurps throne of Judah	c. 842
	—Jehu exterminates house of Ahab, pays tribute to Shalmaneser III of Assyria	
Joel	—Hazael of Syria attacks Assyria, threatens Jerusalem, keeps Israel in subjection	c. 814
	—Israel's three victories over Syrians	
	—Amaziah hires mercenary army to fight against Edom	c. 797
	—Jeroboam defeats Judah, enlarges Israel's borders	c. 785
Amos	—Uzziah conquers Philistines and Arabians	c. 780
Hosea	—Judah in conflict with Assyria under Tiglath-Pileser	c. 748
	—Israel pays tribute to Assyria	
Isaiah	—Jotham in Judah keeps Ammonites in subjection, fortifies Judah and Jerusalem	c. 735
Micah	—Ahaz, defeated by Syria and Israel, makes alliance with Assyria	c. 734
	—Pekah and Rezin (of Syria) enter alliance against Judah	
	—Assyria captures northern and eastern districts of Israel under Tiglath-Pileser	
	—Israel enters alliance with So of Egypt	c. 727
	—Assyria, under Shalmaneser V, besieges Samaria	c. 724
	—Samaria falls to Sargon II of Assyria, captives carried away to far east	c. 722
	—Sargon captures Karkar, defeats Egypt at Raphia	c. 720
	—Sargon captures Ashdod	c. 711

v

THE PROPHETS AND THEIR NEIGHBORS

PROPHET	CONTEMPORARY HISTORIC EVENT	DATE (B.C.)
	—Sennacherib (successor to Sargon) invades Philistia and Judah	c. 701
	—Hezekiah submits to Sennacherib, pays tribute. Providential disaster to Assyrian army	c. 701
	—Sennacherib defeats Egypt at Eltekeh	
	—Assyria, under Esarhaddon, successor to Sennacherib, conquers Egypt	c. 681
	—Tirhakah regains throne and independence of Egypt	c. 670
	—Assyrians, under Assurbanipal, invade Egypt, sack Karnak (No-Amon)	
Nahum	—Josiah seeks Jehovah, books of law discovered in temple Temple repaired, covenant renewed	c. 623
	—Necho, Pharaoh of Egypt, marches through Palestine	
	—Cyaxares founds Median Empire	c. 633
	—Jehoahaz deposed by Necho on his return from Euphrates and carried into Egypt	c. 610
	—Nineveh, capital of Assyria, destroyed by Medes and Persians	c. 609
Daniel	—Nebuchadnezzar captures Jerusalem carries off sacred vessels to Babylon Daniel taken captive	c. 605
	—Necho of Egypt defeated by Nebuchadnezzar.	
	—Jehoiakim rebels against Babylon	c. 602
Ezekiel	—Jehoiachin captured by Nebuchadnezzar, Ezekiel taken captive to Babylon	c. 598
	—Zedekiah placed on throne of Judah by Nebuchadnezzar	c. 594
	—Zedekiah and other petty kings rebel against Babylon	c. 589
	—Nebuchadnezzar invades Jerusalem	
	—Jerusalem captured and destroyed Gedaliah appointed by Nebuchadnezzar to govern Judah	c. 587
Jeremiah	—Jeremiah carried away to Egypt	
	—Death of Nebuchadnezzar	c. 562
	—Cyrus captures Babylon . . . Darius made ruler, Daniel promoted by Darius	c. 538
	—Cyrus becomes sole ruler of Babylon, issues edict to benefit Jews	c. 536
	—Jews return home under Zerubbabel, attempt to rebuild temple	c. 535
Haggai	—Prophets urge people to rebuild	c. 520

THE PROPHETS AND THEIR NEIGHBORS

PROPHET	CONTEMPORARY HISTORIC EVENT	DATE (B.C.)
Zechariah	—Darius Hystaspis succeeds Cambyses, protects and aids Jews in rebuilding.	
	— Temple dedicated	c. 516
	—Battle of Marathon	490
	—Accession of Xerxes	486
	—Battle of Salamis	480
	—Esther becomes queen of Persia	c. 478
	—Accession of Artaxerxes	c. 465
	—Ezra leads caravan of Jews to Jerusalem	458
	—Nehemiah secures appointment as governor of Jews in Palestine.	445
Malachi	—Nehemiah returns briefly to court of Persia and comes back to correct evils of Jerusalem	433
	—Herodotus	444
	—Pericles in Athens	

"The things written aforetime were written for our learning." Romans 15:4

To

"Charlie", "Sue Sue", and "The Tiger"

PREFACE

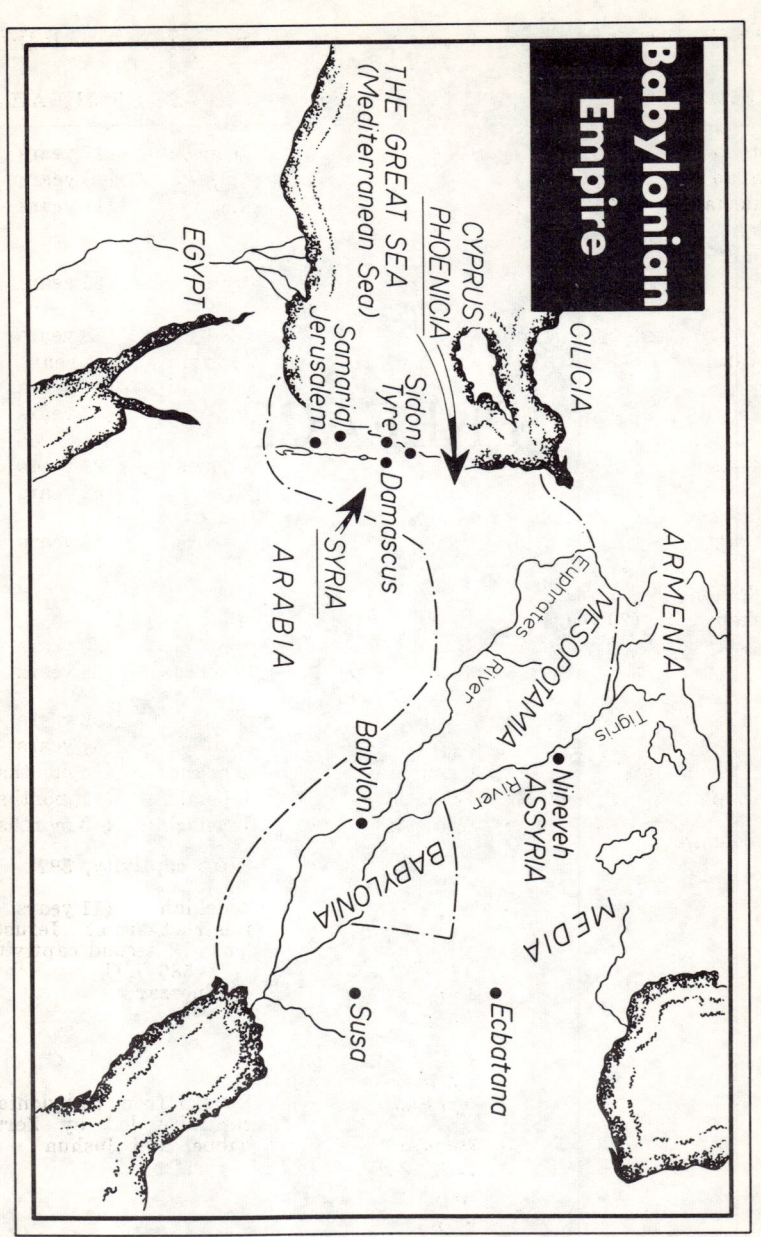

THE PROPHETS AND THEIR CONTEMPORARIES

KINGS OF ISRAEL		PROPHETS	KINGS OF JUDAH	
Jeroboam I	(22 years)		Rehoboam	(17 years)
Nadab	(2 years)		Abijam	(3 years)
Baasha	(24 years)		Asa	(41 years)
Elah	(2 years)			
Zimri	(7 days)			
Omri	(12 years)		Jehoshaphat	(25 years)
Ahab	(22 years)	Elijah		
Ahaziah	(2 years)		Jehoram	(8 years)
Joram	(12 years)		Ahaziah	(1 year)
			Athaliah	(7 years)
Jehu	(28 years)	Elisha	Joash	(40 years)
Jehoahaz	(17 years)	Joel		
Jehoash	(16 years)		Amaziah	(29 years)
Jeroboam II	(41 years)	Amos	Uzziah	(52 years)
Zachariah	(6 months)	Hosea		
Shallum	(1 month)		Jotham	(16 years)
Menahem	(10 years)			
Pekahiah	(2 years)			
Pekah	(20 years)		Ahaz	
Hosea	(9 years)	Isaiah	Hezekiah	(29 years)
		Micah	Manasseh	(55 years)
Captivity by Assyria under Sargon 721 B.C.		Zephaniah	Amon	(2 years)
		Nahum	Josiah	(31 years)
		Habakkuk	Jehoahaz	(3 months)
Fall of Nineveh 612 B.C. during reign of Jehoiakim		Jeremiah	Jehoiakim	(11 months)
		Daniel	Jehoiachin	(3 months)
			First captivity, 597	
			Zedekiah (11 years) Destruction of Jerusalem . . . second captivity . . . 586 B.C. by Nebuchadnezzar	
		Jeremiah Ezekiel		
		Fall of Babylon 539 B.C. to Cyrus of Persia	Return from Babylonian captivity led by Zerubabbel and Joshua	
		Haggai Zechariah Obadiah Malachi		

xi

CONTENTS

DEDICATION viii
PREFACE ix
CONTENTS xiii

Chapter I—HOW TO STUDY THE BIBLE 1
Chapter II—WHAT IS A PROPHET? 5
Chapter III—THE COVENANT THEME IN THE PROPHETS 10
Chapter IV—BAAL WORSHIP 22

— MICAH —

Chapter V—SUPERSCRIPTION 45
Chapter VI—FIRST CYCLE 51
Chapter VII—SECOND CYCLE 77
Chapter VIII—THIRD CYCLE 93
Chapter IX—FUTURE EXALTATION AND MESSIANIC HOPE 105
Chapter X—JEHOVAH'S CONTROVERSY WITH HIS PEOPLE 123

— NAHUM —

Chapter XI—PREFACE 144
Chapter XII—INTRODUCTION 148
Chapter XIII—DETAILS OF NINEVEH'S DOWNFALL 156
Chapter XIV—THE EPITAPH OF NINEVEH 161

— HABAKKUK —

Chapter XV—PREFACE TO HABAKKUK 170
Chapter XVI—HOW CAN GOD ALLOW INJUSTICE TO GO UNPUNISHED 171
Chapter XVII—THE SECOND QUESTION 177
Chapter XVIII—THE PROPHET'S POETIC PRAYER 192

— ZEPHANIAH —

Chapter XIX—INTRODUCTION TO ZEPHANIAH 201
Chapter XX—JUDGEMENT OF GOD 205
Chapter XXI—THE JUDGEMENT OF GOD IS UNIVERSAL 217
Chapter XXII—COMFORT AND CONSOLATION 221

MINOR PROPHETS

— HAGGAI —

Chapter XXIII—PREFACE TO HAGGAI 234
Chapter XXIV—EXPOSITION OF HAGGAI 238

— ZECHARIAH —

Chapter XXV—PREFACE TO ZECHARIAH 258
Chapter XXVI—INTRODUCTION TO SECTION I 262
Chapter XXVII—A VISION OF HORSES 264
Chapter XXVIII—A VISION OF FOUR HORNS AND SMITHS .. 268
Chapter XXIX—A VISION OF A MEASURING LINE 272
Chapter XXX—A VISION OF THE HIGH PRIEST 278
Chapter XXXI—A VISION OF A MENORAH AND
            OLIVE TREES 281
Chapter XXXII—A VISION OF A FLYING SCROLL 288
Chapter XXXIII—A VISION OF A WOMAN IN A
            FLYING BASKET 292
Chapter XXXIV—A VISION OF WAR CHARIOTS 296
Chapter XXXV—THE PROCLAMATION OF THE MESSIAH 300
Chapter XXXVI—TEACHING ABOUT WORSHIP 306
Chapter XXXVII—PREFACE TO SECTION II 321
Chapter XXXVIII—THE TRIUMPH OF ZION THROUGH
            HER MESSIAH 324
Chapter XXXIX—ISRAEL RESTORED 335
Chapter XL—A PARABLE OF SHEPHERDS 344
Chapter XLI—IN THE FIRST DAY 353
Chapter XLII—IN THE SECOND DAY 365

— MALACHI —

Chapter XLIII—INTRODUCTION 380
Chapter XLIV—DENUNCIATION OF UNFAITHFULNESS 381
Chapter XLV—THE COMING DAY OF THE LORD 394

BIBLIOGRAPHY 409

CHAPTER I
HOW TO STUDY THE BIBLE

In II Peter 1:20-21 we are informed; "... *no prophecy of scripture is of private interpretation. For no prophecy ever came by the will of man: but men spake from God, being moved by the Holy Spirit.*" This statement not only flatly affirms the fact of divine inspiration of the scriptures, it gives us a definite clue as to how to study them. It is not the task of the Bible student to interpret but to exegete.

Exegesis is a strange word to most of us. It is from the Greek *exegeomai* which means literally; "to lead out, to unfold." In contrast, to interpret is to "explain the meaning of . . . to have or show one's own understanding, to construe."

To study scripture, by the process of exegesis, is to apply certain scientific principles of investigation in the attempt to arrive at the thought which was in the mind of the inspired writer when he wrote. It is a safe assumption that "the Bible means what it says" when one has applied these principles and ascertained what it does say.

Interpretation, or explaining the meaning according to one's own understanding, should never be attempted until after the interpretor has made a careful exegesis of the passage to be explained. God did not give us a set of generalities which may be interpreted according to our own pre-conceived theology. Through inspired men (the exact method of inspiration is beside the point), He said something definite. It is the task of the Bible scholar to find out what is said.

To accomplish this, one must learn to carefully apply the principles of exegesis, much the same as they would be applied to any other writing . . . especially a writing as old as those which make up the sixty-six books of the Christian Scripture. Because of the age of the Biblical writings, exegesis becomes largely a matter of removing the differences in language, circumstance, custom, etc. which divide the ancient from the modern world. The Bible, and especially, the New Testament, was written in the language which was common to those who first read it. The *Koine* Greek in which the New Testament was written and into which the Old Testament had been translated was the common language of the street and market and household. The mode of self expression, the idioms and figures and allusions used were familiar to those who read. Hence it may be assumed the first readers of Scripture readily understood what may seem a dark saying to the most profound modern English-speaking Bible student. The rules, or principles of exegesis suggested here are the means by which these

1

differences are removed, and the simple yet profound thoughts of God recorded in the Bible made apparent to us.

RULE NO. 1 . . . Use a dictionary. Most Americans are unfamiliar with the Hebrew and Greek of the Bible, and so must rely on English translations. For this reason, it is inadvisable to limit oneself to a single translation. Every translation has its strengths and its weaknesses. By comparing several the student of the English Bible is much more likely to arrive at the thought presented in the original than he is if he uses only one translation.

No matter which translation, or translations one uses, the words in it represent in the opinion of the translator, the best possible transferal of thought from the original scripture text to the language of the reader. It is best not to assume that you know what a particular word means, especially if it is a key word in a verse or passage. An *unabridged* dictionary will usually give, as the first meaning of a word, the meaning of that word in the language from which we have borrowed it.

For an example; the Greek word *baptismo* may be defined in general American usage as "the application of water in the name of The Father, The Son, and The Holy Spirit." (As a matter of fact it is so defined in the MEMBERSHIP MANUAL of the Methodist Church.) WEBSTER'S NEW WORLD DICTIONARY OF THE AMERICAN LANGUAGE, on the other hand, gives the original meaning as "a dipping in (Gr. immersion)." Since God chose to record His Word in Hebrew and Greek, rather than English, it is never safe to be uncertain of the meaning of key words.

The translators of our English Bibles have used words which they believe best represent the original language. By using an unabridged dictionary as a study aid, you may be sure that the English word means to you what it meant to the translator.

RULE NO. 2 . . . Pay attention to grammar. Grammar is nothing more nor less than the organized presentation of thought. The translators usually do not attempt to follow the grammatical construction of the original, because to do so would result in a translation very difficult for an English speaking person to read.

However, just as in the choice of individual words, so in the grammatical constructions, the translators have attempted to represent the *thought* of the original.

Many people do not like to study grammar. Even in elementary and high school they found it very tedious. This is unfortunate because it is impossible to understand a written thought without applying the rules of grammar, either consciously or instinctively. In any event, the serious student of the Word of God cannot afford to ignore this basic rule of exegesis. A very helpful tool to refresh yourself on the rules of English grammar is *Plain English Handbook,* McCormick-Mathers Publishing Company.

RULE NO. 3 . . . Mind the context. Words mean *nothing,* or rather, they may mean *anything* out of a specific context. The word context means literally "to weave together." The thoughts of various words, phrases, clauses, sentences, paragraphs, and chapters are woven into one complete whole. To take a word or a verse out of context is to cut out a small piece from a plaid garment. It does not accurately represent the whole pattern of thought presented by the Author of the book from which it was taken; and so may be made to say something entirely different than which the Author would have us learn.

A rather humorous illustration of the importance of context comes to mind: A verse of Scripture says "muzzle not the oxen that treadeth out the corn." Another verse says "for of such is the kingdom of haeven." The logical conclusion from these two verses is that there are oxen in heaven" . . . the Bible says so." Of course the Bible does not say so unless these particular verses are wrenched out of context. The proof texts of every denominational creed and of every religious cult claiming to be Christian are used in just this way, and with much more serious consequences than the ridiculous conclusion that there are oxen in heaven.

Or take for instance the word "run". In modern parlance it may mean "to move rapidly"; it may refer to a score in a baseball game; or it may refer to a snag in a nylon. The words of the Bible are like that. They mean many things out of context. But in a particular subject in a given set of circumstances they mean only one thing.

RULE NO. 4 . . . Study historically. The books of the Bible were written to real people, at a time and place in history. Their lives were lived under conditions very different from those of twentieth century America.

The culture was the culture of the orient, the middle east, the ancient Egyptians, the Greeks and the Romans. The language was that of the "Partheans and Medes and Elamites and the dwellers in Mesopotamia, in Judea, and Capadocia and Asia" *(Acts 2:9-10)* **and dozens of** other places and peoples which fall like strange sounds on the ears. They lived in the days of Sargon and Shallamanezer and No-Amon and Caesar and Herod. Their concepts of deity were formed in the crucible of Baalism and Jehovah worship, and all the varying degrees of pantheism which fall between. They pledged allegiance not to "The United States of America and to the republic for which it stands," but to Babylonia and Memphis and Athens and Rome . . . and to the God of Abraham and Isaac and Jacob. David was not a little boy who killed a giant in Sunday School, but the great king of Israel in whose image it was hoped the Messiah would come and establish His kingdom as the final world power in the never ending sequence of world powers.

It is amazing, and thrilling to see the Scriptures come alive with real people in real situations . . . and it's relatively easy to transport oneself back into Bible times. For a few dollars one can buy HALLEY'S BIBLE HANDBOOK, and for a few more dollars THE WYCLIFFE HISTORICAL GEOGRAPHY OF BIBLE LANDS. For what most Christians spend on a few years of vacations and fishing and golf and convention going, one ca actually visit the lands of the Bible. Nothing will add the dimension of history to Bible study quite so quickly and profoundly as a few weeks in the land where it all happened. Short of a college education with a Bible major it is doubtful if anything is more valuable to the Christian who would understand the Bible.

RULE NO. 5 . . . Study analytically. There is no more sure way of being certain of one's understanding of a given passage of Scripture than to compare one's conclusions concerning this passage with what the Bible in general teaches on the same subject. If your conclusions concerning a passage clash with what you have learned from the rest of the Bible about the same subject it is time to review *both*. Either you have misunderstood this passage, or you have overlooked something in what the rest of the Bible says. *The Bible does not contradict itself.*

There is an inherent danger in this particular rule of study. To study analytically *before* having applied the other rules of exegesis is to run the risk of misunderstanding the whole Bible on a given subject. One has a tendency, unless one is on his guard, to ignore the historical circumstances and the context of certain verses and fall into the trap of skipping about looking for proof-texts. This is the fundamental weakness in such mythology as premillenialism, adventism, etc.

Such systems are based on "grasshopper interpretation," rather than sensible exegesis. So beware the chart and the outline of proof-texts when studying one passage in the light of other passages.

RULE NO. 6 . . . *Use the commentaries.* This must be done *last* if one is to be free to draw his own conclusions without being unduly influenced by what others think a passage of Scripture means. However, it is always helpful, once one has made his own investigation of Scripture, to know what others have learned.

Throughout the entire process of study, bear in mind that the things of God are spiritually discerned. *(I Corinithians 2:10-15).* A prayer for guidance will not make your understanding of the Bible infallible, but it will open up the channels through which the thoughts of God must pass if they are to enter your heart as well as your head. The process of Bible study is the process of thinking the thoughts of God after Him. By following these simple rules, one places himself in a much more advantageous position to hear what God has said.

CHAPTER II

WHAT IS A PROPHET?

There is a need at the outset to answer the question "what is a prophet"? The current atmosphere in America evidences two views of this question which are poles apart and mutually contradictory. The one tends to make of the prophet a clairvoyant mystic with some unexplicable insight into future events. A popular magazine recently ran a feature article listing the amazing predictions of half a dozen of the more popularly known clairvoyants and describing their more sensational predictions, (eg. the assassination of President Kennedy, the outcome of future presidential elections, etc.)

The mystic insight attributed to these secular seers is closely akin to the "powers" attributed by certain fundamentalists to the prophets of the Bible. In both there is an exaggerated emphasis upon and concern for the foretelling of future events which makes of the prophet little more than a fortune-teller.

At the opposite extreme is the concept of the Biblical prophet as merely a normal man with *above* normal insights into moral, spiritual and ethical truth. This concept plays down, denies or ignores the futuristic aspects of prophecy, according to the theology of the commentator.

MINOR PROPHETS

It would seem that the truth about prophets and prophecy resolves itself to: (1) what did the prophet do, (2) how did he do it, and (3) why did he do it?

We will move a great way toward answering these questions by taking a long look at the word "prophet" itself. As is often the case with key words of Scripture, the translators have chosen rather to transliterate than to translate. Whether this be because such words are often too pregnant to be done justice by a single English word (English is neither a language of religious expression, as is Hebrew, or of philosophic expression, as is ancient Greek), or because the translators are concerned with selling books to widely diverse audiences, the difficulty remains that the word "prophet" is merely a transliteration of the Greek *prophetes*. As such it means nothing to an English speaking reader, excepting as his religious prejudices supply him with a preconceived notion of its meaning.

Since we are presently concerned with the prophets of the Old Testament, who wrote in Hebrew, rather than the New Testament prophets, who wrote in Greek, we must take notice that the Greek *prophetes* (prophet) is used in the Septuagint (the Greek version of the Old Testament popular in the first century) to represent not one but three Hebrew words. Each of these Hebrew synonyms is used, in various contexts, to refer to what our English versions, both Old and New Testaments, call simply by the transliterated "prophet."

First . . . "Prophet" is used to translate the Hebrew *roeh*. When this word is used there seems to be some emphasis upon the *means* by which God communicates His message to the spokesman. It is frequently rendered "seer."

Second . . . The Hebrew *chozeh* seems to share with *roeh* the concern for the means by which the message of God comes to the messenger. It also is translated *seer* as well as prophet.

Third . . . and most frequently used is the word *nabi*. Interestingly, this word means, at its root, "to bubble over." It suggests that the prophet is first himself filled with the Spirit and message of God, and that this filling is so complete that it bubbles over as the spiritual message of God spills out for the benefit of God's people. There seems little justification for the association with this word of the idea of emotional ecstasy. More to the point is Jesus' statement to the woman at the well that ". . . the water that I shall give him shall become in him a well of water springing up (literally, bubbling over) unto eternal life."

Far more than "it shall come to pass," the watchword of the

WHAT IS A PROPHET?

prophets was "THUS SAITH THE LORD!" It is claimed for them and by them that "the Word of the Lord came unto" them. *(Isaiah 38:4, Jeremiah 18:1, Ezekiel 20:2, Hosea 1:1, Joel 1:1, Micah 1:1, Zephaniah 1:1, Haggai 1:1.)* The prophet was a man possessed by God. *(I Chronicles 16:22, Psalms 105:15).* More than merely one who spoke *for* God, he was one *through* whom God spoke. *(Hosea 12:10, Zechariah 7:7, Hebrews 1:1)* His message was not his own. Rather it came directly from God through vision *(II Chronicles 32:32, Isaiah 6, Lamentations 2:9)* and without this prophetic vision the people perished *(Proverbs 29:18).*

It was not the task of the prophet to give counsel and advice. He was rather a bringer of divine command *(II Chronicles 29:25).* It was in this sense that Moses spoke both of himself and The Christ as prophets.

The thunderings of the prophets against sin were not merely those of social reformers who would build a better society, but were warnings of disaster to a people whose disobedience of God's commands threatened not only their ethnic existence but God's own purpose in bringing them into being and sustaining them as a people. *(Nehemiah 9:30)*

It is not surprising that the most succinct statement in the divine record concerning both the prophetic message and its source is to be found in the New Testament. A few moments spent considering this statement in *II Peter 1:20-21* will prove extremely helpful to our present task of understanding the prophets themselves:

Two words come to special attention in this passage. *First* . . . the word *prophecy.* In light of what has been said concerning the overriding purpose of the prophet, we ought never suppose that the word "prophecy" can be limited to what the prophet said about future events. A prophecy is *any* pronouncement made by a prophet . . . on *whatever* subject.

The term prophecy is derived from the word *prophet.* As mentioned, previously, this word is not generally translated in the English versions, but is rather a transliteration, a mere transposing of letters. Its meaning is obscured rather than rendered by such indirectness on the part of the translators.

In the language of both the New Testament and the Septuagint, (from which the New Testament writers quote) *prophetes* (prophet) is a compound of *pro,* meaning "before" in reference *primarily* to place rather than time, as a speaker stands "before" his audience, with *phemi,* meaning "to declare or report, especially quoting *the words of another.*"

A prophet, then, was one who stood before God's people and spoke God's word. A "prophecy" is anything the prophet said.

Second . . . the word Scripture, *(Graphes)* means simply a writing . . . any writing. "Prophecy of Scripture" is simply the written record of the prophet's message.

This recorded message, says Peter, is not a matter of "private interpretation." In this context Peter refers to the *source* of the prophet's message. What he said was not his own interpretation of a given set of historic circumstances and their bearing on the ultimate purpose of God. Rather, "men spake from God, being moved by the Holy Spirit."

By the same token, our understanding of the written account of the prophet's message can never be according to our own views and opinions. It is just here that the most violence is done to the divine record of prophecy by those who would force prophecy, especially those passages dealing with eschatology, into the molds of their own systems.

To say it briefly, the prophet meant what he said. It is our task, through applying the rules of exegesis, to find out what he said rather than trying to make him say what we want him to mean!

There was no greater danger in Israel than that posed by the false prophet. *(Deuteronomy 13:1-5, I Kings 22:22-23, Isaiah 9:15)* The false prophets taught untruths in the name of God. *(Jeremiah 14:14)* That which they taught was not of God but was their own deceived notions *(Jeremiah 23:26)*. They saw false and deceptive visions *(Lamentations 2:14)*. Their personal lives were ungodly *(Jeremiah 23:11)*, wanton and faithless *(Zephaniah 3:4)*. Consequently their prophecying led God's people astray. *(Micah 3:5)*.

In brief, the false prophet was the exact antithesis of the true prophet. The true prophet, since he was to be God's spokesman, was first a man through whom God *could* speak. If the false prophet was faithful, in a sense greater than just being "true to God". He was faithful in that he believed God explicitly and trusted Him to do what He promised, or on occasion threatened, to do.

If the false prophet was ungodly, the true prophet was godly. Godliness, as the prophets lived it, was more than mere mortality; it was a constant conscious awareness of a real, contemporary God, which controlled their every thought and act. If the false prophet was wanton, the true prophet was selfless to the point of martyrdom. Indeed, it has been suggested that martyrdom is the identifying mark of the true prophet. It is not true that every genuine prophet was put to death by those to whom he spoke, yet such was so nearly true that Stephen could challenge his tormentors with "Which of the prophets

WHAT IS A PROPHET?

did not your fathers persecute? and they killed them that showed before of the coming of the Righteous One . . ." *(Acts 7:52)*

It may be said, that the primary function, perhaps the sole function, of the prophet at the time of the minor prophets was to turn God's people back to God's covenant. *(Nehemiah 9:26)* Whatever was said about the future was intended to accomplish this overriding purpose.

Israel, to whom the prophets were sent, were God's people. Ideally they were a theocracy. Though they were headstrong (Stephen would say stiffnecked) to the point of rejecting God's rule over them to clamor for a king, God still endeavored to rule them as His covenant people.

During the period of the judges this rule was direct. In the period of transition from the judges to the kings it was Samuel who acted as kingmaker; and Samuel, the last of the judges, is also called a prophet.

While the kingdom was united, God still spoke to His people through prophets. The king himself was not exempt. It was the prophet who confronted David face to face with his theft of "the little ewe lamb."

Prophetic activity, in so far as the *writing* prophets are concerned, reached its peak during the period of the divided kingdom. There is a note almost of desperation in the voice of God as He tries again and again through His prophets to recall a people who will not be ruled anymore by Him.

Following the return from captivity, the people, and there were pitifully few of them, persisted in their rebellion against the rule of God. The Old Testament closes with a last plaintive warning of the consequences in the message of a prophet.

The sum of the matter is that from Moses to Malachi, the prophets served as the voice of God, first in the giving of the Law and then in the repeated insistence that God must rule, indeed that He *could* rule only through obedience to His law. *Whatever the prophets said about the future was said in the attempt to motivate God's people to obey Him,* either by holding forth the glories of God's eternal purpose toward which His rule was leading or by stern warnings of the consequences of failure to cooperate, by obedience, in the accomplishment of that purpose.

It must be born in mind, as noted by Jack P. Lewis, that "prophecy is conditional *(Jeremiah 18:5-11)* (when it speaks of the future).

The question must be kept before you: have the conditions of this threat or promise been met?"

CHAPTER III

THE COVENENT THEME IN THE PROPHETS

"The Blood Red Thread" which holds the Bible together is the covenant in which God promised to bless all the nations of the earth through the seed of Abraham. To think of the Judaeo-Christian system as "Man's search for God" is to think of a mouse in search of a cat! Not that God is playing cat and mouse, but that the search is so obviously in the other direction. It is God who seeks man, not man who seeks God. Redemption is God's idea, not man's!

The search began with God's cry, "Adam, Where art thou?" *(Genesis 3:9)* The answer came back from Calvary; "My God, my God, why hast thou forsaken me?" *(Matthew 27:46)* Both were the cries of anguish from the broken hearts of parent and child.

When the very best Man cried out from the cross it was because He was face to face with the experience of being lost. The ultimate of this experience is death, "the wages of sin." When Jesus was "made sin on our behalf" *(II Corinithians 5:18-19),* He experienced, in our behalf the meaning of "lost."

Whatever God may have done in the eons of time touched so briefly in the first eleven chapters of Genesis, it was the call of Abram in *Genesis 12:1-3* which set in motion the "Scheme of Redemption" that was to climax at Calvary. In the making of the everlasting covenant, established at this call, God revealed to man the only way back to God by virtue of His unmerited favor made effective through obedient faith.

The covenant was proposed by God, not man. Man can only respons on God's terms. *(Ephesians 2:8)* The heart of the covenant was the promise that through it all the nations of the earth will be blessed in the seed of Abraham. The New Testament identifies that "seed" as Christ, *(Galatians 3:16)* and as those baptized into Him. *(Galatians 3:27-29)*

The theme of the Bible is the history of this covenant, and its fulfillment in Christ, through the new covenant people. It is the record of God's working in the history of His covenant people to "recon-

THE COVENANT THEME

cile the world unto Himself." *(II Corinithians 5:19)*. The Covenant of Promise first began to be fulfilled in "all that Jesus began to do and to teach *(Acts 1:1)* and continues to be fulfilled through the new covenant people, the church *(Galatians 3:29)*.

Jesus indicated that two things stand written in the *Old Testament* Scriptures: (1) that the Christ should suffer and be raised the third day and, (2) that repentance and remission of sins should be preached in His name among all the nations beginning at Jerusalem. *(Luke 24:44-48)* The church thus becomes, under the New Covenant the continuing presence of Christ in the world" . . . His body, the fullness of Him that filleth all in all . . ." *(Ephesians 1:23)*

It has always been God's intent, ultimately, to offer reconciliation to every man who would respond to Him in obedient faith. In the Old Testament, those descendants of Abraham *who remained in the covenant relationship* through obedient faith were His people. Those who went off after strange gods were cut off. It was not physical ancestry that maintained this arrangement, but obedient faith. *Through the covenant* Abraham became the father of the *faithful* under both the Old and New Covenant. *(Galatians 3:6-9)*

Since it was the task of the prophets to call a rebellious people back to obedient faith in order to maintain the covenant through which all the families of the earth would be blessed, we must be familiar with the covenant in order to understand the message of the prophets.

The first mention of the covenant between God and Abram is brief and to the point. Recorded in *Genesis 12:1-3*, this simple statement contains all the essential elements to be found in the expanded records of the covenant seen progressively throughout the rest of the Old Testament. In this sense, Genesis twelve is the beginning of the Bible. The first eleven chapters of Genesis are the preface.

The heart of the covenant, indeed the heart of the Bible is, "For God so loved the *world* that He gave His only begotten Son, that *whosoever* believeth in Him should not perish, but have everlasting life." *(John 3:16)* This is the Gospel which God "preached beforehand unto Abraham, saying "In thee shall all the nations of the earth be blessed." *(Galatians 3:8)*

God's eternal purpose in man, so far as it has been revealed to man, is that God shall rule, as Father, within each man through the obedience of faith. As W. O. Carver has put it, "(the purpose of God) is the *spiritual* ideal wherein all shall know God, from the least to the greatest."

Since man first sinned, it has been God's intent to call, out of the rebellious race, a people for His own possession . . . a people who will commit themselves to Him as Father so as to allow Him to adopt them as sons. *(Ephesians 1:3-5)*

The call began with Abraham, when he lived in Ur. All that is necessary to bring sinful man back into divine sonship is implicit in the covenant made with this man. Whom God *chooses* He *calls,* whom He *calls,* He *blesses,* whom He *blesses* He *commissions.* The *called* continue to receive the *blessings* of God only so long as they continue to carry out the *commission. The commission in every age always moves toward the bringing of men back into God's family by His grace made operative through obedient faith.*

In the case of Abraham, the call was direct. God spoke to him personally and called him out of his home, away from his people. The Hebrew writer reminds us that "by *faith* Abraham, when he was called, *obeyed* to go out, not knowng whither he went.'" This is faith expressing itself in obedience. Upon this obedient faith, Abraham was blessed. God said; "I will make of thee a great nation, and I will bless thee and make thy name great." *(Genesis 12:2* (a) *).*

As the recipient of these blessings, Abraham was commissioned; "Be thou a blessing." *(Genesis 12:2* (b) *).* Being faithful to the commission, he would receive further blessing; "I will bless them that bless thee and curse them that curse thee." *Genesis 2:3* (a) *).*

The conclusion of this brief first account of the covenant is a simple statement of its purpose; ". . . in thee shall all the nations of the earth be blessed."

Throughout this passage *(Genesis 12:1-3)* it is impossible to escape the implication that the call, the blessings, the commission, the continued blessings and the purpose are not intended for Abraham alone, but for all those who by obedient *faith* were to become the sons of Abraham. This implication is to be found in all the great historical epochs of the Bible. As C. C. Crawford points out, "We do not have three religious systems revealed therein . . ." *(ie.* patriarchal, Jewish, and Christian). Rather, we have the record of God at work in His covenant people to accomplish His eternal purpose in man by reconciliation of all humanity through the covenant people in general and the *"Seed"* (singular) of Abraham (*i.e.* Christ) in particular. *(Galatians 3:16)*

The expanded record of the covenant found in Genesis seventeen forcefully reiterates that which is stated in the shorter record of *Genesis 12:1-3.* Here emphasis is placed upon the multiplication of Abraham's descendants. Abraham was to be multiplied exceedingly. Three

THE COVENANT THEME

times it is said he shall be the father of many nations. His name is changed to Abraham (from Abram) for this season. Kings were to come out of him.

The Covenant is to be established not only between God and Abraham, but between Him and Abraham's descendants "in their generations," (*i.e.* each in its own time for an *everlasting* covenant. He will be *God* to these *covenant* people, beginning with Abraham and continuing through his descendants. *His descendants are those who trust and obey God. (Galatians 3:7)*

All the land of Canaan is to be given to Abraham and his seed after him for an everlasting covenant on the condition, *"I will be their God."*

Finally comes the stern directive, *"Thou Shalt Keep My Covenant, Therefore, And Thy Seed After Thee In Their Generations."*

Later, the seed had indeed "multiplied exceedingly" so that a law must be given which would mold the family into a nation. The fundamental condition of the covenant, namely that *He* would be their *God*, became the first commandment of the law "Thou Shalt have no other gods before me." *(Exodus 20:3)* The Law would be given only after the people had sworn to keep the covenant. *(Exodus 19:5-8)*

The *Genesis 17* record of the covenant closes with the giving of the symbol of the covenant, which would later become a command of the Law, *ie.* that every male be circumcised. *(Leviticus 12:3, Deuteronomy 10:16)* It is important that we not miss the symbolism of circumcision. ". . . the uncircumcised manchild whose flesh of his foreskin has not been circumcised, that *soul* shall be cut off from his people; *he hath broken the covenant." (Genesis 17:14)* Circumcision, the symbol of God's agreement with His people was from the beginning intended as a constant warning of the consequences of breaking the covenant. As, in circumcision, flesh was cut off in initiating one into the covenant relationship with God, so a spiritual cutting off from God would result from breaking the covenant. Every Israelite who rejected Jesus, the fulfillment of the covenant, bore in his own body a warning of the consequences! To break the covenant was to forfeit the promise!

Two thousand years after Abraham, the first Christian martyr accused his tormentors of being "uncircumcised in heart and ears," *(Act 7:51)* and later Paul was to write, "We are the circumcision, who worship God in the spirit . . . and have no confidence in the flesh . . ." *(Philippians 3:3* compare *Deuteronomy 30:6)*

From beginning to end, the covenant depended upon *obedient faith,* upon worshipping God "in spirit and truth," rather than upon physical ancestry alone. Any man who failed in this, though he be a direct descendant of Abraham in the flesh and a citizen of the Commonwealth of Israel, could expect to be *cut off* in the spirit from God.

The re-statement of the everlasting covenant to Isaac, Abraham's son, and Jacob, Abraham's grandson, did not change the original purpose of God in calling Abraham and his seed into the covenant relationship with Himself. Nor did the re-affirmation of that same covenant with the nation of Israel at the giving of the Law alter the divine purpose . . . *(cf. Galatians 3:17)*

It *was* a re-affirmation which took place when God molded the family of Abraham into a nation by giving them the law. God did not make a *new* covenant at Sinai. Rather He gave a law which was to govern the nation who had agreed to the covenant. *(Exodus 19:5-8)* The heart of the covenant was still ". . . in thee shall all the nations of the earth be blessed." The covenant relationship still depended upon *the obedience of faith.* This obedience was now to be expressed in obedience to the law.

So, as Paul informs us, ". . . the covenant, confirmed beforehand by God, the law . . . doth not disannul, so as to make the promise of none effect." *(Galatians 3:17)*

Israel, under the law, was to be a nation of priests. *(Exodus 19:6)* The primary function of the priest is to mediate between God and man and offer sacrifices. As a nation of priests, Israel should have been vitally concerned for the relationship of all peoples to God. The failure of national Israel which turned her divine priesthood into bigotry and her Messianic hopes into nationalistic ambition did not alter the purpose of God in those faithful covenant people *within* the nation. Those who were concerned for the *obedience of faith* rather than nationalism and racial pride were still His people, the *real* Israel.

It was because the majority of Abraham's descendants forgot the main thrust of the covenant toward the blessing of all men, that Paul was constrained to write, ". . . they are not all Israel, that are of Israel." *(Romans 9:6)* In God's eyes, true Israel's primary concern was the covenant and its promise of a divine redeeming Seed. These were a minority among the citizens of the nation of Israel.

The real meaning of the covenant is seen in *Genesis 22:22.* Isaac (Abraham's seed) was sacrificed, showing that the blessing of all nations promised by the covenant could only come about through the sacrifice of the True Seed. Here is also demonstrated the truth that the fulfillment of the covenant depended upon *obedient faith* on the part of the covenant people and not *just* upon the seed's being descended from Abraham.

Since the idea of the covenant relationship between Jehovah and His people is the most basic idea in God's dealing with Israel, it profoundly effects the whole moral and ethical outlook of the prophets *(cg. Micah 4:1-3).* The Law of Moses simply codified the ethical and moral precepts implicit in the covenant. It spelled out the meaning of *obedient faith.*

The call of the prophets was a call to moral and ethical repentence, as well as religious obedience to the law. A call to repentence is never the establishment of a *new* ethic. It is necessarily a plea rather to return to the old. The call of the prophets was a call to keep the *everlasting* covenant by obeying the law of God.

Whether it be Jeremiah or John or Jesus or the church preaching "repentance and remission of sins," *(Luke 24:44-47)* the call is the same. God's people, who have missed the mark of eternal morality implied in the covenant and spelled out in the law, must turn once more to the eternal ethic of Jehovah.

We, who would come into God's family under the New Covenant, without the necessity of first having been under the Old, cannot escape the necessity of repentance by pleading ignorance. Having never become familiar with the codified ethic of the Covenant as established in the law we must nevertheless repent, "for when Gentiles that have not the law do by nature the things of the law, these, not having the law are the law unto themselves, in that they show the work of the law written in their hearts, their conscience bearing witness therewith and their thoughts one with another accusing or else excusing them . . ." *(Romans 2:14-15)* The eternal morality of God is universal, else the promise of the covenant to bless all men is not valid.

When Jesus opened the eyes of His apostles to understand the Old Covenant Scriptures in terms of His own identiity, ministry, suffering and resurrection, He concluded that the end of it all is "that repentence and remission of sins should be preached in *all the nations,* beginning at Jerusalem." *(Luke 24:47)* John's comment on Jesus' conversation with Nicodemus, recognized as the "golden text of the Bible" states God's love as universal. *(John 3:16)* God has kept His promise to bless all men in Abraham's Seed.

God's concern that *all* men should hear of the remission of sins and be challenged to return to Him did not *begin* in Luke's Gospel. Nor did God *begin* to love the world the night Jesus was born. In the Old Testament as well as the New, God moves in universal love to redeem *all* men. God loved the whole world of men from the beginning, else Jesus would never have been born!

From the giving of the law it was the nation formed of Abraham's descendants through whom God moved his purpose forward toward the fullness of time *(Galatians 4:4-5),* when the promised Seed of Abraham should appear to bless all men. The task of the prophets was to recall the covenant people to the keeping of the law, not only to preserve their physical national identity but, more significantly, to preserve the spiritual genetic of *obedient faith.* It was this spiritual genetic through which the covenant was to be fulfilled as "they that are of *faith,* the same are sons of Abraham. And the Scripture, foreseeing that God would justify the Gentiles by faith, preached the gospel beforehand unto Abraham, saying 'in thee shall all the nations be blessed." *(Galatians 3:7-8)*

First century (A.D.) Judaism made the law, which was the means to the greater end of fulfilling the covenant, the end in itself. The nation framed by the law came to be the sole object of God's affection in the mind of the Jew. National ambitions and Jewish welfare as a political kingdom overshadowed the greater purpose of God *(ie.* the blessing of all men by calling them to a new covenant).

This narrow nationalism is understandable, when one considers the Roman yoke under which first century Israel galled. However, we must avoid the pitfall which prevented Israel from accepting the promised Seed of Abraham when He came, namely *the reading of Jewish nationalism into the message of the Old Testament prophets.*

Again to quote W. O. Carver, "The answer to Jewish narrowness was the Jew's Bible!" The task of the prophets was to recall God's covenant people to His law to be used of Him to bless all the nations. Not everyone who could trace his physical ancestry back to Abraham certainly not everyone who was a citizen of the first century Jewish commonwealth, was included. Abraham is the father, not of the Jew *per se,* but of the faithful. *(Galatians 3:7)*

THE REMNANT

Faced with the rebellion of both the northern and southern kingdoms and the impending overthrow of each, the 8th century prophets began to realize that *most* of the physical descendants of Abraham, the children of Israel, were simply not going to "make it." Whatever God was going to accomplish through Israel as a covenant people would be accomplished only through those within the commonwealth who remained faithful to the covenant. These the prophets referred to as "the remnant."

Several Hebrew synonyms are used to designate these faithful, but the central idea is the same in each. It is the faithful minority who remain aware of the covenant with God who are to form the "holy seed" for the New Israel (the church) under the new covenant. It is the *remnant alone* who were truly *"Israel."* The term "remnant" is used in several passages to refer only to the historic few who returned from the Babylonian captivity, but in many more passages the remnant takes on distinct Messianic overtones. It is the faithful few through whom God will bless all nations in fulfillment of His covenant.

These faithful few are a holy seed, a spiritual kernal within the nation. They were to survive the calamaties which befell the rebellious nation and become the germ of the eternal people of God. They were to be blessed of God and to be a blessing. The number of the physical descendants of Abraham would be "as the sands of the sea," but only the remnant would be saved. (Compare *Isaiah 10:22* and *Romans 9:27, 11:5*)

Ahijah is the first prophet to utter this idea *(I Kings 16)*. Isaiah connects the remnant with the children *who keep the covenant (II Kings 19:34)*. He recalls the promise to David, (reiterated by the God of the covenant), that the children of the covenant should sit upon the throne, *if the children kept the covenant.*

In *II Kings 21:10-14* is the warning that even the remnant must pass through the captivity because of Baal worship in the land.

Ezra 9:14 expresses concern that the commands of God will again be broken after the return from Babylon and that consequently God would consume them "so that there should be no remnant nor escaping."

Isaiah 10:20-22 records the prophetic visions of the preservation of the remnant: "The people are as the sands of the sea, yet a remnant shall return."

Isaiah 11:11-12 indicates that the remnant includes even some who are of the ten "lost tribes" of the northern kingdom who would be assembled together with the dispersed of Judah.

Isaiah 46:3 promises deliverance to all the remnant of the house of Jacob.

Jeremiah 23:3 sets down the promise of God to "gather the remnant of my flock out of all countries whither I have driven them." This promise is accompanied by another; "Behold the days come, saith the Lord, that I will raise unto David a righteous Branch, and a king shall reign and prosper and shall execute judgment in the earth." The

MINOR PROPHETS

echo of these promises is found in *Acts 2:5* when *devout* Jews from every nation under heaven gathered together to hear the first apostolic sermon.

Jeremiah also pictures the joy among the chief of nations that was to accompany the deliverance of the remnant. *(Jeremiah 31:7-ff)*

Ezekiel is less optimistic. He fears for the "full end of the remnant of Israel." *(Ezekiel 11:13)*

Micah 2:12 looks beyond the captivity to the gathering of the remnant. *Micah 4:7* associates the making up of the remnant with the establishment of the Messianic kingdom, and *Micah 5:7-8* depicts the remnant to be "in the midst of many people . . . among the Gentile.' It was to these that Paul would go first in every city.

Micah 7:18 takes into account the necessity of redemption even on the part of the faithful few as he portrays God passing over the transgressions of the remnant.

Zephaniah 3:13 makes note of the righteousness of the redeemed remnant.

The point of all this is, of course, that the threat of disaster to the commonwealth of Israel could never exhaust the whole purpose of God. The nation might be, indeed finally was, cut off, but God's purpose in his people would find fulfillment through the faithful remnant.

The scope of this writing, as the final volume of the BIBLE TEXTBOOK SERIES, is the last seven of the minor prophets. We shall now review the highlights of the covenant theme in each of these books in turn. It is suggested that the reader study carefully Jesus' approach to the Old Testament by which He opened the eyes of the Twelve "that they might understand the Scriptures" *(Luke 24:44-49)*, and the unfolding of the covenant promise in Acts.

With this approach clearly in mind, it is further suggested that the reader review *all* the Old Testament prophets from Jesus' point of view. It is a rewarding experience to read the Old Testament through His eyes and see the everlasting covenant move forward to its fulfillment in Him and the church, the real Israel of God.

For our present purposes in completing the final volume of the series, we begin with Micah. While the judgments of Micah are leveled against the rebellious covenant people, the *universal* concern of God is seen at once in *Micah 1:2*. Micah's exclamation includes not only "all ye people", the common term for the children of Israel, but ". . . . hearken, O earth, and all that therein is." All the nations of the earth have a stake in the repentance of God's covenant people!

THE COVENANT THEME

When Jesus sat at supper with the two downcast disciples in Emmaus and "beginning from Moses and from all the prophets He interpreted to them in all the Scriptures the things concerning Himself . . ." *(Luke 24:13-35)* He no doubt recited such passages as *Micah 1:4-5* and *5:2-5*.

Micah sees Jehovah as the Master of all the nations. In his prophecy, as well as that of other Old Testament writers may be traced the outline of the way by which God's sway over all men is to be brought about. People from all nations are to willingly answer the call when He who is Abraham's Seed is born in "Bethlehem Ephratah . . . little among the thousands of Judah . . . shall come forth . . . whose goings forth have been from of old, from everlasting . . . (and) the remnant of Israel." *(Micah 5:2-5)*

In *Micah 2:12, 4:7, 5:7, 5:8,* and *7:18,* the prophet focuses attention on those few in the nation who were true to the covenant. These are the remnant. The multitudes of Abraham's physical descendants have gone off after strange gods. They have broken the covenant, by disobeying the law, but there is a remnant whose lives of obedient faith are such that God will yet be able to bless all he nations in the Seed of Abraham.

It is the remnant that the Messiah will "put together as the sheep of Bozrah, as the flock in the midst of their fold." It is they who shall "have passed through the gate . . . and thy King shall pass before them, and the Lord on the head of them." *(Micah 2:12-13)*

It is the remnant, "that was cast off of a strong nation . . ." *(ie.* who actually had little to say about the rebellion of the Jewish commonwealth against God) over whom the "Lord shall reign . . . from henceforth, even for ever." *(Micah 4:7)*

The universal outreach of this remnant to bless all the nations is seen in *Micah 5:7-8.* ". . . the remnant of Jacob shall be in the midst of many people." It was the few faithful Jews in the synagogue who formed the nucleus of most of the churches established by Paul.

In *Micah 7:18,* it is the remnant whose iniquities are pardoned and whose transgressions are passed over. The prophet sees this as the fulfillment of ". . . the mercy to Abraham, which thou hast sworn to our fathers from the days of old." *(Micah 7:20)* In other words the pardoning of the remnant is seen by Micah as a fulfillment of the covenant.

Micah's Messianic message is the accomplishment, through the faithful few, of that which God set out to do in the call of Abraham.

Zephaniah makes less direct reference to the covenant theme than does Micah, yet the mention he does make is enough to show that he to is aware of the importance of his message to the fulfilling of God's promise. His instruction is to "wait ye upon me, saith the Lord, until the day that I rise up . . . that I may assemble the kingdoms . . . that they may all call upon the name of the Lord, to serve Him with one consent." *(Zephaniah 3:8-F)*

The remnant in Zephaniah is more emphatically those who are to return from the captivity *(Zephaniah 2:7)* but even here there are Messianic overtones. "The remnant of Israel shall not do iniquity, nor speak lies; neither shall a deceitful tongue be found in their mouth; for they shall feed and lie down and none shall make afraid." *(Zephaniah 3:13)* Here is a people true to the moral and ethical demands of the covenant and of the spirit more than the letter of the law. Here is the unlimited sway of the Lord over the lives of His people. His law is "written in their hearts." *(cf. Jeremiah 31:33)*

Haggai also sees the end of the covenant as the rule of God over all and His people as a blessing to every nation. *It was their gravest error that the Jews identified God's dominion over all men with their own national ambition to become the dominant world power.* The error did not alter *God's* intent that in Abraham's Seed should all the nations of the earth be blessed.

Haggai's statement in behalf of God is "according to the word that I *covenanted* with you when you came out of Egypt, so my spirit remaineth among you; fear ye not." *(Haggia 2:5)* His assurance is that despite the appearance of defeat in the overthrow of the nation, the resources are His to do what He promised in the covenant. (Read *Haggai 2:5-9)*

In *Haggai 1:12-14* it is again the remnant through whom the purpose of God moves forward.

Zechariah has much to say on the covenant theme. In *Zechariah 2:11* the prophet appeals to Messianic fulfillment as proof of divine origin of His message. "Many nations shall join themselves to Jehovah in that day, and shall be my people; and I will dwell in the midst of them."

This proof is accompanied by the plea "Be silent, all flesh, before Jehovah; for He is waked up out of His holy habitation." *(Zechariah 2:13)*

Zechariah will have none of the nationalistic exclusiveness which developed among the Jews from David to Christ. Rather he gives voice to the assurance that His kingdom shall rule over all and His people shall bless the whole race of men. The Jews identified God's kingdom

THE COVENANT THEME

more and more with their own hopes of political dominion over the earth, but the fulfilling Seed of Abraham was to say, "My kingdom is not of this world . . . my kingdom is not from hence." *(John 18:36)*

The Apostle Paul, wrote to non-Jewish Christians in Colosse that God has delivered us ". . . out of the power of darkness, and translated us into the kingdom of the Son of His love." *(Colossians 1:13)*

In *Zechariah 6:9-15* the fulfilling Seed is called "The Branch." (compare *Isaiah 4:2, 11:1-ff*) Here proof of the divine authenticity of the prophet's message is that "He shall build the Temple of Jehovah, and shall sit on His throne, and the counsel of peace shall be between them both . . . and they that are far off shall come and build in the temple of Jehovah." *(cp. Ephesians 2:19-22)*

Paul, who more than any other New Testament writer (except possibly Luke) is aware of the universal outreach of the covenant, echoes these thoughts in the Ephesian letter. In that epistle, which has been called "the greatest piece of writing in all history," the eternal purpose of God and its fulfillment in the church is outlined in amazing completeness. It is not surprising, therefore, to find in the Ephesian letter the ultimate fulfilling of the message of the Prophets.

To those who once were "separate from Christ, alienated from the commonwealth of Israel, and strangers from the covenants of promise" *(Ephesians 2:12)* Paul wrote "For He is our peace, who made both one, and brake down the middle wall of partition . . . that He might create in Himself of the two (Jew and Gentile) one new man (human kind)." *(Ephesians 2:14)* This is the crescendo of the symphony to which the prophets wrote prelude. Zechariah's statement "the counsel of peace shall be between them both" *(i.e.* the throne and the temple) is here fulfilled in the cross through the church.

Nor is this all; Zechariah says the Branch "shall build the temple." In the Ephesian letter we learn that this temple is the church" . . . being built upon the foundation of apostles and prophets, Christ Jesus Himself being the chief corner-stone; in whom each several building, fitly framed together, groweth into *a holy temple* in the Lord; in whom also ye also are builded together for a habitation of God in the Spirit." *(Ephesians 2:20-ff)*

In *Zechariah 6:15,* the prophet writes a reminder that the promise is conditional; "And this shall come to pass *if* ye will diligently obey the voice of Jehovah your God." The nation of Israel did not diligently obey, but the faithful remnant (true Israel) did.

This is vividly demonstrated in the contrast of the first century Jewish priests and authorities with such men and women as Simeon

(Luke 2:25-35) and Anna *(Luke 2:36-38)*, and Joseph *(Matthew 1-19-ff)* and Nathaniel *(John 1:45-47)* and some five hundred others *(1 Corinthians 15:6)* who formed the first Christian fellowship in Jerusalem.

One of the most glaring contrasts between the Kingly Christ and the kingly amibtions of the post-Babylonian Jews is the description of His final entry into Jerusalem. Zechariah wrote "Rejoice greatly, O daughter of Zion; shout, O daughter of Jerusalem; behold thy King cometh unto thee: He is just, and having salvation; lowly, and riding upon an ass, even upon a colt, the foal of an ass." *(Zechariah 9:9)* John sees the fulfillment of this in Jesus' choice of beasts for His so-called "triumphal entry" and quotes the prophecy exactly. *(John 12:14-15)* The king the Jews expected would have been more fittingly mounted on a war horse!

The covenant theme is less obvious in Malachi, so we shall reserve comment upon it until later. Enough has been said to establish the covenant theme, "in thee shall all the nations of the earth be blessed," as the pole star of the prophets.

CHAPTER IV
BAAL WORSHIP

Much of the Old Testament, certainly much of the message of the prophets, is indiscernable without at least a perfunctory understanding of the worship of Baal. Every reference to idolatry among God's people unless otherwise specified is a reference to Baal worship. Of the seven immediate neighbors of Israel, only Moab worshippd other *major* deities.

Moab's major deity was Chemosh. It is easily demonstrated that Chemosh was simply Baal with a strong *Jeh* (Jehovah) influence.

Judah worshipped Jehovah, but the influence of Baal was so great that the Jehovah of Judah during the period of the minor prophets is scarcely discernable from Chemosh of Moab. *(eg. Isaiah 66:17)*.

Some historians have tried to show that Baal was not one god, but merely a common name ascribed to the local deities of the middle eastern peoples. Careful tracing of the worship performed in his honor, and of the nature ascribed to Baal himself indicates otherwise. The various Baalism worshipped in different localities were one and the same god in various guises and with varying local coloration.

BAAL WORSHIP

From Babylon to Assyria and Syria, to Egypt, to Greece, and finally to Rome, the evidence points to the goddess-mother herself, the child and the father as the same unholy trinity. The child presented as a fullgrown deity is presented under the name of Ninus in Babylon, Baal in Assyria, Syria and Israel, Osiris in Egypt, Dionysus in Greece and Bacchus in Rome are one and the same god. So much so, in fact, that sometimes even the name is the same from place to place.

There are a myriad of other names for Baal. The multiplicity in each locale of worship is multiplied by the far reaching locations of his influence. See the chart at the end of this chapter for a sketchy analysis of some of these names in the locations where they were used.

The roots of Baal worship are buried in the silt of Noah's flood and the confusion of tongues at the Tower of Babel. Its beginnings were apparently brought about, not through the evolution of religious thought, but deliberately as a device to aid in the building of the early Babylonian empire. "Knowing God, they glorified Him not as God." *(Romans 1:21)* The evolution of thought, traceable in the spread of the "Mystery" cults, as this worship is known, throughout the ancient middle eastern world and the Mediterranean basin is to be accounted for on the basis of local coloration and custom as they entered the idolatrous religions from place to place.

It was as the originator of false religion that Babylon earned the title "mother of harlots." *(Revelation 17:5)* The prophets frequently allude to this allegory of Baalism. *(eg. Micah 1:7)*

Wherever the mystery religion spread, there was always to be found three major deities . . . always a father, a virgin mother and a sacrificed son. These were always accompanied by a host of minor gods and goddesses who were believed to exert varying degrees of influence upon the lives of their worshippers.

The similarities shared by the universal triune deities, both in the world of the Bible and throughout the world are too numerous, too obvious and too dominant to be accounted for on the basis of mere coincidence. They point to a common origin of the myths surrounding the father, mother and son.

The scope of this present work will not permit an indepth study of these phenomena . . . by which man, at the dawn of history deliberately turned from the worship of the only God to "The likeness of an image of corruptible man, and of birds, and four footed beasts and creeping things." *(cf. Romans 1:18-23)* throughout the world. We shall limit ourselves to an oversimplified account of the process as it effected the world of the minor prophets.

The abundance of evidence, (though admittedly not conclusive proof,) identifies Nimrod as the founder of the sensuous idolatry which soon became identified with sun worship and spread from the Tigris-Euphrates valley round the fertile crescent to the Nile and thence around the entire Mediterranean world. This son of Cush, grandson of Ham, according to the divine record *(Genesis 10:9)* was first a mighty hunter, (his name means "subduer of the leopard.") who soon "began to be mighty upon the earth." *(I Chronicles 1:10)* "The beginning of his kingdom was Balel." *(Genesis 10:10)* Modern archeology identifies the tower of Babel with the ruins of Bers Nimroud which means "tower of Nimrod."

The first inhabitants of Moab are referred to as "mighty ones" *(Genesis 15:5)*. Those of Ammon were called "crafty, wicked men" *(Genesis 15:15)*. The original dwellers in Edom were the same as those in Moab. *(Genesis 6:4)*

The term *rapha* ("Mighty ones") is the same as that translated "crafty or wicked ones." It is also, unfortunately, translated "giants" in some contexts in the Authorized Version of the Old Testament. *(Eg. Deuteronomy 2:20)* Matthew Henry, in these contexts, has rightly rendered the term "terribles ones" in reference to the Emmins in the land of Moab. *(cf. Deuteronomy 2:11)* The term may be synonomous with *nephilium* fallen ones of *Genesis 6:4* and *Numbers 13:33*.

It seems likely that Nimrod, or some other mighty hunter, realized that a band of hunters, trained in the use of weapons to subdue animals could be disciplined to act together and as easily subdue humans. There is little doubt that, at this point in history, animals were multiplying far more rapidly than men, and Nimrod's exploits against them would assure him the rank of hero among his fellows. They could be easily persuaded to give up a measure of their personal liberty in exchange for protection by this "mighty one." This marked a decisive break with the patriarchal system by which men had theretofore been governed. *(Israel followed suit, probably through the influence of her Baal worshipping neighbors when she demanded a king in the place of the judges . . . I Samuel 8:10)*

Nimrod, fully entrenched as the eminent benefactor of his people, led them to seek their chief good in sensual pleasure, and convinced them that they could enjoy the delights of sin without fear of recrimination from God. His exploits were always accompanied by troops of women, to the sounds of music, revelings and games . . . and whatever else fed the desires of the flesh.

Galling under the righteous rule of God, recently enforced by

BAAL WORSHIP

the flood, these "mighty ones" began to make a deliberate ritual of unrighteousness. Themselves they exalted (Nimrod and his followers, including Simeramis his wife) as leaders of a cult of sensualism. It is quite natural that they be called "fallen ones" by those who did not participate in their debauchery and who still remembered the lesson of the flood.

Diodorus records: "Ninus, the most ancient of the Assyrian kings mentioned in history, performed great actions. Being naturally of a war-like disposition, and ambitious of glory that results from valour, he armed a considerable number of men that were, like himself, brave and vigorous, trained them . . ." Ninus is further described as rising to extraordinary heights and power by bringing the people of Babylon under subjection to him *while it was yet a city*. There is no room for reasonable doubt that Ninus of secular history and the Nimrod of the Bible are one and the same.

Various legends of the death of Nimrod persist throughout the middle east yet today. One such myth among the Arabs says that Nimrod, vexed at God for sending a prophet to warn him against persistance in ritualized immortality, resolved to attack God in heaven. In order to carry out this threat, he built a great tower. Having ascended to the top of the tower, he found himself no closer to heaven than when he started. The following night the tower collapsed, which incident only served to inflame Nimrod's anger. He then devised a plan to fly into heaven in a car drawn by strong birds. The car crashed on Mt. Hermon, and Nimrod was fatally mutilated in the fall. (The mutilation of the god played a prominent role in the worship of Baal.)

Another version of the death of Nimrod, which is far more important in the development of Baal worship, has him being attacked by a wild boar. In this version also Nimrod dies of mutilation

Yet another version says that he went to the rulers of Bab (Babylon) and endeavored to convince them that they should condone and promote his cult of immorality. Still aware of God's wrath through the flood, they reacted violently and sentenced Nimrod to death by mutilation.

Varied as these legends are, they contain a single common element which forms the heart of Baal worship. Nimrod died violently at the height of his career as a "mighty one" and he was mutilated.

Nimrod's wife, Semiramis, who had risen to power and influence with her husband through the promotion of religious immorality was faced with a decision. She must either sink back into obscurity or she must devise a way to transfer her husband's influence to herself. She soon resolved that he should be worshipped as a god. The ancient world in general was familiar with God's promise to send a deliverer to crush the head of the serpent. *(Genesis 3:15)* (Allusions to this promise are found in every major religion.) The followers of Nimrod's cult would be quick to accept Semiramis' presentation of Nimrod reborn through her: as *Zero-ashta* (the seed of woman) *Mithras* the mediator. She was at once his wife and his mother, and is so represented throughout the mystery religions.

The earliest pictures of Baal worship show him crushing the head of the serpent, as do those of his Greek, Indian, Scandinavian and Egyptian counterparts. In all the great idolatrous religions of the world there is the death of a great leader-hero who voluntarily lays down his life for his people, only to be reborn of his wife as *"alma mater"* virgin mother. One of the universal titles of this sacrificed son is "deliverer." Part of the ritual of his worship, as we shall see later, is the mourning over his death. (See *Ezekiel 8:14*, where the prophet alludes to the women weeping over Tammuz. Tammuz is one of the early Assyrian titles for Baal.)

Many ancient evidences point to the fact that men shortly after the flood began to picture the heavens pressed close to the earth that one could not stand upright beneath them. This represented God's demands for righteousness and the supression of physical appetites. Nimrod had led the revolt against this, and now Semiramis could present him as the one who, through his own death, had lifted the burden of righteousness from the backs of his followers. Had not God himself promised a deliverer? By virtue of his death his followers could live for the flesh without fearing the wrath of God.

The Greek version of this pagan emancipation would show Atlas lifting the heavens upon his shoulders, and Homer would write:

*"From the clear vein the immortal Ichor (precious blood) flowed,
Such stream as issues from a wounded god,
Pure Emanation, uncorruptible flood,
Unlike our gross, debased terrestrial blood."*

Having retained her power and prestige through the claim that her hero-husband had actually died as the promised deliverer and been reborn as a god, Semiramis herself soon became elevated above the plain of mortality and venerated as the "Queen of Heaven," "Mother of God." Just as the early pictures of Ishtar (or Semiramis) have her holding the deified babe and pointing toward heaven.

BAAL WORSHIP

This marks the beginning of Zorasterism in Babylon. The true God was not entirely forgotten. As the new religion spread westward he was venerated as "the great invisible," as the "hidden one." He was thought to be unconcerned for the lives of men and was to be worshipped in silence. In Babylon he was known as Belus, Bel (the confounder . . . cf. *Jeremiah 1:3,* Chaos (the god of confusion) and Cush (the father of Nimrod) whose symbol was a club. The idea of confounder and confuser are easily understood as references to the experience at the Tower of Babel, and the club is obviously the symbol of his intolerable wrath.

It was the son and the mother who were the chief objects of worship. He was the great deliverer, and she was, after all, his mother and thus, in a sense, even more to be reverenced because without her he would never have been reborn following his death.

Various names for the son in Assyria were Kronos, Ninus, Monis, Tammuz, and Zero-Ashter. The mother was known variously as Semiramis, Reah, Cyble, and Ishtar, terms denoting her various relationships to her husbnd-son and to her devotees.

In Baalbek, the ancient Syrian city of Baal, this worship became refined, more clearly defined and its rituals more stylized. The father was here referred to as Bel. The name Chaos, ascribed to him as the confuser of tongues, lapsed into disuse. The mother became known at Baalbek as Ashtoreth and the son as Baal or Hadaad.

Here also the cult became identified with sun worship. Baal became the god of the sun, and his chief symbol the halo or sunburst.

In Phoenicia the Assyrian names prevailed largely, with some local variation and coloring. It was from Phoenicia that the name of the mother, Astoreth, came into our western languages. The anglicized form is Easter.

In Egypt, the legend of the sacrificed god added a detail concerning his rebirth which made the Egyptian version of his worship distinct. Legend there had it that the god, known to Egyptians as Osiris, had been torn in pieces when he was killed. In the process of his rebirth his mother, known to Egyptians as Isis, or Mut, was required to bring the pieces back together to refashion his body. She was able to locate all but his reproductive organs and his eyes. Hence the son in Egypt became the un-reproductive god of darkness and ruled over the underworld.

The father, identified first with Re and later, in the middle kingdom, with Amon-re rose to a prominence he did not enjoy in Babylon or Baalbek. He ruled the day and produced life through the mother.

MINOR PROPHETS

The mother, Isis, became the chief object of the sensual ritualism which marked Egyptian sun worship.

The Egyptian symbol of Osiris the son, was a golden calf which retained the spots of the Babylonian leopard skin in which Ninus had been portrayed. The sun burst became the symbol of Amon-re the sun god . . . and the mother retained her everpresent symbol of fertility, the egg. The single symbol which represented best the cult in Egypt was the egg standing atop a tau cross, thus forming the key of life which was ever held in the hand of Amon-re.

His symbol has been revived in modern times by the Hippie-Yippie movements, whose ritualization of fleshly love, sensual dancing and rhythmic music performed to the accompaniment of narcotic induced hallucinations is hardly discernible from the worship of the Egyptian sun cult.

The Greeks added their own peculiar cultural flavor to the worship of the pagan trinity. The deeds of their ancient heroes were attributed to the son, whom they called variously Bacchus (the lamented one), Plutus, Dionysus, (the sin bearer), Kisos, Adonis, and Mercury (the persuasive speaker.)

The mother was, to the Greeks, Irene, Ceres, Artimus, Aphrodite and Diana. In general, Diana was revered as the goddess of chastity and her temple served by vestal virgins. At Ephesus it was a different story. There she was contemplated as the mother of the gods, and her turreted crown was reminiscent of the tower of Babel.

The father was Hephaistis to the Greeks.

The Romans borrowed their religion from the Greeks as they borrowed everything else from the Greeks. The father became Janus, the mother was Venus, and the son retained the Greek titles of Bacchus, Adonis and Mercury.

Throughout the development and spread of the cult, the multiplicity of names for each of the three deities is derived from terms applied to them in their various relationships to one another and to their worshippers.

They appear in various dress and are credited with the heroic deeds of certain local heroes. In every place they maintain the same essential relationship one to the other. The father, for the most part was given little attention, (excepting in Egypt) though the worshippers were careful not to completely ignore him. The son was revered as saviour-deliverer and worshipped for his direct concern with the affairs of men. The mother, in whom resided the wellsprings of life, and to whom the son owed his own life, was the center of the most sensual fertility rites the minds of her depraved priests and priestesses could concoct.

Worshippers were initiated into the cult by ritual which utilized rhythmic music, flashing lights and narcotic potions to induce emotional experiences and physical sensations by which the candidate came to believe he had actually shared, vicariously, in the atoning death and re-birth of the deliverer-god.

In addition to this universal triad, there was in each locale a multitude of minor deities . . . gods and goddesses who had originally been local tribal gods and who were included in the hierarchy of heaven when the worship of the sun god trinity became predominant. Mount Olympus reeled with the rhythm of their reveling.

So it was that the prominent male deity of all of Israel's neighbors came to be known and worshipped as Baal. His influence upon the people of God cannot be overstated.

He claimed several titles throughout Assyria and Palestine, all of which are easily applicable to Nimrod to whom may most probably be traced the first use of his blasphemous title: the meaning of Baal is "Lord!"

The original title of Baal seems to have been *Baal-Abarin*, lord of the mighty ones. Other titles include *Baal-Aph*, lord of wrath, *Baal-lashon*, lord of the tongue, *Baal-hatzim*, lord of arrows, *Baal-Bereth*, lord of fir trees, *Baal-Berith*, lord of the covenant.

Baal-Aph, lord of wrath, depicts the originator of the cult as a man angry against the righteousness of God and His demands, which, as we have seen, were depicted as the oppressive lowering of the heavens. In lifting this oppressive insistence upon righteousness, Baal-Aph became the deliverer of his people.

Baal-Lashon, lord of tongues, depicts the original Baal as persuasive in drawing away a following from the worship of the righteous God. Centuries later his counterpart in Greece and Rome would be known as Mercury, the orator (not messenger) of the gods.

Baal-Hatzim, lord of arrows, depicts Baal as a mighty hunter and warrior. Such prowess in the hunt was the beginning of Nimrod's power.

Baal-Bereth, lord of fir trees, represents Baal as the great deliverer made immortal through his rebirth. The evergreen became the symbol of immortality.

This concept of everlasting power is also described in another title *Baal-Berith*, lord of the covenant, describing his everlasting power and indestructible life as giving him authority over men. This title was itself a direct challenge to Jehovah, the covenant God of the Hebrews.

A final title, probably ascribed to the father rather than the son, was *Baal-Thalath*, the lord of the rib, or husband of the rib. This signifies that he always walked sideways (with a limp). (It is probably the origin of Vulcan's lameness also). Thus the father of the gods was identified with Adam, through an allusion to the creation of his wife from his rib. In memory of this the priests of Baal limped, or walked sideways about the altar. In *I Kings 18:26* the word rendered "leaped" means, literally, to limp. It was a side-ways limping dance performed about the altar as the sacrifices were offered to Baal. In performing it, the priests slashed themselves in memory of Baal's sacrifice, after having first numbed themselves with narcotic potions.

It has been said that Baalism was, at its root, the worship of everything immoral. Its beginnings and evolvement are described vividly as *Romans 1:18-32*. The entire Roman world of Paul's day was permeated with the religious concepts and immoral practices promoted by the Mystery cults. Even the Jews shared them, albeit without associating their concepts with pagan worship *per se*. (*Cf. Romans 1:32*)

The worship of Baal, and his various counterparts in other ancient peoples, centered around certain annual feast days, each of which commemorated some momentous event in the sacrifice of the son and the life-giving virtues of the *alma mater*.

The sacrificial death of Baal for the deliverance of his people was celebrated in connection with the winter solstice, the time when the sun reached its farthest point from the equator. The lengthened period of darkness common to winter months and the abbreviated period of daylight accompanied by the overshadowing of the sun by clouds was taken as commemorative of the death of the sun god.

On *December 24*, after sun set, a huge log was burned to symbolize his suffering and death. Next morning a fir tree stood in its place, symbolizing his immortality. The tree was trimmed with colored eggs, depicting the fertility of the virgin mother through whom he had been reborn.

December 25th was given over to orgies of immortality and drunkeness. Baalbek's Berosus, later known in Greek and Roman times as the *festival of Bacchus* or *Saturnialia* were varied versions of the celebration of the rebirth of the sun god. Slaves were temporarily freed to depict the deliverance of the people by Baal. One slave was chosen and honored as Zoganes, the god of wantoness.

Zoganes found his way to Europe, during the dark ages, in the person of the "Lord of Misrule." It was he who there led the *Christ Mass* festivities *on December 25th*. There also the *fir tree* trimmed with *eggs* commemorated the re-birth of the deliverer and became part of the Christ Mass festivities.

The mistletoe, regarded as a divine branch come down from heaven and growing on the sacred tree which sprang from earth, also figured in the rituals of Baal and became more prominent as the influence of the cult spread through northern Europe. The kiss, symbol of the reconciliation bought by the sacrifice of the sun god signaled the beginning of the sensual rites beneath the mistletoe.

The boar came to figure significantly in the observance of the sacred solstice. He was sacrificed to the god in memory of the legend which said that a wild boar had been the instrument of the death of the sacrificed god. The sacrificed boar then became the "main course" of the feast in honor of Baal. One cannot but be aware of this practice when reading such passages as *Isaiah 66:17* and other Old Testament Scriptures forbidding the eating of pork. The problem in the early church of eating meat sacrificed to idols *(eg. Romans 14)* sprang from this and other animals sacrificed to the Greek and Roman versions of the sun god.

In Egypt the symbol of Osiris (the son in the pagan trinity) was the goose, and in Rome sacred geese were always kept in the temple of Jupiter, as at Baalbek.

The traditional English Christmas dinner consisting of a boars head, goose and yule cakes finds its historic origin in Baal worship.

The worship of Astarte, the mother of Baal was always the worship of fertility and fecundity. The letter *"O"*, symbol of *Zero-Ashta* (the seed of woman) in Babylon, came to represent the egg in her fertility rites.

The rite took place in the spring. Its date was determined using the method established by early Babylonian astrology. Three days after the vernal equinox, when the sun god crossed the equator on his way north for the spring and summer seasons, a feast of forty sacred days began. The period, known in Egypt as Lent and held in honor of Osiris, was later celebrated in Greece and Rome in honor of Adonis. It represented forty days of mourning by Ceres (the mother) over

Prosepine her daughter who had been carried away and raped by her husband-son.

During the Greek period at Baalbek, when Baal was worshipped in the temple of Bacchus, the fusion of the Greek variation of sun worship caused little difficulty as it became identified with the fertility rites connected with the egg and observed by Baal worshippers since the time of the divided kingdom and before. The dyed eggs were eaten with barley cakes following the consecration of both to Baal and Ashteroth (Easter). This feast was eaten to the accompaniment of lewd dances and sacred prostitution.

The feast of the eggs marked the end of the forty days of Lent. Its beginning was signaled in Egypt, in the Temple of Karnak, by the sun light streaming through an aperture in the ceiling at just the right angle once each year to strike the head of Mut, the mother of Osiris.

These and other feasts, observed with variations and refinement throughout the ancient world grew out of the Baal worship with which Israel was surrounded, and to which she more than once surrendered.

Elevated places were selected for the worship of Baal. This may explain Elijah's choice of a mountain as the site for the contest with the prophets of Baal. Meeting them on their own ground he made mockery of their counterfeit religion. Baal worship in high places must also be kept in mind in reading the words of the Psalmist: "I will lift up mine eyes *unto the hills.* From whence cometh my help? My help cometh from the Lord (the real Lord) which made heaven and earth." (and not from Baal, lord of the hills!)

Perhaps the most vivid description of Baal worship, as it confronted the people of God, is evidenced in the worship conducted by the Ammonites. The local name for Baal at Ammon was Moloch. It is likely that it was from the worship of Moloch that the Phoenician name Baal-Hammam, lord of the heat, originated.

Moloch was made of brass, cast with the head of a calf and seated on a brazen throne. Both the throne and the image were hollow, as were its arms and legs. The idol thus shaped, formed a furnace in which the flames were fanned to incredible fury ("seven times hotter than hot") by the draft created as fire swept upward through the limbs to the trunk and through the outstretched arms.

With the arms of Moloch heated red by the flames, the victim, usually a baby girl, was thrown into them where she immediately burned to death. The infant's screams were drowned by the frantic beatings of the drums which signaled the beginning of sensual dances and lewd rituals.

BAAL WORSHIP

References to this horrendous practice may be found in such Old Testament passages as *Ezekiel 16:22, Jeremiah 7:31,* and *Jeremiah 19:5.*

It was from the word *hinnom,* describing the screams of dying infants that the Jews took the name of the Valley of Hinnom. In expression of their disgust for this unspeakable cruelty they made the valley in which it was practiced the city dump of Jerusalem. It was this valley from which Jesus borrowed the word Gehenna . . . translated Hell!

Milton's description of the worship of Moloch is vivid and accurate:

"First, Moloch, horrid king, besmeared with blood
of human sacrifice, and parents tears;
Though for the noise of drums and timbrels loud
Their children's cries unheard, that passed through fire
To this grim idol. Him the Ammonite
Worshipped in Rabba and her watery plain
In Argob and Basan, to the stream
Of utmost Arnon. Nor content with such
Audacious neighborhood, the wisest heart
Of Solomon he led by fraud to build
His temple right against the temple of God
On that opproborious hill; and made his grove
The pleasant valley of Hinnom, Tophet thense
And black Gehenna call'd, the type of Hell'"

The worshippers of the sun, personified in Baal, spiritualized the reproductive powers in the male and female human being. With the image of a virile bull before them, and the egg of fertility as an instrument of worship, they tried to revive the forces of reproduction and life through ritualized fornication. With Baal, at the center of the religion was always the virgin mother . . . perpetually virgin despite her invention of and dedication to sacred prostitution. It was the corruption of Jehovah worship by Baalism which was the chief cause of the downfall of the northern kingdom and the Babylonian captivity of the southern kingdom. It was the culture produced through a corruption of Jehovah worship by Baal worship against which the prophets spoke. It was a people whose covenant relationship to God was compromised by the sensual worship of idols that the prophets sought to call to repentance. The task was over-whelming, and the result all but inevitable.

From the time of Moses Baalism had been a threat to the faith of the covenant people. The first mention of this influence in Scripture is found in *Numbers 22:41,* and the first indication of Israelite participation in it in *Numbers 25:3.*

There can be little doubt that the people from the beginning had been familiar with sungod worship, of which Baalism was one form. Abraham had been called out of the Chaldees, which was the cradle of sun worship. For four hundred years the children of Israel had lived in Egypt, where the worship of Amon-re, Isis, and Osiris, along with a myriad of minor deities literally dominated every facet of life, from the Pharoah to the lowest slave.

In *Judges 2:11, 13, 3:7, 8:33, 10:6, and 1:10 we learn that the* influence of Baal among the people increased rapidly following their occupation of the promised land. From time to time there were periods of repentance (*eg. I Samuel 7:4),* but the temptation of a religion of sensual experience against the worship of an invisible God who must be served in obedient faith was overwhelming. Modern archeology has unearthed little evidence of graven images among the people at this period of their history, but there is an abundance of amulets and charms depicting Asthoreth, the fertility goddess always associated with Baal, which were worn by Israelite women during pregnancy.

It remained for Solomon to introduce sun god worship into Israel to such an extent that it became an integral part of the daily culture of the people. True, Solomon built the temple to Jehovah in Jerusalem and indulged in lavish patronage of Jehovah worship. But it is is equally true that the kingdom of Solomon was most noted among foreign contemporaries, not for his strict worship of Jehovah but for its crass commercialism. It was in this pursuit that Solomon concluded treaties and entangling alliances with polytheistic states. It was to support this policy of national aggrandizement that he levied taxes and conscripted laborers to the extent that, following his death, his successor son's refusal to abandon the policy brought about the permanent division of the kingdom and the ultimate end of the Davidic dynasty.

Religious exclusiveness such as that demanded of Israel under the law, is never the handmaiden of internationalism and power politics. Solomon's alliances were often sealed by opportunistic marriages to pagan princesses, and strange wives, rather than being required to worship and serve the God of Abraham, Isaac and Jacob, were encouraged to continue in their native forms of the sun god worship which dominated the ancient near east. The temple itself, although incorporating

BAAL WORSHIP

the divinely given pattern of the tabernacle in its "floor plan", was essentially a Canaanite structure, built by Canaanite architects on a Canaanite high place. And in its shadow Solomon himself erected, for his Egyptian wife, another temple to the sun god!

Although Solomon must bear the blame for introducing idolatry, (and idolatry in those days, in that part of the world meant sun god worship, of which Baalism was one form) into Jerusalem and so into what was to become the southern kingdom, this despicable religion found fertile soil in the north also. The champion of Baal there was Jezebel whose name has come to be synonymous with everything immoral.

The civil strife which brought about the division of the kingdom following the death of Solomon was instigated by a prophet of God *(I Kings 11:26-29)* who was speaking against the new order in Jerusalem, not only because it demanded unjust levies from the northern tribes but because it had placed paganism in the seat of Jehovah worship. Another prophet warned Rehoboam that the uprising in the north was God's will. *(I Kings 12:21-24).*

When Jeroboam erected in Bethel a shrine to rival the temple in Jerusalem, it was a shrine to Jehovah, and golden bulls placed in it were intended simply as symbolic support for the throne of the invisible Jehovah. But the similarity of the golden bulls to the images associated with Baal worship was too obvious. Many who came to the shrine to worship Jehovah remained to worship the golden bulls. There can be little doubt that this marked the beginning of the strange admixture of Baalism and Jehovah worship which came to be the religion of the northern kingdom. It was by confusing these two mutually incompatible faiths that Jeroboam "made Israel sin." *(I Kings 15:34).*

The attempt of the northern kings to recapture the glories of Solomon led them into an alliance with Phoenician Tyre. Now any student of ancient history is aware that Tyre in particular, and the Phoenesians in general were responsible for bringing Baal worship into the Mediterranean coastlands in the first place. The alliance between Samaria and Tyre was cemented by a marriage of Ahab to the pagan princess Jezebel.

Whatever can be said about Jezebel, and a great deal has been said, both in the Bible and in other writings, she was a woman of deep religious conviction. She was not content to merely be allowed to serve her foreign god in Israel. She became a missionary, determined to turn the entire northern kingdom from Jehovah to Baal. It is to her credit that, unlike the professing Jehovists among whom she lived, she was not interested in a compromise between the two mutually antagonistic religions. She took every measure at her disposal to bring the issue to a showdown. *(1 Kings 18-19).*

The gods and goddesses of Phoenecia were thus arrayed against the one true God. Baal the sun god and his wife-mother Astarte (Ashtoreth) represented the most completely carnal forces of fertility. The rituals performed in their names, especially those to Astarte, were concerned with the control of fecundanty of the earth of animals and of man. The most degrading acts imaginable were performed as acts of public worship to curry the favor of the gods.

The contrast between the absolute morality demanded by the law of Jehovah and the absolute immorality of Baal worship cannot be overstated. If Israel were to be God's people, and keep His laws there could be no compromise with such ritualized lewdness. Men take on the character of the gods they worship. If Israel ever took Baal to his bosom in earnest, it would be the end of Israel as a covenant people.

Yet many did turn from Jehovah, with His demands for righteousness to serve Baal and Astarte—and their own fleshly desires. Some, clinging to tradition, yet indulging in apostacy actually came to address Jehovah as though He were Baal.

After the death of Jezebel, there were a few feeble attempts at reform. Added to these were the warnings of the prophets of God, which were anything but feeble. But the die was cast. It was all downhill—all the way to destruction. When finally the Ashara, high goddess symbol of Baalism, was allowed by Jehu to remain in Samaria, it became apparent that the paganism introduced as a foreign cult now thrived as an Israelite cult . . . the predominant religion, eventually, of the northern kingdom! The influence of this cult upon the ultimate demise of that kingdom cannot be overstated.

It was against this compromised worship and its resultant sinful society that the prophets of the pre-exilic age thundered, in both the north and the south. The only ray of hope which shown through the storms clouds which the prophets saw on the horizons of both Israel and Judah was the conviction that a remnant of the covenant people would repent and remain faithful to the Covenant of Jehovah.

It is possible, at first casual contact, that the essentials of Baal worship will impress the Christian reader as being remarkably similar to those of Christianity. The belief in a trinity, the sacrifice of the son of a god for the deliverance of his people, the birth of the son through a virgin mother may give one a start.

BAAL WORSHIP

A closer look will show these similarities, if indeed they can be called similarities at all, to be those of a counterfeit. The trinity of Baalism was composed of a nearly unknown father god who was for the most part ignored by the worshipper, a son sacrificed to save his people FROM RIGHTEOUSNESS, and a mother who was portrayed as the same time as a virgin and the leader of a cult whose priestesses were public prostitutes. The trinity of the Christian (if this term is permissible at all, being unscriptural,) is composed of an all-powerful, loving Father whose will is the overriding purpose of all, including the life of His Son, a Son whose life was given to save His people FROM RIGHTEOUSNESS, and a Holy Spirit whose nature is entirely non-physical and hence as far from the nature of the sun goddess as is possible. The re-birth of the sacrificed Baal was through the powers of the goddess. The resurrection of Jesus was by the power of the Father. The virgin mother of Baal was elevated as Queen of Heaven, while the virgin mother of Jesus is last seen among the humble worshippers of her Son. (Acts. 1:14) The purpose of Baalism was to thwart the demands of God, the ideal of the Christian faith is to fulfill His eternal purpose.

THE SEPTUAGINT—LXX

We have included in this commentary, instead of the usual paraphrase, a translation of the Septuagint.

This is the earliest version of the Old Testament Scriptures now in existence, or of which modern scholarship possesses any certain knowledge.

Translated from the original Hebrew into Greek in Alexandria, Egypt, beginning under the reign of Ptolemy Philadelphus and being completed under Ptolemy Sater (c. 285 B.C.), the Septuagint filled a critical need in its day. The influence of the Greeks upon the Jews living outside Judea was so great that they no longer spoke or read Hebrew. Putting their Scriptures into one common Alexandrian dialect of the day was an event comparable to our translation of the King James Version in 1611.

As with any attempt to bring thought from one language to another, there is some loss, no doubt there is in bringing Hebrew theological forms into the philosophic language of the Greeks.

However, the version is important to the Christian scholar, not only as the oldest Scripture now in existence, but because it is the version quoted and alluded to by Jesus and the Apostles.

The LXX, as it is called for the 70 Jewish scholars who translated it, was the Bible of the New Testament Church.

MINOR PROPHETS

	BABYLON (Assyria)	SYRIA	PHOENICIA	EGYPT	GREECE	ROME
FATHER	Belus Bel (the confounder) Chaos (god of confusion) Cush	Bel	Bel	Amoun Re Amoun-re	Hephaitis Saturn	Janus
MOTHER	Cybele Semiramis Istar Rhea		Ashtoreth	Astarte Astoreth	Maut Isis	Irene Ceres Artimis Aphrodite Dinah	Venus
SON	Kronos Zero-ashta Mithras Tammuz Ninus Monis		Baal Hadaad	Baal (?)	Osiris Khons	Plutus Bacchus Adaonis Mercury Kisos Iacchus	Bacchus Adonis Mercury Jupiter

38

QUESTIONS OVER INTRODUCTION

Chapter I—*Questions*

How to Study the Bible

1. What is *exegisis?* How is it superior to *interpretation* as an approach to Bible Study?
2. In the science of exegisis, what is meant by "removing the differences?"
3. List and explain the rules of exegisis:
   a. why is a dictionary an important tool to Bible study?
   b. why is an unabridged dictionary preferable?
   c. how do the rules of grammar aid in Bible study?
   d. what is meant by context?
   e. why is it important to study scripture in context?
   f. what is the advantage of studying the Bible in its historical setting?
   g. what is analytical Bible study?
   h. what is the inherent danger of analytical study of scripture?
   i. why should commentaries be used only after the first fives rules of exegisis have been applied to a text?
   j. discuss the importance of prayer as a factor in Bible study.

Chapter II—*Questions*

What Is A Prophet?

1. List two popular views of prophecy and show how each contradicts the other.
2. What three questions must we answer to arrive at a scriptural view of the prophet?
3. What is the literal meaning of the Biblical word **Prophet?**
4. The watch word of the Biblical prophet is not "it shall come to pass" but _____?
5. Explain the Biblical concept of prophecy from *II Peter 1:20-21*.
6. Compare the characteristics of the false and true prophets in Israel.
7. The primary function of the prophet in the time of the minor prophets was?
8. How does the work of the prophet relate to the government of Israel as a theocracy?
9. What is meant by the statement "Prophecy is conditional?"

MINOR PROPHETS

Chapter III—*Questions*

The Covenant Theme in the Prophets

1. What is the "blood red thread" which holds the Bible together.
2. Discuss—"the covenant was proposed by God, not man."
3. The covenant arrangement between God and His prophets was maintained by _____ rather than physical ancestory.
4. Who first received the covenant from God *(Genesis 12: 1-3)*?
5. Whom God choses He _____?
6. Whom God calls He _____?
7. Whom God blesses He _____?
8. The called continue to receive God's blessing only as long as they _____.
9. The historical epochs of the Bible do not record these religious systems. Rather they are the record of _____.
10. The descendants of Abraham are all who _____. *(Galatians 3:7)*
11. How did circumcision constitute a warning concerning the covenant.
12. How should Israel's position as a nation of priests have effected her attitude toward other peoples?
13. In God's eyes, true Israel's primary concern was a convenant and its promise of _____.
14. How does the sacrifice of Isaac show the true meaning of the covenant?
15. _____ is the most basic idea in God's dealing with Israel.
16. Jesus understood the Old Covenant Scriptures in terms of His own _____, _____, _____, and _____. And concluded the end of it all to be _____.
17. What is the relationship of John 3:16 to the covenant theme of the Bible?
18. The "spiritual genetic to be preserved by Israel's obedience of the Law of Moses was _____.
19. The answer to Jewish narrowness was _____.
20. It is the _____ (the faithful few) who were truly Israel, according to the minor prophets and the New Testament.

QUESTIONS OVER INTRODUCTION

Chapter IV—*Questions*

Baal Worship

1. Every reference to idolatry among God's people, unless otherwise specified, is a reference to _____.
2. The various Baalism worshipped in various localities were _____.
3. In the trinity of Baalism, the child is variously called _____ in Babylon _____ in Assyria, Syria and Israel _____ in Egypt, _____ in Greek and _____ in Rome.
4. The beginning of Baal worship was not the result of religious evolution but of _____.
5. Wherever this false religion spread it centered in three major dieties, a _____, a _____, and a _____ son.
6. The abundance of evidence identifies _____ as the founder of idolatry.
7. _____ of secular history and _____ of the Bible are one and the same.
8. all the versions of the death of Nimrod contain a single common element which forms the heart of Baal worship this element is
9. Simcramus wife of _____ became _____ mother of _____ the mediator who in turn became Baal of the Canaanites.
10. Tammuz was _____.
11. What was meant by the ancient picture of heaven pressed so close to earth that a man could not stand upright?
12. What unique element did the Egyptians add on the legend of the sacrificed god.
13. What devices were used to initiaite worshippers into the sun god cults?
14. Baal had many names, derived from his various actions and relationships:
    a. Baal-Aph Lord of wrath signifies _____.
    b. Baal-Lashon Lord of tongues signifies _____.
    c. Baal-Hatzin Lord of Arrows signifies _____.
    d. Baal-Bereth Lord of Fir Trees signifies _____.
15. Baalism at its root, is the worship of everything _____.
16. What is the significance of December 25th in Baal worship?
17. Who was Moloch?
18. How did Solomon influence the rise of Baalism in Israel?
19. The evil queen _____ was a missionary of Baalism.
20. The pre-exilic prophets thundered against _____ worship and its resultant _____.

"Then the king of Assyria came up throughout all the land, and went up to Samaria, and besieged it three years. In the ninth year of Hoshea the king of Assyria took Samaria, and carried Israel away into Assyria..."
(II Kings 17:5–6).
"I besieged and captured Samaria, and carried off 27,290 of its inhabitants as booty."
The Assyrian text of this victory inscription of Sargon II dealing with his campaign in Israel, which is preserved in the original, reads like a confirmation of the biblical statement.

FROM: THE BIBLE AS HISTORY IN PICTURES
By Werner Keller – Wm. Morrow Co.

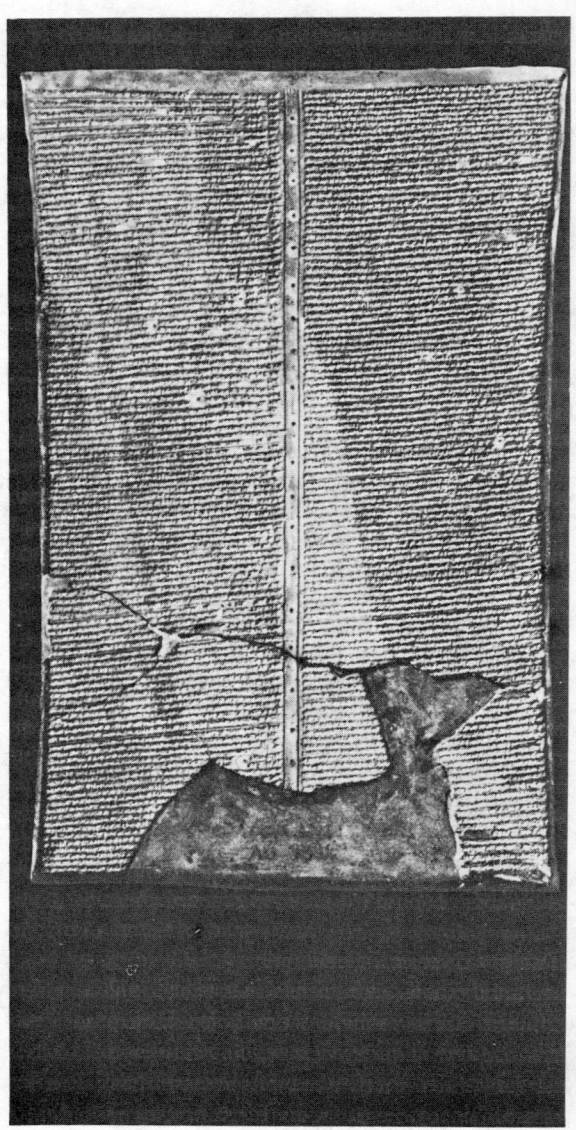

PART II
MICAH

MICAH
OUTLINE OF MICAH

I. The first cycle ... 1:2-4
   A. A call to harken ... 1:2-4
      1. Evidence of universal concern ... 1:2(a)
      2. The Lord to be witness ... 1:2(b)
      3. The Lord from His holy temple ... 1:2(c)-3(a)
      4. Tread upon the high places ... 1:3(b)
      5. Mountains to melt, valleys to melt like wax ... 1:4
   B. Occasion of wrath ... 1:5
      1. Jacob — Israel
      2. Judah
      3. Samaria
      4. Jerusalem ... sin of Judah
      5. Poluted and false religions of Samaria and Jerusalem.
   C. Samaria to be destroyed ... 1:6-12(a)
      1. Samaria ... scene of desolation ... 1:6-7
      2. The husband's lament ... 1:8
      3. The purpose of punishment ... 1:9
      4. Punishment extended to the gates of Jerusalem ... 1:10-12(a)
   D. Warnings to Judah ... 1:12(b)-16
      1. Maroth ... v. 12(b)
      2. Lachish ... v. 13
      3. Moresheth Gath ... v. 14
      4. Mareshah ... v. 15

II. The second cycle ... 2:1-13
   A. Woe to the arrogant misleaders ... 2:1-3
   B. A taunt against the wicked ... 2:4-5
   C. The prophet accused as an enemy ... 2:6-7(a)
   D. The prophet answers his critics ... 2:7(b)-11
   E. Warnings tempered by promises ... 2:12-13
      (The first mention of the remnant by Micah)

III. Third cycle ... 3:1-12
   A. Outrages of civil officials ... 3:1-4
   B. Mercenary prophets ... 3:5-8
   C. Conclusion of the denunciation ... 3:9-12

IV. Future exaltation of the remnant ... chapters 4-5
   A. Zion, center of worship ... 4:1-5
   B. The restoration of the Diaspora ... 4:6-8
   C. Distress and redemption . . . 4:9-5:1

SUPERSCRIPTION 1:1

 D. Focus on the Messiah... 5:2-6
 E. The glorious future of the remnant... 5:7-15
V. Jehovah's controversy with His people... chapters 6-7
 A. Forgotten acts of salvation... 6:1-8
 B. God's justice demands the wicked be punished... 6:9-16
 C. Micah longs for Godliness... 7:1-6
 D. The prophet looks to God... 7:7-13
 E. The prophet prays for his people... 7:14-17
 F. Prayer of prophetic praise... 7:18-20

CHAPTER V
SUPERSCRIPTION... Micah 1:1

RV... The word of Jehovah that came to Micah the Morashite in the days of Jotham, Ahaz, and Hezekiah, kings of Judah, which he saw concerning Samaria and Jerusalem.

LXX... And the word of the Lord came to Michaeas the son of Moraschi, in the days of Joatham, and Achaz, and Ezechias, kings of Juda, concerning what he saw regarding Samaria and Jerusalem.

COMMENTS

 The record of Micah's prophecy begins with a claim to inspiration. There is no description of his call, as in Isaiah and others, but the simple statement that "the word of Jehovah came to Micah the Morashite." It is echoed by *Hebrews 1:1* and *II Peter 1:19-21*.
 Micah is also recognized as a prophet by Jeremiah, *(Jer. 26:18),* who says he speaks to all people of Judah in the day of Hezekiah.
 Pusey makes the significant observation that the title and date are an important part of a prophetic book, since they indicate to people who come after that what the prophet wrote was not written after the event. To say it simply, there is evidence in the prophet's identifying both himself and his time of writing, that what he says is *going* to happen was not in fact written *after* it happened. It is not written *ex post facto*.
 It is impossible to overstate this truth or the importance of it, since fulfilled prophecy represents some of the best possible evidence for the inspiration of the Scriptures. As we have seen, the foretelling of the future was not the *primary* concern of the prophets. Nevertheless, when they *did* deal with the future, they did so with infallible accuracy.

1:1 MICAH

In view of the fact that no mere human can foretell what is going to happen two minutes from now, the accuracy with which the prophets write of the future bespeaks divine guidance. They often dealt with events which were not minutes but years, even centuries into the future, and they did so without equivocation. If they "missed" it would prove they were delivering their own conjectures rather than a divine message . . . but they did not "miss." They preached and wrote what only God could know.

Micah not only claims that what came to him was the "word of Jehovah," he also claims to have seen in a vision those things which he foretold concerning Samaria and Jerusalem. *Hosea 1:1* employs the phrase "the word of Jehovah," while *Nahum 1:1* speaks of his writing as the record of a "vision." Micah employs both terms.

Had a later editor compiled these works they would probably have begun each book with identical headings. The variation with which each of the writers claims divine origin for his message lends weight of evidence to the conviction that what they wrote was *from* God *through* the prophets. One thinks at once of the Hebrew writer's assertion that *God* spoke to the fathers in the prophets in varying degrees and in varying ways. *(Hebrews 1:1)*

The significant thing is that in each of these three cases (Micah, Nahum, Hosea), there is a direct claim to divine inspiration. Micah makes a double claim indicating not only that what he is about to write is the "word of Jehovah" but indicating also the method by which it came to him, *ie.* in a vision. As Matthew Henry has aptly put it, "what is written . . . must be heard and received, not as the word of dying men . . . but as the word of the living God."

Micah's phrase, "in a vision," merits special attention. He claims to have *seen* vividly that which he writes. His record is an eyewitness account of history *in advance!*

This accounts for the unhesitating certainty with which he describes events that at the time of writing lay in the future. History has long since vindicated his confidence in what he wrote by confirming its accuracy.

It is well to note, before attempting a study of this book, that Micah's message is not arranged *chronologically* but *logically*. The emphasis is upon the message rather than upon the calendar of events.

The time of Micah's call is set by his reference to three kings of the southern kingdom. They are Jotham, who reisgned from 750 to 735 B.C., Ahaz, who reigned from 735 to 715, and Hezekiah, who reigned from 715 to 687. Because of the nature of the persons and

SUPERSCRIPTION   1:1

reigns of these kings, Micah saw the leadership of Judah swing from holiness, peace, and prosperity, to crass idolatry and immorality, and then, almost desperately, back again toward righteousness and national respectability.

Jotham, the first of the kings mentioned by Micah, was the eleventh king of the southern kingdom. His contemporaries in the north were Shallum, who reigned one month, Menahem, who reigned two years, and Pekahiah, who reigned two years.

Jotham's reign totaled forty years, the first twenty-five of which were spent as co-regent with his father, Uzziah (also called Azariah). He reigned alone for sixteen years. The record of his rule is found in *II Kings 15:30, 32, 33.*

Jotham is best described as holy, his reign as peaceful and prosperous. *(Cf. II Chronicles 27:2-6)* He was succeeded on the throne of Judah by his son, Ahaz, whose person and administration were the exact opposite of his own.

The twelfth king of Judah, Ahaz, became king at the age of twenty. He was idolatrous in the extreme, to the point of sacrificing his own children to Baal. It was his reign that brought about the conditions which led to the destruction of Judah. Despite the efforts of his successor-son at reform, the seeds of God's wrath were deeply planted.

It was to Ahaz that Isaiah gave the prophecy of the virgin birth of the Messiah. *(Cf. Isaiah 7:14)* The efforts of modern translators (eg. the Revised Standard Version) to deny Isaiah's intent to foretell a birth without benefit of natural father is based solely upon the ambiguous literal meaning of the word *alma,* translated *virgin* in *Isaiah 7:14.* Literally, *alma* may mean, also, young maiden. This overlooks the historic context of the writing, which is set against the backdrop of Baal worship. It also ignores the intended impact of Isaiah's prophecy upon King Ahaz, a devotee of Baal.

The worship of the sun god, in his many guises from Babylon to Rome, always included the *alma mater* or *virgin mother.* Isaiah's use of the term *alma* to describe the birth of the Savior is part of the prophet's attempt to call the king back from idolatry to the worship of the *true* God, Whose Son would *indeed* one day be born of a virgin. (See above section on Baal worship.)

Fearing the northern alliance of Syria and Israel, the idolatrous Ahaz entered into a compact with Tiglath Pileser III, the wily ruler of Assyria. The results were disasterous for Judah. The southern kingdom became a mere satellite nation, a vassal state, tributary to Tigleth Pileser's Assyrian Empire.

1:1   MICAH

The third king mentioned by Micah is regarded as a reformer. Hezekiah, the thirteenth king of Judah, and the son of the Baal-worshipping Ahaz, became king at the age of twenty-five. Most of his energies were given to attempting to undo what his father had done in the corrupting of God's people with idolatry.

What motivated Hezekiah's commitment to Jehovah and the restoration of temple worship, we can only guess. Some interesting fiction could be written describing him as a child, horrified at the sacrifice of his brothers and sisters to his father's pagan god.

Hezekiah's contemporaries in Israel were Pekah, who reigned for twenty years and Hoshea, who ruled for nine years. It was early following Hezekiah's ascension to the throne of Judth that Israel was overrun by Assyria.

Although the fall of Israel left Judah exposed on the north to the Assyrian armies of Sennacharib, the dedicated Hezekiah refused to pay tribute to the invader. As a result, in the fourteenth year of his reign, he found his own kingdom invaded by Sennacharib and his capital city, Jerusalem, threatened.

Because of the king's dedication to God, Jehovah intervened in behalf of Judah and Sennacharib was stopped just short of the city and turned back. *(Cf. II Kings 28* and *Isaiah 36:1-22)*

Just following the deliverance of his kingdom from Assyrian invasion, Hezekiah fell desperately ill. It has been suggested that his illness was of divine origin to prevent him falling prey to his own pride. In any event, God intervened a second time on his behalf, when in answer to prayer, the king's illness was prevented from being fatal, and he was given the promise of fifteen more years of life and prosperity.

For this second deliverance, Hezekiah's gratitude was eloquent, *(Cf. Isaiah 38:10-20)* but short-lived. He shortly made a vain show of pride and possessions before Merodach-baladar of Babylon and as punishment received a message from God that, at a future time, his wealth would be taken to Babylon.

Concerning Micah himself little is known, but that little is enough to give a picture of a God-fearing man from the country, shocked and enraged at the luxurious degeneracy which he found in the capital cities of Samaria and Jerusalem.

He is best described as "a younger contemporary of Isaiah," a country man whose home was in Moresheth, some thirty miles southwest of Jerusalem.

SUPERSCRIPTION 1:1

In the Septuagint Moresheth is referred to as Moresheth-Gath, meaning a possession of Gath. There are those who believe that Moresheth and Gath are one and the same. If this is true, Micah's home is to be identified with Gath southwest of Jerusalem rather than Gath-Gittain which lies about the same distance to the northwest. Jerome places it just east of Eleuheropolis.

Moresheth is mentioned explicity by name only once in the Bible in *Micah 1:14*. There is one other allusion to it in *Jeremiah 26:18*.

The village lay in the Judean piedmont bordered on the north and east by the hill country and on the south and west by the plain which marks the way from Jerusalem to Gaza just on the border of the land of the Philistines.

Micah mentions the towns and villages in this area in such a way as to leave no doubt that he was personally familiar with them. The area is grazing country, with fields of grain and olive groves.

Micah, the prophet, is concerned with the plights of the poor in a land of affluence and plenty. The contrast between the much of the "haves" and the little of the "have nots" is reminiscent of our own unbalanced distribution of wealth.

Micah's answer was not political pressure. He led no "poor people's marches," he burned no businesses, he headed no political pressure group. To him, as he spoke the "Word of Jehovah," social injustice was a symptom of spiritual decay for which repentance of the oppressor was the only solution. The problem was, to him, ethical. The advantage taken of the poor by the rich, of the powerless by the powerful was, in the eyes of this country-bred preacher, an affront to God. He does not preach man's duty to man as a separate ideal from man's duty to God. *Rather the former is the outworking of the latter.*

In keeping with this, Micah's understanding of the work of a prophet was not primarily concerned for the future. His understanding of this mission is best expressed in his own words, "But as for me, I am full of power by the Spirit of Jehovah, and of judgement, and of might, to declare unto Jacob his transgression, and to Israel his sin." (*Micah 3:8*) Whatever he said about what lay in the future, he said it first to move his contemporaries to immediate repentance, and secondly to reassure them that God would not forget His covenants.

As a contemporary of Isaiah and Hosea, Micah's surroundings were those common also to them. It is not strange, then, that his message is also similar to theirs. As background, a reading of *II Kings 15:32-20:21* and *II Chronicles 27:1-32:33* will prove invaluable.

1:1 MICAH

Fifty years of peace and prosperity had ended with the death of Jeroboam II. In 745 B.C. the Assyrians, led by Tiglath Pileser III, began their westward march and expansion. By 738 Damascus had fallen. In 721 the same fate would engulf the northern kingdom and its capital city, Samaria.

Although Judah, the southern kingdom. did not fall at that time, Hezekiah's anti-Assyrian policies later turned Sennacherib and the armies of Assyria on Judah. In 711, as previously stated, the southern kingdom became a tributary, a mere satellite of the Assyrian empire. When Sennacharib marched westward to put down a revolt in the philistine states, he humbled Judah with the same effort.

Thus Micah spoke in a time of social unrest, national insecurity, and religious turmoil not unlike those of the United States in mid-twentieth century. He viewed evil as a failure to grasp the nature of true religion, and believed that the only remedy was to strike at the source by denouncing the wickedness and demanding repentance upon pain of national anihilation. He would have agreed with *James 1:27* completely.

He makes no hesitation in insisting that the demands of God are binding upon the rich and powerful as well as the poor and powerless. He does not preach a "middle class morality" but eternal ethical right determined by Jehovah.

Chapter V—*Questions*

1. Micah"s prophecy begins with a claim to _____.
2. Why is the date of a prophetic statement an important part of the book?
3. Micah's "double claim" to inspiration indicates both _____ _____ and _____.
4. Account for the unhesitating certainty with which Micah describes the events of the future.
5. Micah's message is not chronological but _____.
6. The time of Micah's call is set by his reference to three kings:
   Jotham, who reigned from _____ to _____.
   Ahaz, who reigned from _____ to _____.
   and _____ who reigned from 715 to 687 B.C.
7. The first 25 years of Jotham's reign were as co-regent with _____.
8. Describe Jotham's reign.
9. Ahaz's reign was characterized by _____.

50

FIRST CYCLE 1:2-4

10. _____ is also called _____.
11. Ahaz entered into an alliance with _____ of Assyria.
12. This resulted in the southern kingdom becoming a _____.
13. Hezekiah, the third king mentioned by Micah, was the _____ king of Judah. He was the son of Ahaz, but he did not worship _____.
14. Hezekiah's contemporaries in Israel were _____ and _____.
15. Due to Hezekiah's dedication to Jehovah, _____ was stopped just short of Jerusalem and turned back.
16. Micah is described as a younger _____ of Isaiah.
17. To Micah, social injustice was a symptom of _____.
18. How did Micah understand his mission? *(Micah 3:8)*
19. Micah does not preach a "middle class morality" but _____.
20. The overthrow of the northern kingdom was accomplished by the _____ empire while Judah was conquered later by _____ who were in turn defeated by _____ who released the captive remnant.

CHAPTER VI
FIRST CYCLE
A CALL TO HARKEN ... Micah 1:2-4

RV ... Hear, ye peoples, all of you; hearken, O earth, and all that therein is: and let the Lord Jehovah be witness against you, the Lord from his holy temple. For, behold, Jehovah cometh forth out of his place, and will come down, and tread upon the high places of the earth. And the mountains shall be melted under him, and the valleys shall be cleft, as wax before the fire, as waters that are poured down a steep place.

LXX ... Hear these words, ye people; and let the earth give heed, and all that are in it: and the Lord God shall be among you for a testimony, the Lord out of his holy habitation. For, behold, the Lord comes forth out of his place, and will come down, and will go upon the high places of the earth. And the mountains shall be shaken under him, and the valleys shall melt like wax before the fire, and as water rushing down a declivity.

COMMENTS

A CALL TO HEAR AND HARKEN . . .
EVIDENCE OF UNIVERSAL CONCERN . . . 1:2(a)

At the outset of Micah's recorded prophecy there is evidence of God's universal concern for all men. The prophet's call is to both "ye *peoples,* all of you," and to "(hearken) *earth,* and *all* therein is."

The term "people" is frequently used in Scripture to designate the covenant people of God. It is a term used to delineate between Israel and "the nations." (eg. *Psalm 50:7*)

In verse 2, Micah calls to "ye people, *all of you."* His message is intended for *all* those to whom the expression "the people" may rightly be applied, both in the northern and southern kingdom.

By his use of ". . . earth and all that therein is," Micah calls the whole world to listen to God's indictment of His covenant people. The use of "earth and all that therein is" to describe the non-covenant nations (*ie.* the Gentiles) was one of longstanding precedent.

Moses, in *Deuteronomy 32:1,* uses this expression to declare to all mankind the name and greatness of Jehovah.

Micah's contemporary, Isaiah, used the same phrase to tell all mankind that God's people have rebelled against Him. *(Isaiah 1:2)*

Two reasons are apparent for God's concern that the "earth and all that is in it" hear His charges against both Samaria and Jerusalem; *ie.* against both branches of the covenant people: (1) All men have a vital interest in the fulfillment of the covenant through the people. The more nationalistic the people became, and the more their religious practices became polluted with Baalism, the less aware they became of God's promise to bless, through them, all the nations of the earth. But God never forgot. (2) The time was fast approaching when God would cast off His rebellious people. When this happened, neither the world nor the people themselves would have any reason to say that God was unfaithful. None could say that He had not warned the people of the dire consequence of their failure to keep His covenant and obey His law. (Cf. *Romans 11:1-4*)

A vital lesson is to be learned from this verse by today's "people," the church, namely that he who will not learn from God's past dealings with His people can blame only himself and not God for his own suffering. When the Jews were finally cast off by God it was after they had ignored not only the warning of the prophets but the meaning of the captivity which they endured as a result of not heeding that warning.

FIRST CYCLE 1:2b

THE LORD IS TO BE WITNESS . . . 1:2(b)

The condemnation of God is never arbitrary. The people are to have a "fair trial." The "star witness" for the prosecution is to be the Lord Jehovah Himself.

Moses had issued a similar warning of impending judgment, "And the generation to come, your children that shall rise up after you, and the foreigner that shall come from a far land, shall say, when they shall see the plagues of the land, the sickness wherewith Jehovah hath made it sick; and that the whole land thereof is brimstone and salt, and a burning, that it is not sown, nor beareth, not any grass groweth therein, like the overthrow of Sodom and Gomorrah, Admah and Zebion, which Jehovah overthrew in His anger, and in His wrath: even all the nations shall say, whereof hath Jehovah done this unto this land? Then men shall say, because they forsook the *covenant* of their fathers, which He made with them when He brought them forth out of the land of Egypt, and went and served other gods, and worshipped them, gods that they knew not, and that He had not given them: therefore the anger of Jehovah was kindled against this land, to bring down upon it all the curse that is written in this book; and Jehovah rooted them out of their land in anger, and in wrath and in great indignation, and cast them into another land, as at this day."*(Deuteronomy 29:22-28)*

Anyone who has visited present day Palestine has been amazed that this land was once called "a land flowing with milk and honey." Excepting those sections that have felt the improvements of modern technology and agricultural reclamation, it is a barren rocky wasteland. Such a visitor finds himself asking, "Wherefore hath Jehovah done this to this land?"

The answer of both Moses and the prophets is ". . . because they (God's people) forsook, the covenant of Jehovah . . ." What is true of the land is equally true of the people who once inhabited it. Micah presents the Lord Himself as the chief witness to the justice of God's wrath against His rebellious people.

Nor is the Lord the only witness. The defense of Stephen, the first Christian martyr, was essentially the same testimony against the people as that made by the Lord in the prophetic writings. The burden of Stephen's defense is that God's dealing with the people had always been progressive, toward the accomplishment of His eternal purpose to bless all men rather than static and prejudiced toward the commonwealth of the Jews. This purpose Stephen saw as universal rather than local. Underlying his entire argument is Stephen's insist-

1:2a, 3a   MICAH

ence that God's treatment of Israel has always been ethical, rather than erratic. His actions are governed by the same morality He demands of them. Stephen closes with the classic accusation that the people have always been "stiffnecked and uncircumcised in heart and ears" to the point of murdering the prophets whom God sent to call them back to the covenant. (Cf. *Acts, chapter seven*)

THE LORD IS IN HIS HOLY TEMPLE . . . 1:2(c)-3(a)

The temple here is not necessarily, nor even probably the temple at Jerusalem. *Psalm 11:4* speaks of "Jehovah in His holy temple." The eleventh Psalm is generally recognized as a Psalm of David, and was therefore written *before* there was a temple in Jerusalem.

The temple, or holy dwelling place out of which the Lord comes to testify against His people is His real dwelling place. The sanctuary of Solomon's temple (or its reconstructed post-Babylonian counterpart) was never more than a type of the real habitation of God.

We have this on the word of no less an author than the writer of the New Testament epistle to the Hebrews. *Hebrews 8:5(a)* informs us that the tabernacle (which was given permanence in the building of the temple) was ". . . a copy and shadow of the heavenly things."

God is not an absentee God. He does not "dwell in temples made by hand," *(Acts 17:24)* it is true, but the fact that He is invisible is not to be misunderstood. His judgements in history are evidence that the "Lord of Lords; who only hath immortality, dwelling in light unapproachable; whom no man hath seen, nor can see . . ." *(I Timothy 6:15(b)-16)* does indeed "come forth out of His place, and will come down . . ." *(Micah 1:3)*

There is no need to read the second advent of Christ into these verses. God has always come out of His holy place to chastise His people. Perhaps these historic comings, such as this one spoken by Micah, are a foretaste, a warning, of the final coming of Christ in judgement, but the words of Micah were fulfilled in the judgements of God against the northern and southern kingdoms at the hands of Sargon and Nebuchadnezzar.

TREAD UPON THE HIGH PLACES . . . 1:3(b) +

The "high places" refer to Baal worship. They were generally any natural or man-made projection which stood above their surroundings. (Cf. *I Kings 13:32* and *II Kings 23:15*)

FIRST CYCLE   1:3b

High places were forbidden by the law *(Deuteronomy 12:11-14)* and when Israel entered the promised land they were instructed to destroy them as monuments to Canaanite idolatry. (Cf. *Leviticus 26:30, Numbers 33:52, Deuteronomy 33:29)* These commandments were so completely ignored by the people that they became practically unknown.

By divine command, Gideon built altars in the high places, as did also Manoah. *(Judges 6:25-26, 13:16-23)* Samuel also appears to have violated the commandment against high places in building the altar at Mizpah, *(I Samuel 7:10)* and again at Bethlehem. *(I Samuel 16:5)* Saul transgressed this command at Gilgal and Ajalon. (Compare *I Samuel 13:9* and *14:35)* David ignored the divine ordinance against high places on the threshing floor at Ornan, *(I Chronicles 21·26)* as did Elijah on Mount Carmel *(I Kings 18:30)* and other prophets. *(I Samuel 10:5)*

Some of the above named men violated this command in obedience to directive from God for a special purpose *(eg.* Elijah's contest with the prophets of Baal.)

Rehoboam instituted definite worship in the high places. *(II Chronicles 11:15, II Kings 23:9)*

Hezekiah's reforms included the systematic elimination of these shrines to paganism. *(II Kings 18:4,22, II Chronicles 31:1)* This task was completed under Josiah. *II Kings 23, II Chronicles 34:3)*

After this systematic destruction, there is no further mention of the worship of Jehovah in high places in the Old Testament. However, the "worship in these hills" mentioned by the Samaritan woman at Jacob's well *(John, chapter four)* was probably a vestige of this despicable practice of mixing Jehovah worship with Baal worship. Baalbek, the last surviving center of sun god worship, continued to flourish under the Roman domination of the New Testament period and well into the third century A.D.

The working of God in history has long since trodden down the "high places" of Baal worship and of polluted Jehovah worship, but the influence of Baal among God's people is apparent yet today as Christians continue the observance of the same holy days by the use of many of the same devices and customs.

The more one learns of the abominable practice of Baal worship and of its devastating effect upon the covenant people, the more one questions the wisdom of promoting such days and customs in the church. The history of virtually every major "Christian holiday" is traceable directly to the worship of the sun god in one form or another.

55

MOUNTAINS TO MELT, VALLEYS TO MELT LIKE WAX . . .
1:4

Fire is the traditional symbol of God's purifying judgement. Moses, exhorting Israel against covenant breaking, warned; "Take heed to yourselves lest ye forget the covenant of Jehovah your God, which He made with you, and make you a graven image in the form of anything which Jehovah thy God hath forbidden thee. For Jehovah thy God is a devouring fire, a jealous God. *(Deuteronomy 4:23-24)*

It is fitting that Micah, and other prophets *(e.g. Isaiah 66:15)* in their attempt to call the people back to the covenant through obedience to the law, should remind them of this symbol. The heat of God's wrath is depicted as melting the mountains and turning the valleys to wax. The symbolism is obvious, both the high and the low, the great and the small will be devoured by God's firey wrath. God is no respecter of persons. As the song writer has put it:

> *"The great man was there, but his greatness*
> *When death came was left far behind.*
> *The angel who opened the records*
> *Not a trace of his greatness could find."*

No matter how high or low the station, hearts hard as stone against the pleading of God's prophets become like wax in the presence of His wrath. One of the primary warnings of the prophets is that human greatness does not bring preferential treatment from God.

THE OCCASION OF THE WRATH . . . Micah 1:5

RV . . . For the transgression of Jacob is all this, and for the sins of the house of Israel. What is the transgression of Jacob? is it not Samaria? and what are the high places of Judah? are they not Jerusalem?

LXX . . . All these calamities are for the transgression of Jacob, and for the sin of the house of Israel. What is the transgression of Jacob? is it not Samaria? and what is the sin of the house of Jacob? is it not Jerusalem?

COMMENTS

The purifying wrath of God against "the people" is, in this case, occasioned by "the sins of Jacob . . . and for the transgression of the house of Israel." Here in the "indictment" Micah uses the covenant names which treat both the kingdoms as one people.

Many times the covenant name for God is "the God of Abraham, Isaac and Jacob." The shorter form of reference to the covenant people is simply "Jacob," as used here by Micah. Jacob, as the last of the patriarchs and the father of the twelve tribes, is best representative of the covenant people as a whole.

Indeed, it is his new name, Israel, given to him upon his realization that Jehovah is the universal God rather than a local deity, which came to represent the people as well as the man.

"Israel" was first the name of the man, Jacob. Following his dream on the way to Haran from Beersheba, Jacob awoke to the realization that "surely the Lord is in this place, and I knew it not." *(Genesis 28:16)* It was during the dream that God reaffirmed to him the everlasting covenant which He had made with Abraham and confirmed previously with Jacob's father, Isaac.

As with them, so with Jacob, the heart of the covenant was: "in thy seed shall all the families of the earth be blessed." *(Genesis 28:14)* Some fourteen years later, following his marriage to the daughters of Laban, Jacob turned in prayer to God because of his fear that his brother Esau would seek revenge against him. Subsequently, God granted him the experience of wrestling with an angel. When he prevailed in the combat the angel said to him, "thy name shall be no more called Jacob but Israel (Prince of God) for as a prince thou hast power with God and with men, and hast prevailed." *Genesis 32:28)*

To understand the meaning of the name Israel in any given passage, one must keep in mind the various uses of it throughout the Old and New Testaments. The exact meaning must be determined by the specific context in which it appears.

As we have seen, *Israel* was first the covenant name given to Jacob upon his realization of the universal nature of God. It next came to apply to the whole family descended from this man, then to the twelve tribes into which the family grew, *ie.* the direct descendants of the twelve sons of Jacob.

Israel next came to apply to the nation formed of Jacob's descendants by the giving of the Law through Moses. This is significant, since Israel was the *covenant* name. The attachment of it to the nation points up the truth written by Paul, "a covenant confirmed beforehand by God, the law, which came four hundred and thirty years after, doth not disannul, so as to make the promise of none effect."

1:5   MICAH

(Galatians 3:18) The purpose of God in Israel was not changed by the passing of time and development of a political commonwealth. The very name worn by the nation under the Law was intended to emphasize their covenant relationship to God, and to signify the life, character and mission that was to be theirs as His called-out people.

First the family, then the federation of tribes wore this name. In the beginning the people were held together by a sense of kinship growing out of a common ancestry and a common covenant God.

In the giving of the Law a third factor united them. The Law was, in effect, a national constitution. During the time of the judges, when the Law was applied directly by God through the judges, there was an acute awareness of the nation's covenant relationship to God. Under the reign of Saul, David and Solomon, the covenant awereness waned as the people struggled for national identity among the nations of the world. By the time the kingdom was divided, the term *Israel* expressed almost entirely a nationalistic concept which was nearly devoid of any covenant awareness.

The ideal which runs through both the pre-exilic and post-exilic prophets is the restoration of covenant awareness through obedient faith in God.

Micah's prophecy is addressed to pre-exilic *Israel*. The outlook of the people at this time was strongly nationalistic. Covenant awareness was at perhaps its lowest ebb, yet the prophet uses the ancient covenant name *Israel* in such a way as to remind his readers of its real meaning.

The name *Israel* was taken by the *southern* kingdom during the post-exilic period (following the return from Babylon). *(Ezra 6:16, Nehemiah 11:3)* In the inter-Biblical period, from Malachi to Matthew, the term fell into disuse. In its place the nation and the people were called *Jews* to distinguish them from Greek, Roman, Persian, etc.

In the New Testament, *Israel is used to emphasize relationship to God as a covenant people. (Matthew 9:33, Luke 2:32, John 3:10, Acts 4:10)* When the *nation,* or race, is intended in the New Testament, the term is *"Jews."* This is obviously a distinction vital to the understanding of the relationship of New Testament *Israel* to the Old Covenant and God's people under it.

Before singling out first the northern and then the southern kingdoms to warn each of its particular punishment, Micah calls to them both in terms calculated to remind them wherein they have failed. They will be punished for more than specific sins. The punishment for these sins will be brought about by their failure to keep the covenant. Such had been the warning of Jehovah against His people at the time of the giving of the Law, and earlier at the institution of circumcision.

In both Israel and Judah, Micah equates the sins of the nation with the nature of its capital. The transgression of Jacob (Israel) is Samaria. The sin of Judah is Jerusalem.

JUDAH . . . 1:5(b)

Following the rebellion of the ten northern tribes and the division of the kingdoms, the northern kingdom became known as Israel and the southern as Judah. While the rebellious northern tribes seem to have usurped the "family name" of God's people, it was the southern kingdom through whom the fulfillment of the covenant finally came.

Originally, the name *Judah* designated the fourth son of Jacob and Leah, born in Mesopotamia during the time when his father served his uncle Laban. Judah, the great-grandson of Abraham, became the head of and gave his name to the most powerful of the twelve tribes. In the blessing of Judah, Jacob promised that, ". . . the scepter shall not depart from Judah, nor a law-giver from between his feet, until Shilo come; and unto him shall be the obedience of the people." *(Genesis 49:10)*

The significance of this, as well as the rest of the blessing, *(Genesis 49:8-12)* is seen in the increasing strength of Judah throughout the history of the people. (See *Numbers 2:3, Joshua 9:1, Judges 1:1-2, Isaiah 29:1,* etc.) The capital city, Jerusalem, became the capital of the southern kingdom, with Judah as the predominant tribe, (the southern kingdom also included Benjamin and Simeon) and remained so until the coming of the Christ to the Roman province of Judea. Judea was the first century vestige of Judah, and its capital also was Jerusalem. The scepter had not passed from Judah until He came!

In the occupation of the land of Canaan under Joshua, Judah, the tribe, had occupied the southern section from the Jordan to the Mediterranean as far north as the southern boundaries of Dan and Benjamin. *(Joshua 15)* With the division of the kingdom, it was this territory, along with the greater part of that of Benjamin to the north and Simeon to the south, that formed the southern kingdom.

Samaria . . . transgression of Jacob . . . Micah 1:5(b)

The capital of the northern kingdom of Israel was Samaria. Micah singles out this capital in the north as the personification of the "transgression of Jacob."

Samaria was situated south of the Plain of Esdralon in the vicinity where Abraham had stayed for a while on the plains of Moreh. *(Genesis 12:6)* It was in the territory possessed, in the days of Joshua, by Ephraim and Manasseh. The name, Samaria, came to be applied to that general area following the time of Solomon.

The city from which the territory of Samaria took its name was situated on a hill some forty miles north of Jerusalem. In 880 B.C., Omri moved his capital there from Tirzah. The hill upon which it sits is located adjacent to the fertile *wady esh-Shair,* and towers some 300 feet above the valley which extends from Shechem (Sychar) westward to the coast. The Mediterranean is clearly visible from this vantage point.

Under Ahab, due in a large part to the influence of Jezebel, Baal worship came to dominate both the religion and the general culture of Samaria. *(II Kings 3:2)* Idolatry, sensuality and oppression become the order of the day. (See chapter III, BAAL WORSHIP.)

Modern archeological excavations at Samaria reveal seven Israelite levels. The first and second, or lowest, levels date from the time of Omri and Ahab. The seventh, or highest, level marks the destruction of Samaria by the Assyrians following the three year siege begun by Shalamaneser in the seventh year of Hoshea's reign. The siege was concluded under Sargon II in 722.

It was this destruction of which Micah warns in our text. Sargon claims to have carried away only 27,290 from the entire nation of Samaria (Israel). No doubt, as with Judah later, these were the most powerful and influential citizens.

The sin with which Samaria is particularly identified, when Micah calls her "the transgression of Jacob," is idolatry, particularly the worship of Baal. As Halley puts it, "God had sent Elijah, Elisha and Amos to turn them (the Samaritans) back from idols. But in vain. They were about ripe for the death blow."

JERUSALEM ... SIN OF JUDAH ... 1:5(c)

Manuscript evidence here seems to indicate as the correct reading, ". . . . what are the high places of Judah . . ." rather than "what is the sin of Judah."

If this be true, the sin of Judah is but a variation of the idolatry of Samaria. However, the "high place" of Jerusalem would be the temple and its immediate surroundings as the center of worship. The worship conducted there, rather than being out and out Baal worship, was, during this period, Jehovah worship polluted with Baalism.

FIRST CYCLE   1:5c

It is interesting to note that both *Je* (in Jehovah) and *Baal* literally mean Lord. Itt is often difficult to tell, in some passages, whether the prophets are denouncing Baal worship *per se* or a corruption of Jehovah worship.

The Bible reader is first introduced to the *site* of Jerusalem some one thousand years before the time of David. We are told *(Genesis 14)* that Abraham stopped there shortly after the slaughter of the kings. *(Hebrews 7)* The ancient name of the place was Salem, an abbreviated form of yeru-Shalem foundation, or city, of peace.

It was here that Abraham met and paid tithes to Melchezedek. The name means literally "my king is Zedek." He was priest to the God *El-Elyon,* "God of Peace," *whom* Abraham identified with *Yaweh* (Jehovah). *Genesis 14:18-20)*

It is probable that this also marks the site of the sacrifice of Isaac by his father, Abraham. "The land of Moriah," *(Genesis 22:2)* has not been positively identified. The Septuagint reads, "the highland," while the Syriac has "land of the Amorites." Local tradition, however, identifies Moriah with the mountain on which the temple was built. *(II Chronicles 3:1)*

The Scriptures do not identify the exact location of Isaac's sacrifice, but both Jewish and Arab (Moslem) tradition locate it at the present site of the "Dome of the Rock." This second most sacred shrine in Islaam stands where the Biblical temple once stood.

(Incidentally, it is the possession of this sacred site which furnishes much of the fuel for the present inferno in the Middle East.)

At the time of Joshua, Jerusalem was the domain of Adom-Zedek, the Amorite who, in alliance with four other kings, attempted to prevent the Israelite conquest of southern Canaan. *(Joshua 10)* It was then the home of the Jebusites. *(Genesis 10:15* and *Numbers 13:29)* The city was on the border between the lands assigned to Benjamin, on the north, and Judah, on the south *(Joshua 15:7-8 and 18:10)* It was never occupied by the Israelites until the time of David, by which time it was at least a thousand years old!

The most historic transaction ever to take place in this ancient city took place when David made it his capital. Following the death of Saul at Gilboa, David reigned over Judah from Hebron *(II Samuel 2:1-4)* When the death of Isbosheth opened the way for David to unite the northern and southern tribes, Jerusalem was a more appealing location for two primary reasons.

First, Jerusalem was more centrally located than Hebron, and hence more accessible from both north and south.

1:5c   MICAH

Second, and perhaps more significant, the city belonged to no tribe. Being situated on the line between Benjamin to the north and Judah to the south, it could be made the seat of governmen for the federation without disturbing the *status quo* of any tribe, in much the same way that Washington D.C. was made our national capital without being part of any state.

Jersusalem is one of two cities called, in Scripture, "city of David." The other is Bethlehem. *(Luke 2:11)* The latter was his "home town" by birth, *(I Samuel 1:16)* the former became his city by force of arms. *(II Samuel 5)*

After making Jerusalem his political capital, David determined to make it the religious capital also. He brought the Ark of the Covenant from Shiloh to Jerusalem and placed it with careful preparation. *(II Samuel 6:12-14)* He also purchased the threshing floor of Araunah as the site upon which a permanent housing for the Ark would be built and later erected an altar of burnt offerings upon the site. *(II Samuel 24:25)*

The traditional tomb of David may be seen today on the southwestern slopes of the hill upon which Jerusalem sits. Most scholarship discounts the authenticity of the site, however.

Evidence of early pagan influence in Jerusalem, capital of Jehovah worship, is seen in such activity as the sacrifice offered by Adonijah "by the stone of Zoheleth, which is beside En-rogel." *(I Kings 1:9)* Zoheleth is associated with Baal worship.

(Readers of the English Bible are frequently misled concerning Adonijah by the unfortunate King James translation of *I Kings 1:6*, "he was a very goodly man." Rotherham more accurately renders this passage, "he was of exceedingly handsome appearance."

A part of the sun worship during the festivities of the winter solstice (December 24-25) centered around the burning of a log. (See Chapter III Baal Worship) The log represented the sun god cut down in the midst of his strength. Around the stump of the tree was pictured a serpent, symbol of his reviving life. After the burning of the log on the evening of December 24, the evergreen fir appeared next morning in its place symbolizing the reviving of the slain god. The serpent which twined around the stump was also worshipped as a minor deity. It was at an altar to this pagan god that Adonijah offered sacrifices.

Since Adonijah offered his sacrifices on the eve of an abortive attempt to sieze the throne of his father, David, he could scarcely do so in the proper place. It is highly probable that he was attempt-

FIRST CYCLE 1:5c

ing to sacrifice to Jehovah. If so, his worship of God at a pagan altar is a good example of the pollution of Jehovah worship by Baalism in Jerusalem.

This pollution was multiplied several-fold by Solomon's compromise with paganism. *(1 Kings 11:4-8)* Ashtoreth, Chemosh and Moloch, named in connection with Solomon's unfaithfulness are names associated with the unholy trinity of the sun god. (See again Chapter III BAAL WORSHIP).

During the first hundred years following the division of the kingdom, Jerusalem was in a state of decline. At this time, Baalism increased.

After a period of restoration, from Jehosaphat to Joash (B.C. 871-789), Jerusalem was humiliated again by Jehoash (B.C. 798-789). It was during this period that Ahab and Jezebel, of the Omri dynasty in the northern kingdom, seized the throne of Judah. The temple was laid waste and the priesthood of Baal was supported from the royal treasury.

Jerusalem was revived agian under Uzziah, but the worship of Jehovah was never quite completely purified of the influence of Baalism prior to the Babylonian captivity.

It is quite obvious that the sinfulness of both Samaria and Jerusalem and their subsequent destruction are directly related to the insiduous influence of Baal. Babylon, "the mother of harlots," *(Revelation 17:5)* had succeeded, through her daughter, the religion of Baal, in seducing Israel the "prince of God."

It was this spiritual immorality between the people of God and the religion of men that was the object of God's warning to them through the prophets, and the target of His wrath when they refused to repent.

POLLUTED AND FALSE RELIGION OF SAMARIA AND
JERUSALEM RESULT IN MORAL AND SOCIAL EVILS . . .

The peculiar sins of Israel were personified in Samaria. The moral and social abuses against which Micah prophecied are the same as those listed by Amos, who preached and wrote during the same period. Amos speaks of God's faithful being sold into slavery. *(Amos 2:6-7)* The poor were oppressed. *(Amos 5:7)* Graft in high places was the order of the day *(Amos 5:12)* as was dishonesty in business dealings.

The insatiable drive for status symbols *(Amos 4:1, 3:15, 6:4)* coupled with an intense pre-occupation with entertainment *(Amos 6)* left the people unconcerned for their national welfare.

1:5, 6   MICAH

False confidence in a false god produced a false sense of security from divine judgement. *(Amos 5:14, 9:10)*

As might be expected, the moral fiber of the people was totally rotten. Amos speaks of father and son committing fornication with the same girl. *(Amos 2:7)*

The peculiar sins of Judah were personified in Jerusalem. Micah lists the peculiar sins of the southern kingdom. They vary slightly from those of the north, and the variation may be due in part to the degree of Baal influence. Nevertheless, Judah's sins are heinous and the prophet's warning is sharp just as against Israel. The absence of righteousness noted by Micah *(Micah 7:2)* is reminiscent of Abraham's futile search for one righteous man in Sodom. *(Genesis 18:23-ff)*

In denouncing this unrighteousness, Micah focuses on four principal kinds of evil-doers: (1) There were the land grabbers whom the prophet pictures as lying awake at night and scheming how they may do the small farmer out of his holdings. *(2:1)* Their concern was not for the moral right or wrong of what they were doing, but only for whether or not they would be found out. *(2:9)* This avarice was practiced even at the expenes of one's own relatives. *(7:5-7)*

(2) There were lovers of evil in high office. *(3:1-4)* In their activities, bribery rather than justice decided civil cases *(7:3)* so that the "little man" had no effective recourse against the grabbing of the rich and powerful.

(3) False preachers, who were more concerned with their income than with the truth or with right and wrong, preached what their wealthy listeners wanted to hear.

(4) Hireling priests added to the practice of the false prophets. *(311)* Idolatry was allowed to pollute the worship of the people. *(5:11-2 and 3.7)* As a result of such unholy "clergy," the people believed that their national identity as "God's People" insured them against destruction *(3:11)* and that God's favor could be bought with sacrifice. *(6:5-7)* They could have profited greatly by reading their own Bible. *(eg. Psalm 50)*

No thinking American Christian can read the minor prophets and fail to sense the parallels between Israel and Judah just prior to their downfall and America in the second half of the twentieth century. The sins are the same . . . their causes are the same . . . the public apathy is the same . . . the false sense of security is the same . . . and, because God deals with men in every age on the basis of the same eternal ethic, the danger of destruction is the same. If our nation should fall due to this moral dry rot resulting from polluted and false

FIRST CYCLE 1:6-11

religion, it would be no strange thing when viewed in the light of history. And if God should use a godless power to bring about this destruction, this also would be in keeping with the lessons of history. God is still on His throne exercising authority over nations!

SAMARIA TO BE DESTROYED . . . Micah 1:6-11

RV . . . Therefore I will make Samaria as a heap of the field, and as places for planting vineyards; and I will pour down the stones thereof into the valley, and I will uncover the foundations thereof. And all her graven images shall be beaten to pieces, and all her hires shall be burned with fire, and all her idols will I lay desolate; for of the hire of a harlot hath she gathered them, and unto the hire of a harlot shall they return.. For this will I lament and wail; I will go stripped and naked; I will make a wailing like the jackals, and a lamentation like the ostriches. For her wounds are incurable; for it is come even unto Judah; it reacheth unto the gate of my people, even to Jerusalem. Tell it not in Gath, weep not at all: at Bethleaphrah have I rolled myself in the dust. Pass away, O inhabitant of Shaphir, in nakedness and shame: the inhabitant of Zaanan is not come forth; the wailing of Bethezel shall take from you the stay thereof.

LXX . . . Therefore I will make Samaria as a store-house of the fruits of the field, and as a planting of a vineyard: and I will utterly demolish her stones, and I will expose her foundations. And they shall cut in pieces all the graven images, and all that she has hired they shall burn with fire, and I will utterly destroy all her idols: because she has gathered of the hires of fornication, and of the hires of fornication has she amassed wealth. Therefore shall she lament and wail, she shall go barefooted, and being naked she shall make lamentation as that of serpents, and mourning as of the daughters of sirens. For her plague has become grievous; for it has come even to Juda, and has reached to the gate of my people, even to Jerusalem. Ye that are in Geth, exalt not yourselves, and ye Enakim, do not rebuild from the ruins of the house in derision: sprinkle dust in the place of your laughter. The inhabitant of Sennaar, fairly inhabiting her cities, came not forth to mourn for the house next to her: she shall receive of you the stroke of grief.

COMMENTS

SAMARIA . . . SCENE OF DESOLATION . . . Micah 1:6-7

Samaria had been first to succumb to Baal worship. Before Jerusalem, Samaria had first become shot through with sin as a result of

1:6, 7   MICAH

false gods. Samaria had chosen to break with the government in God's chosen city, Jerusalem. Samaria would be first to feel the wrath of God against a rebellious people.

Micah had actually seen this destruction in the vision by which the word of God came to him. (Cf. *1:1*) *His* description of it bears the vivid stamp of eyewitness testimony. It is as though his eyes smarted from the dust of falling buildings and the stench of death after battle burned his nostrils. He would live to experience the same terrible desolation again in reality. The land would be overrun in 734 B.C. and the city itself wiped out in 721 B.C. by the armies of Shalmaneser and Sargon II.

Micah's God is not a petty national deity commited unconditionally to support the nation of Israel. He is the transcendant God who has called a man and through him created a people to bless all men. He will not brook flagrant disobedience and turning to strange gods. Indeed He cannot, if His eternal grand design for man is to be redeemed in the Seed of Abraham and fulfilled in a called-out family with Him as head.

Nor is He simply a petulant overlord who is in a rage because He has not had His own way. His wrath springs from much deeper wells. His wrath is His love reacting to that which threatens to thwart His blessing all the nations of the world. If He is to bring this redemption about, what He is about to do to Israel, must be done to preserve the covenant by which the blessing is to come to all.

Samaria, *capital* of the northern nation and center of her religion has become also the *capital* of her sin and the center of guilt. So Samaria will become "as a heap of the field . . . as places for planting vineyards . . ."

In the rock-strewn fields of Palestine, such a heap is a common sight, as the farmer gathers the stones into a heap in preparation for planting. The stones of which the once proud *city* of Samaria was built will be cast into the valley below and piled in heaps. This prophecy of desolation was fulfilled so completely that even these heaps of stones have all but vanished today.

Before the building of Samaria by Omri, the three hundred foot hill on which it stood was a vineyard. Because the *city* had turned to strange gods and led its people into *sin,* the site would be returned to its original use.

The hill is surrounded today by terraces, one a narrow wooded mound of earth raised slightly from the hillside. Above it are the

66

marks of smaller terraces which may well be the vestiges of the streets of the city. In place of streets the terraces now support terraced fields.

God will "discover the foundations" of the city. The foundations are the unseen part of any structure. To find or discover them, it is necessary first to destroy the buildings which rest upon them. One who has walked among the ruins of ancient civilizations knows the familiar sight of such foundations . . . they are the last remaining ruin of any overthrown city. God will discover them in Samaria by wiping out this capital of idolatry.

All her graven images are to be beaten to pieces. To borrow a phrase from Abraham Lincoln, we have come to "the nub of the matter." It is Israel's unfaithfulness to her covenant vow with Jehovah in worshipping these images which was to bring about the ruination of Samaria.

The word "hires" (v. 7) refers to all that the worshippers of Baal sought to gain from worshipping him, along with the gifts offered to him as acts of worship. The motive in false worship is always personal gain of one type or another, just as true worship is always the abandonment of self to the purpose and service of God.

In laying waste the idols of Israel, God will be destroying the hires of a harlot. In her overthrow, her wealth, gained from spiritual fornication with idols, would go to another harlot . . . the Assyrian capital of Nineveh.

Micah is not the first to call false religion harlotry, especially when indulged in by the covenant people. (False worship is called harlotry throughout the Bible from its inception in old Babylon.) The allegory is an apt one. The covenant with Israel is treated as a marriage vow; Israel's incessant affairs with Baal as adultery.

Hosea 2:2-13 develops this allegory in the actual marital stress of the prophet's own life. *Ezekiel 16* contains two separate versions of the allegory.

In the first, the foundling child becomes the faithless wife of her benefactor. There the emphasis is upon Judah, but the principle is the same, since all of the people flirted with idolatry. The girlchild is left exposed to die. Jehovah passes by and bids her live and flourish. Later, in womanhood, He solemnly marries her and provides her with wealth and status far above her neighbors. She owes all to Him.

In return His bride plays the harlot *(Ezekiel 16:15)* by offering her children, the children of Jehovah, to idols!

Ezekiel 16's second allegory centers in Jerusalem. Her sin is said to be worse than Sodom or Samaria, since after all, they were not wives of Jehovah as was she. (Micah, however, does not hesitate to use the same allegory against Samaria since the people in the north as well as those in the south stood under the same divine covenant.)

Similar accusations of unfaithfulness are directed against the covenant people in such passages as *Hosea 4:13-14, Amos 2:7-8, Isaiah 30:6, Jeremiah 2 & 3,* etc.

The law required that an unfaithful wife and her lover be put to death. *(Deuteronomy 22:22)* Israel's unfaithfulness is worse than that of a common prostitute who is paid for her services. She invites her lovers and pays them. *(Isaiah 30:6,* etc.) Therefore God, Who is righteous in that He always conducts Himself by the same standards which He sets for His people, will punish His faithless wife. *(Ezekiel 16:35-43)*

The punishment will not be by death. He will expose her to the world and give her over to her lovers, but He will do it to stop her harlotry and save the marriage, *ie.* the covenant. This is carefully spelled out by the prophets. The forthcoming downfall of Israel and the captivity of Judah will be followed by a reconciliation. The covenant will once again become the basis of a happy marriage. The temple will be rebuilt, following the captivity, and the *remnant* of Israel will yet be the means of blessing all the nations of the world through the Seed of Abraham.

THE HUSBAND'S LAMENT . . . 1:8

God does not enjoy punishing His people. Even though He has no choice but to cast off His faithless bride for a time in order to preserve the marriage, He now says, in effect, *"this is going to hurt me worse than it does you!"* Such lamentation ought to put the lie to the theology current in some modern circles which separates the God of the Old Testament from the God of the New Testament on the ridiculous assumption that the God of the Old Testament was not a "God of love." There is no pain equal to the pain suffered when love punishes to preserve!

The deep anguish of God over the state of Israel and the necessity to punish her so violently is spelled out in terms of the public mourning customary at the time. In time of deep distress, the bereaved stripped off his sandals (the Septuagint so translates "stripped" here) and his upper garments (the meaning of "naked" in these verses). Such barefoot, naked condition was a common sign of mourning. *(II Samuel 15:30)*

FIRST CYCLE   1:8,9

To lament was to beat the breast in despair to the accompaniment of a loud mournful howl. The sound is here compared to that of the jackals, (rather wild dogs) which howl when deserted like a human cub when left alone and unloved. It is also compared here with the sound of the ostrich which in distress utters a long shrill sighing cry as though in deep hurt. Another similitude may also be intended by the reference to the ostrich: an ostrich hen will occasionally forget her nest, leaving her eggs to be trampled. So has Israel deserted Jehovah. (Cf. *Hebrews 10:29* where unfaithfulness to Christ is pictured as trampling under foot the Son of God.)

Micah pictures Jehovah as utterly tormented by the plight of His people and with grief for having to punish them so severely. Although He has been deeply wounded by the unfaithfulness of His bride, He still loves her very much. Yet the purpose for which the marriage had been contracted demands her faithfulness to Him and to bring this about she must be punished. He does not glory in her impending suffering . . . He is more torn by it than she!

It would be difficult to find a more vivid example of what it means to hate sin and love sinners. The old cliche of the wife deserting her husband for his best friend is exceeded here when Israel deserts God for His worst enemy . . . Baal. Yet he does not hate her . . . He despises her sin. Even in the punishment there are overtones of forgiveness!

How much more we would appreciate our relationship to God if we could but understand how very much He loves us! How much more we would be like Him . . . and worthy to be called His children . . . if we could learn to so love in spite of sin.

THE PURPOSE OF THE PUNISHMENT . . . 1:9

Leaving the allegory of the faithless wife and the injured husband, the Lord, through Micah, now reveals His ultimate concern. The infection of Samaria is spreading like a deadly contagion to Judah . . . to the Chosen City itself. If the Covenant of Promise is to be redeemed, the infection must be stopped. Since it is already incurable, it must be destroyed.

Moral decay resulting from false religion bears the seed of its own destruction. In the case of Samaria it was time for surgery. The northern kingdom was wiped out, its people scattered, and there was never to be a return.

There is the hope that, seeing the destruction of Samaria, Judah would repent. As the infection, so the therapeutic destruction reached as far as the capital gates when the armies of Sennacherib camped outside the walls. *(Isaiah 36:1, 37:33-37)* God's punishment came step by step, leaving time for repentance. The defeat of Samaria and the scattering of her people, the halting of Sennacharib short of a conquest of Jerusalem were designed to call Jerusalem to her knees in contrition, to turn her away from the idolatry and insuing abandonment of morality which had become uncurable in the north.

But Jerusalem would not repent. She was taken captive to Babylon so that God, through suffering, might force the remnant back to Himself that the covenant might be fulfilled through them.

PUNISHMENT EXTENDED TO GATE OF JERUSALEM . . .
1:10-12

The punishment of God against the northern kingdom is not to stop at Samaria. It will rather roll like a relentless tide until it dashes against the very walls of Jerusalem. This is depicted dramatically by Micah as he lists one village after another, each one slightly nearer Jerusalem.

He begins with Gath, one of the five cities of the Philistines, on the northern borders of Judah and proceeds through Bethle-aphrah, Shaphir, Zaanan, Bethezel and Maroth. The coming invasion by Sennacharib is presented in all its terror as one village after another falls before him, the refugees from one finding no succor in the next.

"Tell it not in Gath!" Gath, the city of the Philistines . . . how the Philistines would delight to hear of the destruction of the Hebrews. The prophet's words are an echo of David's lament over the death of Saul and Jonathan. *(II Samuel 1:20) "Weep not at all."* Do not reveal to the enemies of God's people your inner feelings . . . lest they rejoice!

From Gath the invaders would sweep south. *"At Bethle-aphrah have I rolled myself in the dust."* This is the only mention of Bethle-aphrah in the Bible. Its name is a play on words . . . meaning literally "city of dust." (An appropriate name for many Judean villages!) Rolling in the dust was one of many customary forms of mourning, similar to another such practice . . . that of sitting in sackcloth and ashes.

From Bethle-aphrah the disaster mounts to Shaphir, a village of Judah which lay between Eleutheropolis and Ashkelon. The name means "fair." *"Pass away, O inhabitants of Shaphir, in nakedness and shame."* Nakedness again is to be understood as the removal of the upper gar-

FIRST CYCLE   1:10-12

ment as a sign of mourning. That which was once fair would stand naked and ashamed in the judgement of the Lord!
"The inhabitant of Zaanan is not come forth." Zaanan has not been definitely identified by archeologists. It is probably the same as Zenan, located east of Ashkelon. *(Joshua 18:22)* Its people cannot come forth to console the refugees from the north because they are themselves in the path of Sennacharib. This is reminiscent of Jeremiah's warning, "Thus saith Jehovah, Behold a people cometh from the north country; and a great nation shall be stirred up from the uttermost parts of the earth. They lay hold on bow and spear; they are cruel, and have no mercy; their voice roareth like the sea, and they ride upon horses, every one set in array, as a man to the battle, against thee, O daughter of Zion. We have heard the report thereof; our hands wax feeble: anguish hath taken hold of us, and pangs as of a woman in travail. Go not forth into the field, nor walk by the way; for the sword of the enemy, and terror, are on every side. O daughter of my people, gird thee with sackcloth and wallow thyself in ashes: make thee mourning as for an only son, most bitter lamentation; for the destroyer shall suddenly come upon us." *(Jeremiah 6:22-26)*
"The wailing of Bethezel shall take from you the stay thereof." Bethezel may be the same as Azal. *(Zechariah 14:5)* "The stay thereof" is taken away. That is to say, Bethezel, itself smitten, cannot sustain those who flee from the destruction on the plains. There is no more security near Jerusalem. The rout is complete.

WARNINGS TO JUDAH ... Micah 1:12(b)-16

RV . . . For the inhabitant of Maroth waiteth anxiously for good, because evil is come down from Jehovah unto the gate of Jerusalem. Bind the chariot to the swift steed, O inhabitant of Lachish: she was the beginning of sin to the daughter of Zion: for the transgressions of Israel were found in thee. Therefore shalt thou give a parting gift to Moreshethgath; the houses of Achzib shall be a deceitful thing unto the kings of Israel. I will yet bring unto thee, O inhabitant of Mareshah, him that shall possess thee: the glory of Israel shall come even unto Adullam. Make thee bold, and cut off thy hair for the children of thy delight: enlarge thy baldness as the eagle; for they are gone into captivity from thee.

LXX . . . Who has begun to act for good to her that dwells in sorrow? for calamities have come down from the Lord upon the gates of Jerusalem, even a sound of chariots and horsemen: the inhabitants of Lachis,

1:12-16 MICAH

she is the leader of sin to the daughter of Sion: for in thee were found the transgressions of Israel. Therefore shall he cause men to be sent forth as far as the inheritance of Geth, even vain houses; they are become vanity to the kings of Israel; until they bring the heirs, O inhabitants of Lachis: the inheritance shall reach to Odollam, even the glory of the daughter of Israel. Shave thine hair, and make thyself bald for thy delicate children; increase thy widowhood as an eagle; for thy people are gone into captivity from thee.

COMMENTS

The warning of Micah to Judah, concerning the fall of Samaria and the northern kingdom, is that the punishment from the north is to extend through the Philistine plain to the gates of Jerusalem. In verses 6-11 we saw the encroachment from Samaria's viewpoint. In verses 12-15 we see the invasion of the northern kingdom from the vantage point of several Judean towns which are so situated as to be in the path of Sargon. We might have expected the overthrow of the north to end at the boundary between Israel and Judah, but the conqueror was not so neat in his concerns. Certain towns which lay south of the border would, largely for reasons of topography, be taken along with the northern kingdom. Whatever the attitude of the southern kingdom toward this violation of its territory, it was in no position to do much about it.

The cities mentioned are in the Philistine plain of Shephelah in northwestern Judah, and are the home territory of the prophet Micah. Moresheth-gath was Micah's home town. One can imagine the anguish of heart that came to the prophet as, in a vision, he saw the destruction of people and places filled with personal nostalgia and memories.

The first of the cities of the Philistine plain mentioned is Maroth. The name means *bitterness*. The city is known in modern times as *Unman*. It is located in the hill country bordering the plain of Sephelah near Beth-anoth and Eltekon. (Cf. *Joshua 15:59*)

As with each of the cities and towns named here, there is a play on the literal meaning of the name Morath. The people of Morath (bitterness) are anxiously waiting for the good. There is no bitterness like that felt by those who wait in the path of an invading army, hoping against hope for the intervention of a delivering force. Since this is apparently the first city below the border and on Judean territory to be invaded, the citizenry would no doubt hope for the army of the southern kingdom to intervene on their behalf. In bitterness they waited eagerly for help (goodness) . . . but none came.

To those who stood in the path of the invader, it would seem that Sargon was the originator of their woes. The prophet sees otherwise. That which is to happen, which he has seen already happening in his vision, is "come down from Jehovah." It is punishment, first for sin, and secondly for failing to heed the prophets.

The anxiety of the citizens of Morath over their own plight would be eclipsed by their awareness that Jerusalem itself was threatened.?

The next mentioned city in the line of march is Lachish. The literal meaning of Lachish is *swift beast*. Again there is a play on words in the original text. The inhabitants of Lachish (swift beast) are warned to hitch their swift steed to the chariot. There would be need for speed if any were to successfully flee before the invading host.

Lachish is located at the site of today's Tel-el-Hesey, about sixteen miles east of Gaza and slightly north. (Cf. *Joshua 15:39* and *Jeremiah 34:7)* Her punishment is just, in that she was the "beginning of sin to the daughter of Zion."

We are not sure in what sense Lachish was the "beginning" of sin. Some have thought this was one of Solomon's chariot towns. *(I Kings 9:19, 10:26)* If so, the people of Lachish would have been among the first in Israel to be introduced to the false sense of security which comes from the dependance upon military arms rather than upon the might of Jehovah.

It seems more likely that Lachish was the "beginning" of sin in that she had been among the first cities of the southern kingdom to participate in the newly minted idolatry of Jeroboam. *(I Kings 12: 16-29)*

Whatever the reason, Micah makes Lachish responsible as the beginning of corruption and idolatry in Judah. The term *daughter of Zion* is a personification of all the people of Judah and of Jerusalem in particular. The implication is that Judah has been infected with Israel's sin and that Lachish is the "carrier."

Even though Lachish is a fortified city, Reoboam having made it so by surrounding it with double walls, battlements and towers, it would not escape the judgement of God at the hands of Sargon.

Micah's home town, Moresheth-gath, is next on the list of cities receiving the prophetic warning. It is difficult to know just who is being addressed in verse 14(a). There is apparently no historic connection between Lachish and Moresheth-gath and so no reason apparent why such a statement should be directed to Lachish. It seems more

1:12-16   MICAH

likely that *"you must give parting gifts"* is directed to Judah who must watch another Judean town overrun in the downfall of the northern kingdom.

It was (and still is) customary in that part of the world for members of the family to bring goodbye gifts to a daughter who has been given in marriage, and especially to one whose marriage will take her to a far away place never to be seen again by her family. The goodbye to Moresheth-gath will be like that . . . permanent.

The literal meaning of *Moresheth* is "possession," and again, in the giving of gifts, there is the play on words which is typical of this passage.

Achzib is mentioned, along with Mareshah, in *Joshua 15:44*. It may be the Chezeb of *Genesis 38:5* and also the Cozeba of *I Chronicles 4:42*. It is probably to be identified with modern Aen-Kezbah, situated eight miles north and east of Beit Jibrin in the Philistine plain.

The plural "houses of Achzib," is taken by some to indicate two Achzibs. If so it would be translated "the two Beth-Achzib." If this is true, the second Achzib is probably the one mentioned in *Joshua 29:29* and *Judges 1:13*. It is located in Asher and situated at or near the present site of Ez-zib on the coast between Acco and Tyre.

As with the other locations mentioned here, the name Achzib is a play on words. The Hebrew form of the word is *akhzabh*, meaning "a deceitful thing." It is applied in *Jeremiah 15:18* to a stream which seasonally dries up and which would deceive a weary traveler who expected to refresh himself. (Compare *Job 6:15*)

So Achzib shall be a deceitful thing to the king of Israel. The members of the royal family, fleeing to the town or towns of Beth Ach-achzib will not find a way of escape or refreshment.

It might be well to recall just here, that Sargon claims to have carried off only some 27,000 people from the northern kingdom. If so, it was the members of the royal family along with the social, political and cultural leaders. In this way the conquered people would be leaderless and unlikely to rebel. The flavor of fleeing royalty is found throughout the prophecies of the downfall of Israel.

In verse 15 we again find the usual play on words; this time found in the use of *yoresh*, "him that shall possess," with *Mareshah*, "a possession." *Joshua 15:44* pictures Moreshah as located near Achzib. Archeologists identify it with a ruin called Merash near Beit-Jibrin . . . about one mile to the south.

The Israelites had taken the city from the Canaanites. It will once more be possessed by a new possessor.

FIRST CYCLE   1:12-16

Adullam identified with the ruins at present day Aid-el-ma, three miles southeast of Soco and northeast eight miles from Mareshah, is, in a sense, the high water mark of the invasion at the time of the fall of Israel. Later, the entire southern kingdom would fall to Sennacharib, but for the present, the Assyrian tide stops here.

Adullam, as its location indicates, is in the lowlands of Judah *(Joshua 15:55)* and is characterized by an abundance of caves. It was here that David had fled from Saul. *(1 Samuel 22:1-ff)*

Now, centuries later, the same caves are to provide refuge for the northern nobility as they flee before the Assyrians. If there is to be a safe hiding place it will be here. So the "glory of Israel" *ie.* the valuables which are to be hidden from foreign plunder, are to come to the caves of Adullam.

Self-inflicted baldness was a symbol of mourning among the worshippers of Baal. *(Amos 8:10, Isaiah 3:24)* It is forbidden in the Law of Moses, *Leviticus 19:27-28* and *Deuteronomy 14:1)* probably because it was associated with the surrounding paganism. The demand that those here receiving the punishment of Jehovah shear their heads and the heads of their children is repeated three times for emphasis. The punishment is essentially for worshipping pagan gods. The fitting form of mourning for such is the mourning practiced by the original worshippers of Baal.

The word "eagle" in the English translation is misleading. The bird referred to here is probably the Carrion Vulture which populates Egypt (where it was worshipped) and Palestine. Its head is completely bald in front, and has only a very thin covering in back. Micah's rebuke is vivid and scathing.

The terrors of war have not changed. Insert new names for the towns and villages in this passage and we have a description of Europe cringing before Atilla the Hun, or Hitler . . . and of the people of the East trembling before the Japanese Imperial Army as it advances down the Pacific island chain toward Australia. Or, to make the allegory more contemporary yet . . . here is a picture of the Czech people shuddering as the Russian tanks roll by, or of Yugoslavia and Hungary bracing for a similar invasion.

The difference is that the invasion of Sargon and later of Sennacharib had been announced in advance by the prophets of God. They had been made aware that the pillage of war was their just punishment for having been unfaithful to God. Perhaps it is only this awareness that distinguishes them from more recent victims of conflict.

MICAH

Chapter VI—*Questions*

First Cycle

1. What evidence does Micah give in the early verses of his book concerning God's universal concern for all men?
2. The term "the people" is used frequently to designate————.
3. The term "the nations" indicates ———— in contrast to "the people."
4. What long precedent does Micah have for his use of "earth and all that therein is" to call the whole world to listen to God's indictment of His covenant people?
5. ————, Micah's contemporary, uses the same phrase.
6. What two reasons are apparent for God's concern that the "earth and all that is in it" hear His charge?
7. Who is the "star witness" for the prosecution against God's unfaithful people?
8. Show how Stephen's defense (Acts 7) seconds the accusation of Micah against the people.
9. Discuss, in connection with Micah 1:2(c)-3(a), "God is not an absentee God."
10. What is signified by the term "high places" (Micah 1:3(b))?
11. Discuss Micah's statement that the mountains shall melt and the valleys melt like wax. Micah 1:4
12. The purifying wrath of God against the people is to be occasioned by ———— and ————.
13. Trace the eight ways in which the name Israel is used historically in the Bible.
14. What is meant by pre-exilic? by post exilic?
15. Trace the Biblical history of the name Judah and its development into the word Jew.
16. Describe the situation of the city of Samaria.
17. How is Samaria the "transgression of Jacob"?
18. How is Jerusalem the "sin of Judah"?
19. Both *Je* and *Baal* mean ————.
20. Compare the sins of the northern and southern kingdoms.
21. Why was Samaria to be first to feel God's wrath?
22. Discuss the significance of Samaria's graven images.
23. How is spiritual harlotry an apt allegory of idolatry?
24. How does the lament of Micah 1:8 relate to our understanding

"*In the ninth year of Hoshea the king of Assyria took Samaria*" (II Kings 17:6).
This was Sargon II, conqueror of the capital of the northern kingdom of Israel. His portrait has been preserved on this limestone relief for over two thousand five hundred years.

FROM: THE BIBLE AS HISTORY IN PICTURES
By Werner Keller - Wm. Morrow Co.

Dur-Sharrukin—"Sargon's citadel"—was inscribed on cuneiform tablets which Emile Botta, the great French archaeologist, discovered at Khorsabad north of Nineveh in 1842. They were found among the ruined walls of what had been a gigantic royal establishment. Its builder was "Sargon, the king of Assyria", referred to in Isaiah 20: 1. The frontage of the city wall itself with its twenty towers—not counting the entrance gateway—was over 2000 feet long. The palace, which can be seen farther back, with its temple-tower, was built on an artificial platform 45 feet high (reconstruction).

FROM: THE BIBLE AS HISTORY IN PICTURES
By Werner Keller - Wm. Morrow Co.

SECOND CYCLE 2:1-3

that the God of the Old Testament is the same loving God as that of the New Testament?
25. What is the purpose of the punishment promised by Micah?
26. The warning of Micah to Judah is ——————.
27. List the cities of the Philistine plains mentioned by Micah. Locate them on a map.
28. Micah's home town was ——————.
29. Why did Sargon carry off the social, political and cultural leaders of Israel?
30. Self-inflicted baldness by the worshippers of Baal was a symbol of ——————.

CHAPTER VII
SECOND CYCLE
WOE TO THE ARROGANT MISLEADERS . . . Micah 2:1-3

RV . . . Woe to them that devise iniquity and work evil upon their beds! when the morning is light, they practise it, because it is in the power of their hand. And they covet fields, and seize them; and houses, and take them away: and they oppress a man and his house, even a man and his heritage. Therefore thus saith Jehovah: Behold, against this family do I devise an evil, from which ye shall not remove your necks, neither shall ye walk haughtily; for it is an evil time.

LXX . . . They meditated troubles, and wrought wickedness on their beds, and they put it in execution with the daylight; for they have not lifted up their hands to God. And they desired fields, and plundered orphans, and oppressed families, and spoiled a man and his house, even a man and his inheritance. Therefore thus saith the Lord; Behold, I devise evils against this family out of which ye shall not lift up your necks, neither shall ye walk upright speedily: for the time is evil.

COMMENTS

Micah now turns from the generalities of judgement impending against the northern and southern kingdoms, their capitals and their cities, to the personal denouncement of those who sit in high places in them. The punishment of Jerusalem and Samaria are the result of sin. Sin is an individual thing. If a society or a city is sinful, it is because it is inhabited by sinful people. If the individual is subject to

77

undue pressure and temptation in such surroundings, it is because he must associate with sinful people. In the case of the kingdoms denounced by Micah, the people were pressed toward sin and idolatry by sinful social leaders. It was these leaders who were disbursed from Israel by the Assyrians. It was the leaders of Judah who were led captive to Babylon.

(*Verse 1*) The evil of those in power was well thought out. They lay awake nights scheming, and the next day they eagerly put their plans into action. Micah accuses them of doing these evil things simply because the power to do so was in their hands. Power is the determining factor in both their intentions and their practices. There is not even a pretense at justice. An old adage says, "power corrupts and absolute power corrupts absolutely." It was true in Israel and Judah.

Plutarch wrote, "It is an observation no less just than common, that there is no stronger test of a man's character than power and authority, exciting as they are to every passion, and discovering every latent vice." Those in authority among God's people at the time of the minor prophets simply failed to pass the test. Rather than using their power and riches to the common good, they used them as an occasion of avarice and greed and debauchery.

(*Verse 2*) Pascal is quoted as saying, "power without justice is tyranny." Those in power in Israel and Judah were tyrants in the worse sense of the word. In the words of Wendell Phillips, "Power is ever stealing from the many to the few." The iniquity devised upon the beds of the powerful in Jerusalem and Samaria was designed to rob more and more of the possessions of the poor.

The prophet accuses them of coveting fields and seizing houses, of oppressing men and their families or heritage. The verse has a familiar ring to anyone who is aware of the cases common in American civil courts. In Israel and Judah there was no recourse to the courts.

(*Verse 3*) Therefore . . . because the powerful spend their time devising evil schemes against this people . . . I devise an evil from which ye shall not remove your necks, neither walk haughtily.

It has been said often that sin carries in its nature the seeds of its own punishment. One of the basic tenets of American jurisprudence is that the punishment shall fit the crime. The Law of Moses taught the principle "an eye for an eye, a tooth for a tooth." The evil which Jehovah devised against the avarice and greed of the powerful must be counted just by any standard.

Jehovah devised an "evil time" as the just punishment of these oppressors. Amos used the same terminology to describe the same impending judgement. *(Amos 5:13)*

Those against whom this particular "evil time" was devised as punishment would find no escape from it. They would not be able to "remove their necks," or to walk proudly. As they had taken lands and houses and possessions from the poor to add to their own pleasures, so, in the day of their captivity, were their houses and lands to be taken from them. Just as their power left no legal recourse for those who were oppressed by them, so their captors would have no mercy upon them.

We have previously noted that, both at the destruction of Israel and the later captivity of Judah, it was the rulers, the social elite and the influential rich who were actually led away, first by Assyria and then by Babylon. The full weight of God's punishment thus fell upon exactly those people who were directly responsible for the evil which brought it about.

A TAUNT AGAINST THE WICKED . . . Micah 2:4-5

RV . . . In that day shall they take up a parable against you, and lament with a doleful lamentation, and say, We are utterly ruined: he changeth the portion of my people: how doth he remove it from me! to the rebellious he divideth our fields. Therefore thou shalt have none that shall cast the line by lot in the assembly of Jehovah.

LXX . . . In that day shall a parable be taken up against you, and a plaintive lamentation shall be uttered, saying, We are thoroughly miserable: the portion of my people has been measured out with a line, and there was none to hinder him so as to turn him back; your fields have been divided. Therefore thou shalt have no one to cast a line for the lot.

COMMENTS

Napoleon once wrote, "Even in war, moral power is to physical as three parts to one." It was so in the case of those against whom Micah spoke the message of God. The power by which they enforced their social abuses was related directly to the moral power of a false religion. It is the exercise of power that most clearly reveals what is at the base of the true character of a man. In their case, the foundation of their abusive character was Baalism.

Having compromised God's truth with the falsehood of Baalism, the character of these rulers and social leaders was not forged of any real metal. Having first given way to the temptation to flirt with a false god, they found no real standard of ethics by which to govern their own lives. The inevitable result was the extreme cruelty against their fellows to which their greed had driven them. When the wrath of God is released against them, they will feel the sting of their own sins, as their enemies taunt them.

The taunt (or parable) which will be spoken against them by those who see the judgement of God brought upon them is written in advance, by the prophet in *Micah 2:4-5*. ". . . a parable against you, and lament with . . . lamentation," might be more literally rendered, "lament with a lamentation of lamentations." In the Hebrew text it reads *"naha, nehi, nihyah,"* and is reminiscent of the sing-song "yaya, yaya, yaya" with which young children taunt one another in every language. This monotonous insulting derision will be leveled against them repeatedly as their enemies make jest of their hardship, just as they now make sport of those whom they oppress.

Their friends, on the other hand, will cry in their behalf, ". . . we are utterly ruined." Those who now sit "high and mighty" at the expense of the down-trodden will find themselves in total despair. They will exclaim, ". . . He changed the portion of my people, how doth he remove it from me! To the rebellious he divideth our fields."

The irony and justice of God's judgements are magnificent. The powerful have changed the inheritance of the common people by cunning theft. They have removed the lands from them without recourse. In their downfall they will complain against God for doing exactly the same to them. In their straying from Jehovah to Baalism they have rebelled against God, and their rebellion has resulted in their misuse of power and wealth and their trodding down of His people. In that day they will wonder why God has taken the same possessions from them and given them to the "rebellious" Gentiles who will over-run their lands.

In verse five, Micah warns them that, just as they have left no legal recourse to those from whom they have stolen property, so in that day they will have "none that shall cast the line by lot." There will be no legal division of land, because there will be no land left to divide. It will be occupied by the enemies. There will be no courts to establish titles, because the government will be in the hands of the invader. Their misery over the loss of their unjust claims and titles will bring to them a measure of the misery they are now heaping upon

SECOND CYCLE 2:6, 7

others. They have forgotten that the land . . . this land especially, belongs to God. He led their fathers to it for *His* purposes. Now that they have deserted Him for Baal and are grabbing the land for their own greed, He will remove it completely from them.

History records that this warning was fulfilled in the northern kingdom at the dispersion of the ten tribes, and in the southern kingdom at the Babylonian captivity. Although God Himself restored the southern kingdom seventy years later, as a homeland for a remnant through which to fulfill the promise of the covenant, it is extremely difficult to justify any modern claim to the northern territories by the present state of Israel on any Scriptural basis. God removed the land from them in punishment for their despicable idolatry and maltreatment of His people, and because they refused to hear and heed the warnings of the prophets.

THE PROPHET ACCUSED AS AN ENEMY . . . Micah 2:6-7(a)

RV . . . Prophesy ye not, thus they prophesy. They shall not prophesy to these: reproaches shall not depart. Shall it be said, O house of Jacob, Is the Spirit of Jehovah straitened? are these his doings?

LXX . . . Weep not with tears in the assembly of the Lord, neither let any weep for these things; for he shall not remove the reproaches, who says, the house of Jacob has provoked the Spirit of the Lord; are not these his practices?

COMMENTS

V. 6 . . . PROPHESY NOT . . . THEY PROPHESY

These are the words of the false prophets and their followers in response to the warning pronounced by the prophets of Jehovah. Others than Micah had been rebuked in this same way. (eg. *Amos 7:16*)

The warnings of God's spokesmen grate on the ears of those who will not hear. They specifically charge Micah to desist from saying, "reproaches shall not depart from Israel." (Don't talk like that, preacher, it's not nice and it's not tolerant, and we won't listen!")

V. 7 . . . SHALL IT BE SAID, O HOUSE OF JACOB? . . .

Those whom the prophet has warned now turn on him as though he, and not they, were the enemies of God. In effect their challenge is, "we are God's people . . . we wear His name. Are we not the chosen Israel? Are we not the sons of the patriarchs? How can you say that God will act so toward His favorite people?"

Here is a glimpse of the national pride and racial arrogance that was ultimately to prevent the Jews from accepting Christ and which caused them to persecute Stephen and Paul for preaching a Gospel of universal concern. They have had increasing difficulty, throughout the remainder of their history as a nation, and still today as a race, in grasping the fundamental concept of a covenant people. Somehow the idea that God's Israel is composed of those who are related to Him by *obedient faith and not merely by racial ancestry or national origin* seems beyond their comprehension as a people. Modern Zionism is a case in point.

There are some "evangelical" Christians today whose understanding of the prophets is warped by the same erroneous idea. Most of the "far out" schemes and devices dealing with eschatology have at their heart the notion that God is somehow bound to the physical Hebrew race and the citizens of a national Jewish commonwealth. Nothing could be farther from the prophets' understanding of the nature of God's Israel. The insistence of Micah in this particular context is that the race . . . the nation, will suffer non-deferable calamity because they have failed to really *be* Israel. They have failed, by going off after strange gods and by breaking the Law of God, to keep the covenant upon which their peculiar relationship to God depended. (Cf. *Exodus 19:5-6*)

The logic of Micah's accusers is reflected in their retort, "Is the Spirit of Jehovah straitened? are these His doings?" In effect, "is Jehovah's Spirit so constricted and narrow that He would allow the destruction of His chosen people?" One hears much the same reasoning today on the part of those who insist on identifying Israel with a race or a political commonwealth.

The error of such thinking lies in this: it is precisely because the Spirit of God is *not* straitened that He will take such drastic measures to preserve the covenant faith. If God were only the tribal or national God of the Hebrews, He would be bound, or straitened, to defend them as "my people, right or wrong."

But such is not the case. Israel was called into being in the beginning because it was God's purpose through them to bless *all* nations. To do this there must be a once-for-all demonstration that His relationship to His people does not depend upon their racial origin and national identity, but upon their obedient faith. In the captivity there will be no nation, no holy city, no sacred temple. The people will have *only*

SECOND CYCLE 2:7-11

their faith to cling to. Micah will shortly say that out of this experience will come a faithful remnant through whom God's redemption will come.

The tendency manifest here to blame God or His spokesman for the social calamities of a nation are not confined to the dusty ancient archives of Biblical history . . . it is a tendency very much alive and with us today. The person who says, "if there is a God why does He allow poverty and suffering and war and inequality to go unremedied," "if there is a God how can He allow such things to exist in a 'Christian' civilization?" is voicing the same false concept of God as that held by Israel and Judah in the days of the minor prophets.

The failure of such logic lies in its major premise. It assumes that a nation which gives lip service to God and prints "in God we trust" on its coins is a Christian nation. Or, in its modern version, it assumes that all men are the children of God by some inalienable right. Such simply is not, and never has been the case. God's people are those who are faithful to His covenant, who obey His commandments. Ultimately a child of God is one who receives His redemption through the promised Seed of Abraham. (Cf. *John 1:11-12*)

The time had come in Micah's day to place the blame for what was about to happen squarely where it belonged, to "tell it like it is." The suffering and destruction and famine that lay ahead for both Israel and Judah would come as a result of their unfaithfulness, their disobedience and their failure to hear and heed God's call to repentance.

We have arrived at a similar time in the history of western civilization, and especially in "Christian" America.

THE PROPHET ANSWERS HIS CRITICS . . . Micah 2:7(b)-11

RV . . . Do not my words do good to him that walketh uprightly? But of late my people is risen up as an enemy: ye strip the robe from off the garment from them that pass by securely as men averse from war. The women of my people ye cast out from their pleasant houses; from their young children ye take away my glory for ever. Arise ye, and depart; for this is not your resting-place; because of uncleanness that destroyeth, even with a grievous destruction. If a man walking in a spirit of falsehood do lie, saying, I will prophesy unto thee of wine and of strong drink; he shall even be the prophet of this people.

LXX . . . Are not the Lord's words right with him? and have they not proceeded correctly? Even beforetime my people withstood him as an enemy against his peace; they have stripped off his skin to remove hope in the conflict of war. The leaders of my people shall be cast forth from their luxurious houses; they are rejected because of their evil practices; draw ye near to the everlasting mountains. Arise thou, and depart; for this is not thy rest because of uncleanness: ye have been utterly destroyed; ye have fled, no one pursuing you: thy spirit has framed falsehood, it has dropped on thee for wine and strong drink. But it shall come to pass, that out of the dropping of this people . . .

COMMENTS

V. 7(b) . . . DO NOT MY WORDS . . .

The word of God, no matter how stern, is never a threat to those who walk uprightly. Even the warning of inevitable national calamity would issue in the strengthened faith of the faithful, and the return from captivity of a generation dedicated to the re-establishment of true Jehovah worship. Centuries earlier David had written, "With the pure thou wilt show thyself pure; With the perverse thou wilt show thyself froward, For thou wilt save the afflicted people, But the haughty eyes thou wilt bring down." *Psalm 18:26-27)*

V. 8 . . . BUT OF LATE . . .

The Hebrew here translated "of late" may also mean, literally, "from of old," "since yesterday," or "long ago." The thought seems to be "from of old," or from the beginning my people have risen up as an enemy. There is no more vivid description of the history of Israel. The cycle of rebellion is seen throughout the Old Testament record. God blesses . . . enjoying the blessings, the people forget their source; forgetting, they turn from God to idolatry and disobedience; as a result they are brought low; in their low estate they cry out for deliverance; in answer to their cry, God sends a deliverer; in their blindness they reject the deliverer; and in the rejection their sufferings are multiplied the more. This pattern is clearly seen in Stephen's resume *(Acts, chapter seven)* of God's historic dealing with them.

God's answer, to their plea that Jehovah cannot so treat the people who wear His name, is to remind them of their consummate mistreatment of those in their midst who are truly His.

V. 8 . . . YE STRIP THE ROBE, ETC. . . .

The *eber* or robe is the garment worn next the body. The *salmah*, or garment is the large flowing coverlet worn as an outer garment in the day time and used as a blanket at night. The haughty followers of the false prophets treat the humble passers-by as enemies . . . stripping them of all their garments.

This stripping of the garments of a defenseless enemy was not an uncommon practice in Bible times. Jesus was careful to instruct His followers as to the proper response when their Roman overlords did this to them. "If any man," He said, ". . . take away your outer garment, give him your inner garment also." *(Matthew 5:40)*

The idea that must not be overlooked just here is that *the proof of enmity with God is the mistreatment of His people*. He has accused them of forever rising up like enemies against Him, and now offers as proof that they are treating His people not only as enemies, but as conquered enemies. For such people to claim immunity from God's chastisement on the grounds that they are the descendants of the patriarchs is an affront not only to God's mercy but to His intelligence!

V. 9 . . . THE WOMEN OF MY PEOPLE . . .

Not only are the passers-by stripped of their garments by these enemies of God, the women are driven from their sheltering homes and the glory of God is kept from their children.

Pehraps the prophet has in mind here the widows and orphans of those men mentioned in verse two of this chapter as having been done out of their fields and houses and having their families oppressed.

V. 9 . . . YE TAKE AWAY MY GLORY FOREVER . . .

From the point of view of God's purpose in Israel, the denial of His glory to their children is absolutely intolerable. The idea of taking away Jehovah's glory from the children obviously refers to the plight of the children in a household denied of shelter, proper clothing, and in many cases the presence of a father. The denial of these physical necessities is deplorable, but worse is the denial of the proper upbringing of the children to assure their faithfulness to the covenant and obedience to the law.

These children were the children of the patriarchs! They were Abraham's progeny through whom the promised Seed must come. If God allows these conditions to prevail unchecked there will *be* no remnant through whom the Seed *can* come.

It has been said that the church is always but one generation from extinction. The generation of parents which allows a whole generation of children to grow up unaware of their duty to God will be the last generation of the church. If it takes national calamity to drive such parents to their knees for the sake of their children, so be

2:10, 11   MICAH

it. One thing was characteristic above all else of the Israelites during the Babylonian captivity; they taught their children the way of God!

V. 10 ... ARISE AND DEPART ...

Here is the direct command of God casting from His land those despicable people who had cast others from their homes. As those who "erred" in their hearts, and did not know God's ways in the wilderness were not allowed to enter this land *(Psalm 95:10-11)* so those who have turned from His ways will not be allowed to remain in it. Because of their sins *(Micah 2:4-5)* the sentence will not be revoked.

V. 11 ... NOT YOUR RESTING PLACE ...

The land had become a resting place after the wilderness wanderings, but it was not to be so now because of their abuses. The reason the land is not to be their resting place is, in the words of the American Standard Version, "because of uncleanness that destroyeth." Rotherham has, "Because it is defiled it shall make desolate." Some translators prefer "it shall destroy you." The sense of the statement seems to be that, because they have defiled the land which the Lord gave their fathers for the accomplishment of His covenant purpose, the land is now spewing them out. The law demanded that the land be not defiled, and stated the punishment for such defilement as ". . . the land vomiteth out her inhabitants." *Leviticus* 18:25) The idea that these people, by virtue of their race, are permanently bound to this land is refuted.

The phrase, "not your resting place," is reminiscent of *Hebrews 13:14*.

V. 12 ... IF A MAN WALKETH ... DO LIE
... HE SHALL BE THE PROPHET OF THIS PEOPLE ...

Micah now describes the kind of prophet who is always in demand among a depraved people. "He walks in a spirit of falsehood." His whole life is a lie! He presents himself as a prophet of God, knowing that the prophet's primary business is to tell the truth of God to God's people, while he has no such intention. Rather he says to the people, "I will prophecy unto thee of wine and strong drink."

The Hebrew *ruach* here translated "spirit" (of falsehood) also means wind as does the Greek *pneuma,* which in the New Testament is variously translated both wind and spirit. In *Micah 2:11* the Revised Standard Version, has "If a man should go about and utter wind and lies, etc."

SECOND CYCLE 2:12, 13

Why wine and strong drink? It is possible that these refer to the intoxicants and narcotic potions given to the candidate for initiation into Baal worship to induce the emotional experience by which he became identified with the death-resurrection myth of that god. Since the Jews, at this juncture, had so polluted Jehovah worship with Baalism, they would have given heed to a prophet who preached the validity of this practice.

It seems more likely, however, that the terminology here refers to the hollow words of the false prophet which were designed to tickle the itching ears of his listeners by telling them that they would continue in affluence and plenty, while the true prophets were warning against famine and want and captivity. Wine and strong drink are available in a situation of over-abundance. In the presence of famine and want, people turn their attention to the food and shelter which are necessities of life.

JUDGEMENTS TEMPERED BY PROMISES . . . Micah 2:12-13

RV . . . I will surely assemble, O Jacob, all of thee; I will surely gather the remnant of Israel; I will put them together as the sheep of Bozrah, as a flock in the midst of their pasture; they shall make great noise by reason of the multitude of men. The breaker is gone up before them: they have broken forth and passed on to the gate, and are gone out thereat; and their king is passed on before them, and Jehovah at the head of them.

LXX . . . Jacob shall be completely gathered with all his people: I will surely receive the remnant of Israel; I will cause them to return together, as sheep in trouble, as a flock in the midst of their fold: they shall rush forth from among men through the breach made before them: they have broken through and passed the gate, and gone out by it: and their king has gone out before them, and the Lord shall lead them.

COMMENTS

A word must be said here regarding the textual unity of the Scriptures. The sudden shift from threats and warnings of doom to glowing promises of restoration is seen by some scholars as evidences that the book of Micah was not actually written by the prophet, or that it was not all written by the same man no matter what his identity. An example of this is seen in Professor J. E. McFayden's statement made as part of his comments on *Micah 2:12-13*. Dr. McFayden wrote, "It is curious to find so gracious a promise following immediately upon denunciation and threat. This, however, is not an uncommon feature in prophecy. Sometimes it is open to suppose the promise was appended by a later hand: here, the scattered sheep seem to suggest the Exile, note that a century after Micah's time . . . whoever added these and similar promises was inspired by the sound conviction that threat and disaster could never exhaust the whole purpose of God."

The idea that, because the stern judgements of the prophet are interspersed with promises, the book must have been compiled by an editor, completely fails to grasp the distinction in the mind of the prophet between the unfaithful majority who are the objects of God's wrath and the faithful remnant who are the recipients of His promises.

The idea of a restored remnant presupposes the capture and destruction of the political commonwealth and the rejection of the race-*per se*. If it was ever in the purpose of God to redeem a total political commonwealth or a race as an ethnic unit, that concept is abandoned with the introduction of the remnant idea. Few real students of the Bible believe such was *ever* the intent of God in the nation or race.

The remnant concept so dominated the thought of Isaiah that he named his son *Shear-Jashub*, "the Salvation of the Remnant." (Cf. *Isaiah 7:3; 8:2,18; 9:12; 2:21; 6:9-13*) It is not strange to find the same idea voiced by Isaiah's contemporaries such as Micah.

In *Romans 11:5*, Paul refers to *Isaiah 10:22* in his exposition of the final grafting together of the faithful Gentiles and the faithful remnant of Israel into a single people of God. In referring to the rejection of the race and commonwealth *per se*, Paul insists that God has not rejected His true people.

In identifying the remnant, as distinct from the whole of the race and nation descended from Abraham, Paul refers to Elijah's "seven thousand men, who have not bowed the knee to Baal," *ie*. those Israelites indeed who had refused to compromise their covenant relationship to Jehovah. So, says Paul, the present remnant (the faithful of the first century) is the people chosen by the grace of God. This choice, or "election," of grace is everywhere in the Bible related to the covenant.

Paul's argument is that God has not repudiated His true people, in allowing the Gentiles access to the ranks of the election. He has rather identified them! His true people, the real Israel of God prior to the beginning of the gospel age as well as now, are not marked off from other men by their semetic ancestry or their national citizenship. They are those within the national-racial structure of the commonwealth, as well as those Jews now citizens of other nations, who are faithful to the covenant of God. As Barclay has it, "The prophet began to see that there never was a time, and there never would be a time, when the whole nation was true to God, but at the same time, always within the nation there was a remnant left who had not forsaken their loyalty or compromised their faith."

Amos 9:8-10 sees the separation of the remnant from the race. *Zephaniah 3:12-13* sees the gathering of the remnant people from among the dispersed Jews throughout the world. *Ezekiel 14:14,20,22* sees salvation itself not as a national matter but as an individual matter; not determined by racial origins of family heredity, but based on personal righteousness. Righteousness which is acceptable to God is always related to God through the covenant on the basis of obedient faith. All else, as Isaiah says "is as filthy rags."

As we have seen, Isaiah's entire concept of the people of God is dominated by the remnant idea.

In our present text, and later in chapter 5, verse three, Micah conceives of God gathering the remnant first from Babylon and then in specific Messianic terms.

The threats against the northern and southern kingdoms, coupled with the promises of salvation to the faithful remnant should serve a real purpose today. We need to know, for our own sakes, and to shout from the rooftops for the sake of others . . . *NO* nation or race is saved *per se*. God commands all men everywhere to repent. The remnant . . . the real Israel of God is the fellowship of individuals related to one another on the basis of a common covenant with God. God has not, and never will reject His people, regardless of outward appearances to the contrary. No nation or religious institution *is* his people. The remnant of the human race, as well as of the commonwealth of Israel is saved by grace through faith.

The sin of denominationalism is essentially the sin of counting oneself part of God's people on the basis of identity with a religious institution just as the Jews of Micah's day, and Jesus' day, and Paul's day, and one suspects even of our day, counted themselves as God's people because they were citizens of a kingdom whose identity was based on a religious law.

The sin of racism is the twin brother to the sin of denominationalism. The Jews could trace their ancestry back to a common origin in Abraham. God had worked with them, through the influence of faithful men, in special ways. To prevent the entrance of paganism into their thinking as a deterent to faith, He had forbidden them to marry non-Hebrew mates. All this and many other similar factors combined to bring them to the conclusion that *as a race* God considered the Hebrews superior to all others. During the reign of terror that was Nazi Germany this race found itself threatened with extinction by the very same kind of thinking that historically they had exercised toward other races and which they today evidence toward their middle-eastern neighbors. The conclusion of the Christian Gospel is that, among God's people there is no East or West, North or South, Jew or Greek, Black or White. God's covenant people are one in the promised Seed of Abraham.

Micah's first mention of the remnant has as its primary concern the promise that God's people would not be brought to extinction in the judgements just pronounced. Rather, a remnant would return from the captivity. The restoration, as history shows, was to be only partial. The deeper meaning of the words; "I will assemble, O Jacob, all of thee . . ." is to be realized in the Messianic fulfillment of the everlasting covenant. In chapters four and five Micah will expound this theme in some depth.

Those who did return from Babylon were Judah, Benjamin, and Levi, the components of the southern kingdom, which God had preserved for His covenant purposes. (Cf. *I Kings 12:23-24*) It is doubtful if even all of these who returned were true Israelites in the covenant sense of the word. At the beginning of the nation, all its people had been given the opportunity to be true Israel. From the captivity on, Israel's national identity was (and is) important *only* as it bears directly on the fulfillment of the everlasting covenant.

Another indication of the Messianic overtones of Micah's remnant is the "great noise by reason of the multitude of men." This would seem to indicate a much more numerous gathering than the faithful few within the small number who actually returned after the captivity. The terminology is more reminiscent of the "multitude whom no man could number," *ie.* all God's covenant people through all time, finally gathered together in His presence. (Cf. *Revelation 7:9*)

In connection with the remnant, Micah pictures Jehovah by the use of three figures; the *shepherd*, the *breaker* (or lead ram), and the *king*. He is pictured as the shepherd of the "sheep of Bozrah." "The sheep of Bozrah" was a popular saying, like the "kine of Bashan" *(Amos 4:1)*, and alludes to the fine flocks which were the wealth of Bozrah, a key city of Moab. Jehovah is pictured as shepherd of the finest of flocks, and the remnant is that flock.

The "breaker," or lead ram, was the ram who went before the flock to butt or break down any and all barriers. So the Lord, leader of the remnant flock, will break through all barriers to the ultimate accomplishment of God's purpose in the covenant people. "If God be for us, who can stand against us?"

The Messianic overtones expressed in the figure of the Lord passing as king before the remnant are obvious. It was in David particularly that the Messianic prophecies of the Lord's kingship found their personification. From David's reign on, the Messiah was expected to sit upon "the throne of His father David." There have been many and conflicting ideas as to the nature of His kingship and His kingdom, but there is a unanimity of conviction among God's people that the Lord *is* King over His people.

Beginning with Abraham and the Patriarchs, the covenant emphasis was nearly, if not entirely, upon the development of a people. In David is added the idea that this people are to compose a kingdom. The "king idea," which became the obsession of the first century Jew, was introduced by God only after He had made it crystal clear that all His dealings with Israel, including the establishment of a king over them, were primarily concerned with the fulfillment of His promise to Abraham to bless all the people of the earth, through the people of the covenant.

David was taken from his father's pasture to become a prince over the people of God. To this end God was with him and reduced his enemies to defeat. For this reason God made the name of David ring out even above that of Moses in the assemblies of Israel. And it was for the accomplishment of His eternal purpose that the Lord promised David, "And it shall come to pass when the days are fulfilled that thou must go to thy fathers, that I will set up thy seed after thee who shall be of thy sons and I shall establish his kingdom . . . and his throne shall be established forever." *(I Chronicles 17:7-14)*

Two things are to be noted here. *First,* the throne of the son of David is to be established forever. In view of what happened just following the death of Solomon, who succeeded David on his earthly throne, and of the subsequent desolation of the commonwealth, the fulfillment of God's promise to David must be found elsewhere than in the perpetuation of an earthly dynasty. The eternal, or everlasting throne of David is to find its fulfillment in the King of Kings.

Secondly, the promise to David that his seed would sit upon the everlasting throne of His people was unconditional! The promises made to Abraham were conditioned by obedient faith. Among these was the promise of a land in which to dwell. To break the covenant was to forfeit all claim to the land. God's determination to set the seed of David over this faithful people was absolute and unconditioned.

From David on the faithful within Israel, who were of the Davidic line became the particular branch of Abraham's progeny through which the Promised Seed would come.

It must be kept in mind that the Davidic covenant is simply the Abrahamic covenant restated. As with the conditional promise to Abraham, so the unconditional promise to David had universal purposes in the blessing of all men. That Micah was aware of this is obvious in *Micah 4:1-ff* as we shall see in a later chapter. In his presentation of the fulfillment of the Kingly promise, Matthew identifies the two covenants as one and the same. *Matthew 1:1* begins the genealogy of the Eternal King with the words, "The book of the generation of Jesus Christ, the Son of *David*, the Son of *Abraham*." (Italics mine)

From the demise of Solomon and the division of the kingdom onward, God preserved the institutions of Israel "for David's sake." The southern kingdom is established to preserve the Davidic line *(I Kings 11:11-13)* Jerusalem was saved "for David's sake." *(II Kings 19:34)* Throughout the prophets, the Messianic hope is Davidic. (Cp. *Isaiah 55:1-3, Amos 9:11, Hosea 3:5, Zechariah 12:17-21*)

And so, for at least a thousand years before the birth of the King, God's concern is seen to be not with the race or the national political entity but with the unconditional promise to set the Seed of David upon the throne of His people. More than ever, the people existed for the sake of the Seed. When the time came that the Jews as a nation and the religious institutions of that nation rejected the Christ, God would cast them off. But the promise which was the heart of the covenant would be fulfilled through a covenant remnant ruled by the promised Seed of David.

It does violence to the awesomeness of this promise to limit it to *any earthly experience* of God and His people.

Chapter VII—*Questions*

Second Cycle

1. Discuss the relationships between individual and "social" sins.
2. Discuss "power corrupts and absolute power corrupts absolutely" in reference to the situation denounced by Micah.
3. How do power and authority test a persons character?
4. Discuss Pascal's statement "power without justice is tyranny."

5. How is this evidenced in the circumstances addressed by Micah?
6. How can a just God devise evil? (Micah 2:3)
7. What was the power by which the social leaders of Micah's day enforced their evil designs?
8. How does God's punishment predicted by Micah "fit the crime" of those He will punish? (Micah 2:5)
9. What is the relationship between the wickedness addressed by Micah and the false prophets of the day?
10. What part did national pride and racial arrogance play in the downfall of the wicked northern and southern kingdoms?
11. How does God's purpose in Israel rule out such pride and arrogance on the part of the faithful?
12. How do you answer the tendency to blame God for social calamities?
13. Discuss mistreatment of people as evidence of enmity with God.
14. What single fact made God's punishment of social sin in Israel and Judah necessary to the accomplishment of His purpose in the covenant?
15. What single characteristic of the Israelites during the Babylonian captivity stood out above all else?
16. Describe the kind of prophet the people desired in Micah's time. (Micah 2:11)
17. Discuss the problem of textual unity of the scriptures. (cf. Micah 2:12-13)
18. The idea of a restored remnant, as presented by Micah, presupposes the destruction of _____ and the rejection of the _____ *per se*.
19. The doctrine of election, divine choice, is, in the Bible, always related to the _____.
20. What is the similarity of modern denominationalism and the attitude of racial and national priority with God on the part of the Jewish people of Bible times?
21. Discuss the figures of the "shepherd," the "breaker," and the "king" in connection with the remnant.

CHAPTER VIII

THIRD CYCLE

OUTRAGES OF CIVIL OFFICIALS . . . Micah 3:1-4

RV . . . And I said, Hear, I pray you, ye heads of Jacob, and rulers of the house of Israel: is it not for you to know justice? ye who hate

3:1-4 MICAH

the good, and love the evil; who pluck off their skin from off them, and their flesh from off their bones; who also eat the flesh of my people, and flay their skin from off them, and break their bones, and chop them in pieces, as for the pot, and as flesh within the caldron. Then shall they cry unto Jehovah, but he will not answer them; yea, he will hide his face from them at that time, according as they have wrought evil in their doings.

LXX . . . And he shall say, Hear now these words, ye heads of the house of Jacob, and ye remnant of the house of Israel; is it not for you to know judgement? who hate good, and seek evil; who tear their skins off them, and their flesh off their bones: even as they devoured the flesh of my people, and stripped their skins off them, and broke their bones, and divided them as flesh for the caldron, and as meat for the pot, thus they shall cry to the Lord, but he shall not hearken to them; and he shall turn away his face from them at that time, because they have done wickedly in their practices against themselves.

COMMENTS

(Verse 1) Micah's concern for the return of the people to the covenant reaches its highest pitch in chapter three, as he pleads with the official leaders of the people. He has dealt in chapters one and two with the economic and social leaders of the northern and southern kingdoms. Now he turns his attention to the *official* leaders. He is acutely aware that no nation can rise any higher than the moral standards of its officials, especially of its courts.

Repeatedly Micah couches his appeal to people in high places in terms calculated to remind them that they are the temporal rulers of God's people. He addresses them as the "heads of Jacob" and "the rulers of the house of Israel." To these he addresses a warning of imminent doom, but with the underlying hope that they will repent.

The King James version has "princes" of the house of Israel in this verse. This is unfortunate, since it is generally agreed that this passage is intended for the magistrates and judges rather than for the royal family.

These are obviously not included in the remnant mentioned in the closing verses of chapter two. The prophets warning to them follows immediately the glowing hope expressed for the deliverance of the remnant so that they will make no mistake about their own predicament. They must not mistake themselves for inclusion in the real Israel of God just because they sit in the seats of temporal judgement over the people.

"IS IT NOT FOR YOU..."

In *Micah 2:1-ff,* we saw Micah's denunciation of the wealthy and influential for their merciless mistreatment of the poor. The prophet now challenges the judges that they have the responsibility of preventing and dealing with such injustice. The wealthy could not do what they do were it not for corrupt courts. (See above on *Micah 1:5*) Magistrates and judges above all others should be aware of the penalties of wrong doing and injustice. Micah's warning is that the laws apply equally well to the lawyers.

"YOU WHO HATE GOOD AND LOVE EVIL"... v. 2

These corrupt judges not only hate good men and love evil men, worse than that, they hate good as a principle and love evil as a principle.

Modern existential philosophy and situation ethics notwithstanding, there *is* such a thing as absolute good and absolute evil . . . as abstract reality as well as in tangible experience.

That the early church fathers believed this to be true is seen in such ancient writings as that attributed to Jerome, the translator of the Latin Vulgate, "It is sin not to love good; what guilt to hate it. It is faulty not to flee from evil, what ungodliness to love it."

"PLUCK OFF THEIR SKIN AND FLESH FROM THEIR BONES ... v. 2(b)-3

Such alluusions as this to describe the cheating advantage taken by one man over another are to be found in every culture. Examples of it in the historic writings of Israel are to be seen in such passages as *Psalm 14:4* and *Proverbs 30:14.* We still speak of such practices as "skinning" someone.

A proverb attributed to the American Indian says, "The Indian scalps his enemies, the white man skins his friends." It seems the white man cannot claim to be original in this maltreatment of his fellowman. The judges of Israel are warned here of the consequences of it.

This particular passage in Micah, denouncing the loving of evil and the hating of good brings to mind a very significant change in civilized man's evaluation of right and wrong. In 1867, Robert Milligan wrote, "It will, I presume, be generally conceded that the will of God is the natural and only proper standard of all that is right. If God is our Sovereign King and Lawgiver, it is His right to command, and it is our duty to obey."

To this the Christian will readily say "amen!" To this also the ancient pagans would agree, although their confusion of deities could furnish no uniformly acceptable standard of right and wrong. To this even the evil doers addressed by Micah gave lip service, else the prophet could not have appealed to them on the ground of a clear cut distinction between good and evil.

We are something more than naive if we believe we can approach modern man, and especially the members of the intellectual and academic communities or young people on this basis today.. Beginning with Hegel (1770-1831) through Kierkegaard (1813-1855) to the existential thinking of Karl Jaspers Sarte, Camus, Julian and Aldous Huxley, *et al*, to the ultramodern (now passé) God-is-dead cult, twentieth century man has reached the rationale which says there not only *is not* but that there *cannot be* any absolute good or evil. Everything is relative. Absolutism is dead and man must decide in the context of a given set of circumstances the situation ethics of the moment.

To try to cut through such layers of ignorance by quoting the dictums of God from the Bible is to try to sweep back the tide with a broom. To give up in despair of being able to reach those who think like this is to abandon an entire generation, and possibly an entire civilization to spiritual darkness forever.

Somehow modern Christians must learn, as it is said the early Christians did, to "out-think, outlove and outdie" those whose spiritual eyes have been blinded by the self-acclaimed wisdom of men. The warnings of the prophets concerning the consequences of loving evil and hating good must be gotten through to modern man, but our task is twice as difficult as that of Micah and the others. They at least shared with those whom they sought to warn the common presupposition that there is a Sovereign God and His word determines the difference between objective good and objective evil. It is no longer so in our day. We share no such common ground with those whom we seek to turn from the error of their ways.

MERCENARY PROPHETS . . . Micah 3:5-8

RV . . . Thus saith Jehovah concerning the prophets that make my people to err; that bite with their teeth and cry, Peace; and whoso putteth not into their mouths, they even prepare war against him: therefore it shall be night unto you, that ye shall have no vision; and it

THIRD CYCLE   3:5-8

shall be dark unto you, that ye shall not divine; and the sun shall go down upon the prophets, and the day shall be black over them. And the seers shall be put to shame, and the diviners confounded; yea, they shall all cover their lips; for there is no answer of God. But as for me, I am full of power by the Spirit of Jehovah, and of judgement, and of might, to declare unto Jacob his transgression, and to Israel his sin.

LXX . . . Thus saith the Lord concerning the prophets that lead my people astray, that bite with their teeth, and proclaim peace to them; and when nothing was put into their mouth, they raised up war against them: therefore there shall be night to you instead of a vision, and there shall be to you darkness instead of prophecy; and the sun shall go down upon the prophets, and the day shall be dark upon them. And the seers of night-visions shall be ashamed, and the prophets shall be laughed to scorn: and all the people shall speak against them, because there shall be none to hearken to them. Surely I will strengthen myself with the Spirit of the Lord, and of judgment, and of power, to declare to Jacob his transgressions, and to Israel his sins.

COMMENTS

As in the case of the arrogant misleaders *(Micah 2:1-3)* so with the unjust magistrates *(Micah 3:1-4)*, the prophet relates their sin to false preachers.

(Verse 5) Here the accusation is direct. It is the false prophets who "make my people err." By not denouncing sin, the false prophet encourages his hearers to sin. By flattering sinners in their sin and telling them that God is not really all that demanding, the false preacher leaves the impression desired by his hearers. Namely, that sin will not really be punished.

When these false prophets do denounce some action or inaction in their hearers it is not because of the righteous demands of God but because they do not feel their salaries are big enough. This reveals them to be part of the total picture of a decadent social order. They are as mercenary as those who lay awake nights figuring how to cheat someone of his possessions.

The agreeableness of the message of a false prophet was determined by the size of the "bite" placed in his mouth by his hearers. When the "religious payola" was sufficient they foretold peace and prosperity. When it was not, they sanctified war as a judgement against those who failed to feed them. In such pronouncements they sounded like the true prophet, but they would change their "tune" when the offerings were good. Such preaching is not calculated to bring about repentance on the part of the hearer.

(Verse 6) Micah's warning concerning such despicable practices on the part of those who claim to speak for God is that the light of God will be withheld from them. There will be no vision. The implication is clear, for where there is no vision, the people perish. *(Proverbs 29:18)*

The calamities which Micah has predicted for Israel and Judah will be shared by the false preachers as well as the social and official misleaders. When the calamity strikes they will no longer be able to claim to speak for God. When the judgements of God come, as they have promised His judgements will not come . . . when it is learned that God is not, after all, the tolerant benevolent benefactor the false teachers have made Him out to be, but rather the God of the covenant demanding faithful obedience to His will and His law, no one will listen any longer to those who made Him out to be what their hearers hoped He was.

(Verse 7) In that day of judgement, the false seers will be put to shame and confounded. Everything of which they have been warned will have come to pass . . . the laxity of judgement on the part of God which they have predicted will be shown for what it is . . . wishful thinking.

They will be put to shame. The covering of the lips may be explained in one of several figures. In the custom of the day, the moustache and beard were matters of great pride. The covering of them was an act expressing shame.

Another reference to the covering of the lips is found in *Leviticus 13:45*. There the command is that the leper is to "cover his upper lip and cry unclean unclean." This was one of the laws of God pertaining to hygiene. In *Micah 3:7* the implication seems to be that spiritual and moral infection being spread by the false prophet will finally be stopped when the calamity predicted by Micah finally stops their mouths.

In verse eight, Micah constrasts himself, as a true prophet to the false prophets he has just denounced. Three things characterize him. He has within himself the *POWER* of God's Spirit, without which no one can speak accurately and effectively concerning the will of God. (Cp. *Acts 1:5,8*)

He possesses JUDGEMENT, *ie.* a sense of justice which moves him to speak the truth no matter how unpopular as opposed to the false prophet whose motivation was money.

He possesses *MIGHT* or courage to say what needs saying in the face of ridicule and even persecution. (Cp. *II Timothy 1:7*)

He possesses these three graces "to declare unto Jacob his transgression, and unto Israel his sin." Jacob and Israel originally referred to the same individual. Jacob was his name before God confirmed to him the everlasting covenant. Israel was his covenant name. Micah apparently intends to distinguish here between the physical descendants of Jacob and the faithful covenant people among them to whom he refers by the covenant name, Israel.

Transgression is a specific term for the deliberate infraction of God's law. For these deliberate transgressions Micah has the power and the judgement and the might to speak out against those unfaithful to the covenant. Sin is a more general term. Even those who were faithful to the covenant were not free from sin completely. The prophet also has the power and the judgement and the might to speak to the covenant people whenever necessary.

One can scarcely read this denunciation of false and mercenary preachers without being aware of the present religious climate of our day. I have before me as I write the most recent publication of COCU (the Consultation On Church Unity). It is entitled *A Plan of Union*. Its authors make bold to claim that what they are doing in their eccumenical designs and ambitions is led by the Spirit of God. They claim the enlightenment of the Holy Spirit while they are denying the same to the writers of the Bible. They are teaching theology and proposing practices which are diametrically opposed to the Scriptural teaching and order of things in the church. One suspects their motivation, like that of those false prophets of whom Micah spoke, is something less than the selfless desire to see God's people do God's will.

One does not have to be a prophet of doom to foresee the possible collapse of our culture which is following the lead of such men. Just as those who misled the eighth century Jews into believing that God would not exact judgement against the followers of false teachers, so these twentieth century clergymen have denied the judgements of God. If our culture should collapse it will owe much of its failure to the teaching of these men. And, in that day as in the day of Judah's fall, the false prophet will be shown for what he is.

CONCLUSION OF THE DENUNCIATIONS . . . Micah 3:9-12

RV . . . Hear this, I pray you, ye heads of the house of Jacob, and rulers of the house of Israel, that abhor justice, and pervert all equity. They build up Zion with blood, and Jerusalem with iniquity. The heads thereof judge for reward, and the priests thereof teach for hire, and the prophets thereof divine for money: yet they lean upon Jehovah, and say, Is not Jehovah in the midst of us? no evil shall come upon us. Therefore shall Zion for your sake be plowed as a field, and Jerusalem shall become heaps, and the mountain of the house as the high places of a forest.

LXX . . . Hear now these words, ye chiefs of the house of Jacob, and the remnant of the house of Israel, who hate judgment, and pervert all righteousness; who build up Sion with blood, and Jerusalem with iniquity. The heads thereof have judged for gifts, and the priests thereof have answered for hire, and her prophets have divined for silver: and yet they have rested on the Lord, saying, Is not the Lord among us? no evil shall come upon us. Therefore on your account Sion shall be ploughed as a field, and Jerusalem shall be as a storehouse of fruits, and the mountain of the house as a grove of the forest.

COMMENTS

To this point, Micah has denounced specifically the wealthy whose wealth is gained by cheating the poor, the false prophet who preaches what his listeners want to hear while he ignores their sins, the judges who are unconcerned with justice and the political officials who, like their constituents, hate good and love evil. In this passage he summarizes and concludes the list of those whose greed for power and wealth, along with their unconcern for human misery have brought God's covenant nation to her downfall.

The list of their sins has an ominously familiar ring to anyone aware of the present spiritual condition of our own nation. They abhor justice and pervert all equity. They judge for reward, teach for hire and divine for money. And through it all they have the audacity to "lean upon Jehovah." Rather than repent and obey His laws, they presume to believe that they are yet His people, so that no evil can befall them.

False teaching is always recognizable by its emphasis on the goodness of God accompanied by the denial of His wrath . . . its proclamation of the promises of God while denying the condition of those promises. The preaching of such lies only makes the judgements of God the more certain.

(Verse 9) "Hear" is here resumed from verse one, indicating that Micah is about to sum up his denunciation of the evils of those who claim to be God's people.

The term "heads of Jacob" as in verse one calls attention to the civil rulers of the commonwealth, while "rulers of the house of Israel" here as there refers to the religious leaders. The sum of all of which he has accused them is that they "abhor justice and pervert all equity."

Pusey remarks concerning verse 9, "They abhored judgement he says, as a thing loathsome and *abominable,* such as men cannot even bear to look upon; they not only dealt wrongly, but they *perverted,* distorted, all *equity* . . . whatever was right by conscience or by God's laws, they distorted, like the sophists making the worse appear the better cause."

A rather sadistic anecdote will illustrate how this attitude toward social justice is very much alive today. The story is told of two black men walking along a limited access highway in the deep south. A wealthy plantation owner's Cadillac struck them both, throwing one into a nearby cotton field and the other through the car's windshield and onto the back seat. A sheriff soon arrived on the scene and announced, "We'll charge one with leaving the scene of an accident and the other with breaking and entering." The humor of this story lies not in the judgement of the sheriff against the unfortunate blacks, but in the unlikely circumstances of the accident. Perversions of justice just as "far-fetched" are matters of court record throughout the United States. The reasons are the same as those which brought about the corruption of Micah's day.

(Verse 10) Maintaining his distinction between the civil and religious authorities, Micah accuses the latter of building up Zion with blood and the former of building up Jerusalem with iniquity.

Religion consisted of meticulously observing the formal sacrifices daily in the temple while ignoring the moral implications of the law, particularly the matter of human relations. The charge is reminiscent of that leveled against the religious leaders of first century Zion by Jesus, "Woe unto you, scribes and Pharisees, hypocrites! for ye tithe mint and anise and cummin, and have left undone the weightier matters of the law, justice and mercy and faith: but these things ye should have done and not to have left the other undone." *(Matthew 23:23)* Both Micah and Jesus would have agreed with *Proverbs 15:8,* "The sacrifice of the wicked is an abomination to Jehovah . . ." The covenant purposes of God, symbolized here in the term Zion, cannot be built upon the blood of religious sacrifices offered by evil men.

We cannot but note in passing that one of the chief reasons for the disenchantment of modern man with the institutionalized church is that the religious people who are members of the churches have too often failed to relate their duty to God to their duty to man and particularly to the social injustices exacted from the poor and the ignorant. It is easy to say that the purposes of God are redemptive rather than reformative . . . that the business of the church is to preach the gospel and win the lost, but it is not so easy to reach the lost whose stomach is empty because some influential member of the church has denied him work because of the color of his skin. It is easy to say the church's business is to proclaim the redemption of Christ to those outside the church, but it is not so easy to get the outsider to listen to a recital of his spiritual needs while we remain aloof and unconcerned for his physical needs. No doubt this is why Jesus' only detailed account of the judgement has to do with those who fed and visited and clothed the downtrodden in His name . . . or who while performing great religious works had failed to do so. *(Matthew 25:31-46)* In the prophecy of Micah, as well as that of the Lord, the punishment of such evil is severe and total.

Just as the religion of Zion was built upon the blood of mockingly meaningless sacrifices, so the political structure of Jerusalem's civil government was built upon social iniquity. Matthew Henry's comment here says it about as well as it can be said, "They pretend in justification of their extortion and oppressions, that they have built up Zion and Jerusalem: they add new streets and squares . . . and adorn them; they establish and advance the public interests both in church and state, and think therein they do God and Israel good service."

Could there be any more accurate illustration in an ancient writing of the social injustices of modern America? In the name of progress we move underprivileged people out of inadequate homes for which we pay them little or no renumeration to make way for our expressways and urban renewal projects . . . we exact exorbitant taxes to subsidize such urgent projects as the scientific study of earthworms while many who pay the taxes are forced to deprive their children of the necessities of life . . . the list of our iniquities is as long as that charged by Micah against the leaders of his society. We will be something less than wise if we fail to understand that the moral dry rot which destroyed Israel and Judah in the eighth and seventh century B.C. will also destroy ours in the 20th and 21st centuries A.D.

"HEADS . . . PRIESTS . . ." v. 11

Following still farther his denunciation of both the civil and religious leaders of the nation, Micah again accused the judges of being corrupt, deciding cases on the basis of bribes rather than justice.

THIRD CYCLE 3:9-12

To this charge, the prophet adds a new note. Heretofore, he has denounced the false prophet as representative of the corrupt religious system. Now he turns to the priest. The priest, he alleges, teaches for hire. The duty of the priest was to teach the law and decide controversy with justice. *(Leviticus 10:11, Deuteronomy 17:11)* Instead, these spiritual representatives of God among His people were emmeshed in the same materialism that polluted the rest of the upper classes of society.

Nor does Micah forget the false prophet in making this summary of his charges. He again asserts that the prophets preach only to fill their purses. They divine, that is they proclaim what they know the people want to hear as the will of God in order to receive pay.

And while they do this, they tell the people that God is among them, that the doom predicted by Micah and Isaiah and others cannot come to pass because they are, after all, the chosen people of God.

Such a claim brings up a rather moot question, very relevant in our day: Who is the real patriot? Who is really concerned for his country? The person who says "my country right or wrong" or the person who, like Micah, sees the faults of his homeland and sets about in the name of God to do something about those faults?

Is should be apparent from the subsequent doom pronounced against Zion and Jerusalem, as well as from the testimony of more recent history, that God's relationship to the Jews as a race or as a nation is not unconditional. They have rejected Jehovah for Baal . . . they have abandoned spiritual justice for materialistic gain and fleshly pleasure. As their ancient uncle Esau, they have sold their birthright for a mess of pottage and so no longer have any claim to the promises of Jehovah!

"THEREFORE . . ." v. 12

In consequence of the sin of those in high places, the sacred mountain, Zion, is to be plowed as a field, and Jerusalem their capital is to be as any other high place in the forest. ("On the 6th September, A.D. 70, Jerusalem fell and the Romans destroyed it so completely that they drove a plough across the ruins. As a nation the Jews had come to an end; and their own mad folly had brought their end upon them." Barclay)

The kingdom is finished. The north will go first, the south will soon follow. And God will recall a remnant through whom to accomplish His promise ". . . in thee shall all the families of the earth be blessed." *(Genesis 12:3 (b))*

One hundred years later another prophet, Jeremiah, would quote these verses from Micah in defense of his own denunciations of an equally sinful generation. *(Jeremiah 26:18)*

Chapter VIII—*Questions*
Third Cycle

1. Discuss Micah's concern for the covenant in light of his plea in *Micah 3:1-4*.
2. Discuss the concept of absolute good and evil in contrast with modern situation ethics (new morality). *Micah 2:1-ff*
3. What is meant by "pluch off their skin and flesh from their bones *(Micah 2:2(b)-3)?*
4. Discuss the will of God as "the only natural and proper standard of all that is right."
5. Discuss ways to penetrate the "layers of ignorance" in modern philosophies with the truth of God's sovereignty.
6. Are the prophetic warnings of the consequences of loving evil and hating good relevant to our current moral revolution?
7. What three classes of people does Micah denounce? *(Micah 2:1-3, 3:1-4, 3:5)*
8. What specific class of leaders are accused of making the people to err?
9. What seems to have been the chief concern of the false prophets?
10. What is God's warning to mercenary prophets?
11. Comment on the idea that God *is* a "tolerant benevolent benefactor."
12. What is to be the fate of the false prophets in the day of the judgement against the wicked nations as pronounced by Micah?
13. What three things characterize Micah as a true prophet as opposed to the false prophets?
14. Compare the false prophet syndrome of Micah's day with our present religious climate in America.
15. What is the relationship between false religious teaching and the cultural collapse of a civilization?
16. What are the specific sins with which Micah charges the wealthy, the false prophet, the magistrates, the political officials?
17. False teaching is always recognizable by its emphasis on the_____ _____of God accompanied by a denial of His_____.
18. The term "head of Jacob" calls attention to_____.
19. "Rulers of the house of Israel" refers to _____.

FUTURE EXALTATION & MESSIANIC HOPE   4:1-5

CHAPTER IX
FUTURE EXALTATION AND MESSIANIC HOPE

XION, CENTER OF WORSHIP . . . Micah 4:1-5

RV . . . But in the latter days it shall come to pass, that the mountain of Jehovah's house shall be established on the top of the mountains, and it shall be exalted above the hills; and peoples shall flow unto it. And many nations shall go and say, Come ye, and let us go up to the mountain of Jehovah, and to the house of the God of Jacob; and he will teach us of his ways, and we will walk in his paths. For out of Zion shall go forth the law, and the word of Jehovah from Jerusalem; and he will judge between many peoples, and will decide concerning strong nations afar off: and they shall beat their swords into plowshares, and their spears into pruninghooks; nation shall not lift up sword against nation, neither shall they learn war any more. But they shall sit every man under his vine and under his fig-tree; and none shall make them afraid: for the mouth of Jehovah of hosts hath spoken it. For all the peoples walk every one in the name of his God; and we will walk in the name of Jehovah our God for ever and ever.

LXX . . . And at the last days the mountain of the Lord shall be manifest, established on the tops of the mountains, and it shall be exalted above the hills; and the peoples shall hasten to it. And many nations shall go, and say, Come, let us go up to the mountain of the Lord, and to the house of the God of Jacob; and they shall shew us his way, and we will walk in his paths: for out of Zion shall go forth a law, and the word of the Lord from Jerusalem. And he shall judge among many peoples, and shall rebuke strong nations afar off; and they shall beat their swords into ploughshares; and their spears into sickles; and nation shall no more lift up sword against nation, neither shall they learn to war any more. And every one shall rest under his vine, and every one under his fig-tree; and there shall be none to alarm them: for the mouth of the Lord Almighty has spoken these words. For all other nations shall walk every one in his own way, but we will walk in the name of the Lord our God for ever and ever.

COMMENTS

(Verse 1) "It will come to pass" gives us transport to the future (from Micah's day). We leap the centuries far beyond the captivity to Messiah's day.

"In the latter days" is the English rendering of the phrase which fixes the time when it shall come to pass. The phrase is reminiscent of *Hebrews 1:2*. There we are told that God, having spoken to the fathers in the prophets has spoken to us in a Son. No more conclusive evidence is needed to connect Micah's prophecy with the Messianic age The rabbis so understood this term. (The age was to be final and eternal. Nothing lies beyond it so far as earthly history is concerned. It is itself the final goal of history.) "Upon the last of the days" is the exact opposite of "in the beginning" of *Genesis 1:1* (LXX) and *John 1:1*. As Lange points out, it denotes "the completion of the world in contrast to its beginning."

John indicates that we are in this end time. (CF. *I John 2:18-f)* *(See my comment in *Hereby We Know,* College Press, pp. 59-ff)

In this end time, says Micah, the mountain of Jehovah's house shall be established on top of (or at the head of) the mountains. In the place of the literal mountain which is to be plowed as a field *(Micah 3:12),* the ideal of God will be established.

Those who would take Micah literally here see "the ultimate establishment of the kingdom with Jerusalem as the capital" *(The New Scofield Reference Bible).* This is, of course, not in keeping with Jesus' concept of true Jehovah worship. Just as Micah predicts that all peoples shall flow into God's exalted mountain, so Jesus said "Neither in these (Samaritan Gerazim and Ebal) mountains, nor in Jerusalem (Mt. Zion and Mt. Moriah) shall ye worship the Father . . . but the hour cometh *and now is* (italics mine) when the true worshippers shall worship the Father in spirit and truth . . . God is spirit: and they that worship Him must worship Him in Spirit and in truth."

The psalmist used this same metaphor in *Psalm 68:17* to indicate the eminence of Jehovah worship on Mt. Zion over the other high places. The emphasis upon and contrast of high places, or mountains, is set against the backdrop of the tension between Jehovah worship on Mt. Zion and Baal worship on the various surrounding high places. In the last times, or Messianic age, true worship is to be firmly and finally exalted above all else.

In verse 5, Micah says "all the peoples walk everyone in the name of his god, but we will walk in the name of Jehovah our God for ever and ever." The coming of the Messianic age has not eliminated false religion. The very site of Jehovah's temple is now the second most holy spot in Islaam. But true Jehovah worship, *ie.* Christian worship, has been exalted above them all.

(Verse 2) "Many nations" here is not be understood in terms of political empires. *The people* in the Old Testament are generally all those in covenant relation to God while the *nations* are all those not in covenant relationship.

Many who in Micah's day were "seperate from Christ, alienated from the commonwealth of Israel, and strangers from the covenant of promise . . . " *(Ephesians 2:12)* are now "made nigh in the blood of Christ." *(Ephesians 2:13)*

Isaiah looked forward to this same glorious day *(Isaiah 2:2)* when the universal concern of God for all men would be realized.

Significantly, both Micah and Isaiah see the movement of Gentiles toward the exalted "mountain of Jehovah's house" as voluntary. The religion of the prophets is of such quality as makes it independant of nationality or election. As the Jews understood election, any interpertation of prophecy which overlooks this basic truth cannot be correct.

The statement ". . . out of Zion shall go forth the law and the word of Jehovah from Jerusalem" is not to be understood as limited to or even indicative of the law of Moses. Rather it is the "law of the Spirit of life." *(Romans 8:1,2)* It is in keeping with Jesus' ascertion that "thus it is written . . . that repentance and remission of sins should be preached in His name unto all the nations, beginning at Jerusalem." *(Luke 24:45-47)* There is little doubt that such passages as this in Micah were in Jesus' mind when He taught the apostles to so read and understand the Old Testament.

(Verse 3-4) Men are at war with men because men are at war with God. In the Messianic age (our own time included) the ideal is peace based on His judgement. He will judge between peoples . . . He will decide concerning strong nations. When and if the leaders of nations seek His will together . . . when His judgement is taken seriously, there can be peace.

History has demonstrated in blood that this peace will not prevail so long as each nation believes God has only its own national interests at heart. When asked if he did not believe that God was on the side of the north, Abraham Lincoln answered that it was more important that we be on God's side than He on ours. This is the Messianic ideal.

Both in the matter of war as described in verse 3 and the relation of races described in verse 2, the church, as Messiah's kingdom does not *have* the answer. The church *is* the answer. In the true church there is no Jew nor Greek, east nor west, male nor female. We are all one, and until we *are* all one, we are not truly the church!

The implements of war will be beaten into implements of peace, not by voting funds for welfare rather than warfare, but by seeking the will of God's Messiah in international relations.

The ideal described in verse 4 of every man in the security and plenty of his own vine and fig tree will come not by civil rights agitation and legislation but by seeking the will of God's Christ in human relations. God must become the ruler of our economy as well as our church doctrine!

(Verse 5) On this verse we noted above that all false religion would not be obliterated in the age of the Messiah. This is obvious to anyone with definite conviction concerning the "faith once for all delivered . . . " We would simply add here that this verse is evidence Micah is not describing the final "summing up of the ages" when all false religion will be forever wiped out. When Micah says " . . . all the peoples walk everyone in the name of his god, and (but) we will walk in the name of Jehovah our God . . . " he is not condoning false religion. He is describing an era of tolerance or religious freedom unknown in the ancient world. It is, after all, better to discuss religious differences than to kill over them, as in the great religious wars of western European history.

THE RESTORATION OF THE DIASPORA . . . Micah 4:6-8

RV . . . In that day, saith Jehovah, will I assemble that which is lame, and I will gather that which is driven away, and that which I have afflicted; and I will make that which was lame a remnant, and that which was cast far off a strong nation: and Jehovah will reign over them in mount Zion from henceforth even for ever. And thou, O tower of the flock, the hill of the daughter of Zion, unto thee shall it come, yea, the former dominion shall come, the kingdom of the daughter of Jerusalem.

LXX . . . In that day, saith the Lord, I will gather her that is bruised, and will receive her that is cast out, and those whom I rejected. And I will make her that was bruised a remnant, and her that was rejected a mighty nation: and the Lord shall reign over them in mount Zion from henceforth, even for ever. And thou, dark tower of the flock, daughter of Sion, on thee the dominion shall come and enter in, even the first kingdom from Babylon to the daughter of Jerusalem.

COMMENTS

(Verse 6-7) "In that day" refers us back to 4:1. What Micah is about to say is to take place during the same "last of the days" which, as we have seen, is the Messianic age.

(Verse 6) "That which is lame . . . " Micah uses here the image of the covenant people as God's flock. His sheep are pictured as limping or halting as the result of much wandering. These will be assembled. Part of the worship of Baal, the chief cause of their impending captivity, was a limping, halting dance about the altars of Baal in the high places. When God finished punishing them they will have real cause to limp!

HER THAT HALTED IS TO BECOME A REMNANT . . . v. 7

The covenant people are no longer identified with the race of Abraham's descendants nor the political commonwealth which was national Israel. From this point forward, true Israel is the faithful remnant. (See above on 2:12)

There is a distinction here between two groups. The one Micah calls "that which was lame" (LXX "bruised"). The other he styles "that which is driven away . . . afflicted . . . cast off."

The lame or bruised are the faithful obedient few. Although they will be bruised in the captivity and dispersion of the nation, God will make of them a remnant. Through them He will yet fulfill His covenant promise.

That which is cast off He will make a strong nation. Paul informs us emphatically *(Romans 11:1)* that God *has* not (from Micah's point of view, *will* not) cast off His people. His people are the remnant. Those whom He cast off are the rebellious majority.

Of both, the remnant and the strong nation composed of those cast off, Micah says, "Jehovah will reign over *them."*

TOWER?OF THE FLOCK . . . v. 8

The flock is the remnant , God's faithful covenant people, Zion out of whom shall proceed the law of God to all people. (Cf. *4:2* above.) The tower of the flock . . . the hill of the *daughter* of Zion (not Zion herself) is the cast-off ones who shall become a strong nation. As the tower of the flock was a lookout post to guard the shepherd's flock, so the nation would shield within her the covenant remnant until the time of Messiah's coming.

The term "tower of the flock" is literally the "tower of **Ophel.**"

4:6-8   MICAH

Ophel is not Mt. Zion, but a percipitous slope on the south of the temple mount. This brings to sharper focus the distinction between Zion, the *remnant,* and the tower, the *nation.*

It is to the nation that "the former dominion" shall come. The remnant shall become the nucleus of the Christian church.

DISTRESS AND REDEMPTION . . . Micah 4:9-5:1

RV . . . Now why doest thou cry out aloud? Is there no king in thee, is thy counsellor perished, that pangs have taken hold of thee as of a woman in travail? Be in pain, and labor to bring forth, O daughter of Zion, like a woman in travail; for now shalt thou go forth out of the city; and shalt dwell in the field, and shalt come even unto Babylon: there shalt thou be rescued; there will Jehovah redeem thee from the hand of thine enemies. And now many nations are assembled against thee, that say, Let her be defiled, and let our eye see our desire upon Zion. But they know not the thoughts of Jehovah, neither understand they his counsel for he hath gathered them as the sheaves to the threshing-floor. Arise and thresh, O daughter of Zion; for I will make thy horn iron, and I will make thy hoofs brass; and thou shalt beat in pieces many peoples: and I will devote their gain unto Jehovah, and their substance unto the Lord of the whole earth. Now shalt thou gather thyself in troops, O daughter of troops: he hath laid siege against us; they shall smite the judge of Israel with a rod upon the cheek.

LXX . . . And now, why hast thou known calamities? was there not a king to thee? or has thy counsel perished that pangs as of a woman in travail have seized upon thee? Be in pain, and strengthen thyself, and draw near, O daughter of Zion, as a woman in travail: for now thou shalt go forth out of the city, and shalt lodge in the plain, and shalt reach even to Babylon: thence shall the Lord thy God deliver thee, and thence shall he redeem thee out of the hand of thine enemies. And now have many nations gathered against thee, saying, We will rejoice, and our eyes shall look upon Zion. But they know not the thought of the Lord, and have not understood his counsel: for he has gathered them as sheaves of the floor. Arise, and thresh them, O daughter of Zion: for I will make thine horns iron, and I will make thine hoofs brass: and thou shalt utterly destroy many nations, and shalt consecrate their abundance to the Lord, and their strength to the Lord of all the earth. Now shall the daughter of Zion be completely hedged in: he has laid siege against us: they shall smite the tribes of Israel with a rod upon the cheek.

FUTURE EXALTATION & MESSIANIC HOPE 4:9, 10

COMMENTS

WHY DOST THOU CRY ALOUD? ... v. 9-10

The term "tower of the flock" (*v. 8*) appears also in *Genesis 35:16-ff.* There is the record of Rachel, beloved of Jacob, dying in childbirth as they journeyed from Bethel to Bethlehem.

Just as Rachel died in childbirth, so the nation of Israel would die at the hands of Titus (70 A.D.) and Hadrian (135 A.D.) in the height of her Messianic expectancy. First century Israel looked for a king, but could find none. Micah's question is pertinent, "Is there no king in thee?" The king would indeed be in her, but she would die in travail without seeing (recognizing) Him just as Rachel died.

The nation, even in Micah's time, in pain would go away into Babylon . . . there to be rescued. To all outward appearances the Hebrew nation was dead when they were led away into Babylon. In truth, however, it was there they were molded into a people who never again forgot God.

True, their national ambition blinded them to the Christ. He was recognized only by the *remnant*, not the *nation*. Nevertheless, there is a real sense in which Micah can truly use the plural, both the remnant and the nation (*v.* 7) shall be ruled over by Jehovah.

In all this, Micah is looking beyond the Assyrian Dynasty to the sypremacy of Babylon, and through Babylon to the Persians, and beyond Persia to the Messianic Age.

(Verse 11) It is the prophet's purpose in these verses to return to the warnings of *3:12*. Before there can be a national restoration and a deliverance of the remnant there must be the captivity.

Having projected hope which lay nearly two centuries in the future in its first instance *ie.* the deliverance from Babylon, and some eight centuries in the future in its Messianic fulfillment, Micah returns in verse 11 to the situation immediately before him. Between the present and the blessed future was an array of enemies bent on Israel's destruction.

In Micah's own time the Assyrians dominated the international scene. They would wipe out the northern kingdom and in their turn be replaced by Babylon. Babylon would enslave the southern kingdom, only to be destroyed by the Persians.

The Medo-Persians would themselves yield to Alexander and the Greeks.

Against the oppression of the Greeks would rises a blood bath known to history as "The Maccabean Period," including a Jewish civil war, to be ended only by Roman occupation.

(4:12-5:1 . . .) This array of foreign powers who, from the beginning of recorded history, have used the land of Israel as a military pawn and buffer state have reckoned without God's thought and counsel. *He has gathered them, ie.* the nations arrayed against Israel, *as sheves to the threshing floor.* Jerusalem, "daughter of Zion," is called to arise and thresh. Jehovah will make her horn iron and her hoofs brass.

Thus, against the figure of oxen treading out grain, God promises power which will beat many people "in pieces."

Nothing in history to date, fully accords with the prediction. The only period of history since Micah in which Israel has had any military power was the Maccabean period of victory over Antiochus Epiphanes and that victory was on nothing like the scale indicated here in the threshing of many nations.

To find the fulfillment of this prophecy, we must look to more recent history. We have previously referred to *Romans 11* in reference to the first group here presented by Micah *ie.* the true Israel, the covenant people called the *remnant.* But what of the cast off ones who are to become a *strong nation* to whom the former dominion shall come?

It is concerning *them* that Paul writes "as touching the Gospel, they are enemies for your (Christians) sake, but as touching the election, they are beloved for the father's sake. For the gifts and calling of God are not repented of. For as ye in time past were disobedient to God, but now have obtained mercy by their disobedience, even so have these also now been disobedient, that by the mercy shown you they also may now obtain mercy." *(Romans 11:24-ff)* (See Don DeWelt, *Romans Realized,* p. 174-f)

The Jews are precious to Jehovah because of His past relations with them. There is little doubt that the Bible predicts another period of national life and prosperity. To recognize this ought, not, however, to engender in us such earthly, material and sordid hopes as proved their undoing in the rejection of Christ two thousand years ago. Whatever is in store for the Jewish nation in terms of earthly identity, it can in no way preclude the longing of God and His church to win them to Christ.

It is my opinion that in our day, which is called the latter days, the time of the Messiah (Cp. *Micah 4:1 & 6*), we are seeing the fulfillment of *Micah 4:9-5:1* in the present history of the Israeli nation.

FUTURE EXALTATION & MESSIANIC HOPE 4:10—5:6

As we have previously indicated, no time in the interval between Micah and the present has met the fullness of this passage. From Assyria to now many nations have been assembled against the Jews (v. 11). In all this historic desire to see these people defiled, the nations have not considered God's will nor known His counsel (v. 12). The present Arab-Russian-Chinese coalition against modern Israel certainly takes none of this into account.

Yet, in a strength unbelievable, reported by every news media of our time, this little postage stamp country has not once but four times in turn defied the strength of Britain and all the Arab world could hurl against her and has each time "threshed" them soundly (v. 12). In six days in June, 1967, Israel literally *"beat in pieces many people."*

Micah promised this would come to pass *during the Christian era.* It ought be no great source of amazement that we are seeing it happen!

(5:1) But before the remnant shall be gathered by Messiah, before those cast off can become a strong nation, the inevitable must happen. The kingdoms will gather their armies together and attempt in vain to hold off the armies of Assyria and of Babylon. But it will be to no avail. The price of their apostacy must be paid.

FOCUS ON THE MESSIAH . . . Micah 5:2-6

RV . . . But thou, Bethlehem Ephrathah, which art little to be among the thousands of Judah, out of thee shall one come forth unto me that is to be ruler in Israel; whose goings forth are from of old, from everlasting. Therefore will he give them up, until the time that she who travaileth hath brought forth; then the residue of his brethren shall return unto the children of Israel. And he shall stand, and shall feed his flock in the strength of Jehovah, in the majesty of the name of Jehovah his God: and they shall abide; for now shall he be great unto the ends of the earth. And this man shall be our peace. When the Assyrian shall come into our land, and when he shall tread in our palaces, then shall we raise against him seven shepherds, and eight principal men. And they shall waste the land of Assyria with the sword, and the land of Nimrod in the entrances thereof: and he shall deliver us from the Assyrian, when he cometh into our land, and when he treadeth within our border.

LXX . . . And thou, Bethlehem, house of Ephratha, art few in number to be reckoned among the thousands of Juda; yet out of thee shall one come forth to me, to be a ruler of Israel; and his goings forth were from the beginning, even from eternity. Therefore shall he appoint them to wait till the time of her that travails: she shall bring forth, and then the remnant of their brethren shall return to the children of Israel. And the Lord shall stand, and see, and feed his flock with power, and they shall dwell in the glory of the name of the Lord their God: for now shall they be magnified to the ends of the earth. And she shall have peace when Assur shall come into your land, and when he shall come up upon your country; and there shall be raised up against him seven shepherds, and eight attacks of men. And they shall tend the Assyrian with a sword, and the land of Nebrod with her trench: and he shall deliver you from the Assyrian, when he shall come upon your land, and when he shall invade your coasts.

COMMENTS

(Verse 2) In the Hebrew text this verse is the *first* verse in chapter five. In the Septuagint it appears, as in all subsequent texts as verse two of this chapter. Actually, 5:1 belongs with the last paragraph, beginning with verse nine, of chapter four.

When the bloodied-handed Herod sent to the rabbis to ask the place of Messiah's birth, he was pointed to Bethlehem. *(Matthew 2: 4-6)* It was on the strength of this passage *(5:2-ff)* of Micah's prophecy. No prophecy concerning His coming is more clear. No predictive Scripture is more universally agreed upon as to its meaning.

Having described the nature of the Messianic age *(4:1-13)* and having inserted a reminder of the punishment which must come first *(5:1)*, Micah now focuses our attention on the birth and work of the Messiah Himself.

Bethlehem! Birthplace of David. Ancient Ephratah of the Gentiles. *(Genesis 35:16)* The entire race of men have an acute interest in what will happen there. To the Jew first but also to the Greek, there will be born in the city of David a Saviour who is Christ the Lord.

As villages go, Bethlehem is no more nor less than average. Nestling on the eastern slopes of a ridge some five miles southwest of Jerusalem, this was, among other things, the traditional home of many whose trade was carpentry. Compared to many districts in Judea, the prophet calls Bethlehem little.

We might have expected the Son of God to be born in Jerusalem, or the King of Kings to be born in Rome, or some other center of power and influence. Instead, He came to a peaceful little Judean town, so insignificant in worldly eyes that Josephus doesn't bother to mention it. Nor for that matter, is it included in the catalogue of Joshua in late Hebrew manuscripts.

Jerome suggested Bethlehem was stricken from the later Hebrew texts to obscure the evidence of Jesus' Messiahship. In light of the fact that the Septuagint does include Bethlehem in the text of Joshua, Jerome may have been right.

In any event, the selection of this humble village of shepherds and carpenters as the birthplace of God's Messiah speaks volumes concerning the value of human status symbols and pride of ancestry. *(Luke 1:52)*

It is also not without significance that the sheep tended on the slopes of Bethlehem's hills were traditionally those intended for temple sacrifice. He who was born there was the lamb of God! The shadow of a cross fell across the manger bed.

So firmly fixed was Bethlehem as the birthplace of the Messiah in the minds of the Jews that Hadrian would allow none of them to live in or near the town.

ONE . . . THAT IS TO BE RULER IN ISRAEL . . .

Perhaps no other single term in the Old Testament has been more grossly misunderstood or the subject of more theological controversy. To the post-exilic Jewish mind it conjured up dreams of one who would establish the Jewish nation as the final worldpower. Upon this dream was based most of the nationalistic pride, the religious narrowness and the racial bigotry which marked the Jewish contemporaries of Jesus.

It was this ambitious vision of world conquest and Gentile enslavement that brought about the death of Jesus (humanly speaking) for He would have no part of such an earthly kingdom. It was this same racio-nationalistic ambition that brought about the death of the first Christian martyr, and which hounded Paul across three continents.

It is this same materialistic concept of Messiah's kingdom which today preoccupies many Christians with eschatological charts and prooftexts whose time might more profitably be spent preaching the Gospel.

On the other hand, it is the failure of many to recognize the kingly office and authority of Jesus that has brought about the spiritual uncertainty of the modern church. It was a *king* who was to be born in Bethlehem, not merely a Galilean carpenter or a pale religious philosopher.

So aware was Jesus of His royal office that even He was tempted by Satan to fulfill the Jewish dream of power by setting up a worldly kingdom. This is the meaning of Jesus' temptations at the opening of His public ministry *(Luke 4:1-12)*. His awareness of His kingship was so intense that His preaching is termed "the gospel of the kind-

5:2, 3   MICAH

dom." *(Mark 1:14-15)* (cp. *Luke 4:43)* It requires more than a little carnal imagination to force Jesus' Gospel of the kingdom into the rabbinical doctrine of an earthly kingdom. Regretably, since the advent of the Plymouth Brethren (1830), the teaching of John Nelson Darby (1800-1882) and the publication of the Scofield Reference Bible, many preachers (particularly of the "faith only" persuasion) have spent a great deal of time and energy doing just that.

The real issue here is the assurance that, just as the return of the remnant will insure the fulfillment of God's promise to Abraham to bless all the nations of the earth, so the one who shall rise out of Bethlehem shall assure the fulfillment of His promise to David. (Cf. *II Samuel 7:16)* Peter saw the fulfillment of this promise in the resurrection of Jesus. *(Acts 2:30-31, 34-36)*

He was to be "ruler in Israel." He was to rule over the house of Jacob forever. *(Luke 1:1-2)*

The Jews object that Jesus could not be Messiah because He was so far from being ruler in Israel that Israel ruled over Him . . . put Him to death. But He Himself answered this objection, and in doing so put the lie to all who would claim for Him a materialistic kingdom. He said, "My kingdom is not of this world." *(John 18:36)*

It is a spiritual Israel He reigns over, the children of the promise . . . all the followers of believing Abraham. *(Galatians 3:7)*

Concerning the One to be born in Bethlehem, Micah says His "goings forth are from of old, from everlasting." Literally the term means "from the days of ages."

There could scarcely be a more forceful statement of the preexistence of Christ. It denotes His existence "in the form of God." (Cp. *Philippians 2:5-ff)* It is fitting such a term should be used in connection with a prediction of His birth. We will see the same words in *Habakkuk 1:12.*

Jesus laid claim to the truth of this designation when He claimed to have been before Abraham *(John 5:58).*

THEREFORE WILL HE GIVE THEM UP UNTIL THE TIME
THAT SHE WHO TRAVAILETH HATH BROUGHT FORTH
. . . v. 3

God will not fully vindicate His people and exalt them until, through suffering, Israel brings forth His Son.

"Then the remnant (residue) shall return unto the children of Israel." The covenant people, within the race and nation and without

FUTURE EXALTATION & MESSIANIC HOPE   5:4-6

. . . the genuine children of Israel in covenant with God . . . all believers shall all be incorporated into the Israel over which Messiah shall rule. And He shall not be ashamed to call them brethren. (Cp. *Hebrews 2:11*)

AND HE SHALL STAND AND SHALL FEED . . . v. 4

He shall be a glorious prince, but His relationship to His people is that of shepherd. (Cp. *John 10:11-ff*) It is no coincidence that the Twenty-third Psalm is the most dearly beloved Old Testament passage among Christians.

He shall do this, not as other men, but in the strength and majesty of Jehovah. It would be said concerning Him that He taught "as one having authority, and not as the scribes." The prophets prefaced their message with "thus saith the Lord," Messiah would say, "verily, verily I say unto you!"

"And they shall abide . . ." The nation of Israel was perishing. Soon the northern tribes would be disbursed so completely as to make them, in subsequent history, unidentifiable. The southern kingdom would endure longer . . . even be in a measure re-established following the captivity, but any hope of national honor related to God's covenant promise had gone up with the smoke of their sacrifices to Baal. But Messiah's flock would abide.

Jesus' own words re-affirm this, "and this is the will of Him that sent me, that of all that which He hath given me I should lose nothing, but should raise it up at the last day."

It is most regrettable that those who teach the Calvinistic nonsense of "eternal security" should be allowed to so pervert this doctrine of assurance as to deprive God's people of its blessing.

". . . He shall be great unto the ends of the earth . . ." He *alone* is great. (Cp. *Joel 2:21-* and *Luke 1:32*) And His greatness shall be to the ends of the earth. Here is another of the myriad evidences in the Old Testament of God's universal concern for all men. The Messianic intent of God has ever been that "all the nations of the earth shall be blessed."

AND THIS MAN SHALL BE OUR PEACE . . . vs. 5-6

In the original here there is no word for man. It is simply and emphatically *this one* . . . He alone . . . who is our peace, The words "our peace" are reminiscent of *Ephesians 2:14*. It is only the Messiah who can bring peace . . . who can bring an end to the warfare between God's people and those who, before He came were "separate from

5:5, 6   MICAH

Christ, alienated from the commonwealth of Israel and strangers from the covenants of promise, having no hope and without God in the world." (Cf. *Ephesians 2:11-15)*

Assyria, being Israel's most powerful enemy at the time of Micah's ministry is made here to represent all the enemies of God's people. When Messiah appears, He will destroy them. (Cf. *Ezekiel, chapter 38)*

"Seven shepherds . . . eight principal men." A strange array, it would seem, to send against the Assyrians. Micah is obviously using well understood figures to convey the truth of Messiah's conquest over the enemies of God's people.

"Seven" expresses perfection. We shall raise against (or depend upon) the Messiah . . . the perfect shepherd.

"Eight" is seven plus one. The Messiah plus those "principal men" or "anointed men," such as the twelve, (Cp. *Isaiah 32:1)* "shall lay waste the land of Assyria with the sword, and the land of Nimrod in the entrance thereof . . ." The Lord's strength is more than enough.

Lange points out that the terms "palace," "seven," and "eight" connect themselves with the threatening formula employed by Amos *(Amos, chapters 1-2)* to announce the approach of the destruction which was about to break. God's grace will be greater than the sin; hence, instead of three and four sins which make the judgement necessary *(Amos 2:4)* seven and eight heroes are named who shall drive away the enemies when Messiah has come.

Just as the Roman empire, *during Pax Romana*, in which period Jesus was born, enforced peace with the Roman sword, so Messiah and those who stand with Him will enforce His peace by subduing His enemies with the sword of the Spirit. (Cp. *Hebrews 4:12, Ephesians 6:17)* Those who stand against the Gospel of Christ, and continue in league with idolatries and witchcrafts, as did Assyria and Babylon of old, shall be consumed by it.

In our day, when tolerance of any and all false teaching has become a sacred cow and when unbelief is regarded as a normal reaction to God, it is difficult to think in these terms. There is, however, a "hard" side to the Gospel. The sword has a cutting edge. There is destruction for those who resist it. (Cp. *I Peter 2:8)*

THE GLORIOUS FUTURE OF THE REMNANT . . . Micah 5:7-15

RV . . . And the remnant of Jacob shall be in the midst of many peoples as dew from Jehovah, as showers upon the grass, that tarry not for man, nor wait for the sons of men. And the remnant of Jacob shall be among the nations, in the midst of many peoples, as a lion

FUTURE EXALTATION & MESSIANIC HOPE   5:7-15

among the beasts of the forest, as a young lion among the flocks of sheep; who, if he go through, treadeth down and teareth in pieces, and there is none to deliver. Let thy hand be lifted up above thine adversaries, and let all thine enemies be cut off. And it shall come to pass in that day; saith Jehovah, that I will cut off thy horses out of the midst of thee, and will destroy thy chariots: and I will cut off the cities of thy land, and will throw down all thy strongholds. And I will cut off witchcrafts out of thy hand; and thou shalt have no more soothsayers: and I will cut off thy graven images and thy pillars out of the midst of thee; and thou shalt no more worship the work of thy hands; and I will pluck up thine Asherim out of the midst of thee; and I will destroy thy cities. And I will execute vengeance in anger and wrath upon the nations which hearkened not.

LXX . . . And the remnant of Jacob shall be among the Gentiles in the midst of many peoples, as dew falling from the Lord, and as lambs on the grass; that none may assemble nor resist among the sons of men. And the remnant of Jacob shall be among the Gentiles in the midst of many nations, as a lion in the forest among cattle, and as a lion's whelp among flocks of sheep, even as when he goes through, and selects, and carries off his prey, and there is none to deliver. Thine hand shall be lifted up against them that afflict thee, and all thine enemies shall be utterly destroyed. And it shall come to pass in that day, saith the Lord, that I will utterly destroy the horses out of the midst of thee, and destroy thy chariots: and I will utterly destroy the cities of thy land, and demolish all thy strong-holds: and I will utterly destroy thy sorceries out of thine hands; and there shall be no soothsayers in thee. And I will utterly destroy thy graven images, and thy statues out of the midst of thee; and thou shalt never any more worship the works of thine hands. And I will cut off the groves out of the midst of thee, and I will abolish thy cities. And I will execute vengeance on the heathen in anger and wrath, because they hearkened not.

COMMENTS

Micah writes glorious things in this passage concerning the remnant. Israel according to the flesh dwelt alone until her destruction. The nearer destruction finally came, the more she dwelt alone, turned in upon herself the less certain it was God's Messiah would save her and make the Gentiles her slaves. Not so the remnant, the true Israel; she will be in the midst of many people . . . as the salt of the earth, or as seed sown upon the ground. (Cp. *Hosea 2:23*)

The remnant shall be as dew from the Lord, covering all as dew in a summer morning. (Cp. *Psalm 110:3*) They shall be pure and clear as dew drops, as the water of life. Dependant upon the Spirit, they shall "tarry not for man, nor wait upon the sons of man." They shall be a great blessing to those people among whom they live, just as the refreshing dew from heaven is a blessing to thirsty earth.

But the remnant shall not be tread upon as is the dew. They shall be "as a lion among the flocks of sheep". . . as a lion "treadeth down and teareth in pieces and there is none to deliver."

Messiah's people shall be silent and gentle and bringers of blessings, as the dew, but they shall be as bold as lions. The forces which today threaten to destroy Christian civilization cannot stand against the power of the Gospel in the lives of commited people any more than a hyena can stand against a lion.

The strength of God's covenant people is that which derives from the Lion of the Tribe of Judah. Israel of old had been instructed to not go to Egypt for horses *(Deuteronomy 17:16)* lest they depend upon chariots and cavalry rather than upon God. *(Psalm 20:7)* From Solomon on they would disregard this command *(I Kings 10:26-28)*. The new Israel has no such arms. She stands or falls upon her trust in Christ. So long as she is faithful nothing can stand against her. (Cp. *Romans 8:31-ff)*

Note those things against which His people are to prevail. *Verse 10* . . . horses and chariots are cut off and destroyed. *Verse 11* . . . Cities and strongholds will be thrown down. The temptation to trust worldly power are so to be eliminated. The church has been slow to relinquish these things, but the circumstances of our day now leave us no choice. Only the Gospel can stand against the armed atheism which threatens our existence.

Witchcrafts and soothsayers *(v. 12)* are also to be cut off. There is a revival of such evil in our day, but not in the hands of the church.

Graven images and pillars and the graven images which are the works of our hand *(v. 13)* are to be eliminated. Even the Roman church has recently "decommissioned" two hundred saints before whose idols thousands have prayed! In the New Testament church such things were an abomination.

Verse 15 must be almost unbelievable to the one today who thinks the God of the Old Testament was only a primative fore-shadowing of the God of Love revealed in the new. Nevertheless, the prophet sees, IN THE AGE OF THE MESSIAH, God executing *"vengeance in anger and wrath upon the nations which hearken not."*

FUTURE EXALTATION & MESSIANIC HOPE 5:7-15

The concept of a God Who does not bring vengeance against anyone is of very recent origin and completely foreign to the Christian God of the New Testament as well as the Old.

Chapter IX—*Questions*
Future Exaltation and Messianic Hope

1. Demonstrate that Micah's prophecy in Micah 4-5 has to do with the day of the Messiah, our own Messianic time.
2. What does John tell us about this end time? *(I John 2:18-f)*
3. What is the meaning of "the mountain of Jehovah's house"?
4. Comment on "all peoples walk everyone in the name of his god, but we will walk in the name of Jehovah our God for ever and ever." *(Micah 4:5)*
5. Discuss "many nations." *(Micah 4:2)*
6. Discuss ". . . out of Zion shall go forth the law, and the word of Jehovah from Jerusalem." *(Micah 4:2 cp. Luke 24:44-f)*
7. Men are at war with men because _____.
8. God must become ruler of our _____ as well as our church doctrine. *(Micah 4:4)*
9. "In that day" *(Micah 4:6-7)* refers us back to _____.
10. "That which is lame" is the image of _____.
11. Discuss "her that halted is become a remnant." *(Micah 4:7)*
12. Distinguish between "that which was lame" and "that which was driven away."
13. Discuss "I will make . . . that which was cast far off a strong nation" in *Micah 4:7* in light of *Romans 11:1*.
14. What is meant by "tower of the flock"? *(Micah 4:8)*
15. Discuss *Micah 4:11* in connection with *Micah 3:12*.
16. In Micah's own time the nation of _____ dominated the international scene.
17. _____ would wipe out the northern kingdom.
18. _____ would enslave the southern kingdom.
19. _____ would conquer the Medo-Persian empire.
20. The Maccabean revolt was against the rule of _____.
21. All these powers, and others since have used the land of _____ as a political pawn and a _____ state.
22. Discuss *Romans 11, Micah 4:11-13* in light of current events in the Middle East.
23. The Jews are precious to Jehovah because _____.

MICAH

24. This does not imply _____.
25. What New Testament reference is made to *Micah 5:2-ff?*
26. What is the meaning of Ephratah? *(Micah 5:2)*
27. Bethlehem nestles on the _____ slopes of a ridge some _____ miles _____ of Jerusalem.
28. Discuss the conditions of Jesus birth in contrast to what might have been expected for the birth of a king.
29. The sheep tended on the slopes of Bethlehem were traditionally intended for _____.
30. Why did the Roman emperor Harian forbid Jews to live in or near Bethlehem?
31. Perhaps no other term in the Old Testament has been more grossly misunderstood than _____.
32. Humanly speaking, it was the Jews' ambitious vision of _____ that was responsible for the death of Jesus.
33. It is the failure of many to recognize the kingly office and authority of Jesus that has brought about the _____ in the modern church.
34. Discuss the temptation of Jesus *(Luke 4:1-12)* in relation to the Jewish dream of world power in the Messianic age.
35. The real issue in *Micah 2:6* is the assurance that _____.
36. Why do the Jews object that Jesus cannot be the Messiah?
37. Discuss the pre-existence of Christ in light of *Micah 5:2.*
38. God would not, Micah promised, fully vindicate His people and exalt them until _____,
39. The Messiah is to be a glorious prince, but His relationship to His people is that of a _____.
40. What is the significance of "His greatness shall be to the ends of the earth"?
41. Discuss "and this man shall be our peace . . ."
42. Discuss "seven shepherds . . . eight principal men." *(Micah 5:5-6)*
43. What is meant by "the remnant shall be as dew in a summer morning"?
44. Messiah's people are to be as bold as _____.
45. *Micah 5:15* must be almost unbelievable to _____.
46. The prophet sees in the age of _____ God executing "vengeance in anger and wrath upon the nations which hearken not."

CHAPTER X
JEHOVAH'S CONTROVERSY WITH HIS PEOPLE

Chapters six and seven are composed of a series of lamentations, threatenings and denunciations. These are directed against all classes of people in Israel and Judah, whereas those which introduce each of the three earlier cycles (chapters 1-3) are directed against the upper classes only. The themes struck there are extended here.

We are pressed to conclude that, just as the sins of society's leaders filter down through all classes so the judgements of God upon those sins are also applied to all classes of people. This is a lesson which is much needed today among revolutionaries who are critical of those in authority. Too many times protests against "the system" are merely "the pot calling the kettle black."

FORGOTTEN ACTS OF SALVATION . . . Micah 6:1-8

RV . . . Hear ye now what Jehovah saith: Arise, contend thou before the mountains, and let the hills hear thy voice. Hear, O ye mountains, Jehovah's controversy, and ye enduring foundations of the earth; for Jehovah hath a controversy with his people, and he will contend with Israel. O my people, what have I done unto thee? and wherein have I wearied thee? testify against me. For I brought thee up out of the land of Egypt, and redeemed thee out of the house of bondage; and I sent before thee Moses, Aaron, and Miriam. O my people, remember now what Balak king of Moab devised, and what Balaam the son of Beor answered him; remember from Shittim unto Gilgal, that ye may know the righteous acts of Jehovah. Wherewith shall I come before Jehovah, and bow myself before the high God? shall I come before him with burnt-offerings, with calves a year old? will Jehovah be pleased with thousands of rams, or with ten thousands of rivers of oil? shall I give my first-born for my transgression, the fruit of my body for the sin of my soul? He hath showed thee, O man, what is good; and what doth Jehovah require of thee but, to do justly, and to love kindness, and to walk humbly with thy God?

LXX . . . Hear now a word; the Lord God has said; Arise, plead with the mountains, and let the hills hear thy voice. Hear ye, O mountains, the controversy of the Lord, and ye valleys even the foundations of the earth: for the Lord has a controversy with his people, and will plead with Israel. O my people, what have I done to thee? or wherein have

I troubled thee? or wherein have I grieved thee? answer me. For I brought thee up out of the land of Egypt, and redeemed thee out of the house of bondage, and sent before thee Moses, and Aaron, and Mariam. O my people, remember now, what counsel Balac king of Moab took against thee, and what Balaam the son of Beor answered him from the reeds to Galgal; that the righteousness of the Lord might be known. Wherewithal shall I reach the Lord, and lay hold of my God most high? shall I reach him by whole-burnt-offerings, by calves of a year old? Will the Lord accept thousands of rams, or ten thousands of fat goats? should I give my first-born for ungodliness, the fruit of my body for the sin of my soul? Has it not been told thee, O man, what is good? or what does the Lord require of thee, but to do justice, and love mercy, and be ready to walk with the Lord thy God?

COMMENTS

The first controversy of Jehovah against His people is occasioned by their having forgotten His saving activities on their behalf in times past. Centuries later, Stephen would level the same charge against them. To him this was the story of their national life. (Cf. *Acts, chapter 7*) *Arise . . . contend . . . (plead your case) before the mountains . . .* vs. 1-2

The judgments pronounced against both the northern and southern kingdoms in the three cycles which compose chapters 1-3 of Micah are harsh. The denunciation of the nation, the casting off of the race *per se* which is evidenced in the promised blessings to the remnant (chapters 4-5) are sure to be decried as unfair by those who are to be cast off. To prove His fairness in these things, God calls the prophet to set the sins of the people before them.

Because the fulfillment of the covenant will issue in God's blessing all the nations of the earth, this controversy is to be before the whole of creation. Thus the prophet comes full circle, connecting this final section of his prophecy to the first (see comment on *1:2-ff*). As the justice of God's judgments against the leaders of the nation was established before all people and nations in the opening cycle, so the fairness of His complaints against the people will now be openly seen of all. The equity of God's cause will be pleaded and sinners themselves forced to confess that God's ways and judgments are fair.

O MY PEOPLE WHAT HAVE I DONE . . . vs. 3-5

In these verses the complaint of God is made. In *6:9—7:6*, the case will be judged.

JEHOVAH'S CONTROVERSY 6:3-5

(Verse 3) The cry of verses 3-5 is not the stern judicial pronouncement of chapters 1-3 against broken law. Here we have rather the plea of a broken heart. "What have I done unto thee?" "Wherein have I wearied thee?" They have sinned against His love as well as His law.

(Verse 4) "I brought thee up . . ." The nation of Israel did not exist until the mercies of God brought an enslaved race out of a foreign land because of the covenant of blessing made with their father! (Cp. *Exodus 2:24*) It was the law, given them through Moses and the priesthood instituted in Aaron that turned the race into a nation . . . the very law whose flaunting now occasioned the heart-break of their God at the necessity of judging His people.

O MY PEOPLE, REMEMBER NOW WHAT BALAK KING OF MOAB DEVISED AND WHAT BALAAM THE SON OF BEOR ANSWERED HIM . . . v. 5(a)

Micah's allusion here is to *Numbers, chapters 22-24*. The prophet places himself in the position of Balaam and asks those to whom he speaks to see the parallel.

Israel, drawing near the promised land had encamped on the plains of Moab opposite Jericho on the east bank of the Jordon. Balak, king of Moab, seeing what Israel had done to the Amorites, was terrified and sent to Pethor near the Euphrates to the prophet Balaam with the request that he come and curse Israel.

When Balaam went before God for direction, he was directed not to return with Balak's messengers, the elders of Moab.

Balak, assuming that Balaam could be bribed, sent ambassadors of higher rank with greater gifts. Again Balaam went to God in prayer and this time was instructed to go with the princes of Moab but to say only what God gave him to say.

Next morning Balaam went with the princes toward Moab. And God was angry, apparently because Balaam had been tempted enough by the bribe to question His first instruction.

As Balaam rode toward Moab, an angel appeared to his ass, but not to him. The animal, seeing the angel block her way, turned aside into a field, whereupon Balaam beat her.

Again the ass saw the angel and, instead of obeying Balaam, crushed his foot against a wall, and Balaam beat her a second time.

A third time the animal saw God's angel blocking the way, and this time she balked, for which Balaam struck her with his rod.

Then the Lord opened the ass's mouth and she asked her master what she had done to be beaten. When Balaam answered it was because she had provoked and ridiculed him and wished for a sword to kill her, the animal reminded him that she had served him well all her life and asked if this had ever happened before.

Then Balaam's eyes were allowed to see the angel standing in the way with drawn sword. He fell on his face before the angel and was asked why he had beaten his ass when the angel had come to stand against him.

The prophet then confessed he had sinned in attempting to force his way past the angel of the Lord.

Understanding that he had done wrong in asking again and again for permission to curse Israel, Balaam asked for instructions and was told to go on to Moab but to say only what the Lord would instruct him to say.

Seeing Balaam coming, Balak rushed to meet the prophet assuming he was going to curse Israel

Balaam ignored the king's rebuke for not having come at once and warned him he would say only what the Lord gave him to say.

Balak took Balaam to Kireath-huzoth, overlooking the outskirts of Israel's encampment. There the Moabite offered sacrifices and sent portions of the sacrifice to Balaam.

Next day Balak took Balaam to the high places of Bamoth-Baal from which he could see the Israelites.

The prophet required the king to again build altars and sacrifice. When this was done, he instructed Balak to wait by the sacrifices while he inquired of God.

God met Balaam and gave him a message, *"How can I curse those God has not cursed. How can I denounce those whom the Lord has not denounced?"*

Hearing this, Balak took Balaam to yet another high place, to the top of Mount Pisgah, hoping he would be permitted to curse Israel from this vantage point. Again Balaam waited on the message of God.

This time the message was, *"God is not a man that He should tell or act a lie nor feel compunction for what He has promised, I have received His command to bless Israel."*

Then follows Balaam's discourse to Balak concerning God's deliverance of Israel out of Egypt. *(Numbers 23:22-26)*

Seeing Balaam would not curse Israel, Balak requests that he neither curse nor bless her, to which Balaam answered, *"All the Lord speaks I must do."*

Again Balak took Balaam to another high place in a last effort to have his way against Israel. But Balaam no longer looked for signs of God's permission to curse His people. Instead he looked the other way.

Then God's Spirit came upon Balaam and the prophet blessed Israel in Balak's presence. Upon this, the king of Moab became angry. In answering Balak's anger, Balaam said, *"I cannot go beyond the command of the Lord to do either good or bad of my own will, but what the Lord says, that I will speak."* (Numbers 24:13, Emphasized Bible)

It is Balaam's progressive willingness and final determination to speak only what the Lord gave him to say that Micah here appropriates to himself. He too has said what his listeners do not want to hear. His reply is, "O my people, remember now what Balak king of Moab devised, and what Balaam the son of Beor answered him . . ."

Micah is also determined to say, good or bad, only what the Lord gives him to say.

". . . REMEMBER FROM SHITTIM TO GILGAL, THAT YE MAY KNOW THE RIGHTEOUS ACT OF JEHOVAH . . ." v. 5(b)

After God had steadfastly forbidden Balaam from cursing Israel and had actually brought this alien prophet to bless Jehovah's people, the people themselves turned to idols! *(Numbers 25:1-ff)*

Having settled down in Shittim the people "began to play the harlot with the daughters of Moab . . . (and) so Israel joined himself to Baal of Peor." *(Numbers 25:1-3,* Emphasized Bible)

As a result, God's anger had been kindled against Israel so that He had instructed Moses to hang their leaders and 24,000 Israelites were smitten.

Micah again asks that those to whom he speaks remember God's past dealing with Israel. He has formerly punished her for unfaithfulness. If they will recall this truth, they will see the validity of Micha's warning of the same wrath. Again Micah's message is timely in our day.

WHEREWITH SHALL I COME BEFORE JEHOVAH . . . v. 6-7

Micah's question is simply whether he, as Balak, shall continually, with animal sacrifices, attempt to alter the will of God. Having placed himself in the way of Balaam's determination to do God's will, whether good or bad, he now implies that his hearers are in the same position as Balak, king of Moab!

. . . SHALL I GIVE MY FIRST-BORN FOR MY TRANSGRESSION . . . v. 7(b)

Micah pursues the issue further, insinuating they would have him turn to Baal in their behalf. It was one of the abominable practices of Baal worship that the first born son of the worshipper be tossed into the fiery bowels of the idol to atone for the parent's sin . . . would they have him resort to this despicable practice to atone for having pronounced the judgment of God against them? The sarcasm is scathing!

HE HATH SHOWED THEE, O MAN, WHAT IS GOOD; AND WHAT DOTH JEHOVAH REQUIRE OF THEE, BUT TO DO JUSTLY, AND TO LOVE KINDNESS, AND TO WALK HUMBLY WITH THY GOD . . . v. 8

Here is one of the classic questions of Scripture. It ranks with that of the Lord, "What is a man profited, if he shall gain the whole world and lose his own life?" (*Matthew 26:16*) And the Hebrew writer's "How shall we escape, if we neglect so great a salvation?" (*Hebrews 2:1-4*)

For such questions there is no answer.

God's insistence upon faithfulness is not unreasonable, particularly when His past blessings and present promises are remembered. Nor is His punishment for unfaithfulness unreasonable when one remembers that it is His purpose through such faithfulness to benefit not only the faithful but all man-kind.

"*What doth Jehovah require of thee?*" The Law set down innumerable requirements. From the direct catalogue of eternal mortality in the decalogue to the detailed requirements of Sabbaths and sacrifices, the sum and substance of such requirements is that God's worshippers shall "do justly, and to love kindness, and to walk humbly with thy God." Failure to keep the commandments and precepts expressed in outward forms inevitably leads to failure to do these simple yet profound elementals: do justly, love kindness, walk humbly.

The Septuagint text contains three terms whose meanings shed much light on this verse: literally "the to be doing the justice;" "love mercy;" and "to be ready, in reference to the go (as on a journey) with your Lord, God."

What is described here is the "life style" required by God. To be doing justice is to have just actions as the habit or style of one's life.

But what is justice? It has to do with the keeping of God's law . . . His commandments and ordinance. Far from removing the necessity for keeping God's commandments, this passage states in simple, yet forceful, terms the necessity to do so.

But to obey the commandments formally—to go through the motions of conformity to God's law without any corresponding effect on one's life makes such obedience a hollow mockery and an affront to God. The second requirement is to love mercy.

Again the Greek of the Septuagint is clear. (And since the Septuagint is the Bible quoted by Jesus and His apostles, it behooves us to understand.) The phrase, "rendered mercy," means—literally, to have pity, to have compassion.

This latter is mentioned as an attribute of God. *(Exodus 33:19* cp. *Romans 9:15)* To have compassion is to place ones' self in the sufferer's situation . . . to suffer with him. This God does.

Micah is not claiming this is required of God's people. Obviously, it is an ideal to be sought, but what is *required* is pity, a feeling sorry for, objectively.

We are to love such mercy! Here is one of those rare pre-Christian uses of the word love—the love of the will, not the emotions. The love that is deliberate self-giving. God requires deliberate giving of self to pity, the objective concern for others. Without this all formal religious obedience is hollow.

Jesus said as much, "These (the keeping of specific commandments) ye ought to have done, and not to have left the other (justice, mercy, trust) undone." *(Matthew 23:23)*

The church member today who is meticulously correct in "doctrinal matters" and unconcerned for mercy where there is human suffering has missed the mark as far as those to whom Micah promised God's wrath missed it.

The third requirement of God is that His people live constantly in an attitude of readiness to go with God as Lord. The phrase "to walk", means literally, proceed or go one's way.

God requires His people to be alert to His authority. As we go our way, we are to do so in the awareness that God is our Lord. This attitude is imperative to the accomplishment of the first two requirements listed by Micah.

6:8-16 MICAH

The Psalmist tells us that "God trieth the minds and hearts." *(Psalm 7:9)* Proverbs 20:27 describes the lamp of Jehovah "searching all His innermost parts." In *Psalm 139:23* the Psalmist prays, "search me, O God, and know my heart." In *I Chronicles 28:9* David informs Solomon, ". . . Jehovah searcheth all hearts, and understandeth all the imaginations of the thoughts."

God does not require by simply issuing commands and edicts. The heart of God's ordinances is His intimate knowledge of the hearts and minds of men. It is for this reason that outward form must always express inner reality, and both must proceed from a constant alertness to the Lordship of Him with Whom we have to do.

GOD'S JUSTICE DEMANDS THE WICKED BE PUNISHED . . .
Micah 6:9-16

RV . . . The voice of Jehovah crieth unto the city, and the man of wisdom will see thy name: hear ye the rod, and who hath appointed it. Are there yet treasures of wickedness in the house of the wicked, and a scant measure that is abominable? Shall I be pure with wicked balances, and with a bag of deceitful weights? For the rich men thereof are full of violence, and the inhabitants thereof have spoken lies; and their tongue is deceitful in their mouth. Therefore I also have smitten thee with a grievous wound; I have made thee desolate because of thy sins. Thou shalt eat, but not be satisfied; and thy humiliation shall be in the midst of thee: and thou shalt put away, but shalt not save; and that which thou savest will I give up to the sword. Thou shalt sow, but shalt not reap; thou shalt tread the olives, but shalt not anoint thee with oil; and the vintage, but shalt not drink the wine. For the statutes of Omri are kept, and all the works of the house of Ahab, and ye walk in their counsels; that I may make thee a desolation, and the inhabitants thereof a hissing: and ye shall bear the reproach of my people.

LXX . . . The Lord's voice shall be proclaimed in the city, and he shall save those that fear his name: hear, O tribe; and who shall order the city? Is there not fire, and the house of the wicked heaping up wicked treasures, and that with the pride of unrighteousness? Shall the wicked be justified by the balance, or deceitful weights in the bag, whereby they have accumulated their ungodly wealth, and they that dwell in the city have uttered falsehoods, and their tongue has been exalted in their mouth? Therefore will I begin to smite thee; I will destroy thee in thy sins. Thou shalt eat, and shalt not be satisfied; and there shall be darkness upon thee; and he shall depart from thee, and thou shalt not escape; and all that shall escape shall be delivered over to the sword. Thou shalt sow, but thou shalt not reap; thou shalt press the olive, but thou shalt not anoint thyself with oil; and shalt make wine, but ye shall drink no wine: and the ordinances of my people shall be utterly abolished. For thou hast kept the statutes of Zambri, and done all the works of the house of Achaab; and ye have walked in their ways, that I might deliver thee to utter destruction, and those that inhabit the city to hissing: and ye shall bear the reproach of nations.

COMMENTS

Verses 9-12 . . .
The prophet, speaking with the voice of the Lord, calls upon the city, Jerusalem, to see the reason why He must punish her wickedness.

"WISDOM SHALL SEE THY NAME . . ." v. 9

The Septuagint, Vulgate and Syriac texts all have "fear" rather than "see." *Proverbs 9:10* tells us "the fear of Jehovah is the beginning of wisdom."

The course of wisdom is to seriously heed God's warnings. He *is* God and is therefore perfectly capable of doing what He says He will do.

"HEAR THE ROD . . ." v. 9(b)

The warning has been given. Micah entreats the people to hear the rod before it falls, before they feel it. They are also entreated to hear Him Who has appointed this punishment for His children.

God's messengers are ever required to explain God's providences and to quicken and direct men to learn the lessons taught by them.

". . . SHALL I BE PURE?" vs. 10-12

Those who had wealth and power abused it. Those who did not have such advantages found other means of defrauding those with whom they dealt. If they could not use force and violence they used fraud and deceit. False weights and measures and deliberate lies were common devices for making a "good bargain." They even spoke falsely concerning God. (Cp. *Ezekiel 8:12*)

How can God remain pure and yet withhold righteous judgment

from such people? Can He be pure and "go along" with such ethics? This is ever the dilemma of God's justice and mercy.

It is very popular today to believe a God of mercy is not capable of stern judgment. There have been other times (eg. the Puritan era) when it seems to have been believed that a just God could not possibly be merciful.

To the informed Christian, or for that matter the informed Jew, the answer has always been God's Messiah. This is the message of *Romans 3:21-26*. It is also the message of Micah as he alternately warns of judgements and promises Messiah's coming.

Verses 13-16 . . .

THEREFORE I ALSO HAVE SMITTEN THEE . . . v. 13

The persistent fact of sin is a prime factor in Micah's message. He did not see it as mere maladjustment or even failure to attain to some objective religious standard. Sin is against the person of God. It is unfaithfulness to His covenant, it is disloyalty to His purpose, it is disobedience to His authority. Exploitation of the poor, bribery, drunkenness, harlotry, idolatry are evil because they are an affront to a moral, ethical God!

The God Who cannot give countenance to sin will not save from destruction those who persist in it.

He will not abandon His mercy. The remnant will be redeemed and received by the Messiah.

But aside from the Messiah, and until He comes, God's rebellious people can expect to reap the consequences of their own evil ways.

. . . EAT . . . NOT BE SATISFIED

As they have swallowed down the riches of ill-gotten gain, so they shall vomit them up again. (Cp. *Job 20:15*) Their unethical affluence will not bring them satisfaction.

Such affluence never does. We are experiencing unparalled social dissatisfaction in the midst of plenty in our time, largely because those who have have been unconcerned for those who have not . . . and because much of our affluence has been gotten at the expense of the poor.

THY HUMILIATION SHALL BE IN THE MIDST OF THEE . . .
v. 14(b)

Their country will not harbor and protect them. God can cast a nation down by what is in the midst of them. They shall not be able to preserve what they have by force nor recover what they will lose. Their tainted wealth shall be removed by a foreign sword.

THOU SHALT SOW . . . BUT SHALL NOT DRINK WINE . . . v. 15

Either their crops will be blasted and withered until there is nothing to reap, or an enemy shall come and reap what they have sown. When they are carried away captive they will not return to harvest what they have tilled.

THE STATUTES OF OMRI ARE KEPT . . . THE WORKS OF AHAB . . . v. 16(a)

Here Micah alludes to the idolatrous reign of Omri *(I Kings 16:21-f)* as symbolic of the current unfaithfulness of the people. Omri had become king in the north, in the dynastic line of Jeroboam. He consolidated his power by defeating Tibni.

Omri reigned six years in Tirzah, after which he bought and fortified the hill of Samaria as his capital city.

It is said he did more evil than all his predecessors, beginning with Baal worship, "that which was evil in the sight of Jehovah."

After a six year reign in Samaria, Omri died and was succeeded by his son, Ahab. Micah here refers to the "works of the house of Ahab." What Bible student could be unfamiliar with "the works of Ahab?" It was he who married the infamous Jezebel whose missionary zeal for her god, Baal, puts the Israelites to shame in their apathetic neglect of Jehovah.

Micah here accuses Jerusalem of following the same idolatrous course as Omri and Ahab. In so doing, he presents us with another evidence that the chief concern of the prophet is to call the people away from idolatry and back to the covenant. There was all sorts of evil rampant in both kingdoms, but the root of it all—the fundamental reason for God's wrath against them—was their going off after Baal and in so doing breaking their covenant with Jehovah.

The Law which made Israel a nation was primarily designed to preserve the covenant and to move it forward toward the time when God, in the fullness of time, would bless all the nations of the earth in Abraham's seed. The gross violations of the law which brought about the preaching of the pre-exilic prophets were simply symptoms of the much deeper and more significant unfaithfulness to the covenant.

DESOLATION . . . HISSING . . . REPROACH

The desolation mentioned here is described vividly in *Micah 3:12.*

The proud city of Jerusalem will lay in ruins for the seventy years of Babylonian captivity, and never again regain the splendor of her former glory.

The term "hissing" is reminiscent of *Lamentations 2:15-f.* There the prophet depicts the sad wonder of those who pass by Jerusalem in her desolation. They clap their hands and suck their breath through closed teeth in expression of their amazement of the sad state of the city once called "the perfection of beauty, the joy of the whole earth."

Because of their haughty claim to be God's only people, while failing in their covenant relationship to Him, the Jews will bear the reproach which comes from such a claim. Because of their disgraceful use of the Law of Jehovah, that which should have been a great honor, *ie.* their "chosen people" status, shall become the occasion of their being despised by the peoples of the earth.

Here, it would seem, is at least a partial key to the historic phenomena mistakenly called "anti-semitism."

MICAH LONGS FOR GODLINESS . . . Micah 7:1-6

RV . . . Woe is me! for I am as when they have gathered the summer fruits, as the grape gleanings of the vintage: there is no cluster to eat; my soul desireth the first-ripe fig. The godly man is perished out of the earth, and there is none upright among men: they all lie in wait for blood; they hunt every man his brother with a net. Their hands are upon that which is evil to do it diligently; the prince asketh, and the judge is ready for a reward; and the great man, he uttereth the evil desire of his soul; thus they weave it together. The best of them is as a brier; the most upright is worse than a thorn hedge: the day of thy watchmen, even thy visitation, is come; now shall be their perplexity. Trust ye not in a neighbor; put ye not confidence in a friend; keep the doors of thy mouth from her that lieth in thy bosom. For the son dishonoreth the father, the daughter riseth up against her mother, the daughter-in-law against her mother-in-law; a man's enemies are the men of his own house.

LXX . . . Alas for me! for I am become as one gathering straw in harvest, and as one gathering grape-gleanings in the vintage, when there is no cluster for me to eat the first-ripe fruit: alas my soul! For the godly is perished from the earth; and there is none among men that orders his way aright: they all quarrel even to blood: they grievously afflict every one his neighbour: they prepare their hands for mischief, the prince asks a reward, and the judge speaks flattering words; it is the desire of their soul: therefore I will take away their goods as a

JEHOVAH'S CONTROVERSY 7:1, 2a

visitation. Woe, woe, thy times of vengeance are come; now shall be their lamentations. Trust not in friends, and confide not in guides; beware of thy wife, so as not to commit anything to her. For the son dishonours his father, the daughter will rise up against her mother, and daughter-in-law against her mother-in-law: those in his house shall be all a man's enemies.

COMMENTS

WOE IS ME . . . THE GODLY MAN IS PERISHED . . . v. 1-2(a)

Chapter seven begins with a cry of despair from the lips of the prophet. His soul is hungry for the fellowship of godly men. In this he is disappointed as a man physically hungry who comes first to the vineyard and then the orchard and finds nothing to relieve his hunger.

Micah sees beyond the confines of the little kingdoms of Israel and Judah. If there are no godly men among the covenant people, then godliness has perished from the earth! Turning to idolatry, as the world worshipped idolatry, the chosen people had brought about a moral situation similar to that which would prevail if there were no God at all!

The statement, "there is none upright . . ." reminds us of David's affirmation concerning those fools who say there is no God. In *Psalm 14:1,* David wrote "The fool hath said in his heart, there is no God. They are corrupt, they have done abominable works . . ." This is repeated in *Psalm 53:1* with the additional statement *"there is none that doeth good."* The fifth and one hundred fortieth Psalms echo this thought and expand it.

In the case of the Psalmist it was the professed athiest who is described in vivid terms as grossly immoral. Micah says that because of the idolatry of the children of Israel the same is now true of the whole world!

In *Romans 3:9-18,* Paul establishes this ungodliness as the universal state of man outside of Christ. There the apostle uses a catena, or chain of references, to prove that the Jews are in no better fix than Gentiles, for all are under sin.

Micah and Paul seem ready to say as Elijah in his time, "I, even I only, am left." *(I Kings 19:10) Their hands are upon that which is evil* . . . v. 2(b)—4(a)

There are, says Micah, not only none who do good, but multitudes that do positive hurt. "They all lie in wait for blood; they hunt every man his brother . . . " They have a thousand cursed arts of ensnaring men to their ruin.

The magistrates, office patrons and protectors of right are the practicers and promoters of wrong. The prince and judge may be hired for bribes to exert all their power to carry out wicked purposes. The great man who has wealth and the power to do good but who desires to do evil does not utter the evil desire of his soul lest his conspiring with the prince and judge become evident.

"The best of them is a brier; the most upright is worse than a thorn hedge . . ." They prick and injure all with whom they come in contact. (Cp. *II Samuel 23:6-7, Isaiah 55:13, Ezekiel 2:6*)

THE DAY OF THE WATCHMAN . . . v. 4(b)

This is the day of the watchman. Just as a policeman comes upon a criminal to arrest him, so the true prophet, God's watchman, comes upon the false prophet and his corrupt followers. The party is over, the piper must be paid. God's wrath is at hand.

TRUST YE NOT . . . vs. 5-6

Here follows a list of those whom honest men (if indeed there were any) could not trust. The list includes "a neighbor," "a friend," "her that lieth in thy bosom," *ie.* one's own wife, "the son," "the daughter," "the daughter-in-law." Such a society in indeed corrupt . . . ready for the wrath of God.

Jesus quotes verse 6(b) in connection with those He expected to persecute the new covenant people. (*Matthew 10:35-36* cp. *Luke 12:53*)

THE PROPHET LOOKS TO GOD . . . Micah 7:7-13

RV . . . But as for me, I will look unto Jehovah; I will wait for the God of my salvation: my God will hear me. Rejoice not against me, O mine enemy: when I fall, I shall arise; when I sit in darkness, Jehovah will be a light unto me. I will bear the indignation of Jehovah, because I have sinned against him, until he plead my cause, and execute judgement for me: he will bring me forth to the light, and I shall behold his righteousness. Then mine enemy shall see it and shame shall cover her who said unto me, Where is Jehovah thy God? Mine eyes shall see my desire upon her; now shall she be trodden down as the mire of the streets. A day for building thy walls! in that day shall the decree be far removed. In that day shall they come unto thee from Assyria and the cities of Egypt, and from Egypt even to the River, and from sea to sea, and from mountain to mountain. Yet shall the land be desolate because of them that dwell therein, for the fruit of their doings.

LXX . . . But I will look to the Lord; I will wait upon God my Saviour: my God will hearken to me. Rejoice not against me, mine enemy; for I have fallen yet shall arise; for though I should sit in darkness, the Lord shall be a light to me. I will bear the indignation of the Lord, because I have sinned against him, until he make good my cause: he also shall maintain my right, and shall bring me out to the light, and I shall behold his righteousness. And she that is mine enemy shall see it, and shall clothe herself with shame, who says Where is the Lord thy God? mine eyes shall look upon her: now shall she be for trampling as mire in the ways. It is the day of making of brick; that day shall be thine utter destruction, and that day shall utterly abolish thine ordinances. And thy cities shall be levelled, and parted among the Assyrians; and thy strong cities shall be parted from Tyre to the river, and from sea to sea, and from mountain to mountain. And the land shall be utterly desolate together with them that inhabit it, because of the fruit of their doings.

COMMENTS

(Verse 7) From the stench of social injustice and personal immorality brought on by false worship, Micah lifts his eyes to God. Like Joshua, when he was confronted with the people's attraction to false gods, *(Joshua 24:14-15)* so the prophet in the face of popular apostacy takes his stand on the side of the Lord.

Not only will he look to the Lord, he will wait *"for the God of my salvation."*

Here is a timely lesson for anyone who would serve God. Whether it be Elijah, despairing in lonliness because of the unfaithfulness of God's people, or Joshua standing like an oak, alone if necessary but steadfast, or Micah declaring his trust to a faithless generation, he who would serve God faithfully must be able to differentiate between God Who is faithful and His people who too often are not. Micah is unshaken in his conviction that "my God will hear me!"

REJOICE NOT AGAINST ME . . . vs. 8-10

Truth is ever in the minority. Error is ever on the throne . . . and with this unnatural imbalance the wicked always boast and scoff and rejoice in the discomfort of God's people. But their joy is as hollow as it is destined to be short-lived.

Though enemies triumph and insult, they shall be silenced and put to shame.

Here is another eternal truth, spoken first in the Old Testament and re-affirmed in the New. *Romans 8:31-39* asks and answers the same question. *"If God is for us, who can be against us? . . . in all these things we are more than conquerors through Him that loved us!"*

The enemies of God's faithful may rejoice for a season in God's chastening of His people, but their joy is to be brief. Micah sees his own plight, as does every true worshipper see such circumstances as a result of sin. Micah confesses himself a sinner *(v. 9)* and stands ready to bear the indignation of Jehovah. This is a common attitude among spiritual giants. David, in his great guilt, felt abandoned by God, yet he knew God had heard and would deliver him. *(Psalm 22 compare vs. 1 and 24.)*

Paul cried out in recognition of his own sin, "wretched man that I am, who shall deliver me out of the body of this death" and immediately rejoiced in the answer "there is therefore now no condemnation to them that are in Christ Jesus." *(Romans 7:24-8:1)*

A DAY FOR BUILDING THY WALLS . . . vs. 11-13

Having stated his trust in God, accepted his discomfiture as the just result of his own sin, and rejoiced in the sure hope of deliverance, Micah now transfers this entire process to the people. Beyond the anticipated exile the prophet sees the decree for deliverance and the rebuilding of the walls of Jerusalem. (Cp. *Amos 9:11* and *Zechariah 12:6*)

. . . FROM ASSYRIA . . . EGYPT . . . TO THE RIVER . . . SEA TO SEA . . . v. 12

In the day of the rebuilding of Jerusalem, following the fall of Babylon, the Jews now to be scattered shall return from throughout the surrounding nations.

THE LAND . . . DESOLATE . . . v. 13

The returning exiles will not find, as did their forefathers, "a land flowing with milk and honey." Rather the land will be desolate, the temple, the walls of the cities in ruins. They must recognize this as "the fruit of their doings." The history of the rebuilding of their lands by the returned remnant is one of the most thrilling chapters in the history of this stiff-necked people. (It is recommended that the reader interrupt the study of Micah here long enough to re-read Ezra and Nehemiah.)

THE PROPHET PRAYS FOR HIS PEOPLE . . . Micah 7:14-17

RV . . . Feed thy people with thy rod, the flock of thy heritage, which dwell solitarily, in the forest in the midst of Carmel: let them feed in Bashan and Gilead, as in the days of old. As in the days of thy coming forth out of the land of Egypt will I show unto them marvellous things. The nations shall see and be ashamed of all their might; they shall lay their hand upon their mouth; their ears shall be deaf. They shall lick the dust like a serpent; like crawling things of the earth they shall come trembling out of their close places; they shall come with fear unto Jehovah our God, and shall be afraid because of thee. LXX . . . Tend thy people with thy rod, the sheep of thine inheritance, those that inhabit by themselves the thicket in the midst of Carmel: they shall feed in the land of Basan, and in the land of Galaad, as in the days of old. And according to the days of thy departure out of Egypt shall ye see marvellous things. The nations shall see and be ashamed; and at all their might they shall lay their hands upon their mouth, their ears shall be deafened. They shall lick the dust as serpents crawling on the earth, they shall be confounded in their holes; they shall be amazed at the Lord our God, and will be afraid of thee.

COMMENTS

If one requires proof of Micah's highest motives in writing the scathing denunciations against his people which make up the greater part of this book, his prayer for the returning remnant certainly provides it amply.

CARMEL . . . BASHAN . . . GILEAD . . . THE DAYS OF THEIR COMING FORTH OUT OF EGYPT . . . vs. 14-15

When Joshua and Caleb returned to Moses after having spied out the promised land, they reported it was a land flowing with milk and honey. Micah's prayer is it shall be that way again when the people return.

One can stand today among the lush forests in the plain of Megiddo at the foot of Mount Carmel and marvel at the beauty of the land as it has recently been reclaimed by today's returnees from exile. They found the region a miserable swamp and turned it into a garden. So does the prophet pray that God's people after Babylon shall reclaim their land.

Bashan was famous for its cattle, Gilead for its healing balm. Micah asks God on behalf of the remnant that it may be so again.

THE NATIONS SHALL SEE AND BE ASHAMED . . . v. 16-17

This prediction concerning the neighbors of Israel is easily seen demonstrated both in ancient and modern times. Just as those who returned from Babylon set about to rebuild, so the modern Israeli loves his land. Hillsides once eroded through neglect and poor husbandry are covered with verdant vegetation. What was formerly barren wilderness now is home for the unique farming communes of Israel.

The nations who mistreated this land, both in ancient and modern times have ample reason to be ashamed. (v. 16)

PRAYER OF PROPHETIC PRAISE . . . Micah 7:18-20

RV . . . Who is a God like unto thee, that pardoneth iniquity, and passeth over the transgression of the remnant of his heritage? he retaineth not his anger for ever, because he delighteth in lovingkindness. He will again have compassion upon us; he will tread our iniquities under foot; and thou wilt cast all their sins into the depths of the sea. Thou wilt perform the truth to Jacob, and the lovingkindness to Abraham, which thou hast sworn unto our fathers from the days of old.

LXX . . . Who is a God like thee, cancelling iniquities. and passing over the sins of the remnant of his inheritance? and he has not kept his anger for a testimony, for he delights in mercy. He will return and have mercy upon us; he will sink our iniquities, and they shall be cast into the depths of the sea, even all our sins. He shall give blessings truly to Jacob, and mercy to Abraham, as thou swarest to our fathers, according to the former days.

COMMENTS

Micah is overwhelmed by the knowledge that, though He must now punish His people for their utter faithlessness, He will not only deliver a remnant, but will bless their lands and humiliate their enemies.

Jehovah is praised for His great glory, His readiness to forgive and His faithfulness to the ancient promises of the covenant.

Although He is just and does punish, He "delighteth in lovingkindness." No one who knows Micah's God can possibly see any contrast between Him and the God of Love revealed in the New Testament.

JEHOVAH'S CONTROVERSY 7:18-20

Chapter X—*Questions*

Jehovah's Controversy With His People

1. Micah chapters six and seven are composed of a series of _____.
2. Just as the sins of society's leaders filter down through all classes so _____ are applied to all people.
3. Jehovah's first controversy with His people is occasioned by their having forgotten _____.
4. God's controversy with His people is before all creation because _____.
5. How does Micah connect the final section of his book to the first section?
6. In *Micah 6:3-5* the _____ is made. In *6:9—7:6*, the case will be _____.
7. The cry of *Micah 6:3-5* is the plea of a _____.
8. Explain Micah's reference to Balaam. *(Micah 6:5)*
9. Why "remember from Shittim to Gilgal"? *(Micah 6:5(b))*
10. Show how *Micah 6:1-5* is timely in our day.
11. What is alluded to by "shall I give my first-born for my transgression"? *(Micah 6:7(b))*
12. Discuss *Micah 6:8* in connection with *Matthew 26:16* and *Hebrews 2:1-4*.
13. God's insistence upon faithfulness is not unreasonable when we remember _____ His _____ and _____.
14. How does Micah answer the question, "what doth Jehovah require of thee?" *(Micah 6:8)*
15. The _____ is the Bible quoted by Jesus and the apostles.
16. *Micah 6:8* does not claim that _____ an attribute of God's character is required of God's people.
17. Rather than compassion, Micah insists that we are required to _____.
18. Discuss *Micah 6:8* in connection with *Matthew 23:23*.
19. Why must the outward forms of obedience always be expressive of inner reality?
20. Compare *Micah 6:9* and *Proverbs 9:10*.
21. What is the significance of "shall I be pure?" *Micah 6:10-12*
22. The persistent fact of _____ is a prime factor in Micah's message.
23. Compare *Micah 6:14* and *Job 20:15*.
24. What is meant by *Micah 6:15*?

MICAH

25. What are "the statutes of Omri"? *Micah 6:15(a)*
26. Compare *Micah 6:16(b)* and *Micah 3:12*.
27. Discuss the historic phenomena known as "anti-semitism" in light of *Micah 6:16*.
28. Compare *Micah 7:1-2(a)* and *Psalm 14:1-2*.
29. Discuss *Micah 7:1-2* in light of *Romans 3:9-18*.
30. *Micah 7:2(b)—4(a)* refers to _____.
31. Compare *Micah 7:2(b)—4(a)* with *II Samuel 23:6-7, Isaiah 55:13,* and *Ezekiel 2:6*.
32. Who are listed as those whom honest men cannot trust? *(Micah 7:5-6)*
33. Discuss *Micah 7:5-6* in connection with *Matthew 10:35-36* and *Luke 12:53*.
34. Discuss *Micah 7:7* in connection with *Joshua 24:14-15*.
35. Despite the wickedness of his time, Micah is unshaken in the conviction that _____.
36. Discuss *Micah 7:8-10* in light of *Romans 8:31-39*.
37. Compare *Micah 7:9* to *Psalm 22:1-24* and *Romans 7:24-8:1*.
38. What is meant by "a day for rebuilding thy walls"? *(Micah 7: 11-13)*
39. If one requires proof of Micah's highest motives in writing his prophecies, his prayer for _____ provides it amply.
40. The nations shall see *what* and be ashamed?

"This same Hezekiah also stopped the upper watercourse of Gihon, and brought it straight down to the west side of the city of David. And Hezekiah prospered in all his works ... and ... he made a pool, and a conduit, and brought water into the city ..."
(II Chronicles 32:30; II Kings 20:20).
View of the tunnel, accidentally discovered in 1880, which King Hezekiah built in 701 B.C. in anticipation of a long siege of Jerusalem by Sennacherib, King of Assyria. The tunnel runs for about 1700 feet through the rock on which the city is built and carries the water of the Gihon spring into the pool of Siloam, inside the old city walls.

FROM: THE BIBLE AS HISTORY IN PICTURES
By Werner Keller - Wm. Morrow Co.

"The boring through is completed."
So begins the inscription, written in ancient Hebrew characters, which was found in the famous tunnel which King Hezekiah built.
"And this was the story of the boring through. While the workmen were hacking their way from opposite ends, and while there were still three cubits to be bored through, they heard voices calling from each side, for there was a crevice in the rock. And on the day when the boring was completed the stone-cutters hacked their way towards each other until they met. Then the water flowed from the spring to the pool twelve hundred cubits, and the height of the rock above the heads of the stone-cutters was a hundred cubits."

FROM THE BIBLE AS HISTORY IN PICTURES
By Werner Keller - Wm. Morrow Co.

PART III
NAHUM

"And (he) will make Nineveh a desolation, and dry like a wilderness. And flocks shall lie down in the midst of her . . . desolation shall be in the thresholds . . ." (Zephaniah 2:13-14). On the east bank of the Tigris massive mounds of ruins are now the sole indication of what was once the great capital city of the Assyrians. Here stood the splendid palaces of Sennacherib and Esarhaddon and the imposing library of Ashurbanipal, surrounded by spacious parklands and game preserves, with stables for the royal livery, with warehouses and government buildings. This mighty city of Nineveh met the fate that Zephaniah and Nahum had predicted when it was destroyed by the Chaldeans and the Medes in 612 B.C.

FROM: THE BIBLE AS HISTORY IN PICTURES
By Werner Keller - Wm. Morrow Co.

"*An oracle concerning Nineveh ... The shatterer has come up against you ... The shield of his mighty men is red, his soldiers are clothed in scarlet. The chariots flash like flame when mustered in array ...*"
(Nahum 1:1; 2:1–3–R.S.V.).

Red was the favourite colour of the Medes and Chaldeans, whose combined forces attacked Nineveh, conquered it and destroyed it. The head of a Mede wearing a round cap (left) and of a Chaldean wearing a headband. "For, lo, I raise up the Chaldeans, that bitter and hasty nation, which shall march through the breadth of the land, to possess the dwelling places that are not theirs. They are terrible and dreadful" (Habakkuk 1:6–7).

FROM: THE BIBLE AS HISTORY IN PICTURES
By Werner Keller – Wm. Morrow Co.

OUTLINE OF NAHUM

I. The coming of the Lord in judgement . . . 1:2—1:15
II. Details of Niniveh's downfall . . . 2:1—3:17
Epitaph of Niniveh . . . 3:18-19

CHAPTER XI

PREFACE

NAHUM, THE PROPHET

Little is known about the prophet, Nahum. His name means *comforter*. He was contemporary with Habakkuk, Zephaniah and Jeremiah. The opening verse of the book which bears his name identifies him as a native of Elkoshite. Unfortunately, modern archeology has thus far been unable to locate Elkoshite. However, strong Jewish tradition places it at Alkosh about thirty miles north of Mosul.

The Galilean city of Capernaum, center of activity during the Roman period and headquarters of Jesus' ministry, has been suggested as Nahum's home. Capernaum means, literally, "village of Nahum." However, there is no proof it is so-called for the prophet Nahum rather than some other with the same name.

The date of Nahum's prophecy is not too difficult to estimate. The capture of Niniveh by Babylon, which Nahum vividly predicts, took place c. 612 B.C. In *Nahum 3:8-10* is the description of the fall of Karnak, or Thebes, (No-Amon) as a *fiat accompli*. Karnak fell in 633 B.C. Nahum's prophecy, then, must have been written between 633 and 612 B.C.

To be a bit more exact, Nahum probably prophecied between the beginning of Josiah's reform, c. 621, and the fall of Nineveh, c. 612. An educated guess places the date at about 614 B.C. Some have dated this work as early as 650 B.C., but this seems unlikely in view of recent information concerning the date of Ashurbanipal's capture of Karnak, as well as the even more recent discovery of a portion of the annals of Nabopolassar, King of Persia at the time Nineveh fell.

According to these annals, Nabopolassar, formerly a vassal of Assyria, and Cyaxares, king of the Medes, were in an allied warfare against Assyria as early as 616 B.C. These allies brought Nineveh

PREFACE TO NAHUM

down in 612 B.C. Egypt was involved in this struggle on the side of Assyria. Following the fall of Nineveh, the Assyrian capital was moved to Haran, which subsequently fell to the Medo-Persian alliance in 610.

From other sources we learn that the war ended in the final defeat of Pharaoh Necho and the remnant of the Assyrian army in the battle of Carchemish by Nebuchadnezzar.

HISTORIC SITUATION

With this secular record of history at hand, and in light of *I Kings 23:29* and *II Chronicles 35:20-24*, we arrive at the following historic situation as prevailing in Nahum's time. By 616 B.C. the Medes and Babylonians on the one hand and the Assyrian-Egyptian alliance on the other had divided the mid-eastern world into two power blocks. The struggle was for the absolute rule of the entire area.

In Judah there were two parties. With the little kingdom caught in the squeeze between the super powers, one party favored the rise of Babylon, hoping thereby to see the demise of Assyria and the guarantee of Judean independence. This party was led by king Josiah and his court.

The other party preached that a pro-Babylonian stance by Judah would only lead to a Babylonian takeover of Judah once the major power struggle was settled. This latter seems to be the position of Jeremiah (cf *Jeremiah 13:21*), while Nahum, an avowed Assyrophobe, favored an alliance with Babylon lest Judah suffer the same fate as Israel at the hands of Assyria.

This apparent difference of political views on the part of Nahum and Jeremiah does not prevent their agreement concerning the judgements of God against Godless nations.

Nahum is not quoted in the New Testament, but it was included in the specific body of writings which Jesus and the New Testament writers called "Scriptures," or "the oracles of God." It deals exclusively with the downfall of Nineveh and makes no Messianic predictions. Recent archeology has vindicated Nahum's description of Nineveh's downfall.

THE NATURE OF NAHUM

It is to be remembered that Nahum's prophecy, in the original, was in the form of an incomplete poetic accrostic. As such, it does not easily lend itself to exegetical commentary. To so dissect any poem is to lose much of its esthetic value and, in the case of prophecy, some of its overall impact.

NAHUM

The theme of Nahum is revenge. History has born testimony to the accuracy of the preview of destruction, but there is little to explain Nahum's attitude. Rejoicing at the bloody destruction of a people who had no opportunity to know God seems out of harmony with God's loving concern for all men.

Perhaps we need to separate the facts of the prophecy from the attitude of the prophet. As in the case of Jonah, God may have not been pleased with Nahum's revelling in Nineveh's destruction.

We cannot but recall Jonah's prejudiced refusal to preach to Nineveh at the outset, and his petulant pouting under a gourd vine when it became evident, upon Nineveh's repentance, that God would rather forgive than destroy. (Cp. *Jonah, chapter four*)

Nahum's prophecy will be appreciated more if two things are kept in mind: (1) the poetic nature of the book and (2) its sequal relationship to Jonah which preceeds it by something more than a century.

NINEVEH

Nineveh, as capital of Assyria, was the leader of an empire whose chief aim was aggressive warfare against her neighbors. Asshur, some fifty miles south of Nineveh, had been the original Assyrian capital, but about the time of Sennacherib, (c. 710 B.C.), and for roughly a century thereafter, Nineveh gained the ascendancy and served as capital.

It was about the time Nineveh became capital of Assyria that Jonah was sent to preach repentance to the city. Then Nineveh heeded Jonah's warning but their repentance was apparently short-lived.

Sennacherib built Nineveh's fortifications, aggrandized her temples and installed a remarkably sophisticated water system. It is estimated that as many as 10,000 slaves worked for twelve years just to build the 15,000,000 ton earthen platform upon which the royal palace was set. Exiles from Israel may have formed part of that work force. (Cp. *II Kings 18:13-16*)

Diodorus describes a defensive wall about Nineveh forming a sixty mile circumferance. This inner defense wall, whose twin may be viewed today among the remains of Nineveh, formed a 7½ mile circuit broken by fifteen gates.

The present ruins of Nineveh seem to be somewhat farther (some 1500 yards) from the Tigris River than was the city in Nahum's day. A growing Arab village is today slowly covering the site of the ancient city.

The city and the empire she ruled were as cruel as her founder, Nimrod (cf. *Genesis 10:11*). Her kings, in their official records, made

PREFACE TO NAHUM

no attempt, as do modern despots, to hide the fact of their fierce atrocities.

However, Nineveh's ability to rule the world did not match her ability to conquer it. No effective administration governed Assyria's conquered territories. Rather, defeated enemies were considered simply the means of gratifying Ninevh's drive for conquest and the spoils of war. Mankind has inherited no positive legacy from the Assyrian empire.

Israel became a vassal of Assyria c. 854 B.C. and was finally destroyed by her in 722 B.C.

Under Ahaz, Judah became vassal to Assyria c. 735 B.C. Jerusalem was threatened by the armies of Assyria under Sargon c. 711 B.C. (cf. *Isaiah 20*) and Judah was severely punished by her c. 701 B.C. The complete submission of Judah to Nineveh was thwarted by the remarkable destruction of Sennacherib's army. (Cf. *II Kings 18:13—19:36*)

After the city of Nineveh was destroyed by the Medo-Persian alliance in 612 B.C., the Assyrian capital moved to Haran where it stayed until destroyed by Nebuchadnezzar in 605 B.C. at the battle of Carchemish.

Nineveh reached its peak, as did the Assyrian empire of which it was capital, under the reign of Ashurbanipal. When he died c. 626 B.C., the downfall began. There are no Assyrian records of the last twenty-five years of her own existence. The final obliteration of Nineveh was total! Two hundred years later the Greek army passed by the site and gave no indication of knowing it had ever existed!

Chapter XI—*Questions*
Preface

1. The name Nahum means _____.
2. The name Capernaum means _____.
3. Was Capernaum the home of the prophet Nahum?
4. List and discuss the date of Nahum.
5. Nineveh was brought down in 612 B.C. by an alliance of _____.
6. The war in which Nineveh was destroyed ended with the defeat of Pharaoh Necho at _____ by _____.
7. By 616 B.C. the _____ and _____ on the one hand and _____ and _____ on the other hand had divided the middle east into two power blocks.
8. In Judah at this time were two parties, one favored the rise of _____ while the other was afraid of this.

1:1   NAHUM

9. Nahum favored an alliance with _____ for Judah.
10. In his political views, Nahum seems to differ with _____.
11. Nahum's prophecy, in the original language, formed an incomplete _____.
12. The theme of Nahum is _____.
13. It is helpful in studying Nahum to separate the facts of the prophecy from the _____ of Nahum himself.
14. Nahum's prophecy is reminiscent of that of _____.
15. The chief aim of the Assyrian empire, of which Nineveh was the capital was _____.
16. Describe the walls of Nineveh.
17. Nineveh's ability to rule the world did not match _____.
18. Israel became a vassal of Assyria in _____ and was destroyed by her in _____.
19. _____ was king of Israel at this time and so became her last king.

CHAPTER XII

INTRODUCTION

NAHUM 1:1 . . .

RV . . . The burden of Nineveh. The book of the vision of Nahum the Elkoshite.

LXX . . . The burden of Nineve: the book of the vision of Naum the Elkesite.

COMMENTS

When Jonah, about 100 years previous to Nahum, foretold the overthrow of Nineveh the great royal seat of Assyrian monarchy, the city repented and was spared. Now, having fallen from their repentance, possibly deceived by their rise to world domination, Nineveh receives a written warning of irreversible doom. The repentance has not been continued, neither will the reprieve from judgement.

As we saw above in the introductory preface (Chapter XI), Elkoshite has not been identified by modern archeology, although Jewish tradition situates it at the site of Alkosh, some thirty miles north of the present town of Mosul. The tomb of Nahum (traditional) is venerated there by present day Judaism.

INTRODUCTION 1:1, 2

Jerome located Elkoshite at the site of Helkesei in Galilee, in his commentary on Nahum. This Helkesei is probably present day El-Kauzeh between Rameh and Biut Jebeih.

The *De Vitis Prophetarum*, of the Pseudo-Epiphanius, locates Elkoshite east of the Jordan river near *Begabor* and connects it with the tribe of Simeon. Nestle concluded that Begabor is to be identified with present day *Beit Jibrim* in southern Israel.

The important words in this verse are *burden of Nineveh* and *vision of Nahum*. They constitute a claim to direct inspiration and a positive identification of the author.

The word *massa* (burden) was most frequently used to denote a threatening prophecy. (eg. *Isaiah 30* and *Zechariah 9:12*)

The idea seems to be that of a burden laid by God upon Nineveh.

The word may also mean to "utter forth" or "call," eg. *Psalm 15:3* and *II Kings 9:27*.

Paul speaks of the beauty of the feet of those who bring God's good news *(Romans 10:15)*. There is a certain inherent ugliness about a bearer of the message of doom. There are few if any passages in the Bible to match Nahum for sheer hopelessness.

"*The book of the vision*" indicates that Nahum *saw* the destruction of Nineveh before it actually took place. The terror of God's wrath cannot be aptly described, it must be experienced for its full deadliness to be grasped.

THE COMING OF THE LORD OF JUDGEMENT . . . Nahum 1:2-8

RV . . . Jehovah is a jealous God and avengeth; Jehovah taketh vengeance on his adversaries, and he reserveth wrath for his enemies. Jehovah is slow to anger, and great in power, and will by no means clear the guilty: Jehovah hath his way in the whirlwind and in the storm, and the clouds are the dust of his feet. He rebuketh the sea, and maketh it dry, and drieth up all the rivers; Bashan languisheth, and Carmel; and the flower of Lebanon languisheth. The mountains quake at him, and the hills melt; and the earth is upheaved at his presence, yea, the world, and all that dwell therein. Who can stand before his indignation? and who can abide in the fierceness of his anger? his wrath is poured out like fire, and the rocks are broken asunder by him. Jehovah is good, a stronghold in the day of trouble; and he knoweth them that take refuge in him. But with an over-running flood he will make a full end of her place, and will pursue his enemies into darkness. LXX . . . God is jealous, and the Lord avenges; the Lord avenges with wrath; the Lord takes vengeance on his adversaries, and he cuts off his

1:2-6   NAHUM

enemies. The Lord is longsuffering, and his power is great, and the Lord will not hold any guiltless: his way is in destruction and in the whirlwind, and the clouds are the dust of his feet. He threatens the sea, and dries it up, and exhausts all the rivers: the land of Basan, and Carmel are brought low, and the flourishing trees of Libanus have come to nought. The mountains quake at him, and the hills are shaken, and the earth recoils at his presence, even the world, and all that dwell in it. Who shall stand before his anger? and who shall withstand in the anger of his wrath? his wrath brings to nought kingdoms, and the rocks are burst asunder by him. The Lord is good to them that wait on him in the day of affliction; and he knows them that reverence him. But with an overrunning flood he will make an utter end: darkness shall pursue those that rise up against him and his enemies.

COMMENTS

JEHOVAH, GOD OF WRATH . . .

The wrath of God is here revealed from heaven against His enemies at the same time His favor and mercy are assured to His faithful, loyal people. His almighty power in both make His wrath exceedingly terrible and His grace very much to be desired.

JEHOVAH IS JEALOUS . . .

The Assyrian empire had desolated Israel and harrassed Judah repeatedly. It seemed their idols had overcome the people of Jehovah. The poetic prophet warns that God is jealous. He will not allow the seeming power of false gods to go unchallenged.

Here is an echo of Jehovah's own evaluation of Himself in *Exodus 20:5, 34:14, Deuteronomy 4:24, 5:9, 6:15.*

There is a certain affection expressed here. Jealousy is of those we love. It is His wounded heart that brings about Nineveh's destruction. God's wrath is always God's love reacting to unfaithfulness.

JEHOVAH AVENGETH . . .

Only God is qualified to avenge. He does so in complete justice. In the case of Nineveh, He had gone to great lengths (cf. *Jonah*) to warn them of the consequence of their sin.

JEHOVAH IS FULL OF WRATH . . .

Paul, in *Romans 1:18-ff*, speaks of God's wrath being revealed from heaven against all ungodliness and unrighteousness. *Romans 2:5-ff*

INTRODUCTION 1:6-8

pictures God's wrath as being stored up against the day of wrath when it will be released in a burst of pent-up power. John the Baptist spoke of fleeing from the wrath to come *(Matthew 3:7, Luke 3:7)*. John, the apostle of love, indicates that the wrath of God remains on those who do not believe and obey the Gospel. Jesus spoke of God's wrath in His foretelling of the destruction of Jerusalem. *(Luke 21:22)*

In light of these, and many more New Testament passages, we must conclude that Jehovah as a God of wrath was not, as some have taught, a primitive notion limited to the Old Testament. The loving God of the New Testament is the same God and wrath is yet one of the facets of His nature.

Verses 2-3(a) indicate that while Jehovah is a jealous God, avenging and full of wrath, His wrath is never impetuous or petulant. His wrath is reserved for His enemies: those who have set themselves against His purposes and His people. He is slow to anger, as indeed a God of love Who demands patience of His people must be. Nevertheless, His patience and slow anger must never be misunderstood as weakness or tolerance of enmity toward Himself.

Verses 3(b)-7 . . . Jehovah is great in power, as witness His control over the forces of nature, the whirlwind, the storm, the clouds, the sea. Even the weather is in His power. The rivers run dry and the most verdant areas of the land, Bashan and Carmel and Lebanon languish and do not produce at His command.

The immovable mountains quake before Him, the hills melt, and the very earth itself is upheaved in His presence . . . even the whole world and all who inhabit it. Rocks break asunder at the outpouring of His wrath.

In the day of God's wrath, they are kept safe who are in Him, but those who attempt to flee will find their hiding places swept away as in a flood.

This entire passage of Nahum is a poetic picture of the wrath of God. Such vividness could scarcely be achieved by the more literal language of prose. It is reminiscent of the apocolyptic description in *Revelation 6:12-17* of the opening of the sixth seal.

(Verse 8) The image of an over-running flood is possibly an allusion to Nineveh's capture by the Medo-Persian armies through a flood in the river which destroyed her walls. More likely it is a poetic reference to the overwhelming armies. The figure is also used quite normally to simply suggest calamity. (cp. *Psalm 32:6, 42:7, 90:5*) *her place* . . . (RV)

This phrase is a direct reference to Nineveh. The city is figured as a queen. Her place (of dwelling) is to be utterly demolished.

THE UTTER ANNIHILATION OF NINEVEH . . . Nahum 1:9-13

RV . . . What do ye devise against Jehovah? he will make a full end; affliction shall not rise up the second time. For entangled like thorns, and drunken as with their drink, they are consumed utterly as dry stubble. There is one gone forth out of thee that deviseth evil against Jehovah, that counseleth wickedness. Thus saith Jehovah: and likewise many, even so shall they be cut down, and he shall pass away. Though I have afflicted thee, I will afflict thee no more. And now will I break his yoke from off thee, and will burst thy bonds in sunder.

LXX . . . What do ye devise against the Lord? he will make a complete end: he will not take vengeance by affliction twice at the same time. For the enemy shall be laid bare even to the foundation, and shall be devoured as twisted yew, and as stubble fully dry. Out of thee shall proceed a device against the Lord, counselling evil things hostile to him. Thus saith the Lord who rules over many waters, Even thus shall they be sent away, and the report of thee shall not be heard any more. And now will I break his rod from off thee, and will burst thy bonds.

COMMENTS

Durant records that two hundred years after the fall of Nineveh, Xenophon's Ten Thousand marched across the site of the city "and never suspected that these (mounds) were the site of the ancient metropolis that had ruled half the world." This utter annihilation is here foresworn by Nahum, as his poetic prophecy moves on.

WHAT DO YE DEVISE? . . . v. 9

There is no defense against Jehovah's wrath, once it has been incurred. The armies of Assyria, led by the great king-general Sennacherib, fell like ten-pins before the walls of Jerusalem in the days of Hezekiah. (Cf. II Kings 18:13—19:36, II Chronicles 32:1—32:22) Nahum envisions Nineveh doing likewise a century later. In both cases the defeat of the Assyrians is attributed to divine intervention.

The destruction would be so final that Nineveh, "the affliction," shall not rise up the second time.

INTRODUCTION   1:10, 11

. . . DRUNKEN WITH THEIR DRINK . . . v. 10

As Babylon would later fall (c. 539 B.C.) with her playboy king in a drunken stupor, so Nineveh fell before Babylon (c. 612 B.C.) with her leaders drunk and "entangled like thorns." They could no more resist the conquering army than can dry stubble resist the spread of a prairie fire.

ONE GONE FORTH OUT OF THEE . . . v. 11

Nahum sees Sennacherib's attempts against Judah as the beginning of her own ruin. He is the "one gone forth . . . that deviseth evil against Jehovah." It was Sennacherib who implemented the designs of Nineveh against God and His people. (cf. *II Kings 19:22-23*)

Sennacherib and his spokesman, Rabshakeh, framed an evil letter and an evil speech, not only against Hezekiah, but against God Himself. He insinuated God was level with the idols of Assyria and unable to protect His people. In this way, the Assyrian sought to dissuade Jehovah's people from confidence in Him, and urged them rather to cast their lot for protection with the great king of Assyria, namely himself.

No one has ever more daringly and blasphemously affronted the Lord than Sennacherib. Nahum therefore counts him a wicked counsellor who has outwitted himself. The great destruction which God will bring against Nineveh because of this wickedness was deferred for a time, but it was the beginning of the end.

(Verse 12-13) In one fatal stroke, when the measure of Nineveh's iniquity was full, the Assyrian empire will be *"cut down and he shall pass away."*

The contrast here between "they" and "his" on the one hand and "thee" on the other delineates between "they," the Assyrians, and "thee," Judah. *Their* punishment was final and utter destruction. Judah's was the chastizing by the Lord of His people. It would therefore be temporary. (cp. *Isaiah 40:1-2, 52:1-2*)

God had used the Assyrians as a yoke on His people, chastening them in the attempt (futile as it proved to be) to call them back to His covenant. But the yoke had been exceedingly wicked and must now be burst asunder. Assyria would burden God's people no more, after the destruction of Nineveh.

DESTRUCTION OF FALSE GODS AND VILE MEN . . .
Nahum 1:14-15

RV . . . And Jehovah hath given commandment concerning thee, that

1:14   NAHUM

no more of thy name be sown; out of the house of thy gods will I cut off the graven image and the molten image; I will make thy grave; for thou art vile. Behold, upon the mountains the feet of him that bringeth good tidings, that publisheth peace! Keep thy feasts, O Judah, perform thy vows; for the wicked one shall no more pass through thee; he is utterly cut off.

LXX . . . And the Lord shall give a command concerning thee; there shall no more of thy name be scattered: I will utterly destroy the graven images out of the house of thy god, and molten images: I will make thy grave; for they are swift. Behold upon the mountains the feet of him that brings glad tidings, and publishes peace! O Juda, keep thy feasts, pay thy vows: for they shall no more pass through thee to thy decay.

COMMENTS
JEHOVAH HATH GIVEN COMMANDMENT . . . v. 14

The decree has gone forth . . . even memory of the Assyrian kings will dim. Their fame will no more be spread abroad. The name *ie.* the house and lineage of Sennacherib, will be sown no more.

Actually, Sennacherib's son succeeded him to the throne in Nineveh. It seems Nahum's poetic prophecy here personifies the empire in the king. It was only shortly after Sennacherib that Nineveh, the capital, was destroyed.

. . . OUT OF THE HOUSE OF THY GODS . . . v. 14

Not only will the king and his country be cut off, the gods he worshipped will also perish. In the ancient near-east, as in the contemporary city states of Greece, the defeat of an empire was not just the disgrace of a people, it was the overthrow of a god.

In the case of Assyria, both the dynasty and the deity fell together. The two sons of Sennacherib were killed in the temple while worshipping their chief god, Nisroch. No doubt the desecration of the temple occured at the same time. Nahum's prophecy that the graven and molten images would be cut off was fulfilled very literally.

Not only in the temple, but throughout the land, the conquerers, unlike the later Greeks and Romans who absorbed local gods, smashed the deities of Assyria wherever they were found.

I WILL MAKE THY GRAVE . . .

Some take the latter part of verse 14 to mean that Sennacherib's

INTRODUCTION   1:14, 15

grave was actually to be made in the temple of Nisroch. In view of the fact that the temple remained in use some time following his death this seems unlikely.

It is more likely Nahum intends here to foretell the ignominious fall of the Assryian dynasty itself. When Babylon was later building on the ruins of Assyria much was said about the grave of that once formidable empire.

Just how despicable were the sins of Nineveh is described in *Ezekiel 31:3, 11, 15, 16*. Her downfall was comensorate with the heinousness of her sin. Nahum says simply "thou art vile" and in this vileness sees the reason for her destruction.

BEHOLD UPON THE MOUNTAIN . . . v. 15

With these words so familiar to the Christian, Nahum introduces the contrasting comfort of God's people in comparison to the utter ruin of her enemies. We find these same words in *Isaiah 52:7* and again in *Romans 10:15*. In each case they are words of deliverance.

The destruction of Nineveh, brought on the marching feet of the Babylonian army, burst asunder the bonds of vassalage and set Jerusalem free, albeit her freedom was short-lived, for her sins, as we saw in Micah, were becoming as great as those of Nineveh.

It is no strange thing that three writers inspired by the same Spirit, should use the same words. By so doing they simply give their *consent to wholesome truths (I Timothy 6:3)* and concur in the *same forms of sound words. (II Timothy 1:13)*

KEEP THY FEASTS . . . PERFORM THY VOWS . . .

Along with Nahum's assurance that they will have no more trouble with Assyria is the subtle warning to remain faithful to God's covenant. He could not but be aware, as were the other prophets, that Judah herself stood in the way of God's wrath unless she stood firm in her faith.

During the troublesome days of Assyria's invasion, the feasts had been interrupted. They had made vows to God, that if He would deliver them out of their distress, they would do Him extraordinary service. Now the poet reminds them to perform that which they have promised.

We may also learn a valuable lesson here from Nahum. We are prone, in times of trouble to plead prayerfully for succor and promise service only to forget when the burden has been lifted.

Chapter XII—*Questions*

Introduction

1. Jonah prophesied to Nineveh about _____ years before Nahum.
2. How do you explain God's destruction of Nineveh in view of her repentance at Jonah's preaching?
3. What two phrases in Nahum 1:1 establish the work as inspired Scripture?
4. God assures His faithful and loyal people of His _____ and at the same time He pronounces His wrath against Nineveh.
5. What had been Nineveh's past dealing with Israel?
6. Comment on the idea that God is a jealous God.
7. Explain *"Jehovah is full of wrath."*
8. In light of Nahum 1:3(b)-7 discuss the power of God.
9. What is meant by the overrunning flood in *Nahum 1:8?*
10. Show how Nineveh's attempts at self-defense were to prove futile.
11. What sort of person was Sennacherib?
12. What was to become of the gods Nineveh worshipped?
13. Discuss *(1:15)* "Behold upon the mountain."
14. Discuss *(1:15)* "keep thy feasts . . . perform thy vows."

CHAPTER XIII
DETAILS OF NINEVEH'S DOWNFALL
WARNING OF WAR . . . Nahum 2:1-7

RV . . . He that dasheth in pieces is come up against thee; keep the fortress, watch the way, make thy loins strong, fortify thy power mightily. For Jehovah restoreth the excellency of Jacob as the excellency of Israel; for the emptiers have emptied them out, and destroyed their vine-branches. The shield of his mighty men is made red, the valiant men are in scarlet: the chariots flash with steel in the day of his preparation, and the cypress spears are brandished. The chariots rage in the streets; they rush to and fro in the broad ways: the appearance of them is like torches; they run like the lightnings. He remembereth his nobles: they stumble in their march; they make haste to the wall thereof, and the mantelet is prepared. The gates of the rivers are opened, and the palace is dissolved. And it is decreed: she is uncovered, she is carried away; and her handmaids moan as with the voice of doves, beating upon their breasts.

DETAILS OF NINEVAH'S DOWNFALL 2:1-7

LXX . . . It is all over with him, he has been removed, one who has been delivered from affliction has come up panting into thy presence, watch the way, strengthen thy loins, be very valiant in thy strength. For the Lord has turned aside the pride of Jacob, as the pride of Israel: for they have utterly rejected them, and have destroyed their branches. They have destroyed the arms of their power from among men, their mighty men sporting with fire: the reins of their chariots shall be destroyed in the day of his preparation, and the horsemen shall be thrown into confusion in the ways, and the chariots shall clash together, and shall be entangled in each other in the broad ways: their appearance is as lamps of fire, and as gleaming lightnings. And their mighty men shall bethink themselves and flee by day; and they shall be weak as they go; and they shall hasten to her walls, and shall prepare their defences. The gates of the cities have been opened, and the palaces have fallen into ruin, and the foundation has been exposed; and she has gone up, and her maid-servants were led away as doves moaning in their hearts.

COMMENTS

HE THAT DASHETH IN PIECES . . . v. 1

The destroyer is at the gates! In his prophetic vision, Nahum shouts the alarm to Nineveh as he sees the soldiers of Babylon's Nebuchadnezzar, allied with those of the Median Cyaxares (or Ahasuerus) approach the very gates of the city.

Destruction is neither distant nor doubtful. Nebuchadnezzar well deserved his common title: he who dashes nations in pieces. *Jeremiah 50:23* calls Babylon the *hammer of the whole earth.*

There is to be no subtlety. The smasher has "come before thy face" in a straight forward attack. Nineveh is therefore called upon to man the towers and magazines and guard the avenues of the city, to encourage her troops and animate herself. There is no way to forestall the stroke of God's judgement. Just as Assyria was used of God to chastise His people, so the Medo-Babylonian alliance will now punish Nineveh.

Will Durant, in his epic *Story of Civilization,* says, ". . . Assyrian history is largely a picture of cities sacked and villages or fields laid waste . . . the weakness of Oriental monarchies was bound up with this addiction to violence." Nineveh's conquerers were simply repaying her in kind.

(Verse two) This verse is something of an enigma. Assyria had been used of God to chasten His people. Now that very activity is published as the manifesto showing the causes of her downfall. We can only understand this by bearing the covenant in mind.

All God has done in human history He has done for the sake of His covenant purpose to ultimately bless all people. The Jews erred in considering national prosperity to be excellence before God. It was never so. God is concerned that His people be faithful. He restores their real excellence by punishing their unfaithfulness. Assyria, who had been used of God to so correct Israel, *ie.* restore the excellency, is now being destroyed by those who will later punish Judah.

The Assyrian policy of "scorched earth" against her enemies had earned her the title "the emptiers."

THE SHIELDS ... MADE RED ... v. 3

Here we begin the prophet's poetic account of the terrors of the invading enemy. Their shields are red with Assyrian blood. The men themselves are drenched scarlet with the gore of battle.

As the chariots approached the city, their charge was swift as lightning and their wheels struck sparks upon the stones.

The spears of the Medes and Babylonians are like a shaking forest of fir trees. As a mighty tree overtops a shrub, so the attackers overwhelm the defenders of Nineveh.

CHARIOTS RAGE IN THE STREETS ... v. 4

The walls are breached . . . the gates are opened and the vehicles of war charge through the defenseless city streets. They are so numerous and driven with such fury that the red tunics of their drivers seem to be the flames of torches and the burning of the city begins.

Much of Nahum's poetic vividness borrows from the literal appearance of the attackers. The dashing in pieces previously alluded to no doubt figures the instruments used to break down the stone and brick walls of the besieged city. The hammer-headed battle-axes of the Medo-Babylonian troops could crush a man's head with even a glancing blow.

The red and scarlet of the bloody attackers was partly due to their uniforms of the same color. This color also would add to the fiery appearance of the chariots.

HE REMEMBERETH HIS NOBLES ... v. 5

Nebuchadnezzar's commanders, here called nobles, are mustered and commanded to take the field immediately. So swiftly do they obey that they stumble over the bloody stone streets. They hasten to secure the walls that are now approached by their troops.

DETAILS OF NINEVEH'S DOWNFALL 2:5-13

The mantelet was a portable shield under which the invader was protected from the besieged defenders on the walls above.

THE GATES OF THE RIVER ARE OPENED . . . v. 6-7

At length the gates of the rivers would be opened. The western defense of Nineveh was the wall along the Tigris river. It was 4,530 yards long and connected to moats on the east, north and south sides of the city.

The Medo-Babylonian army engineers re-routed the river channel and the moats became a dry bed of march into the city. Cyrus would later turn the same trick against its Babylonian originators and so defeat Belshazzar.

Finally the defense of the palace itself dissolves and the Assyrian capital is no more. There remains only the moans of the captives and the doves, like the larks bravely singing over Flanders Field, flap their wings over desolation and death.

THE RUINS OF WAR . . . Nahum 2:8-13

RV . . . But Nineveh hath been from old like a pool of water: yet they flee away. Stand, stand, they cry; but none looketh back. Take ye the spoil of silver, take the spoil of gold; for there is no end of the store, the glory of all goodly furniture. She is empty, and void, and waste; and the heart melteth, and the knees smite together, and anguish is in all loins, and the faces of them all are waxed pale. Where is the den of the lions, and the feeding-place of the young lions, where the lion and the lioness walked, the lion's whelp, and none made them afraid? The lion did tear in pieces enough for his whelps, and strangled for his lionesses, and filled his caves with prey, and his dens with ravin. Behold, I am against thee, saith Jehovah of hosts, and I will burn her chariots in the smoke, and the sword shall devour thy young lions; and I will cut off thy prey from the earth, and the voice of thy messengers shall no more be heard.

LXX . . . And as for Nineve, her waters shall be as a pool of water: and they fled, and staid not, and there was none to look back. They plundered the silver, they plundered the gold, and there was no end of their adorning; they were loaded with it upon all their pleasant vessels. There is thrusting forth, and shaking, and tumult, and heart-breaking, and loosing of knees, and pangs on all loins; and the faces of all are as the blackening of a pot. Where is the dwelling-place of the lions, and the pasture that belonged to the whelps? where did the lion go, that the lion's whelp should enter in there, and there was none to scare him away? The lion seized enough prey for his whelps, and strangled for his young lions, and filled his lair with prey, and his dwelling-place with spoil. Behold, I am against thee, saith the Lord Almighty, and I will burn up thy multitude in the smoke, and the sword shall devour thy lions; and I will utterly destroy thy prey from off the land, and thy deeds shall no more at all be heard of.

COMMENTS

... BUT NONE SHALL LOOK BACK ... v. 8

As with modern, so with ancient warfare, a stream of refugees poured from the fallen city of Nineveh with no idea where to go. The call to them to stay is in vain. Hollow-eyed, they stumble away from all that has ever been home.

Nineveh has always been populace ... as stated by Nahum's picturesque description of her as a pool, the figure of water to symbolize a multitude is a common one. (Cp. *Revelation 17:5*)

A century earlier, in Jonah's time, the population of the Assyrian capital was estimated as including 120,000 small children. *(Jonah 4:11)*

Now, in defeat, the multitude flee. The commanders cry for them to return, but they will not so much as look back. Their one thought is escape.

TAKE THE SPOIL ... v. 9-12

Andrew Jackson is quoted in American history as saying "to the victors belong the spoils." The Medes and Babylonians, and every other invading army to march through the pages of history, agree.

The wealth of the city becomes the prey of its conquerers. The officers stir up their troops to make a thorough job of looting. Nineveh was rich, and the chief source of income to the ancient man of war was such loot.

The Assyrian lion will no longer ravage the world in search of prey for his lioness and her whelps. The poetic symbolism is obvious. The destruction of Nineveh with her armies and chariots will forever prevent her from preying as a wild animal upon the victims of her greed for empire.

BEHOLD I AM AGAINST THEE ... v. 13

The prophet is careful to point out that the sack of Nineveh is carried out at the will of Jehovah. It must be pointed out here that this is a strange idea to the people of the prophet's time. Each nation had its own gods and they were credited with that nation's victories over her enemies. It is not, however, the gods of the Medes and Babylonians to whom Nahum credits the fall of Nineveh. It is Jehovah of Israel! Perhaps Nahum saw, as did Micah, Isaiah and the others that Jehovah is not only the one true God, but that He is Lord of *all* nations.

Chapter XII—*Questions*
Details of Nineveh's Downfall

1. In a prophetic vision, Nahum saw Babylon's _____ and the armies of the Median _____ at the very gates of Nineveh.
2. Nebuchadnezzar's common title _____ was well-deserved.
3. What sort of attack did the Medo-Babylonian alliance launch against Nineveh?
4. We can only understand God's punishing of Assyria for destroying Israel, the purpose for which He had raised up Assyria, by remembering _____.
5. In warfare Assyria had practiced a _____ policy.
6. How does Nahum describe the chariot charge against Nineveh?
7. Much of Nahum's poetic vividness is borrowed from _____.
8. What is meant by "The gates of the rivers are opened"?
9. Compare the refugee situation of Nineveh with that of modern war.
10. Discuss "take the spoil." Is this practice still followed in modern warfare?
11. What is implied in *Nahum 2:13* by the statement "I am against thee"?

CHAPTER XIV
THE EPITAPH OF NINEVEH
WOE TO THE BLOODY CITY . . . Nahum 3:1-3

RV . . . Woe to the bloody city! it is all full of lies and rapine; the prey departeth not. The noise of the whip, and the noise of the rattling of wheels, and prancing horses, and bounding chariots, the horseman mounting, and the flashing sword, and the glittering spear, and a multitude of slain, and a great heap of corpses, and there is no end of the bodies; they stumble upon their bodies;

3:1-3 NAHUM

LXX . . . O city of blood, wholly false, full of unrighteousness, the prey shall not be handled. The noise of whips, and the noise of the rumbling of wheels, and of the pursuing horse, and of the bounding chariot, and of the mounting rider, and of the glittering sword, and of the gleaming arms, and of a multitude of slain, and of heavy falling: and there was no end to her nations, but they shall be weak in their bodies . . .

COMMENTS

Nineveh, for years, had neither been taken nor put in fear. Now she lay, in the prophet's vision, as she would soon really lie, in blood and ashes. Nahum's reaction to her ruin is far from mourning. He rather lists her past glory and rejoices in her destruction. Reading this passage, one can almost hear Jonah joining Nahum in his rejoicing. What Jonah longed to see, Nahum saw. (cf. *Jonah 4:1-5*)

IT IS ALL FULL OF LIES . . . v. 1

Nineveh had aspired to be the capital of the world, by whatever means were at her disposal, whether intrigue in the courts of other nations or by sheer force of arms and the carrying away of conquered peoples. For this Nahum sees her now in ruins.

The God who *made of one blood all the nations of men* never designed any nation to be tyrants and hold others as her slaves. It is He Who will be universal monarch and none other! Yet the chapters of both ancient and modern history are delineated by the records of kings and nations who have tried to rule the world. None have long succeeded.

THE NOISE . . . THE NOISE . . . v. 2-3

The city lies dead. The silence of death is broken only by the sound of enemy arms moving about the streets. There is no regard for the dead . . . the invaders stumble over the fallen corpses.

The carnage seems endless. No attempt is made to count the bodies. They are simply a multitude.

CAUSE OF THE CARNAGE . . . Nahum 3:4-7

RV . . . *because of the multitude of the whoredoms of the well-favored harlot, the mistress of witchcrafts, that selleth nations through her whoredoms, and families through her witchcrafts. Behold, I am against thee, saith Jehovah of hosts, and I will uncover thy skirts upon thy face; and*

These Nahum calls witchcrafts. The world was pictured as full of a host of demons to be warded off by charms and long incantations.

I WILL UNCOVER . . . v. 5

The foreign policy of Assyria, as we have seen, was one of ambitious deceit. This stood first in the list of her harlotries. Now her proud pretentions are to be baffled by Jehovah. Her shame is discovered to her neighbor nations. Her vain hope of universal domination is first revealed and then dashed to pieces.

I WILL . . . SET THEE AS A GAZING STOCK . . . v. 6-7

That great city to which all nations had made court, with which they had coveted alliances, is made a laughing stock.

Abominable filth and vileness is always the aftermath of war. I can still smell the stench of death in the blasted rubble of Europeon cities during World War II. The disease which rises from such putridity causes many to flee . . . and to marvel at the destruction of Nineveh.

No one is left to mourn the passing of Nineveh. Nahum takes delight in it and taunts her with an offer to hire mourners. One cannot but wonder if the Spirit Who inspired Nahum's prophecy approved of the poet's almost sadistic delight in the calamity that befell his enemies. I personally doubt it. More likely God's attitude toward Jonah, when that prophet pouted because Nineveh had been spared, was the same toward Nahum. (*Jonah 4:9-ff*) We do not know.

NINEVEH IS NO BETTER . . . Nahum 3:8-19

RV . . . Art thou better than No-amon, that was situated among the rivers, that had the waters round about her; whose rampart was the sea, and her wall was of the sea? Ethiopia and Egypt were her strength, and it was infinite; Put and Lubim were thy helpers. Yet was she carried away, she went into captivity; her young children also were dashed in pieces at the head of all the streets; and they cast lots for her honorable men, and all her great men were bound in chains. Thou also shalt be drunken; thou shalt be hid; thou also shalt seek a stronghold because of the enemy. All thy fortresses shall be like fig-trees with the first ripe figs: if they be shaken, they fall into the mouth of the eater. Behold, thy people in the midst of thee are women; the gates of thy land are set wide open unto thine enemies: the fire hath devoured thy bars. Draw thee water for the siege; strengthen thy fortresses; go into the clay, and tread the mortar; make strong the brickkiln. There shall the fire devour thee; the sword shall cut thee off; it shall devour

THE EPITAPH OF NINEVEH 3:8-19

thee like the cankerworm: make thyself many as the canker-worm; make thyself many as the locust. Thou has multiplied thy merchants above the stars of heaven; the canker-worm ravageth, and fleeth away. Thy princes are as the locusts, and thy marshals as the swarms of grasshoppers, which encamp in the hedges in the cold day, but when the sun ariseth they flee away, and their place is not known they are. Thy shepherds slumber, O king of Assyria; thy nobles are at rest; thy people are scattered upon the mountains, and there is none to gather them. There is no assuaging of thy hurt; thy wound is grievous: all that hear the report of thee clap their hands over thee; for upon whom hath not thy wickedness passed continually?

LXX . . . Prepare thee a portion, tune the chord, prepare a portion for Ammon: she that dwells among the rivers, water is round about her, whose dominion is the sea, and whose walls are water. And Ethiopia is her strength, and Egypt; and there was no limit of the flight of her enemies; and the Libyans became her helpers. Yet she shall go as a prisoner into captivity, and they shall dash her infants against the ground at the top of all her ways: and they shall cast lots upon all her glorious possessions, and all her nobles shall be bound in chains. And thou shalt be drunken, and shalt be overlooked; and thou shalt seek for thyself strength because of thine enemies. All thy strong-holds are as fig-trees, having watchers: if they be shaken, they shall fall into the mouth of the eater. Behold, thy people within thee are as women: the gates of thy land shall surely be opened to thine enemies: the fire shall devour thy bars. Draw thee water for a siege, and well secure thy strongholds: enter into the clay, and be thou trodden in the chaff, make the fortifications stronger than brick. There the fire shall devour thee; the sword shall utterly destroy thee, it shall devour thee as the locust, and thou shalt be pressed down as a palmerworm. Thou hast multiplied thy merchandise beyond the stars of heaven: the palmerworm has attacked it, and has flown away. Thy mixed multitude has suddenly departed as the grasshopper, as the locust perched on a hedge in a frosty day; the sun arises, and it flies off, and knows not its place: woe to them! Thy shepherds have slumbered, the Assyrian king has laid low thy mighty men: thy people departed to the mountains, and there was none to receive them. There is no healing for thy bruise; thy wound has rankled: all that hear the report of thee shall clap their hands against thee; for upon whom has not thy wickedness passed continually?

COMMENTS

ART THOU BETTER? ... v. 8-10

No-Amon, Karnak, Thebes . . . all names of one of the proudest cities ever built by man. Capital of the middle kingdom of Egypt, she stood majestically on the Nile and guarded the largest temple complex ever built . . . anywhere. Every Pharaoh, from the 12th to the 19th dynasty except the heretic, Ikhnaton, added to her glory. Her civilization, in some instances, advanced beyond that of our own day. Even today the visitor stands in silent awe before her columns and oblisks. One cannot but marvel at the sacred lake at Karnak, where the sprinkling of exorcism and the immersion of Christian baptism first became confused in the fourth century A.D.

But No-Amon, Karnak fell! And it was the Assyrians themselves who in 674 B.C. swept down from the north and subjected the proud Egyptians to tribute . . . and the taunt of the prophet to Nineveh who herself is now to be destroyed is "Art thou better than No-Amon?"

Art thou better? It is a question that sends chills along the spine of any thinking American who is fortunate enough to stand amidst the ruins of fallen civilizations. Are we better than they, that our international harlotries, our internal immoralities, our worship of false gods should not one day bring down upon our heads the wrath of Jehovah? Is it a strange idea, reserved for crackpots and prophets of doom, that God may one day use a heathen nation to fill the streets of Washington, D.C. and New York and Chicago and our other proud cities with corpses even as He used the Medes and Babylonians to lay Nineveh in the dust for her sins?

THOU ALSO ... v. 11

The words fall like the knell of doom on the proud capital of Assyria. The leaders literally were drunken when the Medes and Babylonians came, but they had been in a stupor of a different kind long before. They were "made drunken with the wine of Nineveh's fornication." (Cp. *Revelation 17:1-2* and *Jeremiah 25:17-27*)

ALL THY FORTRESSES ... v. 12-15

All those things in which Nineveh trusted would fail her. Did they trust in bravery and daring? Their hearts would sink and fail them, so that they should abscound for shame, being in disgrace. For fear they will not be able to face invaders because of whose strength they shall sneak to their neighbors to beg assistance.

THE EPITAPH OF NINEVEH 3:14-19

Did they depend on the garrisons and strongholds? These shall prove to be paper walls. Like the first-ripe figs, if you give the tree a little shake, they will fall in your mouth.

Having seen the vanity of the efforts to defend the doomed city, Nahum nevertheless taunts them to make ready to stand off the invader. They are admonished to lay in quantities of water against a siege. New bricks are to be made to strengthen the fortifications.

THEN SHALL A FIRE DEVOUR THEE . . . v. 15

By fire set to buildings and death sown by hand weapons are cities conquered. It is still the same . . . from Nineveh to My Lai.

Though the defenders of Nineveh are as numerous as canker-worms and as locusts . . . yet they shall be over-run.

There is a scathing irony in Nahum's choice of vermin to illustrate the multitudes of Nineveh's defenders. Both the cankerworm and the locust leave devastation wherever they go. So had Assyria spread destruction throughout the world. Now—to use a cliche "the worm has turned."

The Assyrian merchants who once fleeced the populace of surrounding nations will be seen no more, they are like the canker-worm who "ravageth and fleeth away."

The princes also, and the marshalls, those who enforced the Assyrian sway over conquered peoples will be seen no more. Like swarms of grasshoppers which destroy while they are present, but fly away to be seen no more, the Assyrian authorities will, like the merchants, not be seen anymore in lands once ruled as defeated people.

THY WOUND IS GREVIOUS . . . v. 18-19

The destruction of Nineveh will prove the mortal wound of the entire empire. It is all in Nahum's future, but he has seen it in a present vision. History has verified his prophetic pronouncement.

In 612 B.C. the alliance between the Medes and Babylonians did indeed march into the city and that which Nahum foresaw became reality. The alliance was short lived and the victors shortly began to war among themselves. But the fatal blow had been struck.

Never again would Nineveh, or Assyria, play an important role in world affairs. Today the location of the city itself is scarcely discernable, rising as two tels on the valley of the Tigris.

God's prophetic word once more is vindicated by history.

NAHUM

Chapter XIV—*Questions*

The Epitaph of Nineveh

1. Why does Nahum say Nineveh is "full of lies?"
2. In Nahum's vision of fallen Nineveh, the silence is broken only by_____.
3. Discuss *Nahum 3:4-7* in light of the modern question, "If there is a God, why does He not halt or prevent war?
4. What are the "sins of Nineveh" as listed in this paragraph?
5. What is indicated by Nahum's term "witchcrafts?"
6. How does God intend to make Nineveh a "gazing stock?"
7. Who are No-Amon, Karnak, Thebes?
8. Where did the sprinkling of exorcism first become confused with the immersion of Christian baptism? When did this occur?
9. Compare the fate of No-Amon with that of Nineveh.
10. Who defeated No-Amon in 674 B.C.?
11. Discuss Nahum's question "art thou better?" as applied to modern America.
12. In what physical condition were the leaders of Nineveh when the Medes and Babylonians fell upon them?
13. What were "all thy fortresses" in *Nahum 3:12-15?*
14. What is the irony of Nahum's choice of vermin to illustrate the multitudes of Nineveh's defenders?
15. The destruction of the city of Nineveh was the mortal wound of_____.
16. How is God's word in Nahum vindicated by history in the destruction of the Assyrian Empire?

PART IV
HABAKKUK

HABAKKUK

OUTLINE OF HABAKKUK

Introduction . . . 1:1
I. (1:2-11) Habakkuk questions God . . .
"How long can God allow lawlessness to go unchecked?"
II. (1:12-2:20) A second question . . .
"How can God use cruel power to punish people less wicked than the punisher?"
(Answer is five woes)
III. Poetic prayer . . . Chapter 3
   A. v. 1-16 . . . vision of God in judgement
   B. v. 17-19 . . . hymn of faith

CHAPTER XV

PREFACE TO HABAKKUK

HABAKKUK THE PROPHET

We know nothing of Habakkuk, the man. He prophesied just before the rise of the Neo-Babylonian empire. The complaints he makes in the early part of his message seem to date him as contemporary with Jehoiachem (608-597 B.C.) although this is by no means conclusive. (cp. *Jeremiah 22:13-19*) He may have been a contemporary of Jeremiah and Zephaniah. If so, he prophesied shortly after Nahum.

This last seems most likely, since both Nahum and Habakkuk speak of the Neo-Babylonian power as in the imminent future.

Habakkuk is mentioned nowhere in the Scriptures outside the book which bears his name. The Rabbis taught that he was the son of the Shunamite woman mentioned in *II Kings 4:16-f*. This is supported only by tradition, not by historic evidence.

Jewish tradition further says of Habakkuk that he fled to Egypt at the capture of Jerusalem in 586 B.C., which seem plausible. The same tradition says he was carried from Egypt to Babylon to wait upon Daniel in the lions' den. This seems highly fictitious.

HABAKKUK'S QUESTION

Brief as Habakkuk's writing is, it contains some valuable insights regarding two questions very much alive in our day. How can God allow, or rather how long will God allow social evil and violence to go unchecked? And how can a just God use the warfare of wicked men to punish those apparently less wicked than the punisher?

HOW CAN GOD ALLOW INJUSTICE TO GO UNPUNISHED? 1:1

These questions are being asked repeatedly today, and the church's failure to answer them has turned many, especially many of the young, to practical atheism.

As we approach the text, perhaps we should ask ourselves these questions in today's language;
1. How, if there is a Christian God, can He allow economic iniquity and social injustice. Why doesn't He put a stop to such things?
2. How, if there is a Christian God, can He allow war to punish and cripple and deprive "innocent" people?

God gave Habakkuk the answers for which men have long sought. Job discusses the first of these questions as it pertains to the individual. The Psalmist raised it again and again (cf. *Psalm 37, 49, 73*). Jeremiah also addresses it briefly. (*Jeremiah 12:1*)

The aprocraphal book of *IV Ezra 3:29-36* concludes there is no answer to the problem posed by these questions. *II Baruch 11:1-7* (also apocraphal) prefers death over God's answer to Israel's dilemma.

How does one explain the seeming inactivity of God in the presence of the cruel historical fact of social injustices and war? Habakkuk received our answer from God. Do we have the faith and the courage to accept God's answer?

Chapter XV—*Questions*
Preface to Habakkuk

1. Habakkuk is contemporary with what king of Judah?
2. This dates Habakkuk about when?
3. Babylon captured Jerusalem in _____ B.C.
4. Habakkuk demands from God the answer to two questions: _____ and _____

5. Restate these questions in your own words.

CHAPTER XVI
HOW CAN GOD ALLOW INJUSTICE TO GO UNPUNISHED?
INTRODUCTION ... Habakkuk 1:1

1:1   HABAKKUK

RV . . . The burden which Habakkuk a prophet did see.

LXX . . . The burden which the prophet Ambacum saw.

COMMENTS

Habakkuk introduces his written prophecy in words calculated to establish it as authentically from God. Translated "oracle" as often as burden, the introductory noun of verse one is a technical term to describe prophecy. Cp. *Isaiah 13:1, Jeremiah 23:33-40, Zechariah 9:1, Malachi 1:1*) The prophet saw what he was about to write as a vision. (Cp. *Amos 1:1, Micah 1:1*)

One must either accept the prophecy as God's written word or reject it as the halucination of a madman. Since history has long since proven its accuracy, the former seems more likely!

THE FIRST QUESTION . . . Habakkuk 1:2-4

RV . . . O Jehovah, how long shall I cry, and thou wilt not hear? I cry out unto thee of violence, and thou wilt not save. Why dost thou show me iniquity, and look upon perverseness? for descrution and violence are before me; and there is strife, and contention riseth up. Therefore the law is slacked, and justice doth never go forth; for the wicked doth compass about the righteous; therefore justice goeth forth perverted.

LXX . . . Hoy long, O Lord, shall I cry out, and thou wilt not hearken? how long shall I cry out to thee being injured, and thou wilt not save? Wherefore hast thou shewn me troubles and griefs to look upon, misery and ungodliness? judgment is before me, and the judge receives a reward. Therefore the law is frustrated, and judgement proceeds not effectually, for the ungodly man prevails over the just; therefore perverse judgement will proceed.

COMMENTS

The prophet addresses God, significantly by the name "Jehovah," revealed at the beginning of Israel's national existence. During the days of the patriarchs it was unknown. (cf. *Exodus 6:3*) At that time He was called El Shaddai. (cf. *Genesis 17:1*) Habakkuk's use of Yaweh, or Jehovah, here seems calculated to imply that God is neglecting a nation to whom He owes special concern.

HOW CAN GOD ALLOW INJUSTICE TO GO UNPUNISHED? 1:2-11
HOW LONG SHALL I CRY . . . v. 2

We usually phrase the question differently, "How can God allow . . . etc." Habakkuk says "How long." How long will God allow . . . etc. The thought is the same. If God is God, and we are His people . . . how, or how long can He allow us to suffer at the hands of unrighteous men or an unrighteous governmental system such as ruled Judah in the days of the prophet?

For a detailed discussion of the specific conditions that caused the prophet to so cry to God, read Amos or Micah. These wrote earlier, but the situation in Judah has not changed since they wrote, excepting perhaps to get progressively worse. Those who sought evil gain for themselves at the expense of their neighbors did not desist at Micah'a warning of destruction.

Those who built the luxury of their metropolitan affluence upon the blood of the downtrodden had not repented at the preaching of the earlier prophets.

The drunkenness and excesses of the wealthy and powerful had not diminished since the Shepherd of Tekoah expressed his shock and predicted God's punishment.

Habakkuk's question is simply "why doesn't God do something about the situation?" He has more courage than we moderns. He addresses his questions directly to God Himself. He accuses God of not hearing when he prays. His prayers have lifted the specific sins of violence before God. In return he sees more and more of that about which he has prayed.

JEHOVAH'S ANSWER . . . Habakkuk 1:5-11

RV . . . Behold ye among the nations, and look, and wonder marvellously; for I am working a work in your days, which ye will not believe though it be told you. For, lo, I raise up the Chaldeans, that bitter and hasty nation, that march through the breadth of the earth, to possess dwellingplaces that are not theirs. They are terrible and dreadful; their judgement and their dignity proceed from themselves. Their horses also are swifter than leopards, and are more fierce than the evening wolves; and their horsemen press proudly on: yea, their horsemen come from far; they fly as an eagle that hasteth to devour. They come all of them for violence; the set of their faces is forwards; and they gather captives as the sand. Yea, he scoffeth at kings, and princes are a derision unto him; he derideth every stronghold; for he heapeth up dust, and taketh it. Then shall he sweep by as a wind, and shall pass over, and be guilty, even he whose might is his god.

1:5-11   HABAKKUK

LXX . . . Behold, ye despisers, and look, and wonder marvellously, and vanish: for I work a work in your days, which ye will in no wise believe, though a man declare it to you. Wherefore, behold, I stir up the Chaldeans, the bitter and hasty nation, that walks upon the breadth of the earth, to inherit tabernacles not his own. He is terrible and famous; his judgement shall proceed of himself, and his dignity shall come out of himself.. And his horses shall bound more swiftly than leopards, and they are fiercer than the wolves of Arabia: and his horsemen shall ride forth, and shall rush from far; and they shall fly as an eagle hasting to eat. Destruction shall come upon ungodly men, resisting with their adverse front, and he shall gather the captivity as the sand. And he shall be at his ease with kings, and princes are his toys, and he shall mock at every strong-hold, and shall cast a mound, and take possession of it. Then shall he change his spirit, and he shall pass through, and make an atonement, saying, This strength belongs to my god.

COMMENTS

. . . LO, I RAISE UP THE CHALDEANS . . . v. 5

Jehovah's answer is not what the prophet expected. The answer to such prayers seldom is! Rather than magically producing Utopia for the nation by miraculously wiping out all the sin and injustice, God challenges Habakkuk to take a good look at the world situation . . . to consider the nations that lay beyond the border of Judah. The answer to the prophet's question lies beyond his narrow horizons. Just as the question is larger than one man or a single nation, so is the answer.

It is easy to overlook a very basic principle which is apparent again and again in Scripture. The principle is simply that God is the God of the whole world. He is not an absentee creator who has gone away and left us after having set certain forces and laws in operation. Nor is He the local God of Judah alone. Centuries after Habakkuk, Paul will tell the wisest men of his day, " . . . He made of one every nation of men to dwell on all the face of the earth, having determined their appointed seasons (times) and the bond (boundaries) of their habitation . . . " (*Acts 17:26*)

This Jehovah of Judah is the God of all nations. He is Lord, not just of a single nation, but of all human history. Therefore, the answer to questions that plague all men are to be found in the larger arena of international and world activity, rather than in the confines of local

HOW CAN GOD ALLOW INJUSTICE TO GO UNPUNISHED? 1:6, 7

self-concerns. If we believed this, we would have missionaries in every corner of the globe.

So wide in scope and so universal in application is God's answer to injustice and social exploitation, that He tells the prophet, *"I am working a work in yoru days, which you will not believe though it be told you For lo, I raise up the Chaldeans . . . "*

The Chaldeans were a Semitic tribe from the south of Babylonia. Galling under the yoke of Assyria, they revolted in 625 B.C. against seemingly insuperable odds, and freed themselves from Assyrian domination. In alliance with the Medes and Scythians, they demolished the Assyrian capital of Nineveh in 612 B.C. (See Nahum) As rulers of the Neo-Babylonian empire, the Chaldeans soon broke off the alliance with the Medes.

In 609 B.C. the Baylonian army defeated Pharaoh Necho at Megiddo and broke the back of the Assyrian-Egyptian alliance. King Josiah died in this battle in a vain attempt to aid the delining Assyrian empire. (Cf. *II Kings 23:29-30)* Three years later the final defeat of Assyria came at Carchemish when Nebuchadnezzar led the Babylonians in a decisive encounter with Assyria and Egypt. (Cf. *Jeremiah 46:2*)

Having cast her lot with the Assyrian-Egyptian alliance, Judah soon fell prey to Babylonian domination. In 597 B.C. Nebuchadnezzar dismembered Judah. He destroyed Jerusalem and the temple in 586 B.C.

It is this that Jehovah foretells in answer to Habakkuk's first question. Significantly, the Chaldean dominated Neo-Babylonian empire virtrally began with the subjugation of Judah and ended when Cyrus, the Persian, in 539 B.C. overthrew the capital and decreed freedom for the Jews. God had prepared the Chaldeans (whose empire Babylon was) to redress His grievances with His people. This done, God raised up Cyrus to wipe out Babylon. We shall see latter how this came about in answer to Habakkuk's second question.

THEY ARE TERRIBLE AND DREADFUL . . . v. 7

Here begins Jehovah's description to Habakkuk of the empire He is raising up to punish Judah. We need to read these verses not so much for the details, although they are vividly accurate, but for the overall impression the description made upon Habakkuk. Keeping the prophet's question in mind, we must agree with Jehovah's statement that He is working a work Habakkuk will not believe. (v. 5) Modern man also refuses to believe a just God of love will do such things!

The Chaldeans are described as irresistible in power and military methods. Wherever they went there was havoc. They were famous for

1:7-11 HABAKKUK

swift cavalry. Their bent for conquest would become the scourge of the earth. Kings and castles, to whom others looked for defense, were to them a laughing stock. They captured cities as easily as throwing up a mound of earth and advancing over it. Ominously, one of their chief characteristics was the taking of numberless slaves.

The Neo-Babylonians were essentially a commercial people, and one of their chief commodities was human chattel. Prices ranged from $20 to $65 for a woman and from $5 to $100 for a man, and the traffic was strictly controlled by law.

Babylonian slavery is of particular interest to us, for it was into this that Nebuchadnezzar led Judah. Female slaves belonged to their masters completely and most of them bore many children for their masters.

All of a slave's belongings were his master's. He could himself be sold at any moment or pledged for a debt. He could be put to death if it seemed good business to his owner. A reward for his capture was set by law, should he try to escape. He was subject to military conscription and for forced labor on roads. Most of the exquisite cities, especially Babylon herself, were erected by slave labor.

A slave might marry a free woman, and their children's freedom was guaranteed by law. He might be set up in business by his master, as indeed many of the Jews did, and liberated as a reward for faithful service.

The religion of Babylon has already been described in the introductory chapter on Baal worship. This despicable idolatry which earned for Babylon the name "Mother of Harlots," finds its roots in the earliest history of the "land of Nimrod." It flourished in the age of Babylon's great lawyer, Hammurabi (2123-2081 B.C.) and spread like a cancer round the fertile crescent, to Asia Minor, Greece and finally Rome. It seeped into northern Europe, and after the fall of Rome, when the Roman Catholic religio-political monolith ruled over the European dark ages . . . the saints and idols and even the lord to whom Europe prayed was not the covenant God of the Bible or His Son, but the reincarnation of Babylonian deities. As Will Durant so clearly states in his *Story of Civilization,* "Ishtar (the mother of Babylon's gods) interests us not only as analogue of the Egyptian Isis and protoype of the Grecian Aphrodite and the Roman Venus, but as formal beneficiary of one of the strongest Babylonian customs . . . and though her worshippers repeatedly addressed her as "The Virgin," "The Holy Virgin" and "The Virgin Mother," this merely meant that her amours were free from all taint of wedlock. *Note with what fervor the Babylonians could lift up to her throne*

THE SECOND QUESTION 1:11-17

litanies of laudation only less splendid than those which a tender piety once raised to the Mother of God." (Italics mine)

Such was the religion and such were its worshippers whom God raised up to punish His people for their failure to keep His covenant and *for the social immorality which existed among them because they because they turned to the same gods.*

Habakkuk's first question is answered! Jehovah will not long tolerate the evils that repel the prophet. He will raise up one of the most wicked nations in history to punish them.

Chapter XVI—*Questions*

How Can God Allow Injustice to Go Unpunished?

1. Habakkuk's opening words are calculated to established what?
2. What is the significance of Habakkuk's use of the name "Jehovah?"
3. What caused Habakkuk to ask the first of his two questions?
4. What is God's answer? Summarize.
5. Who were the Chaldeans?
6. Why were the Chaldeans named here when it was Babylon who would chastise Judah?
7. What king of Judah died in the vain attempt to preserve Assyria against Babylon?
8. How does Jehovah describe the Chaldeans? (vs. 7-11)
9. What do you know of the religion of the Babylonian empire of Habakkuk's concern?

CHAPTER XVII
THE SECOND QUESTION
HABAKKUK 1:12-17

RV . . . Art thou not from everlasting, O Jehovah my God, my Holy One? we shall not die. O Jehovah, thou hast ordained him for judgement; and thou, O Rock, has established him for correction. Thou that art of purer eyes than to behold evil, and that canst not look on perverseness, wherefore lookest thou upon them that deal treacherously, and holdest thy peace when the wicked swalloweth up the man that is more righteous than he; and makest men as the fishes of the sea, as the creeping things, that have no ruler over them? He taketh up all of

177

them with the angle, he catcheth them in his net, and gathereth them in his drag: therefore he rejoiceth and is glad. Therefore he sacrificeth unto his net, and burneth incense unto his drag; because by them his portion is fat, and his food plenteous. Shall he therefore empty his net, and spare not to slay the nations continually?

LXX . . . Art thou not from the beginning, O Lord God, my Holy One? and surely we shall not die. O Lord, thou hast established it for judgement, and he has formed me to chasten with his correction. His eye is too pure to behold evil doings, and to look upon grievous afflictions: wherefore dost thou look upon despisers? wilt thou be silent when the ungodly swallows up the just? And wilt thou make men as the fishes of the sea, and as the reptiles which have no guide? He has brought up destruction with a hook, and drawn one with a casting net, and caught another in his drags: therefore shall his heart rejoice and be glad. Therefore will he sacrifice to his drag, and burn incense to his casting-net, because by them he has made his portion fat, and his meats choice. Therefore will he cast his net, and will not spare to slay the nations continually.

COMMENTS

O JEHOVAH, MY GOD, MY HOLY ONE . . . v. 12(a)

God had warned Habakkuk he would not believe the answer to his question. *(1:5)* The prophet, upon hearing Jehovah's description of the Chaldeans whom He is raising up to punish the sins of Judah, recoils in shocked horror and incredulity.

The first half of verse twelve is, to the prophet, a rhetorical question. It answers itself in the asking of it. Jehovah *is* from everlasting! He *is* the God of Israel's prophets! He *is* Holy! Therefore, His people shall not die.

Here is the most succinct statement in all the Bible of the gross misconception the Jews had of their relationship to God. Their major premise, *ie.* the everlasting holy nature of God is correct, but their false conclusion, *ie.* that *they,* as a people, could not, therefore, die was based on a minor premise of their own devising!

In *The Story of the Jew Briefly Told,* published by Bloch Publishing Company with Jewish confirmation manual, Dr. Maurice H. Harris says, "It took centuries to grasp the concepts that *God is wholly spirit and without material form, that He is the sole ruler of the universe, not sharing this power with other divinities;* that He is omniscent,

THE SECOND QUESTION 1:12a

Omnipresent, and eternal; that He is absolutely righteous and just in dealing with His children—*not favoring Israel more than other people, though they were the first to recognize Him.*" (Italics mine)

Dr. Harris here places his finger on the problems of both the nation of Judah and the prophet Habakkuk. The first question asked by the prophet grew out of circumstances fostered by the failure of the people to understand that "*. . . God is wholly spirit and without material form, that He is the sole Ruler of the universe . . .*" This failure allowed the Jews again and again to fall into the worship of Baal. (See the discussion of Micah.)

The second question posed by the prophet (v. 12) resulted from their failure to understand that God ". . . is absolutely righteous and just in dealing with His children—*not favoring Israel more than other people . . .*"

Nahum's question to Nineveh on the eve of her doom was *"Art thou better than No-Amon . . . ?" (Nahum 3:8)* As we saw in our study of Nahum, No-Amon, the capital of Egypt, had been devastated by the Assyrians. Nahum would have the Ninevites know they are no better and hence no more assured of national survival than No-Amon. Had someone asked this same question of Judah on the eve of the Babylonian captivity, or of Habakkuk when he entered into his debate with God concerning God's use of the Chaldeans to punish Judah, both the nation and the prophet would have answered a resounding, "Yes!" They believed they *were* better.

If their superiority over other people was not evidenced in their unfaithfulness or their moral corruption, they believed that God's past dealings with their father's proved it.

They were mistaken. John the Baptist, centuries later, challenged the same attitude. (Cf. *Luke 3:7-9)*

The fundamental Jewish error is a misunderstanding, not only of the nature of God, but as well a misunderstanding of a doctrine which runs through both the Old and New Testaments. It is often called the "doctrine of Election." (We suggest just here that the reader review the chapters on the covenant in the introductory section and also my book, *Thus It Is Written,* College Press.)

This doctrine, that God is calling out of every kindred and race of man a people for His own possession, is inherent in the unfolding inspired interpretation of the work of God in history and makes up the bulk of the Old Testament Scripture. It is the entire burden of the Luke-Acts narrative and comes in for a detailed analysis in the writings of Paul, especially Ephesians, Romans, and Galatians. The Jews "were made a heritage of God, having been foreordained according to the plan of Him who effects all things according to the council of His will." *(Ephesians 1:11)* This plan of God, which is the mystery hidden in times past to be revealed in Christ through the church, *(Ephesians 3:1-16)*, never included the Jews or the nation of Israel simply for their own sakes or as an end in themselves.

God chooses whom He will *eg.* Abraham, Isaac, Jacob, Moses, David, *et al.* His choice is made not primarily from the standpoint of its advantage to the chosen.

Nor is His choice, even in the Old Testament, limited only to the physical descendants of Abraham. Paul illustrates this truth in *Romans 9:14* by referring to *Exodus 9:16*. There God says to the Egyptian Pharaoh (who was anything but a Jew), "For this very purpose did I raise thee up, that I might show in thee my power, and that my name might be published abroad in the earth." In a similar vein, Jehovah might well have made a similar statement to the Chaldeans. *(Habakkuk 1:6)*

The perversion of the Biblical doctrine of election reaches its climax in those who commit themselves to a "dispensationalism" which makes the Jew *per se* the center of God's concern, both in the Bible and in the age to come. Such people believe about the Jew exactly what the Jew came to believe about himself. This belief blinds men to the revealed purpose of God's intervention in human history.

The point is, of course, that the *elect* or more accurately the *called* of God, whether individuals or nations, are never chosen for their own sakes merely, but that they are rather called to participate in God's eternal plan to offer the blessings of Abraham to all mankind.

O JEHOVAH ... O ROCK ... v. 12(B)

Habakkuk does not doubt God for a moment. Difficult as it is for him to accept the idea that God should raise up such as the Chaldeans to judge His people, the prophet immediately concedes: "Thou hast ordained him (the Chaldeans, particularly Nebuchadnezzar) and thou . . . hast established him for correction."

We must also not fail to recognize Habakkuk's conviction that God's people could not be wiped out is related to his understanding, quite correctly, that God is Himself eternal. His error was in identifying that people with a race and a nation, and in objecting to God's use of another nation and race to bring about His purposes.

The term "O Rock" applied to Jehovah is reminiscent of *Deuteronomy 32:4* His use of it reflects Habakkuk's conviction that God's

THE SECOND QUESTION   1:12b-17

work is perfect . . . His ways are just, even though they are beyond the prophet's own understanding.

Indeed, it is precisely because of what he knows about God, coupled with his Jewish nationalism that has caused him to so question Jehovah.

THOU THAT ART OF PURER EYES .. v. 13

Habakkuk knows God to be a pure God who cannot tolerate the presence of evil in His sight. Whatever else the Word teaches about God, it certainly affirms this truth, from Eden to Calvary.

How, then, the prophet asks, can such a God look on such perversiveness as is present among the Chaldeans? Why will He look on Babylon's destruction of Judah and hold His peace? His bias shows through when he asserts that the Jews of his day are more righteous than the Babylonians.

Two fallacies should be recognized at this point. First, Jehovah, in revealing His intention to raise up the Chaldeans against Judah, did not say He would overlook Babylon's evil. Divinely recorded history proves He did, in fact, no such thing.

Secondly, the insistence that Judah is more righteous than the Babylonians raises a moot question. They had adopted the Baal worship which originated in the Chaldeas. They had been unfaithful to Jehovah when they were the only people on earth who had His written word. Their behavior had consequently become so corrupt that it was the very reason God chose to raise up a pagan people to smite them.

. . . HE MAKEST MEN AS FISHES . . . v. 14-17

The prophet reinforces his argument by changing his emphasis from the holy nature of God to the unholy nature of the Chaldeans' treatment of people He first says that the incursion of the Chaldeans causes confusion. Like a school of fish or a swarm of insects, those struck by Babylon are left purposeless and leaderless. Then, in the confusion, the Chaldeans capture slaves like catching fish with various nets and devices.

It was indeed the practice of Nebuchadnezzar to lead away to slavery those who were the leaders of a conquered people. As we say, Micah promised that exactly this would happen. The practice, according to Micah, was *God's* device to punish those whose leadership had corrupted the nation.

In verse sixteen, Habakkuk adds that the success of the Chaldeans is the force of their own skill and power (rather than dependance upon God). They idolize themselves because of this (Cf. *Deuteronomy 6:17,* cp. *Isaiah 10:13, 37:24-25).* To Habakkuk this is further evidence that Jehovah cannot use such a nation against his own people.

(Verse 17) Furthermore, asks the prophet, will there ever be an end to it, if God allows such a people as the Chaldeans to succeed against His chosen ones? This argument sounds extremely familiar to us today as we are asked to believe that God cannot control the evil forces of communism if these forces are allowed to prevail against us. Perhaps we, as Habakkuk, need to give serious attention to God's answer.

JEHOVAH'S ANSWER . . . Habakkuk 2:1-20

RV . . . I will stand upon my watch and set me upon the tower, and will look forth to see what he will speak with me, and what I shall answer concerning my complaint. And Jehovah answered me, and said, Write the vision, and make it plain upon tablets, that he may run that readeth it. For the vision is yet for the appointed time, and it hasteth toward the end, and shall not lie: though it tarry, wait for it; because it will surely come, it will not delay. Behold, his soul is puffed up, it is not upright in him; but the righteous shall live by his faith, Yea, moreover, wine is treacherous, a haughty man, that keepeth not at home; who enlargeth his desire as Sheol, and he is as death, and cannot be satisfied, but gathereth unto him all nations, and heapeth unto him all peoples. Shall not all these take up a parable against him, and a taunting proverb against him, and say, Woe to him that increaseth that which is not his! how long? and that ladeth himself with pledges! Shall they not rise up suddenly that shall bite thee, and awake that shall vex thee, and thou shalt be for booty unto them? Because thou hast plundered many nations, all the remnant of the peoples shall plunder thee, because of men's blood, and for the violence done to the land, to the city and to all that dwell therein. Woe to him that getteth an evil gain for his house, that he may set his nest on high, that he may be delivered from the hand of evil! Thou hast devised shame to thy house, by cutting off many peoples, and has sinned against thy soul. For the stone shall cry out of the wall, and the beam out of the timber shall answer it. Woe to him that buildeth a town with blood, and establisheth a city by iniquity! Behold, is it not of Jehovah of hosts that the peoples labor for the fire, and the nations weary themselves for vanity? For the earth shall be filled with the knowledge of the glory of Jehovah, as the waters cover the sea. Woe unto him that giveth his neighbor drink, to thee that addest thy venom, and makest him drunken also, that thou mayest look on their nakedness! Thou art

THE SECOND QUESTION 2:1-20

filled with shame, and not glory: drink thou also, and be as one uncircumcised; the cup of Jehovah's right hand shall come round unto thee, and foul shame shall be upon thy glory. For the violence done to Lebanon shall cover thee, and the destruction of the beasts, which made them afraid; because of men's blood, and for the violence done to the land, to the city and to all that dwell therein. What profiteth the graven image, that the maker thereof hath graven it; the molten image, even the teacher of lies, that he that fashioneth its form trusteth therein, to make dumb idols? Woe unto him that saith to the wood, Awake; to the dumb stone, Arise! Shall this teach? Behold, it is overlaid with gold and silver, and there is no breath at all in the midst of it. But Jehovah is in his holy temple: let all the earth keep silence before him.

LXX . . . I will stand upon my watch, and mount upon the rock, and watch to see what he will say by me, and what I shall answer when I am reproved. And the Lord answered me and said, Write the vision, and that plainly on a tablet, that he that reads it may run. For the vision is yet for a time, and it shall shoot forth at the end, and not in vain: though he should tarry, wait for him; for he will surely come, and will not tarry. If he should draw back, my soul has no pleasure in him: but the just shall live by my faith. But the arrogant man and the scorner, the boastful man, shall not finish anything; who has enlarged his desire as the grave, and like death he is never satisfied, and he will gather to himself all the peoples. Shall not all these take up a parable against him? and a proverb to tell against him? and they shall say, Woe to him that multiplies to himself the possessions which are not his! how long? and who heavily loads his yoke. For suddenly there shall arise up those that bite him, and they that plot against thee shall awake, and thou shalt be a plunder to them. Because thou hast spoiled many nations, all the nations that are left shall spoil thee, because of the blood of men, and the sins of the land and city, and of all that dwell in it. Woe to him that covets an evil covetousness to his house, that he may set his nest on high, that he may be delivered from the power of evils. Thou hast devised shame to thy house, thou hast utterly destroyed many nations, and thy soul has sinned. For the stone shall cry out of the wall, and the beetle out of the timber shall speak. Woe to him that builds a city with blood, and establishes a city by unrighteousness. Are not these things of the Lord Almighty? surely many people have been exhausted in the fire, and many nations have fainted. For the earth shall be filled with the knowledge of the

2:1, 2 HABAKKUK

glory of the Lord; it shall cover them as water. Woe to him that gives his neighbour to drink the thick lees of wine, and intoxicates him, that he may look upon their secret parts. Drink thou also thy fill of disgrace instead of glory: shake, O heart, and quake, the cup of the right hand of the Lord has come round upon thee, and dishonour has gathered upon thy glory. For the ungodliness of Libanus shall cover thee, and distress because of wild beasts shall dismay thee, because of the blood of men, and the sins of the land and city, and of all that dwell in it. What profits it the graven image, that they have graven it? one has made it a molten work, a false image; for the maker has trusted in his work, to make dumb idols. Woe to him that says to the wood, Awake, arise; and to the stone, Be thou exalted! whereas it is an image, and this is a casting of gold and silver, and there is no breath in it. But the Lord is in his holy temple, let all the earth fear before him.

COMMENTS

Having presented what sounds to himself like a conclusive argument against God's use of the Chaldeans to punish Judah, Habakkuk now declares he will simply stand and wait for Jehovah's answer. We do not know what answer he expected. Perhaps he thought Jehovah would acquiesce, as He did when Moses interceded following the unfaithfulness of the people shortly after the exodus. *(Exodus 39:9-ff)* In any event, the answer was not long in coming. The prophet is to write the vision (which is how the book of Habakkuk came into being). He is to make it plain upon tables.

National dealings were engraved upon wooden tables covered with wax. The engraving was made with a hot iron writing instrument and the plaque—or tablet thus engraved was hung in public in the temple. (cp. *Luke 1:63*) It is to be written so plainly that one running past could read it without stopping.

The idea seems to be that whoever reads the tablet engraved with God's answer to Habakkuk's complaint will run to whomever he can with the news. "Run" is used elsewhere for the urgent announcing of God's revealed truth. (cp. *Jeremiah 23:21, Revelation 22:17*)

In view of modern insistence upon the same complaints against God, it would seem that we too should adopt a sense of urgency. God's answer is still valid. Men need to know it now as in the day of the prophet.

THE EPITAPH OF NINEVEH   3:4-7

I will show the nations thy nakedness, and the kingdoms thy shame. And I will cast abominable filth upon thee, and make thee vile, and will set thee as a gazing-stock. And it shall come to pass, that all they that look upon thee shall flee from thee, and say, Nineveh is laid waste: who will bemoan her? whence shall I seek comforters for thee?

LXX . . . because of the abundance of fornication: she is a fair harlot, and well-favoured, skilled in sorcery, that sells the nations by her fornication and peoples by her sorceries. Behold, I am against thee, saith the Lord God Almighty, and I will uncover thy skirts in thy presence, and I will shew thy nations thy shame, and the kingdoms thy disgrace. And I will cast abominable filth upon thee according to thine unclean ways, and will make thee a public example. And it shall be that every one that sees thee shall go down from thee, and shall say, Wretched Nineve! who shall lament for her? whence shall I seek comfort for her?

COMMENTS

The cry of the modern social revolutionist is "if there is a god, why does he not halt or prevent war?" The paragraph before us deserves serious study in answer to this questioning. The God Who declares Himself against Nineveh has not changed in His righteous wrath upon wicked nations.

BECAUSE OF THE MULTITUDE OF WHOREDOMS . . . v. 4

Here is a listing, brief and to the point, of the sins of Nineveh. No doubt the term "whoredoms of the well-fovored harlot" could be a literal description of the immorality of the Assyrian capital. Such corruption always preceeds the downfall of an empire, just as it now eats the fibre out of the strength of the United States.

However, it is more likely Nahum intends here the more profound harlotry that brought on war. Nineveh had courted neighboring nations with the design to ruin their liberties and property.

Nor must we omit from the "multitude of her whoredoms" her mystery redigion. (See chapter on Baal worship.) In her heyday, Assyria was one of the most brutal empires ever to cross the pages of history. Will Durant points out that her religion did nothing to molify this tendancy to violence. Ashur was the name of the national version of the sun god. He was warlike, merciless and was believed to take a divine satisfaction in the sacrifice of captured enemies before his shrine. The worship of Ashur was largely one of omens and exorcism.

(Verse 3) The message is to be commited to writing because the fulfillment of what is said lies in the future, from the point of view of those who first read it. "Write it down just as you receive it," says God, in effect, "then see if it doesn't happen just this way."

In this verse is stated a point which needs to be imprinted indelibly on the mind of anyone who ever doubted the divine inspiration of Scripture. What God said and the prophets wrote about the cataclysmic events of history was written well in advance of the events themselves. That these predictions were fulfilled to the letter years, sometimes centuries, later is conclusive proof to any honest scholar that they were not of human origin.

The predictive element of prophecy was one of the strongest evidences offered by the apostles of the truth of the Gospel. (eg. *Acts 2:22-ff*)

A generation ago it was the fad among the critics of the Bible to say that the predictive prophecies of the Bible were actually written after the fact, but recent scholarship, even of the most liberal persuasion, tends to accept the traditional dates of Scriptural writings. These dates place all predictive prophecies well before its fulfillment.

What God answers here, in reply to Habakkuk's second question, is a case in point. Having answered the first question with a prediction of Judah's punishment at the hands of the Chaldeans, He answers the second by predicting the destruction of the Chaldeans themselves by the Persians!

The years of Babylonian captivity will make the fulfillment of this vision seem to tarry. Nevertheless, those who read are to wait for it. It will surely come. It will not delay.

(Verse 4-5) Jehovah begins His answer by setting forth a general principle. Whoever is puffed up in his own soul (whether Jew or Chaldean) will be punished. "The righteous," whether Jew or Chaldean (Paul will later say "to the Jew first but also to the Greek," *Romans 1: 16117*) "shall live by faith."

The contrast of the Bible between the godly and the ungodly is set forth in verse four in bold relief. It is not a contrast between "good" and "bad" *per se* but between the haughty soul who sets his will against that of God on the one hand and the one who lives by faith on the other. The New Testament will make this contrast even more sharply in terms of the carnal as opposed to the Spirit-directed. (eg. *Galatians 5:16-25*)

A word needs to be said here concerning the statement "the righteous shall live by his faith." As indicated above, Paul alludes to this statement in *Romans 1:17*. In so doing, he quotes the Septuagint. There the text reads literally "but the righteous, out of my faith shall be living." The Greek of the New Testament in *Romans 1:17* reads literally "but the righteous out of faith shall be living."

There is a minor textual problem here. The Hebrew text, as represented in our American Standard Version has "his" faith in *Habakkuk 2:4*. The Septuagint in the same place has "my" faith. Paul's Greek omits both possessive pronouns and says simply "by (not my or his) faith."

The apostle has captured the essential truth of Habakkuk. In contrast to the overwhelming military might in which the Chaldeans trusted *(Habakkuk 1:13(b)-16)* and the Assyrian-Egyptian alliance upon which Judah had based her national security, the righteous shall stake his life upon his trust in God.

The Chaldeans would lay waste to Judah who trusted in Assyrian and Egyptian arms. Cyrus would one day bring the Chaldean empire of Babylon to her knees. Through it all, God would preserve His real people . . . the true Israel. (cf. discussion of Micah's prophecy concerning the remnant.)

Here is an eternal truth, and one God's people in the closing decades of the twentieth century would do well to learn. God deals with people on the basis of obedient faith not on the basis of misplaced national loyalty and military power, whether Chaldean, Jewish or American!

(Verse 6) There is an intriguing reference to wine here. The haughty, who depend on military might and alliances are pointed out as deceived by the treachery of it. When Babylon attacked Nineveh, the leaders of that city were indulging in a drunken revelry. When Babylon herself was taken, it was during Belshazzar's feast when he dared drink wine from the golden vessels of the temple of Jehovah. (cf. *Daniel 5:2-4, 30* cp. *Proverbs 20:1, 30:9*)

The United States may one day fail in her own defense while our leaders are enjoying themselves in the endless round of Washington cocktail parties.

Of course one who objects to such things in our day is looked upon as being somewhat strange and fanatic . . . as were the prophets who tried in vain to warn Israel and Judah of the consequences of the same thing.

In verse five there begins a general description of those things characteristic of the Neo-Babylonian empire which carried in them the seed of the destruction that awaited her. Cocktail party diplomacy was only one of those characteristics. The empire is presented as a haughty man. Just as Judah's pride went before her fall so would Babylon's contribute to the downfall of the empire.

Every ancient nation shared this weakness of pride. Each imagined itself to be the select or chosen people of a god who was superior to all other gods. This national deity would preserve his people and subordinate all other peoples to them. The Jews' flirtation with Baal, along with certain other influences, made them mistake Jehovah for such a nationalistic god. This is why Habakkuk asked his second question *(1:12-f)*. Such haughtiness blinds any nation to the realities of international life.

The second characteristic of Babylon which contributed to his (the haughty man's) downfall was the inability to stay home. As Habakkuk pointed out *(1:14-ff)*, the Chaldeans swept all people into their sphere of dominance as a fisherman snares a school of fish.

Here Jehovah agrees with the prophet's evaluation. The haughty man "enlarges his desire as Sheol." Sheol is the Hebrew equivalent of the Greek Hades; the abode of the dead. It is never full but always seems eager to receive more and more people. Babylon is like this. Just as death is never satisfied, so Babylon is never satisfied . . . always seeking more victims.

This is a fatal obsession for any nation. Every world conqueror, from Alexander (or those who divided his kingdom following his untimely death) to Hitler has learned too late that he cannot encompass the earth and successfully control it.

A classic example is the British Empire. There was a time when Brittania could boast that the "sun never set on the Union Jack." But it did not last. Today England is at best a second rate power.

Even our own attempt to build a world wide economic empire has brought to us problems that seem insoluable and that threaten our national vitality beyond endurance.

The lust for power, as any other lust, carries in it the elements of its own death. (cf. *James 1:15)* It was indeed an attack upon Babylon by those who had once been her ally that brought the empire to destruction in the end.

So Jehovah predicts that those whom the Chaldeans conquer will one day take up a parable (or taunt) against them. This taunt forms the first of a series of woes through which Jehovah answers Habakkuk's second question.

THE FIRST WOE ... v. 6(b)-8

As God's providential guidance of history will bring about Judah's chastisement at the hands of the Chaldeans, so it will bring about, in turn, the destruction of the Chaldeans. Just how this is to come about is described in the woes which Jehovah now pronounces against them.

The first woe is "to him that increaseth that which is not his." To see this principle in operation against the Babylonians, we must bear in mind that Judah was not the only nation to fall prey to the Chaldean's military expansionism. The Medes and Persians also came under the influence of Babylonian greed. And the time was not long in coming when they would together find the strength to do something very final about it.

This uprising reached its climax c. 532 B.C. when Cyrus and his Persians in collusion with certain Babylonian clerics made Babylon subject to the enlightened domination of Persia. For two subsequent centuries Babylon was ruled by the Persians.

God's promise to Habakkuk, in answer to the prophet's second question, is (v. 8) that this downfall of Babylon will be in punishment for her plundering and violence done not only to Judah but to other people as well.

THE SECOND WOE ... v. 9-11

The second in the series of woes pronounced against Babylon in answer to Habakkuk's questioning is stated in verses 9, 10, and 11. It emphasizes the covetousness of Babylon in her aggressions against other peoples. The covetousness is beyond the "normal" greed of an aggressor nation. It is so extreme as to be fatal not only to the invaded nations, but to the invader.

Not content with national aggrandizement and the enriching of his own coffers, the ruler of Babylon steals enough from conquered peoples to enrich his whole nation or family.

This is precisely the sin of Jehoiachem for which God raised up Babylon in punishment (cf. *Jeremiah 22:31*) It will also destroy Babylon in turn.

The "nest on high" is figurative of the eagle (Job 39:27). Here it refers to the royal citadel. Babylon was famous for its towered ziggurats.

To Babylon Jehovah says (v. 10) "Thou . . . hast sinned against thy soul." The empire raised up by God thus becomes guilty of her own destruction.

THE SECOND QUESTION   2:12-14

The very towers of Babylon, built by the blood of conquered peoples and supported by stolen loot, will cry out against her (v. 11). Her splendor is her downfall. Her glory is in her shame!

THE THIRD WOE . . . v. 12-14

The third woe, pronounced in verses twelve through fourteen, is brought about by the extreme cruelty of Babylon. Like her covetousness, her mercilessness against conquered people also contains the fatal poison of the empire.

This blood-thirstiness of Babylon was infamous throughout the ancient world. John uses it, as a familiar fact, in the symbolism of Revelation. *(Revelation 17:6)*

Those who are now laboring to build Babylon are laboring for the fire. (v. 11) That is, they are simply erecting those things which will be burned in the destruction of the city.

The significant truth here, for the sake of the prophet's question, is that it is *of Jehovah of hosts.* The moral principles which bring about the rise and fall of people and nations in the flow of history are not accidental. Neither are they the product of any process of social evolution. These principles are fixed by God. They are the same from age to age in all of man's international relationships. The nation which fails to recognize them and govern itself accordingly may expect to join all previous empires on the rubble heap of dead civilizations!

There is a purpose to God's rigid insistance that nations as well as men recognize and submit to His moral judgements. (v. 14) "The earth shall be filled with the knowledge of the glory of Jehovah . . ."

A word about "glory" may be helpful here. The term itself means literally "the essential nature" of a person. God's glory is His essential character *ie.* that which causes Him to be held in high repute among those who know Him.

By dealing with men and nations on the basis of fixed moral laws, Jehovah is revealing Himself to them. That nations are more often than not blind to this truth is to their detriment, not His!

Just as surely as God was preparing for the coming Christ by revealing Himself to Israel through the prophets and His written word, so He was preparing the nations for Christ through His dealings in history. That both Israel and the Gentile nations failed to learn what Jehovah taught simply underscores man's universal need for salvation. It certainly is not, as Habakkuk's questions would imply, and as modern agnostics insist, an indictment against God as unfair or unjust.

2:15-18   HABAKKUK

THE FOURTH WOE . . . v. 15-17

The fourth woe, with which Jehovah answers the prophet's second question, has to do with the drunkenness of the Babylonians. We have already remarked briefly on this. (see above on 2:5)

Against the practice of excessive drinking in Babylon, God sets in figurative speech the downfall of the empire. Babylon is pictured here as a drunken man. He is not only drunken himself, but like most drunkards, he influences others to share in his revelings.

The accusation is that the drinker shares the drink in order to look on his neighbor's nakedness. There is no genuiness of friendship here. Babylon only pretends to share "the good life" so as to lure his neighbors into alliances which will ultimately expose them to loss and shame.

Proud Babylon, the drunk, is himself not filled with glory as he supposes. His own nakedness is exposed and it is revealed to all the world that he is uncircumcised. He is not God's covenant people!

God will do to Babylon what Babylon has done to others. He will allow the empire to become corrupt to the extent that "foul shame" (literally vomit) will cover its glory.

Ironically, Babylon's final collapse came in the midst of a drunken revel. *(Daniel 5)* The imagery here is very appropriate!

In verse 17 the figure changes. From describing Babylon as a shameful drunk, Jehovah turns to describing him as a beast caught in a net trap.

"The violence done to Lebanon" reminds us that Lebanon was the gateway to Judah for the armies of Babylon. Also that the temple destroyed by the Babylonians was built of the cedars of Lebanon.

Just as men threatened repeatedly by the incursion of wild beasts become driven by fear to destroy the beasts, so Babylon's neighbors, subjected repeatedly to the brutalities of Babylon will one day be driven to destroy him.

THE FIFTH WOE . . . v. 18-20

The fifth woe against Babylon is introduced by a question (v. 18). "What," Jehovah asks, "is the profit of a graven image even to the one who makes it?"

As with all nations of ancient time, Babylon created gods in their own image and then relied upon these gods of their own making to lead, empower and preserve them. It is the futility of this practice that God points to in this woe.

Not only the covetousness and bloody violence of Babylon will contribute to the overthrow of the empire. The trust in man-made gods also will conspire to bring it about. The god in which they trust is dead, *"There is no breath in all the midst of it."* Because they serve a dead god, they too shall die!

"Christian America" woke one day a few years ago to hear on television and read in major publications that "God Is Dead!" Perhaps there was more truth to the pronouncement than we realized. The gods of Roman and Protestant institutionalism . . . the god of economic materialism . . . the god of permissiveness and pleasure . . . the whole American pantheon is dead. Perhaps as we need to learn from the first four woes, so we need to learn from the fifth. The nation is doomed who worships a dead god!

In contrast (v. 20) to the dead god of Babylon, Jehovah is in His holy temple. Strange words, since the temple would, when the vision of Habakkuk came to pass, be in ruins. The obvious intent is that God does indeed not dwell in temples made with hands, whether those hands be Jewish or Babylonian.

A brief listing of the five woes may be helpful:
1. (v. 6) Woe to him who increases his possession of that which is not his.
2. (v. 9) Woe to him who gets evil gain in order to set himself above others.
3. (v. 12) Woe to him who builds his great cities on the suffering of downtrodden people.
4. (v. 14) Woe to him who involves others in his sin in order to exploit them.
5. (v. 19) Woe to those who worship dead gods.

These woes reveal eternal truth which explains in varying degrees the downfall of every collapsed civilization.

Chapter XVII—*Questions*
The Second Question

1. Show how God's answer to Habakkuk's first question gave rise to the second question.
2. State the prophet's second question in your own words.
3. Show how the Jews' misconception of themselves as God's people is reflected in Habakkuk's second question.

4. What two concepts did the Jews find hard to grasp? (As stated by Dr. Maurice Harris)
5. Show how Nahum's question to Nineveh *(Nahum 3:8)* could be asked here of Judah.
6. What do you understand is the Biblical doctrine of "election?"
7. How does dispensationalism pervert the doctrine of election?
8. What word more accurately states the idea of election?
9. What is implied by Habakkuk's use of the term "O Rock" in reference to Jehovah?
10. What two falacies combine to confuse Habakkuk in reference to God's purity and Babylon's impurity?
11. Describe the activity of the Babylonians toward neighboring nations.
12. In a sentence, what is Jehovah's answer to Habakkuk's second question?
13. List the five woes with which God gives His answer.
14. Show how these woes describe eternal principles in God's dealing with nations in history.

CHAPTER XVIII
THE PROPHET'S POETIC PRAYER
VISION OF GOD IN JUDGEMENT . . . Habakkuk 3:1-15

RV . . . A prayer of Habakkuk the prophet, set to Shigionoth. O Jehovah, I have heard the report of thee, and am afraid: O Jehovah, revive thy work in the midst of the years; In the midst of the years make it known; In wrath remember mercy. God came from Teman, and the Holy One from mount Paran. His glory covered the heavens, And the earth was full of his praise. And his brightness was as the light; He had rays coming forth from his hand; And there was the hiding of his power. Before him went the pestilence. And fiery bolts went forth at his feet. He stood, and measured the earth; He beheld, and drove asunder the nations; And the eternal mountains were scattered; The everlasting hills did bow; His goings were as of old. I saw the tents of Cushan in affliction; The curtains of the land of Midian did tremble. Was Jehovah displeased with the rivers? Was thine anger against the rivers, Or thy wrath against the sea, That thou didst ride upon thy horses, Upon thy chariots of salvation? Thy bow was made quite bare; The oaths to the tribes were a sure word. Thou didst

THE PROPHET'S POETIC PRAYER 3:1-15

cleave the earth with rivers. The mountains saw thee, and were afraid; The tempest of waters passed by; The deep uttered its voice, And lifted up its hands on high. The sun and moon stood still in their habitation. At the light of thine arrows as they went, At the shining of thy glittering spear. Thou didst march through the land in indignation; Thou didst thresh the nations in anger. Thou wentest forth for the salvation of thy people, For the salvation of thine anointed; Thou woundedst the head out of the house of the wicked man, Laying bare the foundation even unto the neck. Thou didst pierce with his own staves the head of his warriors: They came as a whirlwind to scatter me; Their rejoicing was as to devour the poor secretly. Thou didst tread the sea with thy horses, The heap of mighty waters.

LXX . . . A PRAYER OF THE PROPHET AMBACUM, WITH A SONG. O Lord, I have heard thy report, and was afraid; I considered thy works, and was amazed: thou shalt be known between the two living creatures, thou shalt be acknowledged when the years draw nigh; thou shalt be manifested when the time is come; when my soul is troubled, thou wilt in wrath remember mercy. God shall come from Thaeman, and the Holy One from the dark shady mount Pharan. His excellence covered the heavens, and the earth was full of his praise. And his brightness shall be as light; there were horns in his hands, and he caused a mighty love of his strength. Before his face shall go a report, and it shall go forth into the plains, the earth stood at his feet and trembled: he beheld, and the nations melted away: the mountains were violently burst through, the everlasting hills melted at his everlasting going forth. Because of troubles I looked upon the tents of the Ethiopians: the tabernacles also of the land of Madiam shall be dismayed. Wast thou angry, O Lord, with the rivers? or was thy wrath against the rivers, or thine anger against the sea? for thou wilt mount on thine horses, and thy chariots are salvation. Surely thou didst bend thy bow at sceptres, saith the Lord, The land of rivers shall be torn asunder. The nations shall see thee and be in pain, as thou dost divide the moving waters: and deep uttered her voice, and raised her form on high. The sun was exalted, and the moon stood still in her course: thy darts shall go forth at the light, at the brightness of the gleaming of thine arms. Thou wilt bring low the land with threatening, and in wrath thou wilt break down the nations. Thou wentest forth for the salvation of thy people, to save thine anointed: thou shalt bring death on the heads of transgressors; thou hast brought bands upon their neck. Thou didst cut asunder the heads of princes with amazement, they shall

3:1, 2 HABAKKUK

tremble in it; they shall burst their bridles, they shall be as a poor man devouring in secret. And thou dost cause thine horses to enter the sea, disturbing much water.

COMMENTS

Having been answered in no uncertain terms by God Himself, Habakkuk bows in prayer. There are no further questions, only the recognition of God's sovereign authority over nations and peoples and a hymn of faith.

The prayer of recognition comprises verses 1-15 of chapter three. The hymn of faith comprises the remainder of the book. This chapter will become well used by the Jews in intercession and meditation during the years of Babylonian captivity.

(Verse 1-2) Habakkuk owns the receipt of God's answer to his questions and the impression made upon him by the answers. He confirms having heard Jehovah's speech. *(v. 2)*

In *2:1* he had set himself to see how God would answer his unanswerable logic. Now he knows. He is struck with consternation by Jehovah's response. His concern now turns to Judah during the impending captivity. He is concerned lest they be utterly rooted out from being kept so long. He prays that, as God has manifest Himself in this vision, so He will strengthen the people "in the midst of the years."

The prophet prays earnestly that *for the elects'* sake these days of trouble may be shortened or the trouble of those days mitigated and the people supported and comforted.

Interestingly, this intercessory prayer is couched in terms of concern for "thine own work" rather than in the terms of national pride as was used in challenging God with the second question. *(1:12-ff)* Apparently Habakkuk has become convinced that the people were for God's sake rather than their own.

Rather than praying for national or racial glory, he now entreats God to act for His own honor and praise.

Even those who are under God's wrath must not despair of His mercy! The prophet has learned the ultimate lesson. Men must *trust* God rather than instructing Him.

(Verse 3-15) It has been the usual practice of God's people, when in distress and ready to fall in dispair, to help themselves by recollecting their experiences, and reviving them, (cp. *Psalm 77:5*) and pleading

THE PROPHET'S POETIC PRAYER 3:3-7

them with God in prayer, as He seems sometimes to plead with Himself. (cp. *Isaiah 63:11*)

So the prophet here looks back to God's first forming of His people, when He brought them miraculously out of Egypt into Canaan, which was then possessed by mighty nations. These words and wonders done in time past are magnificently described here to encourage greater faith on the part of the people during captivity.

1. God appeared in His glory, as never before nor since (*v. 3,4*). The visible display on Mount Sinai (*Deuteronomy 33:2*) is meant. Then "the Lord came down . . ." in a cloud (*Exodus 19:20*). He appeared as a devouring fire. His glory covered the heavens which glowed with the reflection of His appearance. "The earth was full of His praise" (or splendor) as people at a distance saw the cloud and fire on Mount Sinai and marvelled at Israel's God.

His brightness outshown the sun. Even Moses' face glowed when he came down from the Mount. The rays shone not directly from the face of God but around the side of His hand as He hid His face. There was a hiding of His power.

2. The prophet's prayer turns (v. 5) to the plagues by which God had delivered the people from Pharaoh. The pestilence which slew the first-born, the burning coals when the plague of hail mingled with fire, the diseases which blasted Egypt . . . these were "at His feet". . . at His coming . . . at His command.

3. He divided Canaan to His people Israel, and expelled the nations before them. (v. 6) (cp. *Deuteronomy 32:8-9*) He exerted such power that the nations which stood in Israel's way crumbled and fell as the walls of Jericho. The mountain shook, even Sinai. (*Psalm 68:7-8*)

And "His ways are everlasting." He has lost none of His terrible power. All the nations still rise and fall at His command. (Habakkuk has learned his lesson well.)

Jehovah's covenants are unchangeable, despite outward appearances. His mercy endures forever.

All the inhabitants of the neighboring nations are called to note the lesson the prophet has learned. Cushan and the Midianites are especially to take warning.

In the days of Othniel, God delivered Cushan into his hand. (*Judges 3:8*) In the days of Gideon, a barley cake, in a dream, overthrew the tent of Midian. (*Judges 7:18*) Habakkuk sees in these historic events the same principles Jehovah has set forth in the five woes.

3:8-11   HABAKKUK

4. He divided the Red Sea and the Jordan when they stood between Israel and God's purpose in the people. (v. 8) One might have thought God was displeased with the rivers and that His wrath was against the sea, had one been unaware of God's purpose in this activity.

As a general at the head of an army, so God rode at the head of Israel in His chariots of salvation. Habakkuk returns to this in v. 15. When they came to enter Canaan, the Jordan, which at that time of year overflows its banks, was divided. *(Joshua 3:15)* When the difficulties in the way of Israel's salvation seem insuperable as an overflowing river, then God in His might breaks them as He divided the waters.

"The deep uttered his voice" (v. 10), *ie.* the Red Sea and the Jordan were divided, the waters roared and made noise as though sensible to Jehovah's restraint. *"They lifted up their hands* (or sides) *on high,"* for the waters *"stood upon a heap."* *(Joshua 3:16)* The Lord was mightier than they. *(Psalm 90:3-4)*

With the dividing of the Jordan and the sea, notice is again given to the *"trembling of the mountain"* as if the stopping of the waters gave a shock to the adjacent hills. *(Psalm 114:3-4)* The whole creation is yielded to God.

5. He arrested the sun and the moon to bring about Israel's victories (v. 11). (Cp. *Joshua 10:12-ff)* Attempts have been made by defenders of the Bible to explain this phenomena on scientific terms. Some such attempts have smacked of dishonesty. We will do better to take God at His word in such matters. Once we have accepted the principle of direct divine intervention in human history, such "miracles" are no problem.

6. He carried on and completed Israel's victories over the nations of Canaan. *(Psalm 136:17-18)* This is largely insisted upon here as a proper plea with God to enforce the present petition, that He will restore them again to the land of which they were put in possession at the cost of so many lives and miracles.

Many expressions are used here to describe the conquest of Canaan. God's *bow was made naked, ie.* drawn from its case. He *marched through the land in indignation,* as scorning to let the Canaanites any longer possess it. He *threshed through the nations,* despising their confederacies. He *wounded the head . . . of the house of wicked men, ie.* he destroyed the families of the Canaanites.

Some question how a loving God could do what He did to the Canaanites. God answered that question to Habakkuk's satisfaction in chapters one and two.

THE PROPHET'S POETIC PRAYER   3:12-19

In giving Israel so many bloody victories, God made good His promises to their fathers. (v. 9) The promises were made for the sake of the entire world (as we have seen).

HYMN OF FAITH . . . Habakkuk 3:16-19

RV . . . I heard, and my body trembled, My lips quivered at the voice; Rottenness entereth into my bones, and I tremble in my place; Because I must wait quietly for the day of trouble. For the coming up of the people that invadeth us. For though the fig-tree shall not flourish, Neither shall fruit be in the vines; The labor of the olive shall fail, And the fields shall yield no food; The flock shall be cut off from the fold, And there shall be no herd in the stalls; Yet I will rejoice in Jehovah, I will joy in the God of my salvation. Jehovah, the Lord, is my strength; And he maketh my feet like hinds' feet, And will make me to walk upon my high places.

LXX . . . I watched, and my belly trembled at the sound of the prayer of my lips, and trembling entered into my bones, and my frame was troubled within me; I will rest in the day of affliction, from going up to the people of my sojourning. For though the fig-tree shall bear no fruit, and there shall be no produce on the vines; the labour of the olive shall fail, and the fields shall produce no food: the sheep have failed from the pasture, and there are no oxen at the cribs; yet I will exult in the Lord, I will joy in God my Saviour. The Lord God is my strength, and he will perfectly strengthen my feet; he mounts me upon high places, that I may conquer by his song.

COMMENTS

Within these few lines, we have the prophet in the highest degree of trembling and triumphing. In this world, God's people experience both. In heaven there is only triumph.

1. When we see a day of trouble approaching, it concerns us to lay up something in store for that day. The best way to so prepare is to tremble within ourselves at the Word of God.

Habakkuk's fear was that when the Chaldean came to lead off the people, he will break them up as Assyria broke up the northern kingdom. Should this happen, God's people would be no more and God's covenant would go unfulfilled. The fig-tree (v. 17) would not flourish, the vine would bear no fruit, the flock would be cut off and no herd would be in the stalls. Apart from His covenant people, God's purpose would not be realized.

3:16-19   HABAKKUK

    Of course, the truth of this concern is seen historically in that God did not allow it to happen. The captives of Babylon were not scattered. Their children returned to rebuild God's temple.

    2. The prophet had looked back on the experiences of the people in former ages, and had recalled great things God had done for them. From his trembling, he recovered himself. His fright gave way to faith and he was overwhelmed with holy joy. Despite the calamities he foresaw in the vision God granted him, he saw beyond it to the day of restoration.

    It was the joy of faith. A century of suffering lay between the vision and the return of the remnant. Other centuries lay beyond before the coming of Him Who is the ultimate fulfillment of God's purpose in Israel.

    Habakkuk closes on a note of optimism only possible to one who has finally learned to take God at His word despite outward appearances.

Chapter XVIII—*Questions*
The Prophet's Poetic Prayer

1. Habakkuk's final chapter is a poetic prayer. Its two sections are _____ and _____.
2. How does God's answer to his second question strike Habakkuk?
3. With what is the prophet primarily concerned in the first section of his prayer?
4. Why does the prophet recall the past events of God's people?
5. List the past events alluded to here.
6. How can a loving God do what Jehovah did to the Canaanites in their overthrow by Israel?
7. The second section of Habakkuk's prayer . . . the Hymn of Faith, shows the prophet progressing from _____ to _____.
8. What is the best way to prepare for a day of adversity?
9. In remembering God's past dealing with Israel, Habakkuk's fright gave way to _____.
10. How do you account for the optimism with which Habakkuk closes?

"For Gaza shall be forsaken, and Ashkelon a desolation: they shall drive out Ashdod at the noonday, and Ekron shall be rooted up ... In the houses of Ashkelon shall they lie down in the evening ..."
(Zephaniah 2:4,7).
It was about this time that wild hordes of mounted nomads from the Caucasus swept into Mesopotamia, looting and ravaging. They forced their way through Palestine as far as the frontiers of Egypt. These were the Scythians.
The Prophet Zephaniah foresaw with horror the havoc they would wreak in Palestine.
Galloping Scythian horsemen, practising their characteristic shooting over the shoulder, decorate the lid of this bronze Etruscan urn.

FROM: THE BIBLE AS HISTORY IN PICTURES
By Werner Keller - Wm. Morrow Co.

"And he will stretch out his hand against the north, and destroy Assyria"
(Zephaniah 2:13).
This prophecy of Zephaniah was fulfilled only twelve years after the
death of Ashurbanipal. The Chaldeans, one of whom had been
Merodach-baladan, the ally of King Hezekiah of Judah, had succeeded
at last after a long and fruitless struggle against their mortal enemies
the Assyrians, in making themselves masters of Babylon, and had
allied themselves with a people from Iran, the Medes. The first city
to fall before their joint assault was Ashur, which was taken in 614 B.C.
This reconstruction shows the north-west side of this impressive
metropolis, the oldest of the great cities of the Assyrian empire,
lying on the west side of the Tigris, with its massive Temple of the god
Ashur, who was its patron deity.

FROM: THE BIBLE AS HISTORY IN PICTURES
By Werner Keller – Wm. Morrow Co.

PART V
ZEPHANIAH

OUTLINE OF ZEPHANIAH

Introduction: Zephaniah's identity
  A. Family
  B. Date
I. Doom of Judah
  A. Removal
    1. of things of value
    2. of all life
    3. of idolatry
      a. Baal worshipers
      b. animal worshipers
      c. plant worshipers
      d. backsliders
      e. no defense for rebellion
  B. Judgement is certain and soon
    1. powerless strong
    2. wrath
    3. mounting troubles
    4. day of alarm
    5. no protection in position or riches
II. Divine Judgement Universal
  A. Assembly
  B. Gentile cities judged
    1. named
    2. designated
    3. land to change
    4. new dwellers in land
    5. God's blessing
  C. Opposition judged
    1. reproach to God's people
    2. wasted land
    3. prey of residue
    4. punishment for pride
    5. change in worship
  D. Universal retribution
    1. Ethiopia to Nineveh
    2. Habitation for beasts and birds
    3. Humbling the proud
    4. By word instead of praise

INTRODUCTION TO ZEPHANIAH

III. Comfort and Consolation
  A. Not too filthy
  B. A just and Holy God
  C. Endurance counts
  D. Song of Joy

CHAPTER XIX
INTRODUCTION TO ZEPHANIAH
THE DATE

Zephaniah is a companion book to Nahum in two respects: (1) The two were contemporary and (2) the judgements against the nations surrounding Palestine are general in Zephaniah. Nahum singles out one of these objects of God's judgement and deals with it specifically and in detail. What Nahum described in Nineveh at the time of her downfall was in some measure true of all the cities and nations mentioned by Zephaniah.

Zephaniah probably wrote in the latter half of Josiah's reign. Josiah came to the throne at the age of eight, following the death of his father, Amon c. 639 B.C. His reform of Judah began c. 621 with the discovery of the book of the law which some scholars identify as Deuteronomy. (Cf. *II Kings 22*) It seems likely that Zephaniah's prophecy was meant to assist in Josiah's reform.

Some argue for an earlier date, *ie.* the first part of Josiah's reign, on the ground that such pronouncements were more needed prior to Josiah's reform. This seems a rather spurious argument, since it was precisely the pre-reform conditions at which the reform was aimed. Such a reform would be greatly enhanced by the appearance of a prophet of God on the scene after some seventy-five years of divine silence.

Not since Isaiah, Micah and Amos had an inspired spokesman for Jehovah stood in the midst of His people.

ZEPHANIAH THE PROPHET

We know little about Zephaniah aside from the first verse of his book. Three other Old Testament men wore the same name, which means "Jehovah hides," but there is no reason to identify the prophet with any of the three.

He was born some time, probably late, in the reign of the bloodthirsty Manessah c. 687-641 B.C. *(II Kings 21:16)*

ZEPHANIAH

Zephaniah's ancestry is stated in the first verse of his writing. He is a fourth generation descendant of Hezekiah (716-687 B.C.). He was, therefore, of royal blood and very familiar with the court of Judah *(1:8, 3:3)*. No doubt he calls attention to Hezekiah rather than his most recent royal relatives because of their departure from the faith. The most recent, before Zephaniah's contemporary, Josiah, was Amon who was actually named for the pagan god of Egypt.

ZEPHANIAH'S MESSAGE

Like the other writing prophets of the Old Testament, Zephaniah was acutely aware of the international circumstances of his day. It is impossible to understand him without some knowledge of the world situation in which he lived.

In the last quarter of the seventh century B.C. the world stood in terror of a federation of wild tribes from what is now southern Russia. The Sythians smashed Syria and poured over all of western Asia. They pressed to the Egyptian delta before being bought off by Pharaoh Psammitichus I.

They rode bareback on wild horses, drank their enemy's blood and used his scalp for a napkin. The women rode with their men as warriors until they married and marriage was forbidden until a woman had killed three enemies.

The Sythians finally became relatively civilized, inheriting the remnants of the earlier Hittite culture. Their second king was the legendary Midas of the golden touch.

Acutely aware of the Sythian threat, Zephaniah nevertheless seems to have seen it for what it was, *ie.* relatively minor and short-lived. He looks beyond this immediate danger and, without naming the empire, describes the Babylonian domination of the world. This, of course, is only reasonable, since it was the Babylonians (Chaldeans) whom God revealed to Habakkuk as those He was raising up for judgement.

Some have said Zephaniah foretold the Sythian invasion of Judah, but if he was inspired as we believe, he could make no such historical blunder. The Sythians did not invade Judah.

The time before Josiah's reform and, therefore, the conditions to which Zephaniah addressed himself, constitute what has been called the dark age of Judah. Following the death of the good king Hezekiah, his son Manasseh set about to throw the nation into complete idolatry. It became a crime to preach the God known to Isaiah and Micah. The high places of Baal, destroyed by Hezekiah, were rebuilt. Altars to the unholy trinity of the sun cult were erected everywhere in the

INTRODUCTION TO ZEPHANIAH

names of Ashtoreth, Chemosh, Milcom and the other local titles for Baal. (See introductory chapter on Baal Worship.)

The temple itself was desecrated by heathen altars, and to Baal worship was added the abominable Assyrian worship of the planets, the sun and the moon. Witchcraft ran rampant throughout Judah and sacred prostitution was the order of the day. Even the sacrificing of babies to Baal was revived. (Cf. *II Kings 21*)

Manasseh himself seems later to have repented but the damage was done. *(II Chronicles 33:22)*

Manasseh's son, whom he had named Amon for the Egyptian version of the sun god, succeeded his father to the throne of Judah, but his two year reign was so brief as to be unimportant. At the age of eight, Josiah the reformer ascended the throne.

Nothing changed during the years of Josiah's regency, but when he reached the age of twenty-six, he initiated a wide-ranging reform. *(II Kings 22:3-ff)* Zephaniah's prophetic ministry no doubt played a large role, both in bringing about the reform and in implementing it.

The idolatrous priests, the worship of strange deities, the adoration of heavenly bodies, all come in for their share of denunciation by Zephaniah. So also do those who forsake the true worship of Jehovah, the atheists who have altogether abandoned worship, those who give only lip service to God, and those who believe Jehovah will passively do neither good nor evil to anyone.

God's judgement against Judah Zephaniah sees as accompanied by universal judgement. Assyrian power was crumbling. The Sythians, fierce though they were, would not become a major power. The Chaldean empire of Babylon would be raised up by God to smite not only Judah but those nations north, south, east and west of her. Both those afar off and those who were near neighbors would feel the wrath of God.

The message addressed to the world of his time is summed up in Zephaniah's repeated use of the term "day of Jehovah." Two major ideas are included in this term: (1) the universal judgement of God and (2) the comfort and hope reserved for the remnant.

In addition there seem to be two minor ideas which are never clearly defined in Zephaniah: (1) The Messianic period and (2) the final judgement of all nations.

Special attention must be given the term "day of Jehovah" if we are to understand the prophecy of Zephaniah. He did not coin the phrase. It had been in popular usage for at least a century. Amos had attempted to correct a popular misunderstanding of it. *(Amos 5:18-20)*

To the Jews of Amos' day, the day of Jehovah was a day when the Hebrews would finally overcome their enemies. God would utterly destroy all Gentile power, and the world would be ruled from Jerusalem. Such Jewish nationalism and racism are not unknown today. Dispensationalism, so wide-spread among today's Evangelical denominations also propagates this mistaken concept.

Throughout the Old Testament the term *yom YHWH* (day of Jehovah) denotes the time when God's kingdom will be finally consummated and free from attack from without or corruption within. (Cf. *Isaiah 2:12, 13:6-9, 34:8, Ezekiel 13:5, 30:3, Joel 1:15, 2:11, Amos 5:18, Zephaniah 1:14* and *Zechariah 14:1*)

To bring this consummation to its fullness four characteristics are described in various contexts, both in the Old and New Testaments: (1) The judgement of Israel, Judah and the nations of the pre-Christian world; (2) The deliverance and preservation of the remnants during and after the captivity; (3) The first coming of the Messiah; and (4) The second coming of the Messiah and His final judgement of all men and nations.

Conceived of in terms of judgement, the day of the Lord is described as a "day of wrath" or "day of judgement." In its ultimate fulfillment it is "that great and notable day." In general reference it is "that day," "the day of the Lord," "day of God." In terms of Christ's second coming it is "the day of Jesus Christ" or "the day of Christ."

In keeping with the nature of His kingdom, which is "not of this world," the Scriptural teaching concerning the "day of Jehovah" is concerned more with the qualities of the day than with the time of its fulfillment. God is thought of as manifesting Himself in His fullness, punishing wrong, especially wrong worship and social injustice, then rewarding faithfulness and loving service. The final fulfillment of the "day of Jehovah" is the final triumph of righteousness and truth over sin and falsehood.

Any period of history in which God raised up a nation to punish wickedness or unfaithfulness answers to the first characteristic of "that day." Indeed, considering God's constant rule over the history of man, it could not be otherwise.

It is in this sense that Zephaniah places most of his emphasis on "the day of Jehovah." There is a ferver of wrath revealed in the overthrow of wicked Judah and her equally wicked neighbors. There is an unrelenting certainty to Jehovah's judgements in the ebb and flow of international relationships. There is the over-riding warning that a nation which does not turn from sin to God is "living on borrowed time."

On the other hand, we cannot overlook the Messianic and eschatological overtones of Zephaniah's "day of Jehovah." Dr. G. A. Smith is quoted by T. Miles Bennett in this regard: "In short, with Zephaniah the Day of the Lord tends to become the Last Day. His book is the relation of prophecy with apocalypse. That is the moment which it supplies in the history of Israel's religion." Nebular and undefined though it seems, Zephaniah's eschatology marks a definite step forward in the nature of prophecy.

Chapter XIX—*Questions*
Introduction to Zephaniah

1. Zephaniah is a companion book to _____.
2. Zephaniah probably wrote in the _____ half of Josiah's reign.
3. Discuss the relationship between Zephaniah's prophecy and Josiah's reform.
4. Why does Zephaniah mention Hezekiah particularly in listing his own ancestry?
5. Why does Zephaniah discuss the rise of Babylon rather than the Sythian threat?
6. In addition to the corruption of their worship by turning to Baal, the people of Judah also worshipped _____.
7. God's judgement against Judah, Zephaniah sees as accompanied by _____.
8. The two major ideas presented by Zephaniah are (1) _____ and (2) _____.
9. Two minor ideas never clearly defined by Zephaniah are (1) _____ and (2) _____.
10. Discuss the four characteristics of the fullness of the "day of Jehovah."

CHAPTER XX
JUDGEMENT OF GOD
SALUTATION . . . Zephaniah 1:1

1:1, 2   ZEPHANIAH

RV . . . The word of Jehovah which came unto Zephaniah the son of Cushi, the son of Gedaliah, the son of Amariah, the son of Hezekiah, in the days of Josiah the son of Amon, king of Judah.

LXX . . . The word of the Lord which came to Sophonias the son of Chusi, the son of Godolias, the son of Amorias, the son of Ezekias, in the days of Josias son of Amon, king of Juda.

COMMENTS

As in other prophetic writings, Zephaniah's opening verse leaves no room for doubt as to the origin of his message. He does not describe his call, as does Isaiah, nor claim to have seen a vision, as, for example, Nahum. But the claim to inspiration is never in doubt.

It is not in the scope of this work to prove the validity of this claim. The reader is referred to the Moody Press (1963) publication, *Can I Trust The Bible*, edited by Howard F. Vos for an excellent series of treatises on the subject as it pertains to the entire Bible.

We shall simply proceed on the presupposition that Zephaniah was among those described by Peter as "men (who) spoke from God, being moved by the Holy Spirit." *II Peter 1:21*)

The prophet's opening words "the word of Jehovah" are calculated to establish the authority of what he is about to say. He claims royal lineage and has easy access to the courts of Judah, but these are not the authority to which he appeals. He will write down the word of Jehovah God.

Zephaniah identifies himself as son of Cushi . . . of Gedaliah . . . of Amariah . . . of Hezekiah. We know virtually nothing of either Cushi or Gedaliah or Amariah. The important name here is Hezekiah, the last God-fearing king of Judah prior to Josiah with whom Zephaniah is contemporary. (See introductory Chapter 19 for discussion of ancestry and date of Zephaniah.)

UNIVERSAL JUDGEMENT PROCLAIMED . . . Zephaniah 1:2-3

RV . . . I will utterly consume all things from off the face of the ground, saith Jehovah. I will consume man and beast; I will consume the birds of the heavens, and the fishes of the sea, and the stumblingblocks with the wicked; and I will cut off man from off the face of the ground, saith Jehovah.

LXX . . . Let there be an utter cutting off from the face of the land, saith the Lord, Let man and cattle be cut off; let the birds of the air

JUDGEMENT OF GOD 1:2,3

and the fishes of the sea be cut off; and the ungodly shall fail, and I will take away the transgressors from the face of the land, saith the Lord.

COMMENTS

I WILL UTTERLY CONSUME . . . v. 2

The apostle Paul reminds us that the " . . . whole creation groaneth and travaileth in pain together until now. . . " (*Romans 8:22*) as a result of man's sin. Peter informs us " . . . the day of the Lord will come as a thief; in the which the heavens shall pass away with a great noise, and the elements shall be dissolved with fervent heat, and the earth and the works that are therein shall be burned up." (*II Peter 3:10*) John adds, " . . . I saw a new heaven and a new earth: for the first heaven and the first earth are passed away; and the sea is no more." (*Revelation 21:1*) Whatever the chronological relationship of Zephaniah's "Day of Jehovah" to the final summing up of all history by God, it certainly prefigures the ultimate destruction of all the sinful works of man in preparation for the establishment of the universal reign of God.

THE STUMBLING BLOCK . . . v. 3

Along with the wicked, God will wipe out those things which have *caused* man to sin. This is, no doubt, an allusion to the idolatrous worship of the beasts, fishes and birds mentioned here. (cp. *Romans 1:18-ff*) Ezekiel uses similar language in condemning idol worship. (*Ezekiel 14:3-7*)

SAITH JEHOVAH . . . v. 2-3

Zephaniah will allow none of the nonsense current in our time regarding his prophetic insight. Those who today would tell us that this insight came from an informed political prognosticator, do so only by ignoring the prophet's claim, "(thus) saith Jehovah." Here is the watchword of all Old Testament prophecy. The message is from God.

JUDGEMENT OF JUDAH . . . Zephaniah 1:4-2:3)

RV . . . And I will stretch out my hand upon Judah, and upon all the inhabitants of Jerusalem; and I will cut off the remnant of Baal from this place, and the name of the Chemarim with the priests; and them that worship the host of heaven upon the housetops; and them that worship, that swear to Jehovah and swear by Malcam; and them that are turned back from following Jehovah; and those that have not sought Jehovah, nor inquired after him. Hold thy peace at the presence of the Lord Jehovah; for the day of Jehovah is at hand; for Jehovah hath prepared a sacrifice, he hath consecrated his guests. And it shall come to pass in the day of Jehovah's sacrifice, that I will punish the princes, and the King's sons, and all such as are clothed with foreign apparel. And in that day I will punish all those that leap over the threshold, that fill their master's house with violence and deceit. And in that day, saith Jehovah, there shall be the noise of a cry from the fish gate, and a wailing from the second quarter, and a great crashing from the hills, Wail, ye inhabitants of Maktesh; for all the people of Canaan are undone; all they that were laden with silver are cut off. And it shall come to pass at that time, that I will search Jerusalem with lamps; and I will punish the men that are settled on their lees, that say in their heart, Jehovah will not do good, neither will he do evil. And their wealth shall become a spoil and their houses a desolation: yea, they shall build houses, but they shall not inhabit them; and they shall plant vineyards, but shall not drink the wine thereof. The great day of Jehovah is near, it is near and hasteth greatly, even the voice of the day of Jehovah; the mighty man crieth there bitterly. That day is a day of wrath, a day of trouble and distress, a day of wasteness and desolation, a day of darkness and gloominess, a day of clouds and thick darkness, a day of the trumpet and alarm, against the fortified cities, and against the high battlements. And I will bring distress upon men, that they shall walk like blind men, because they have sinned against Jehovah; and their blood shall be poured out as dust, and their flesh as dung. Neither their silver nor their gold shall be able to deliver them in the day of Jehovah's wrath; but the whole land shall be devoured by the fire of his jealously; for he will make an end, yea, a terrible end, of all them that dwell in the land. Gather yourselves together, yea, gather together, O nation that hath no shame; before the decree bring forth, before the day pass as the chaff, before the fierce anger of Jehovah come upon you, before the day of Jehovah's anger come upon you. Seek ye Jehovah, all ye meek of the earth, that have kept his ordinances; seek ye righteousness, seek meekness: it may be ye will be hid in the day of Jehovah's anger.

LXX . . . And I will stretch out mine hand upon Juda, and upon all the inhabitants of Jerusalem; and I will remove the names of Baal out of this place, and the names of the priests; and them that worship the host of heaven upon the housetops; and them that worship and swear by the Lord, and them that swear by their king; and them that turn aside from the Lord, and them that seek not the Lord, and them that cleave not to the Lord. Fear ye before the Lord God; for the day of the Lord is near; for the Lord has prepared his sacrifice, and has sanctified his guests. And it shall come to pass in the day of the Lord's sacrifice, that I will take vengeance on the princes, and on the king's house, and upon all that wear strange apparel. And I will openly take vengeance on the porches in that day, on the men that fill the house of the Lord their God with ungodliness and deceit. And there shall be in that day, saith the Lord, the sound of a cry from the gate of men slaying, and a howling from the second gate, and a great crashing from the hills. Lament, ye that inhabit the city that has been broken down, for all the people has become like Chanaan; and all that were exalted by silver have been utterly destroyed. And it shall come to pass in that day, that I will search Jerusalem with a candle, and will take vengeance on the men that despise the things committed to them; but they say in their hearts, The Lord will not do any good, neither will he do any evil. And their power shall be for a spoil, and their houses for utter desolation; and they shall build houses, but shall not dwell in them; and they shall plant vineyards, but shall not drink the wine of them. For the great day of the Lord is near, it is near, and very speedy; the sound of the day of the Lord is made bitter and harsh. A mighty day of wrath is that day, a day of affliction and distress, a day of desolation and destruction, a day of gloominess and darkness, a day of cloud and vapour, a day of the trumpet and cry against the strong cities, and against the high towers. And I will greatly afflict the men, and they shall walk as blind men, because they have sinned against the Lord; therefore he shall pour out their blood as dust, and their flesh as dung. And their silver and their gold shall in nowise be able to rescue them in the day of the Lord's wrath; but the whole land shall be devoured by the fire of his jealously; for he will bring a speedy destruction on all them that inhabit the land. Be ye gathered and closely joined together, O unchastened nation; before ye become as the flower that passes away, before the anger of the Lord come upon you, before the day of the wrath of the Lord come upon you. Seek ye the Lord, all ye meek of the earth; do judgement, and seek justice, and answer accordingly; that ye may be hid in the day of the wrath of the Lord.

MY HAND UPON JUDAH . . . v. 4

Unlike some others (Amos) whose pronouncements of judgement begin with Judah's neighbors and then focus on her, Zephaniah begins

1:4, 5   ZEPHANIAH

at home. All the world is wicked. The sin of God's people is worst of of all, precisely because they are God's people. As Peter has it, "Judgment must begin at the house of God." (*I Peter 4:17*)

The prophet immediately turns to listing those specifics which have brought God's judgement against Judah. At the top of the list is Baal worship. (See introductory chapter on Baal worship.)

The last vestige, or remnant, of Baal worship is going to be obliterated from "this place" *ie.* Jerusalem.

If this prophecy is indeed related to Josiah's reform, the obliteration of Baalism proceeded a pace before the Babylonian scourge actually executed judgement against Judah. However, thorough though the reform was, it did not remove *all* the remnants of Baal worship. This was accomplished only by the destruction of Jerusalem by Nebuchadnezzar.

CHEMARIM WITH THE PRIESTS . . .

Chemarim in Aramaic means priests. Its literal meaning is "black." It applied to the priests because of their black robes.

Probably both the priests of Baal and the apostate priests of Jehovah are meant here. Just as Zephaniah begins his pronouncement of universal judgement by focusing on Judah, within Judah the focus is on Jerusalem, within Jerusalem "this place" or the temple, within the temple the priesthood. The prophet obviously believes in coming directly to the source of Baalism among God's people.

THE HOSTS OF HEAVEN ON THE HOUSETOPS . . . v. 5

In addition to Baal, the perenniel blight on Judah's faith, the Assyrian worship of the planets, has also infected the people of God. This despicable practice, enjoying an American revival in modern preoccupation with horoscopes, was imported from Nineveh in the days of the wicked Manasseh. (cf. *II Kings 21:3*) It continued to the last in Judah. (cf. *Jeremiah 32:29*)

The housetops mentioned here are the flat roofs of Palestinian homes which were the ideal vantage point from which to worship "the hosts of heaven."

SWEAR TO JEHOVAH . . . SWEAR BY MALCOM . . .

Malcom (Milcom) here means literally "their king." It is etomologically related to Moloch, the Phoenician name for Baal. As sun god, Baal was king of all the heavenly hosts!

JUDGEMENT OF GOD 1:5, 6

Those who swear to Jehovah and swear by Malcom are practicing a religious syncretism similar to that advocated in our day. In Zephaniah's day religious syncretism was a mixture of Jehovah worship and Baal worship. Both "Baal" and "Jehovah" mean "Lord." The worshippers, by appealing (swearing) to the authority of both, were attempting to serve two masters.

This same approach is advocated today as Christianity searches for some peaceful co-existence with Islam, Judaism, Buddhism, etc. W. A. Visser-Hooft, in his book *No Other Name,* 1963, makes an heroic effort to call attention to this influence. His efforts seem to have been in vain, possibly because of his stance as a former general secretary of the World Council of Churches, which is itself a form of religious syncretism.

Colin W. Williams, dean of Yale Divinity School, is quoted as saying, " . . . I hold open that what is true for the Buddhist in his situation may be as valid for him as mine is for me."

Max Therian, speaking before the World Council in New Delhi, echoed this same approach to Islam on the ground that truth and charity were taught by both Mohammed and Jesus and that both are recognized as Master and Prophet.

In both Zephaniah's day and ours the problem of syncretism is a problem of authority. In Judah there was a willing compromise of Jehovah's authority with that of Baal. In our time the premise is situationalism in which the presupposition of absolute authority is summarily dismissed. In either case, the Biblical answer is *"thus saith the Lord!"*

THEM THAT . . . TURN BACK . . .
HAVE NOT SOUGHT . . . NOR INQUIRED . . . v. 6

Indifference to and unconcern for Jehovah are described here. Then as now, there were those who, surrounded by evil heinous enough to merit the judgement of God, were simply satisfied to live out their lives without considering God at all.

To inquire of God is to attend formal worship, particularly the hours of prayer. (cf. *Psalm 10:4*)

In pronouncing punishment against such indifference (v. 12) the prophet describes it as "men that are settled on their lees that say in their heart Jehovah will not do good, neither will He do evil." This amounts to spiritual stagnation just as fermented wine was left for a time on the "lees" to allow solid matter suspended in it to settle, so the unfeeling indifference of some in Judah has left them with a

1:7-9   ZEPHANIAH

congealing of the soul. Perhaps God's judgement will surprise none so much as these.

HOLD THY PEACE . . . v. 7

As the indifferent have had nothing meaningful to say for, to, or about God, they are to be dumb in the presence of His judgement.

The Lord has prepared these evil backsliders as a sacrifice. (cp. *Isaiah 34:6, Jeremiah 46:10, Ezekiel 39:17*) The despised Chaldeans are called to be His guests. They will feast on the remains of Judah as the priests feasted on the remains of sacrifices on feast days. Nebuchadnezzar was invited to come to take vengeance on Jerusalem. (*Jeremiah 25:9*)

SUCH AS ARE CLOTHED IN FOREIGN APPAREL . . . v. 8

Jehovah had regulated the attire of His people in a measure. (*Numbers 15:38-f, Deuteronomy 22:11-f,* cp. *Matthew 23:5*) Special dress was designed to remind them they were in a special relationship to God.

Beyond the mere copying of foreign dress is the implied aping of foreign customs which inevitably accompanies it. The adopting of foreign dress and customs led to the acceptance of foreign religions. There was a gradual blending of Judah with her neighbors until there was little to distinguish the one from the other.

ALL THOSE THAT LEAP OVER THE THRESHOLD . . . v. 9

Several possible implications are suggested here. The priests of the Philistine god, Dagon, avoided stepping on the threshold of their temple because their god had fallen across it (*I Samuel 5:5*). When the Judeans emulated this practice, they were yielding to idolatry.

Household deities may have entered into this leaping over the threshold. Sacrifices of food were left on the threshold for such gods so that the threshold constituted an altar. As such, it was not to be desecrated by stepping directly on it.

Perhaps Zephaniah intends rather to single out by this phrase those who in their haste to intrude on the privacy of their neighbors or to rob and ransack their houses, leaped across the threshold.

In any of these cases, the offense is worthy of punishment.

THAT FILL . . . WITH DECEIT . . .

The house of the master refers to the household in which one was employed. Those who are disloyal to their employers, who enrich themselves at their employer's expense are to suffer God's judgment.

JUDGEMENT OF GOD 1:10-13

THERE SHALL BE THE NOISE OF A CRY ... v. 10-13

The fish gate was located in the north wall of Jerusalem. When the invading Babylonians came against Jerusalem they would come from the north. From that direction the alarm would sound throughout the city.

The second quarter was a northern suburb of Jerusalem, new in Josiah's day. It also would be in the line of Babylonian march.

"The hills" likely refers to the hills immediately north of Jerusalem. Scopus, northeast of the city has long been inhabited as a section of Jerusalem, but without the city walls. Invading armies captured this hill and, because of its commanding view of the city, made it their field headquarters.

YE INHABITANTS OF MAKTESH ... v. 11

Between the easter and western hills on the northern outskirts of Jerusalem is the valley of Maktesh. The name means "hollow place." (*Judges 15:19*) Those who dwelt there would be directly in the path of any invader from the north.

"*People of Canaan*" here probably means merchants. Not only those who lived in the northern outskirts of the city, but those who came there to trade would be caught in the judgemental onslaught.

Zephaniah describes the sudden anguished cry of all who stood in the path of the Babylonians.

I WILL SEARCH ... WITH LAMPS ... v. 12

God's judgement will be exhaustive; none will escape. This searching is directed against those whose sin was indifference. (See above on v. 6) By their non-commitment they have sought to escape from responsibility for the sins against which God's wrath is directed. They have remained obscure ... the "silent majority" will not be held unaccountable for the evil all about them. God will search them out for their own punishment.

THEIR WEALTH SHALL BECOME ... SPOIL ... v. 13

Indifference not only is no assurance of lack of moral responsibility. It actually becomes a danger in itself. Non-commitment cannot protect property from an invading army.

Because these have remained indifferent to God and to conditions about them, they will not be allowed to reap what they produced by their labor. Others will lay waste their vineyards. (Cp. *Deuteronomy 28:30, Amos 5:11, Micah 6:15*)

1:13-15   ZEPHANIAH

The indifferent are self-content in their suburban homes. They have escaped the immediate consequence of the evil of the city. But in God's judgement against the city all they have secured by their indolence will be lost. Modern suburbia take heed!

THE GREAT DAY OF JEHOVAH IS NEAR . . . v. 14

Here again is the prophetic "Day of the Lord," the day in which Jehovah would directly intervene in the affairs of man's history in such a way as to reveal His judgement and redemption. The Jews, smug in their racial identity, were prone to view the day as one of extreme gladness for themselves and of extreme discomfiture for the Gentiles.

Zephaniah's warning is that the day will be one of anguish for the unfaithful among God's people.

Perhaps the most important idea just here is the nearness of the day. This same urgency was evident in the first century church. Both in regard to the prophets and to the New Testament church, modern theologians have insinuated that those who felt such a nearness of the "Day of Jehovah" were mistaken. The passage of time, it is said, proves that mistake.

No so! In every age of history, God works in human affairs on the basis of the same principles. Hence there is evidence in every age of the impending judgements of God. One need only visit the lands of the Bible and walk among the ruins of twenty-two fallen civilizations to realize that urgency concerning God's judgement is well-founded. When the final curtain is about to fall on the history of humanity, and the last "Day of the Lord" is indeed imminent, the "signs of the times" will be the same.

We live in a time when these "signs" are all about us. Whether they portent the declining days of our culture and the beginning of another era, or the soon coming of the final "last Day" is irrelevant. In either case, we would be fools not to share with the prophets and the New Testament church the sense of urgent need for repentant preparation. We, as Zephaniah, need desperately to know the day is so near that the "voice" of it can already be heard.

THAT DAY IS A DAY OF WRATH . . . v. 15-18

In his powerful book, *"Death In The City"* (Inter-Varsity Press, 1969). Francis Schaeffer says " . . . anyone who is unwilling to speak of the wrath of God does not understand the Christian faith." If we allow "the Christian faith" to include those covenant people who looked forward to His coming as well as those who look to it as a *fait accompli,* Mr. Schaeffer's statement could have been directed to Zephaniah's readers. It is precisely because they, and we, are under God's wrath that the judgement must come. It is because we stand guilty and unfit for His presence that He must come to us. As Dr. Schaeffer points out " . . . there is a moral law of the universe and that basic law is the character of God Himself." So then, whether it is Zephaniah or Paul (eg. *Roman 1:18-f)* or a twentieth century preacher who speaks of judgement day and God's wrath, he is discussing the inevitable. Whether the syncretistic denial of this truth comes from a Baal worshipper or a modern existentialist, it is false prophecy and needs to be denounced as such.

Zephaniah's description of the day of wrath in these verses pictures the physical destruction occasioned by God's wrath implemented by Nebuchadnezzar. It may describe what lies in our own future. Figuratively, it certainly depicts the spiritual suffering in the last judgement day by those who know not God.

CALL TO REPENTANCE . . . 2:1-3

God's threatenings are always designed to call men back to Him. Even though He knows few will repent, He is "not willing that any should perish." (*II Peter 3:9*)

Probably these three verses belong to chapter one. They form the usual high note upon which the prophets close a section of threatenings. The purpose of such denunciations as we have just considered is always to bring about repentance and cleansing. Therefore the prophet concludes with a note of hope.

The meek, *ie.* the humble before God, those with the moral courage to see the truth of the prophet's preaching are called to act in concert, to gather together. Here is the remnant on the eve of judgement, drawn together in a common repentance which bespeaks the truth that even the faithful have not always acted according to their faith.

The word "gather" describes a stooping such as is done in the gleaning of fields. It is to be done "before the day pass as the chaff." The day of judgement is a time of harvest. Not only are the unfaithful punished but the faithful are rewarded.

The nation, *per se,* has no shame, Judah's submission to the wooing of Baal marks her as no different from other nations. However, the meek within her still may find hope in gleaning themselves from the whole.

Verse three is a bridge between the pronouncements against Judah in chapter one and the following declaration of judgement against Judah's neighbors. *All* the meek of the earth are called upon to seek Jehovah. Peter's discovery that " . . . in every nation he that feareth him, and worketh righteousness, is acceptable to Him," (*Acts 10:35*) is the discovery of eternal truth.

The "meek of the earth" are presented by Zephaniah as they "that have kept His ordinances." This same concept is found in Paul's Roman letter. *Romans 2:14-15* states, "When Gentiles that have not the law do by nature the things of the law, are a law unto themselves; in that they show the work of the law written in their hearts. their conscience bearing witness therewith, and their thoughts one with another accusing or else excusing them."

The Jews' own Bible was indeed the answer to the Jews' narrowness. *Micah 6:8 (b-c)* has been lived by others. In all the prophets, escape from God's wrath, and conversely the receiving of His mercy are matters of ethics and morality rather than nationality. The admonition is to seek meekness.

Meekness, we repeat, is the moral courage to be humble before God. Jesus' statement is that the meek shall inherit the earth. (*Matthew 5:5*) The achievements of those who are haughty before God are always temporary because they will not stand in the day of Jehovah.

Chapter XX—*Questions*
Judgement of God

1. Discuss Zephaniah's claim to inspiration.
2. Trace the idea of judgement by fire.
3. What are the stumbling blocks which cause man to sin? (1:3)
4. Who are "the hosts of heaven on the housetops?"
5. Discuss the religious syncretism of Zephaniah's day as seen in Judah's compromise with strange gods as it typifies modern religious syncretism.
6. Who will likely be most surprised by God's judgement? (1:6)
7. Discuss Zephaniah's pronouncement of judgement against Judah in light of the principle set down in *I Peter 4:17*.
8. Who are those "clothed in foreign apparel?" (v. 8)
9. Who are "those that leap over the threshold?" (v. 9)
10. When the invading Babylonians came against Jerusalem they came from the _____.

JUDGEMENT OF GOD IS UNIVERSAL 2:4-15

11. Discuss "I will search with lamps." (v. 12)
12. Were the apostles and the prophets mistaken as to the soon coming of the final Day of the Lord? Explain.
13. How do you reconcile the wrath of God and the love of God?
14. God's threatenings are always a call to _____.
15. Who are "the meek?"
16. Meekness is _____ _____.

CHAPTER XXI
THE JUDGMENT OF GOD IS UNIVERSAL
ZEPHANIAH 2:4-15

RV . . . For Gaza shall be forsaken, and Ashkelon a desolation; they shall drive out Ashdod at noonday, and Ekron sholl be rooted up. Woe unto the inhabitants of the seacoast, the nation of the Cherethites! The word of Jehovah is against you, O Canaan, the land of the Philistines; I will destroy thee, that there shall be no inhabitant. And the sea-coast shall be pastures, with cottages for shepherds and folds for flocks. And the coast shall be for the remnant of the house of Judah; they shall feed their flocks thereupon; in the houses of Ashkelon shall they lie down in the evening; for Jehovah their God will visit them, and bring back their captivity. I have heard the reproach of Moab, and the revilings of the children of Ammon, wherewith they have reproached my people, and magnified themselves against their border. Therefore as I live, saith Jehovah of hosts, the God of Israel, Surely Moab shall be as Sodom, and the children of Ammon as Gomorrah, a possession of nettles, and saltpits, and a perpetual desolation: the residue of my people shall make a prey of them, and the remnant of my nation shall inherit them. This shall they have for their pride because they have reproached and magnified themselves against the people of Jehovah of hosts. Jehovah will be terrible unto them; for he will famish all the gods of the earth; and men shall worship him, every one from his place, even all the isles of the nations. Ye Ethiopians also, ye shall be slain by my sword. And he will stretch out his hand against the north, and destroy Assyria and will make Nineveh a desolation, and dry like the wilderness. And herds shall lie down in the midst of her, all the beasts of the nations: both the pelican and the porcupine shall lodge in the capitals thereof; their voice shall sing in the windows; desolation shall be in the thresholds; for he hath laid bare the cedar-work. This is the joyous city that dwelt carelessly, that said in her heart, I am, and there is none besides me; how is she become a desolation, a place for beasts to lie down in! every one that passeth by her shall hiss, and wag his hand.

LXX . . . For Gaza shall be utterly spoiled, and Ascalon shall be destroyed; and Azotus shall be cast forth at noon-day, and Accaron shall be rooted up. Woe to them that dwell on the border of the sea, neighbours of the Cretans! the word of the Lord is against you, O Chanaan, land of the Philistines, and I will destroy you out of your dwelling-place. And Crete shall be a pasture of flocks, and a fold of sheep. And the sea coast shall be for the remnant of the house of Juda; they shall pasture upon them in the houses of Ascalon; they shall rest in the evening because of the children of Juda; for the Lord their God has visited them, and he will turn away their captivity. I have heard the revilings of Moab, and the insults of the children of Ammon, wherewith they have reviled my people, and magnified themselves against my coasts. Therefore, as I live, saith the Lord of hosts, the God of Israel, Moab shall be as Sodoma, and the children of Ammon as Gomorha; and Damascus shall be left as a heap of the threshing-floor, and desolate for ever: and the remnant of my people shall plunder them, and the remnant of my nation shall inherit them. Thus is their punishment in return for their haughtiness, because they have reproached and magnified themselves against the Lord Almighty. The Lord shall appear against them, and shall utterly destroy all the gods of the nations of the earth; and they shall worship him every one from his place, even all the islands of the nations. Ye Ethiopians also are the slain of my sword. And he shall stretch forth his hand against the north and destroy the Assyrian, and make Nineveh a dry wilderness, even as a desert. And flocks, and all the wild beasts of the land, and chameleons shall feed in the midst therof: and hedgehogs shall lodge in the ceilings thereof; and wild beasts shall cry in the breaches thereof, and ravens in her porches, whereas her loftiness was as a cedar. This is the scornful city that dwells securely, that says in her heart, I am, and there is no longer any to be after me: how is she become desolate, a habitation of wild beasts? every one that passes through her shall hiss, and shake his hands.

COMMENTS

Just as God's mercies are universal, so is His wrath. Those who have not the law not only may keep the essential moral requirements of it and thus be excused by their consciences, they may likewise also

JUDGEMENT OF GOD IS UNIVERSAL 2:4-15

violate this moral reality to their own detriment. (*Romans 2:15*) In fact this is precisely what the Bible claims they have done. (*Romans 3:9-23*)

The often heard argument made by those who do not believe in missions; that the people who have not heard are excused somehow by their ignorance will not stand up in light of either the Old Testament or the New. They have violated the light of their own consciences and so stand as objects of God's wrath along with those who have access to His written Word. Surely the love of Christ in us ought to drive us to give them the same chance to repent as ourselves.

(Verses 4-7) In verses four through seven, Zephaniah names the areas to the south and west of Judah who are to feel God's wrath along with the Hebrews. The statements are general rather than descriptive as had been Nahum's rather delighted picture of Nineveh's downfall. Nevertheless, the names roll from the prophet's pen like the muffled drums of a funeral dirge. Gaza . . . forsaken, Ashkelon . . . desolation, Ashdod . . . driven out at noon, Ekron . . . rooted up, the Cherethites . . . woe, the Philistines . . . destroyed. The entire coast will be pasture land.

Those who are left behind of Judah will pasture their flocks in the lands and cities of the condemned peoples. The shepherds will sleep at night in their deserted homes. The remnant shall return from Babylon to inhabit their land.

Four of the cities mentioned here, Gaza, Ashkelon, Ashdod and Ekron are chief cities of the Philistines. The fifth, Gath, was wiped out earlier by the Assyrians and so is not mentioned by Zephaniah in regard to the Babylonian invasion.

These sea people, whose entrance into Canaan had been contemporary with that of Abraham and who had been a constant thorn in the Hebrews' side, would now feel the devastating wrath of God as never before.

Verses eight through eleven pronounce judgement against the nations of trans-Jordan. For centuries they have spoken against God's people. Now Ammon and Moab will feel His wrath. (cp. *Jeremiah 48:27-29, Isaiah 16:6, Ezekiel 21:28, 25:3, 6, 8*) They had long boasted they would annex land belonging to the Hebrews. Now, lest they carry out their boast during the captivity of Judah, they will share that captivity! The desolation described here is evident today.

The gods who once were worshipped in Ammon and Moab are no more. Jehovah worship, even when He is called Allah, as in Moab and Ammon today, is a far cry from the pagan abomination called Moloch.

Zephaniah's promise is that, when all the false gods are made desolate, famished by God, every man will worship Jehovah in his own place, even all the isles and nations.

There are Messianic overtones here. Jesus said concerning His coming as Messiah that " . . . neither in this mountain (Samaritan Gerazim) nor in Jerusalem shall ye worship the Father . . . but the hour cometh and now is, when the true worshippers shall worship the Father in spirit and truth . . . " (*John 4:23-f*) The universal worship of Jehovah in every place rather than in a particular "holy land" was more than an after-thought on Jesus' part. It was the main thrust of the Old Testament.

Zephaniah, in verses twelve and following, broadens the scope of this pronouncement. Not only are Judah and her near neighbors to feel the sting of God's wrath, far way Ethiopia and Assyria and Nineveh shall feel it also.

The Hebrew *Kushim,* translated Ethiopians in verse twelve, included parts of Arabia and all of Nubia. It may possibly also include Egypt at this period when the Nile was ruled by Ethiopic dynasties.

Nineveh, five hundred miles to the northeast of Judah, is singled out by Nahum and her final judgement predicted in vivid detail. Here Zephaniah includes her among the other far flung Gentile peoples. Brief though it is, Zephaniah's picture of Nineveh's desolation is every bit as expressive as Nahum's.

All those included in this sweeping indictment shall feel the sword of the Lord, just as the Philistines, Moab, and Ammon. "My sword" is whatever instrument of judgement God uses. (cp. *Isaiah 34:5, Ezekiel*

Ethiopia was neither an enemy nor a neighbor of Israel or Judah. It is apparently named here to indicate the universality of God's judgement. It is in this sense that the entire passage is frought with undefined but very definite Messianic and eschatological overtones.

Chapter XXI—*Questions*

The Judgement of God is Universal

1. Just as God's mercies are universal, so is His _____.
2. How do you answer the opinion that those who have never heard the Word of God will be saved in their ignorance?
3. Locate, on a map, the cities and areas mentioned in chapter 2:4-15.

4. Why does the prophet pronounce God's judgement against people who were neither neighbors nor enemies of Judah?
5. Discuss the Messianic overtones of this passage . . . eschatological overtones.

CHAPTER XXII
COMFORT AND CONSOLATION

REAFFIRMATION OF JUDGEMENT . . . Zephaniah 3:1-8

RV . . . Woe to her that is rebellious and polluted! to the oppressing city! She obeyed not the voice; she received not correction; she trusted not in Jehovah; she drew not near to her God. Her princes in the midst of her are roaring lions; her judges are evening wolves; they leave nothing till the morrow. Her prophets are light and treacherous persons; her priests have profaned the sanctuary, they have done violence to the law. Jehovah in the midst of her is righteous; he will not do iniquity; every morning doth he bring his justice to light, he faileth not; but the unjust knoweth no shame. I have cut off nations; their battlements are desolate; I have made their streets waste, so that none passeth by; their cities are destroyed so that there is no man, so that there is no inhabitant. I said, Only fear thou me; receive correction; so her dwelling shall not be cut off, according to all that I have appointed concerning her: but they rose early and corrupted all their doings. Therefore wait ye for me, saith Jehovah, until the day that I rise up to the prey; for my determination is to gather the nations, that I may assemble the kingdoms, to pour upon them mine indignation, even all my fierce anger; for all the earth shall be devoured with the fire of my jealously.

LXX . . . Alas the glorious and ransomed city. The dove hearkened not to the voice; she received not correction; she trusted not in the Lord, and she drew not near to her God. Her princes within her were as roaring lions, her judges as the wolves of Arabia; they remained not till the morrow. Her prophets are light and scornful men: her priests profane the holy things, and sinfully transgress the law. But the just Lord is in the midst of her, and he will never do an unjust thing: morning by morning he will bring out his judgement to the light, and it is not hidden, and he knows not injustice by extortion, nor injustice in strife. I have brought down the proud with destruction; their corners are destroyed: I will make their ways completely waste, so that none shall go through: their cities are come to an end, by reason of

3:1-8   ZEPHANIAH

no man living or dwelling in them. I said, But do ye fear me, and receive instruction, and ye shall not be cut off from the face of the land for all the vengeance I have brought upon her; prepare thou, rise early: all their produce is spoilt. Therefore wait upon me, saith the Lord, until the day when I rise up for a witness: because my judgement shall be on the gatherings of the nations, to draw to me kings, to pour out upon them all my fierce anger: for the whole earth shall be consumed with the fire of my jealousy.

COMMENTS

In chapters *1:2-2:3,* social sin and injustice are hardly noted. In the section before us, Zephaniah briefly but emphatically indicates that it is social injustice, such as that spelled out by Micah, Amos and Isaiah, for which Israel will be led captive. This supreme sin, "man's inhumanity to man," is the inevitable consequence of the false religion dealt with in Zephaniah's first two chapters.

HER THAT IS REBELLIOUS . . . v. 1

Jerusalem is not named, but is obviously intended. Her rebellion against Jehovah worship has caused her social pollution. The oppression of the "have nots" by the "haves" is the consequence of the religious syncretism of the "haves."

The twentieth century nonsense that "it doesn't make any difference what one believes so long as he is sincere" is proven erroneous in the history of Judah's punishment. The social evil in America today is in large measure the result of the same sort of religious non-commitment that brought about the downfall of Judah. No culture can remain just and equitable that does not have a certain moral and spiritual base. The social inequity resulting from a lack of religious certainty is the dry rot which destroys civilizations. Mere lip service to Jehovah is not enough.

OBEYED NOT . . . RECEIVED NOT . . . TRUSTED NOT . . . DREW NOT . . . v. 2

The prophet's charge of rebellion against Jerusalem is spelled out in verse two. Four failures have brought her to the brink of destruction. *First,* she *obeyed not* the voice of God. *Hebrews 1:1* tells of God speaking to the fathers in the prophets. Their voice was His voice. His people did not obey.

COMFORT AND CONSOLATION   3:2-4

Moreover, when God sent other prophets to correct her failure to hear, Jerusalem (the spiritual center of Judah) did not *recieve* the correction. This stiff-necked attitude compounded to sin and pushed the nation farther down the slopes toward disaster.

She *trusted* not Jehovah. This would seem, in light of the first two charges, to be self-evident. No one really trusts God who does not heed His spokesmen. The prophet, in this third indictment, calls attention to Judah's alliances with foreign powers. Rather than trust Jehovah's might for her national security, Jerusalem aligned herself with the Assyrian-Egyptian power block in the struggle with Babylon. She would find herself on the losing side. America, whose currency bears the inscription "in God we trust," seems unable to learn this lesson.

The final charge against Judah is that she *drew not* near to God. Instead, she sought Baal. The failure of Judah was not passive merely. She not only failed to hear and trust, she actively sought false gods.

HER PRINCES . . . HER JUDGES . . .
HER PROPHETS . . . HER PRIESTS . . . v. 3-4

These verses are reminiscent of Micha's denunciation of the various influential classes in the culture of the people. Her *princes, ie.* those who held political authority over the people, are roaring lions. They, as Satan, go about "seeking whom they may devour." (cp. *Ezekiel 25:27*)

Her *judges* are as wolves in the evening. Wolves feed at night, beginning at dusk and by morning there is little left of their victims. So with the common people who are at the mercy of corrupt courts. A corrupt judicial is ever the companion of an evil executive.

Her *prophets* are light and treacherous persons. These, more than any other, must answer for Judah's corrupt religion. As Micah accused them, they preached what their wealthy listeners wanted to hear rather than thundering forth God's truth. They proclaimed the imaginings of their own minds rather than God's Word. A dangerous parallel could be drawn here by comparing the practice of these prophets to the modern preacher of topical sermons who neglects the expository treatment of God's Word.

Her *priests* have profaned the sanctuary. The present day American church-goer, with his blase' attitude toward things sacred cannot appreciate the seriousness of this offense. One of the functions of the priests of Levi was to guard the sanctity of the Holy Place. The priests to whom Zephaniah writes have become so worldly-minded, so tolerant of false religion, they are no longer concerned for the sacredness of the temple. (cp. *Ezekiel 22:26*) They perverted the law to suit their own advantage while practicing a narrow legalism generally. They had forgotten the dramatic lesson of Uzzah who was struck dead for placing unclean hands on the sacred ark. (*II Samuel 6:7*)

JEHOVAH IN THE MIDST . . . v. 5

God has not left His people. In the midst of rebellion and injustice, He is faithful to the covenant. He has not been turned aside from His purpose by the unfaithfulness of the people.

"*Every morning He brings justice to light . . .* " The worship of Baal began with greeting him at dawn in the rising sun. At this very hour when the people's unfaithfulness reached its daily pinnacle, Jehovah brings justice to light. His moral standards and His righteousness are as reliable, and more so than the rising of the sun. But the people refuse to see.

"*The unjust knoweth no shame.*" Even the constancy of Jehovah in the midst of their unfaithfulness does not shame them. They are unmoved in their pursuit of unrighteousness and error.

I HAVE CUT OFF THE NATIONS . . . v. 6

God's righteous judgements are not limited alone to Judah. The prophet has already listed the sentences of God against the surrounding Gentiles. It is God, not Zephaniah, who has cut off the nations. The desolation and ruin of those named in the previous chapter are not the result of Jewish nationalism but of God's universal judgement.

The archives of history are filled with the records of those nations cut down by God's righteous judgement because "knowing God, they glorified Him not as God . . . "(*Romans 1:21*) Judah had but to look north to Israel to remember how true this is and how certain are God's judgements.

ONLY FEAR THOU ME . . . v. 7

God still speaks through Zephaniah. He calls the Hebrews back to the rudimentary beginning of wisdom. (cp. *Proverbs 9:10*)

Paul, quoting Psalm after Psalm, will prove that all social evil such as that against which the prophets spoke are the result of failure to fear God. He will list lack of righteousness, and understanding, failure to seek God, turning aside from His purpose, failure to do good, all spiritual uncleanness, deceitful speech, cursing and bitterness, war and destruction and misery and the futile search for peace as the consequences of not fearing Him. (cf. *Roman 3:9-18*)

COMFORT AND CONSOLATION 3:7-9

One can only shudder today at the church member whose twisted misinformation about God's love has led him to a contemptuous familiarity which does not believe one should or must fear Jehovah. God's plea through Zephaniah is *only fear me.* Only . . .just . . . please! A deep and genuine fear of God will bring about the correction of the evil against which judgement must otherwise come

BUT THEY ROSE EARLY AND CORRUPTED . . .

Despite God's plea to fear Him, the people ignored His plea and rose up early to greet the sun god. In so doing, they paved the way for all other corruption.

UNTIL THE DAY . . . v. 8

Here Zephaniah returns to the theme struck in *1:14.* The great Day of Jehovah is again called to mind as the decisive day on which He will gather the nations before Him in wrath.

The meek . . . those who are humble before God (*Zephaniah 2:3*) . . . are called to wait for that day when He will prey upon His enemies. In that day when Jehovah's wrath is poured out to devour the earth with fire (cp. *II Peter 3:7*) the meek shall inherit the new earth.

The idea of destruction by fire in relations to God's judgement is fairly distributed throughout the Bible. Joel spoke of a time which would be revealed in blood and fire and vapor of smoke (*Joel 2:30*). *Psalm 50:3* depicts God's coming in company with a devouring fire. Isaiah wrote of similar phenomena. (*Isaiah 29:6, 30:30, 66:15-16*) We have heard Nahum speak of the hills burning and the earth burning in His presence. (*Nahum 1:5, 6*) Malachi will tell us of the day of the Lord burning as an oven.

We are something less than wise not to fear Him!

Those nations found guilty in Jehovah's court of justice will feel the fiery fierceness of fire that is to devour the adversary. (*Hebrews 10:27*)

This gathering need not be seen as taking place in Jerusalem. There is no Biblical proof for the tradition that the final judgement will take place in the Kidron valley. The idea is that all nations simultaneously and universally are judged by God. His righteousness will flow across the earth as the fiery lava of a volcano consuming all that stand in the way of His covenant purpose.

THE PROMISE OF REDEMPTION . . . Zephaniah 3:9-13

RV . . . For then will I turn to the peoples a pure language, that they may all call upon the name of Jehovah, to serve him with one consent.

225

3:9-13   ZEPHANIAH

From beyond the rivers of Ethiopia my suppliants, even the daughter of my dispersed, shall bring mine offering. In that day shalt thou not be put to shame for all thy doings, wherein thou hast transgressed against me; for then I will take away out of the midst of thee thy proudly exaulting ones, and thou shalt no more be haughty in my holy mountain. But I will leave in the midst of thee an afflicted and poor people, and they shall take refuge in the name of Jehovah. The remnant of Israel shall not do iniquity, nor speak lies; neither shall a deceitful tongue be found in their mouth; for they shall feed and lie down, and none shall make them afraid.

LXX . . . For then will I turn to the peoples a tongue for her generation, that all may call on the name of the Lord, to serve him under one yoke. From the boundaries of the rivers of Ethiopia will I receive my dispersed ones; they shall offer sacrifices to me. In that day thou shalt not be ashamed of all thy practices, wherein thou hast transgressed against me: for then will I take away from thee thy disdainful pride, and thou shalt no more magnify thyself upon my holy mountain. And I will leave in thee a meek and lowly people; and the remnant of Israel shall fear the name of the Lord, and shall do no iniquity, neither shall they speak vanity; neither shall a deceitful tongue be found in their mouth: for they shall feed, and lie down, and there shall be none to terrify them.

COMMENTS

The purpose for which God's wrath is poured out in human history is a redemptive purpose. Zephaniah sees, as do the other prophets, the promise of repentance and consequent redemption. He is just, not arbitrary. He does not punish out of vindictive petulance but out of love. *(Hebrews 12:6)* His judgements are therapeutic, not merely punitive. Ultimately He chastens to save.

The hope comes to Zephaniah like a calm after a hurricane.

A PURE LANGUAGE . . . v. 9

"For then" *ie.* following the judgement just described, there is reason for hope.

I will "turn" *ie.* I will change the nature. The Psalmist cried, "Create within me a pure heart, O God." *(Psalm 51-10)* Paul wrote ". . . if any man is in Christ, he is a new creature: the old things are passed away; behold they are become new." *(II Cor. 5:17)*

COMFORT AND COSOLATION   3:9-11

Evidence of this redemptive reconciliation is a "pure language" or more accurately, a *clean lip*. Isaiah, called by God to speak for Him, cried out "I am a man of unclean lips." *(Isaiah 6:5)* And after he had been purged with fire from the altar, God said to him, "Thine iniquity is taken away, and thy sin is forgiven."

A purified heart, redeemed and reconciled to God always results in pure speech.

... SERVE HIM WITH ONE CONSENT ...

Those who are redeemed not only *may* but *will* serve Him. Jesus promised that the living water of redemption would, in him who drinks, become a fountain, bubbling over to eternal life. (cf. *John 4:14*)

And their service will be with "one consent" . . . more literally with *one shoulder*. As several oxen pushing against a single yoke, they will serve as one. Both the redeemed of Israel and the purged nations will "in that day" serve Him as one. Here is a glimpse of the unity which characterized the New Testament church which, from Antioch forward was a fellowship of those redeemed from Israel and those purified from among the nations.

FROM BEYOND THE RIVERS . . . v. 10

From the long list of those to whom God's wrath would be revealed in judgement Zephaniah selects Ethiopia (see above on *2:12*) to represent the redeemed from among the nations.

This company of the reconciled is also to include Jews from among the dispersion, *ie.* those who were scattered among the nations. It was to the synagogues of the diaspora that Paul first took the gospel in every city. The church, fifteen years after her birth in Judaism, had become a fellowship of redeemed from every kindred and nation.

This concept of universal salvation is not unknown to the Old Testament. In fact, Jesus saw in such prophetic passages the meaning of the entire Old Testament. (Cp. *Luke 24:44-f)*

The reader will do well here to review *Isaiah 2:2-4, Micah 4:1-4, Isaiah 11:9, 19:23-25, 49:5-6*. To pursue the idea of universal salvation in the Old Testament, an excellent reference work is Wm. O. Carver's, *Missions In The Plan of The Ages*, Broadman Press, Nashville, Tenn.

IN THAT DAY THOU SHALT NOT BE PUT TO SHAME . . .
v. 11

In the day when the fires of divine judgement shall have purged men of all nations, promises the prophet, you will not be made ashamed for those things in which you have transgressed. What a promise! Paul exalted in this truth, "There is therefore now no condemnation to them that are in Christ Jesus!" *(Romans 8:1)* When Jesus received in our behalf the judgement of God upon our sin *(II Corinthians 5:21)*, He purged us of all those things for which we need be ashamed.

Zephaniah points out that the lack of any reason for shame on the part of the redeemed is due to God's removal from their midst the boastful and proud. Again we are reminded of Paul's letters. Again and again he reminds the redeemed that all reason for boasting is removed in the processes of redemption. (eg. *Romans 3:27, I Corinthians 3:21, 4:7, Galatians 6:14)* Since Christ received for all of us the wrath of God for our sins, none among the redeemed has any reason to boast. Therefore, no one has any reason to be ashamed of the sin from which he was redeemed, since there are no exceptions. All have sinned and all, in Him, have been redeemed. No Christian has any right to a guilt complex or an inferiority complex.

I WILL LEAVE . . . AN AFFLICTED AND POOR PEOPLE . . . v. 12

"Blessed" . . . said Jesus, "are the poor in spirit, for theirs is the kingdom of heaven." *(Matthew 5:3)* To be poor in spirit—"afflicted and poor" as Zephaniah has it—is to recognize that we are of ourselves unprofitable to God—fit subjects for His wrath. Having exacted our due punishment on Calvary, God leaves us poor—wholly dependant upon Him, but in this dependance we are rich beyond our fondest hopes. O, the depth of the riches of God's love!

THE REMNANT OF ISRAEL SHALL NOT DO INIQUITY . . . v. 13

The remnant is again, as in Isaiah and Micah *et al,* God's redeemed covenant people on the redemption side of God's wrath. They were those who passed through the captivity, God's punishment for former sin . . . they are now those who have passed through Calvary, by being united with Christ's death. In any context the remnant are God's covenant people.

The impure speech of an un-redeemed heart is not to be found among God's people. Those whom God has cleansed will remain after all others have been burned away in the consuming wrath of God's judgement. The redeemed are to become like their God. No untruth, *ie.* unreality, is to be found among them.

Here, as in many other Old Testament passages, God's people are pictured as a flock, lying down in the security of His fold. (cp. *Psalm*

COMFORT AND CONSOLATION   3:14-20

23, Isaiah 17:2, Ezekiel 34:25,28)   This security is only for those who have their refuge in Jehovah.

PORTRAIT OF THE REDEEMED . . . Zephaniah 3:14-20

RV . . . Sing, O daughter of Zion; shout, O Israel; be glad and rejoice with all the heart, O daughter of Jerusalem. Jehovah hath taken away thy judgements, he hath cast out thine enemy: the King of Israel, even Jehovah, is in the midst of thee; thou shalt not fear evil any more. In that day it shall be said to Jerusalem, Fear thou not; O Zion, let not thy hands be slack. Jehovah thy God is in the midst of thee, a mighty one who will save; he will rejoice over thee with joy; over thee with singing. I will gather them that sorrow for the solemn assembly, who were of thee; to whom the burden upon her was a reproach. Behold, at that time I will deal with all them that afflict thee; and I will save that which is lame, and gather that which was driven away; and I will make them a praise and a name, whose shame hath been in all the earth. At that time will I bring you in, and at that time will I gather you; for I will make you a name and a praise among all the peoples of the earth, when I bring back your captivity before your eyes, saith Jehovah.

LXX . . . Rejoice, O daughter of Sion; cry aloud, O daughter of Jerusalem; rejoice and delight thyself with all thine heart, O daughter of Jerusalem. The Lord has taken away thine iniquities, he has ransomed thee from the hand of thine enemies: the Lord, the King of Israel, is in the midst of thee: thou shall not see evil any more. At that time the Lord shall say to Jerusalem, Be of good courage, Sion; let not thine hands be slack. The Lord thy God is in thee; the Mighty One shall save thee; he shall bring joy upon thee, and shall refresh thee with his love; and he shall rejoice over thee with delight as in a day of feasting. And I will gather thine afflicted ones. Alas! who has taken up a reproach against her? Behold, I will work in thee for thy sake at that time, saith the Lord; and I will save her that was oppressed, and receive her that was rejected; and I will make them a praise, and honoured in all the earth. And their enemies shall be ashamed at that time, when I shall deal well with you: for I will make you honoured and a praise among all the nations of the earth, when I turn back your captivity before you, saith the Lord.

COMMENTS

The closing verses of Zephaniah are in contrast to the bulk of the book. To this point the judgements have been harsh. The closing paragraph is tender and gentle.

But there is no contradiction. As we have seen . . . God's judgements are redemptive. He does not rejoice in such suffering. He only does what must be done to call His people back to Himself and purge the Gentiles from their sin.

Here is the anticipation of the day when such affliction shall be over, when God's people shall be reconciled to Himself. There is ample reason for such rejoicing.

SING O DAUGHTER OF ZION . . . v. 14

Cities were, and are, frequently referred to as women poetically to express affection. (eg. *Isaiah 47:1, Psalm 45:12*) Daughter of Zion and daughter of Israel are synonymous terms. Daughter of Jerusalem also seems interchangeable with these terms. All are freighted with covenant significance.

THE KING OF ISRAEL IS IN THE MIDST . . . v. 15

An end shall be put to all their trouble and distresses. Though some grievances remain, they shall be only afflictions, not judgements, for sin shall be pardoned.

The term *"cast out"* here is literally *"swept out."* When they sweep out their sin by reformation, God will sweep out their enemies by destruction.

Our Lord is called *"King of Israel" (John 1:49)*. There is no doubt of the Messianic significance of these verses. He is always in the midst of His people. (cf. *Matthew 28:20*) Because He is in our midst we need not fear evil. (cp. *Romans 8:31-39*)

Zephaniah sees Israel, purged from sin by the fires of judgement, now ready for God's presence which she has heretofore rejected.

LET NOT THY HANDS BE SLACK . . . v. 16

With the King, even Jehovah, in their midst, God's covenant people need not slump in despair. An awareness of His presence is cause for courage and strength even in adversity.

A MIGHTY ONE WHO WILL SAVE . . . WILL REJOICE OVER THEE . . . v. 17

God will delight in His people. After all, this is the reason He created man. When the purging of sin is accomplished and His people at last are His, He will have reason to rejoice! God not only loves

COMFORT AND CONSOLATION   3:18-20

us . . . He loves to love us. If we love Him as we ought, we will have as our strongest desire His good pleasure, just as He has ours.

I WILL GATHER THEM THAT SORROW . . . v. 18

The prophet here promises reprieve to those of Israel who are scattered abroad. Their absence from the sacred feasts is a reproach to Jerusalem. After the purging of their sins, He will bring the faithful into the assembly. In God's eternal Israel . . . the redeemed . . . there will be no reproach or burden.

I WILL MAKE THEM A PRAISE AND A NAME . . . v. 19-20

In these closing verses the Messianic light of Zephaniah burns brightest. There has been a gradual turning from the contemporary and the mundane. In some of the verses we have just read it is difficult to know whether the prophet speaks of the circumstances in which he himself lived, of the captivity and return or of the future Messianic deliverance of the covenant people. Here there is no doubt. The enemies of the people have been destroyed, the gathering of the faithful has been accomplished. Jehovah is in their midst. A praise and a name are theirs among all the people of the earth.

The people, righteous and blessed by God, are known throughout the earth. Even the people of earth's nations praise them. (cp. *Acts 2:47, 5:17, etc.*)

Isaiah also spoke of a new name which God would give His own in the Messianic age. *(Isaiah 62:1-2)* The fulfillment of this promise is seen at Antioch when the covenant people are called Christian. *(Acts 11:26)*

In the intervening ages, before these promises are fulfilled, there would often be cause for sorrow. There would not be the liberty to meet together to keep the public ordinances. During the captivity, the Jews were denied what previously they had neglected. They were reproached and made the objects of derision.

But despite the darkness of judgement, Zephaniah at last sees an end of suffering and a day of universal praise to God and of His people. The faithful will come from distant nations and the remnant will live in the presence and security of Jehovah the King.

Chapter XXII—*Questions*
Comfort and Consolation

1. The sin for which Judah will be led captive is _____ sin.
2. Social sin is inevitably the result of _____.

ZEPHANIAH

3. Though not specifically named in v. 1, _____ is obviously intended by "Her that is rebellious."
4. In light of Zephaniah's pronouncement of judgement against social evil which results from false religion, discuss the statement "it doesn't make any difference what one believes, so long as he is sincere."
5. According to Zephaniah 3:2, four failures have brought her to the brink of destruction. They are: (1) _____, (2) _____, (3) _____, and (4) _____.
6. Zephaniah condemns four classes of cultural leaders in Judah. They are: (1) _____, (2) _____, (3) _____, and (4) _____.
7. The _____ _____ _____ is the beginning of wisdom.
8. Should a Christian fear God? Explain.
9. What is meant (v. 7) by "rose early and corrupted?"
10. Why is God's wrath poured out in human history?
11. What is meant by "turn?" (v. 9)
12. "Pure Language" is evidence of _____.
13. In v. 10 Ethiopia represents _____.
14. Is the idea of universal salvation found in the Old Testament? Discuss.
15. What is meant by "in that day?" (v. 11)
16. The closing verses of Zephaniah are in contrast to _____.
17. Who are the daughter of Zion . . . the daughter of Israel . . . the daughter of Jerusalem (v. 14)?
18. Discuss the Messianic significance of the closing verses of Zephaniah.
19. Discuss "God will delight in His people."
20. Discuss "a praise and a name." (v. 19-20)

PART VI
HAGGAI

HAGGAI

OUTLINE OF HAGGAI

The first message 1:1-15
The second message 2:1-9
The third message 2:10-19
The fourth message 2:20-23

CHAPTER XXIII

PREFACE TO HAGGAI

The purpose of this prophet was to motivate those who had returned from the Babylonian captivity to rebuild the temple. His problem was to overcome their discouragement and indifference.

The often foretold destruction of Jerusalem had finally come in 586 B.C. Nebuchadnezzar ascended the throne of Babylon in 605 B.C. after the victorious battle of Carchemish. In 597 he captured Jerusalem. In 586 the city was demolished and the temple pulled down.

In 605, following his defeat of the Egyptians at Carchemish, Nebuchadnezzar proceeded to Jerusalem. *(Daniel 1:1)* He carried off the royal treasures and a few select young men including Daniel to serve in his court. *(Daniel 1:3-7)*

In 597 Nebuchadnezzar again laid siege to Jerusalem. This time he carried away all the ruling class and leaders of Jewish society, among them the prophet Ezekiel. Remarkably, he did not destroy Jerusalem at that time. (Read *II Kings 24:10-20* and *II Chronicles 36:8-10* and *Ezekiel 33:21*)

In 586 B.C. all those who remained in Judah, with the exception of Jeremiah and a few of the very poorest people, were carried away to Babylon and Jerusalem, with the temple, was destroyed. (Read *II Kings 25:11-12, Jeremiah 40:6*)

The seventy years of captivity predicted by Jeremiah *(Jeremiah 29:10-14)* date from the first transport of prisoners to Babylon in 605 B.C. to the decree of Cyrus that the Jews be released in 538 B.C.

Isaiah had predicted the coming of Cyrus *(Isaiah 44:28, 45:1)*. Cyrus had become king of Persia, the vassal state of the Medes in 559 B.C. To gain freedom from and finally dominance over the Medes, Cyrus allied himself with Nabonidus, king of Babylon.

With this added strength, Cyrus rebelled against Media in 550 B.C. capturing the capital city of Ecbatona.

PREFACE TO HAGGAI

Cyrus's lust for power brought an end to his alliance with Babylon and Babylon now turned to Egypt and Lydia for aid against the rising power of Persia. Lydia was defeated by Cyrus in 546 B.C. and Babylon surrendered without a struggle in 539 B.C.

A significant policy of Cyrus was the return of all images held captive by Babylon to their rightful owners. Since the Jews had no such images, they received rather the sacred vessels from the temple which had been part of the loot taken by Nebuchadnezzar.

In keeping with the practice of restoring fallen gods, Cyrus also returned captured people. The province of Syria, of which Palestine was part, came under the dominance of the Persian monarch in 539 B.C. with the fall of Babylon. The following year in 538 B.C., Cyrus issued the now famous first decree permitting the Jews to return to their homeland.

In this Cyrus was not motivated entirely by humanitarian sentiments. Palestine is a natural buffer zone between Persia and Egypt. Having it populated by friendly, even grateful Jews is symptomatic of Cyrus' political finesse.

His treatment of the Jews was not unexpected. Jehovah's prophets had predicted it before the beginning of the captivity!

The captivity had been such that, when the decree of freedom finally came, not many Jews responded to it. In exile they had been allowed to enter business, marry, raise crops, and establish homes. The synagogue had come into being, replacing the temple as the center of worship. Their property, coupled with a widespread apathy toward spiritual things detained most of them in Babylon.

Those who did return were the spiritually concerned. Idolatry would never again rear its ugly head among God's people until the fourth century A.D. These were the remnant, a handful of faithful people returning to a strip of land no more than twenty-five miles in length . . . all that remained of the once proud kingdom of David and Solomon.

Before the captivity there were twenty-four orders of priests. Only a small number, representative of only four of the orders returned . . . a total of 4,289.

The first call to return to the homeland was totally unheeded by the Levites. (cf. I *Chronicles* 24:3, *Ezra* 2:40) Only seventy-four Levites finally returned.

In all, about 50,000 were the total remnant, and these were largely from the servant classes. The response was similar to the present day migration of Jews to Israel. A very small minority of world Jewery

235

HAGGAI

is concerned enough, or willing to give up the material security in other lands, to help rebuild the Jewish homeland. It is much easier to send money to plant trees!

When this small remnant returned, their first act was to re-erect the altar and re-institute the ancient feasts. *(Ezra 3:23)* Workmen and materials were gathered for the reconstruction of the temple in the second year. *(Ezra 2:68, 69, 3:7-13)*

The surrounding nations, quite naturally, opposed the re-entry of the Jews into Judea. The Samaritans, who now inhabited the old northern kingdom territory, offered help at first, but when they were rebuffed, they mounted a strong opposition to the Jews. *(Ezra 4:1-5)* Thus began an enmity between Jew and Samaritan which carried over into New Testament times, and is still alive today, although few Samaritans remain.

The Samaritans intrigued against the Jews. Both were vassal to Cyrus and the Samaritans accused the Jews of planning revolt. The reconstruction of the temple, connected as it was to Messianic aspiration, supplied them with ample fuel for such rumors.

With this pressure against them, and spiritual indifference mounting, the Jews soon left off the reconstruction and the temple stood less than half-finished.

In 529 B.C., upon the death of Cyrus, Cambyses ascended the Persian throne. He conquered Egypt in 625 B.C., but was thwarted in attempting to conquer Carthage and Nubia. This military campaigning brought Persian armies through Judea with increasing frequency with demoralizing effects upon the Jews.

Cambyses died in 522 B.C. and his death was followed by a brief period of anarchy in the Persian Empire under his weakling successor Smerdis.

Smerdis was assasinated by Darius in 521 B.C. This triggered a number of revolts among Persia's vassal states. These left a mark on Palestine as Darius criss-crossed the land for two years before finally restoring order.

In Darius's second year, the Jews resumed construction of the temple in 520 B.C. Tattenai, the Persian governor of the province, objected that they had no official authority to do so. They appealed to Cyrus' decree which was thereupon discovered in the royal archives *(Ezra 5:1-17)* and Darius ordered Tattenai to allow the reconstruction.

Even with the encouragement of Darius, the Jews waited another year to resume the building. They did this only when God had sent Haggai and Zechariah to persuade them to do so.

PREFACE TO HAGGAI

As a result of the prophecies of these two, the second temple was finally completed in 516 B.C.

HAGGAI THE PROPHET

Haggai, as a person, remains obscure. No one else in the Old Testament shares the name, the literal meaning of which is "festival." He is mentioned in *Ezra 5:1* and *6:4* and referred to in *Zechariah 8:9*. He is named two times in the apocraphal *I Esdras* and in *Sirach 49:11*.

Jewish tradition says that all three post-exilic prophets died in the same month. Haggai, Zechariah and Malachi all passing in the same month the temple was completed.

In addition to the book which bears his name, Haggai is traditionally the author of several ceremonial regulations. The Vulgate credits him as author of Psalm 111. The Peshitta text credits him with Psalms 125 and 126. The Septuagint attributes Psalm 137 to his authorship, and all three credit him as author of Psalms 146, 147, 148, and 145.

HAGGAI'S MESSAGE

Haggai's burden is the spiritual indifference of God's people. The discontinuation of the rebuilding of the temple gave an opportunity for the people to become pre-occupied with their own interests and the erection of their own homes. Some even argued that the seventy year captivity would not really end for two years, so the time had not yet come to re-build the temple. They had, after all, erected an altar and in so doing had recognized their allegiance to God. It was enough!

Harvest failures plagued them also and so added to their preoccupation. (*Haggai 1:6, 9-11, 2:15, 19*) The repeated criss-crossing of their land by armies which, though not attacking them, interferred along with Samaritan interference too, gave them pause as did internal dissensions. (*Zechariah 8:10*)

It was a critical moment. The remnant must be revived or God's covenant would yet fail. The temple, "the shrine within which was kept inviolate the faith of the Old Testament," was symbolic of the remnant's continuation as the reason for the existence of the Jews. Without it, the prophetic symbolism of the sacrificial system could not be resumed.

With this covenant hope in mind, Haggai prods their consciences with Messianic promises. Finally, with Zechariah, he succeeded in persuading the returned exiles to set aside their private interests and get to work.

Chapter XXIII—Questions

Preface to Haggai

1. What was the purpose of Haggai's prophecy?
2. Trace the three incidents from 605 B.C. to 586 B.C. in which increasing numbers of Jews were led to Babylon.
3. _____ had predicted that the Babylonian captivity would last seventy years.
4. _____ had predicted the coming of Cyrus who issued the decreeing which ended the Babylonian captivity.
5. How do you account for Cyrus' return to the Jews of the sacred vessels from the temple?
6. What moved Cyrus to allow the Jews to return to their homeland?
7. Most of the Jews did or did not return to Palestine? Why?
8. What was the first act of the remnant upon returning?
9. What was Samaria's reaction to the return of the Jews? Trace the consequences of the Jew's response.
10. What three prophets encouraged the Jews to rebuild the temple?
11. In addition to the Book of Haggai the prophet is credited with what other writing?
12. The burden of Haggai is _____.
13. How do you account for the Jews' indifference to the task of re-building the temple?
14. Why was this reconstruction critical?

CHAPTER XXIV

EXPOSITION OF HAGGAI

THE FIRST MESSAGE . . . Haggai 1:1-15

RV . . . In the second year of Darius the king, in the sixth month, in the first day of the month, came the word of Jehovah by Haggai the prophet unto Zerubbabel the son of Shealtiel, governor of Judah, and to Joshua the son of Jehoozadak, the high priest, saying, Thus speaketh Jehovah of hosts, saying, This people say, It is not the time for us to come, the time for Jehovah's house to be built. Then came the word of Jehovah by Haggai the prophet, saying, Is it a time for you yourselves to dwell in your ceiled houses, while this house lieth waste? Now therefore thus saith Jehovah of hosts: Consider your ways. Ye have sown much, and bring in little; ye eat, but ye have not enough; ye drink, but ye are not filled with drink; ye clothe you, but there is none warm; and he that earneth wages earneth wages to put it into a bag with holes. Thus saith Jehovah of hosts: Consider your ways. Go up to the mountain, and bring wood, and build the house; and I will take pleasure in it, and I will be glorified, saith Jehovah. Ye looked for much, and lo, it came to little; and when ye brought it home, I did blow upon it. Why? saith Jehovah of hosts. Because of my house that lieth waste, while ye run every man to his own house. Therefore for your sake the heavens withhold the dew, and the earth withholdeth its fruit. And I called for a drought upon the land, and upon the mountains, and upon the grain, and upon the new wine, and upon the oil, and upon that which the ground bringeth forth, and upon men, and upon cattle, and upon all the labor of the hands. Then Zerubbabel the son of Shealtiel, and Joshua the son of Jehozadak, the high priest, with all the remnant of the people, obeyed the voice of Jehovah their God, and the words of Haggai the prophet, as Jehovah their God had sent him; and the people did fear before Jehovah. Then spake Haggai Jehovah's messenger in Jehovah's message unto the people, saying, I am with you, saith Jehovah. And Jehovah stirred up the spirit of Zerubbabel the son of Shealtiel, governor of Judah, and the spirit of Joshua the son of Jehozadak, the high priest, and the spirit of all the remnant of the people; and they came and did work on the house of Jehovah of hosts, their God, in the four and twentieth day of the month, in the sixth month, in the second year of Darius the king.

LXX . . . In the second year of Darius the king, in the sixth month, on the first day of the month, the word of the Lord came by the hand of the prophet Aggaeus, saying, Speak to Zorobabel the son of Salathiel, of the tribe of Juda, and to Jesus the son of Josedec, the high priest, saying, Thus saith the Lord Almighty, saying, This people say, The time is not come to build the house of the Lord. And the word of the Lord came by the hand of the prophet Aggaeus, saying, Is it time for you to dwell in your ceiled houses, whereas our house is desolate? And now thus saith the Lord Almighty; Consider your ways, I pray you. Ye have sown much, but brought in little; ye have eaten, and are not satisfied; ye have drunk, and are not satisfied with drink, ye have clothed yourselves, and have not become warm thereby; and he that earns wages has gathered them into a bag of holes. Thus saith the Lord Almighty; Consider your ways. Go up to the mountain, and cut timber;

build the house, and I will take pleasure in it, and be glorified, saith the Lord. Ye looked for much, and there came little; and it was brought into the house, and I blew it away. Therefore thus saith the Lord Almighty, Because my house is desolate, and ye run every one into his own house; therefore shall the sky withhold dew, and the earth shall keep back her produce. And I will bring a sword upon the land, and upon the mountains, and upon the corn, and upon the wine, and upon the oil, and all that the earth produces, and upon the men, and upon the cattle, and upon all the labours of their hands. And Zorozabel the son of Salathiel, of the tribe of Juda, and Jesus the son of Josedec, the high priest, and all the remnant of the people hearkened to the voice of the Lord their God, and the words of the prophet Aggaeus, according as the Lord their God had sent him to them, and the people feared before the Lord. And Aggaeus the Lord's messenger spoke among the messengers of the Lord to the people, saying, I am with you, saith the Lord. And the Lord stirred up the spirit of Zorobabel the son Salathiel, of the tribe of Judah, and the spirit of Jesus the son of Josedec, the high priest, and the spirit of the remnant of all the people; and they went in, and wrought in the house of the Lord Almighty their God, on the four and twentieth day of the sixth month, in the second year of Darius the king.

COMMENTS

The first message of Haggai to the indifferent and discouraged remnant merits special examination for the simple reason that it got results! Those whose concern is for the building of the spiritual temple of God, the church, will do well to learn from this prophet of action. (cp. *Ephesians 2:19-22*)

THE WORD OF JEHOVAH CAME . . . v. 1

It was exactly twenty-three days from the time Jehovah delivered the message through Haggai until they began to work. That kind of response to a sermon today would leave most preachers speechless!

Darius had assumed the Persian throne by asassinating his predecessor in 521 B.C. Even with his approval, there was no movement to resume building the temple. So God spoke to Haggai (and to Zechariah and Malachi) with a message for the people, beginning with the civil and religious leaders, Zerubbabel the governor and Joshua the high priest.

EXPOSITION OF HAGGAI   1:1

The name Zerubbabel means "born in Babylon" . . . no special significance. He was the son of Shealtiel, according to Haggai.
This presents a problem. In Chronicles Zerubbabel is called the son of Pedaiah, brother of Shealtiel and grandson of Assir. (*I Chronicles 3:17-19*) In Luke's genealogy Zerubbabel is the son Shealtiel and the grandson of Neri. (*Luke 3:27*)

Zedekiah, son of King Jeconiah had no children. Assir, another son of Jeconiah (cf. *Jeremiah 22:30*) had a daughter, but no son. (*I Chronicles 3:16*) Legally, Assir's daughter was heir to the throne, and so must marry a man from her father's tribe. (*Numbers 27:8, 36:8,9*)

She married Neri, of the Davidic line through Nathan's branch. Luke makes no mention of Assir who descended from David through Solomon, but traces the lineage rather through Nathan of whom Zerubbabel was the grandson. This fulfills the prediction of *Jeremiah 22:30*.

Neri and Assir's daughter produced a son named Shealtiel and others as mentioned in *I Chronicles 3:18*. Shealtiel had no children, so, according to law, his brother, Pedaiah must marry his widow to produce an heir for Shealtiel. (cp. *Deuteronomy 25:5-10*)

Zerubbabel was the son of this Levirate marriage. Legally Shealtiel was Assir's son and Jeconiah's grandson. Actually he was the son of Neri. Zerubbabel was legally the son of Shealtiel, but actually was Pedaiah's son. See the diagram below.

Jeconiah

Assir   Zedekiah
                                                 (no child)

Daughter & Neri

Shealtiel, Pedaiah
(no child)

Legal   Actual

Zerubbabel

Since Joshua the high priest and his father, Jehozadek, are not mentioned elsewhere in the Bible excepting for Haggai's contemporary,

241

Zechariah, we do not know anything about them other than Joshua's influential responsibility as spiritual leader during the rebuilding of the temple.

IS IT TIME . . . v. 2-4

The message is not Haggai's but God's. The claim to inspiration is unmistakeable.

It is addressed to those who are responsible for the attitudes and actions (or inaction) of the people. (v.1) The civil and spiritual leaders are responsible for the spiritual and moral fibre of any nation. As water rises no higher than its source, a nation is no stronger than its leaders.

THIS PEOPLE . . . NOT "MY PEOPLE" . . .

The terminology seems designed to express dissatisfaction with the remnant God does not disclaim them, but He is stern. He will not tolerate the kind of attitudes which brought about the captivity from which they were so recently returned.

The message immediately attacks the excuses being made for not building the house of God. *"It is not time."* There has not been sufficient time since our return from exile. We have built an altar as our first act upon return. It is enough until we get "settled in." Seventy years have not lapsed, as Jeremiah predicted, since the destruction of the first temple. Two more years are needed, then we will build. With so much uncertainty in the international situation effecting the national economy, it is a poor time to build.

If you've ever been on a fund drive for a church building, you've heard all this! Our own needs are not met, we have a place of worship, the Bible doesn't allow for church buildings, there may be another war or an economic recession, etc.

What it all amounts to, whether in Haggai's day or our own is simply that God's people are more concerned with their own interests than with providing an adequate house of worship. Haggai tells his people this in no uncertain terms. *"Is it time for you to dwell in your ceiled (paneled) houses while this house lieth waste?"* Then as now, those who object most to building an adequate house of worship are those who spend most on their own houses.

Actually, the message becomes even more pointed in our time if we read *Ephesians 2:19-22.* Whereas Haggai is concerned with building a building of wood and masonry, we are concerned with building the *real* temple of God, the church constructed not of materials but of men.

To make these excuses for not getting on with *this* task is to tamper with and neglect the most important work in the world. Jesus Himself has spoken to this neglect, "Seek ye first the Kingdom and take no thought saying What shall ye eat? or What shall we drink? or Wherewithal shall we be clothed? After all these things do the Gentiles seek." (*Luke 12:29*)

CONSIDER YOUR WAYS . . . WHY? . . . v. 5-11

Stop and think, God's word through Haggai challenges the people. *"You have sown much, and bring in little."* You work hard in the fields, you plant and till and labor for the harvest, but the harvest is scant and meager.

"You eat, but you have not enough." You are not starving but you are not satisfied, there is never enough of the right food on your tables.

"You drink, but you are not filled." There is a drought. Drinking water is scarce and must be used sparingly. In such dry times the vineyards do not produce properly and the wine is in scant supply.

"You clothe you, but there is none warm." No one is naked; you have clothes, but they are not adequate. You are not warm. Your clothes do not provide comfort.

"He that earneth wages earneth wages to put into a bag with holes." There are jobs. Men are employed, but their wages are inadequate. No one is able to "make ends meet." There is too much month left, at the end of the paycheck.

Again "consider your ways," look how things are. *You looked for much."* Your expectations were high when you started home from Babylon. But *"it came to little."*

You were able to bring home crops and wages, but *"I did blow upon it."* instead of blessing and magnifying it.

WHY? SAITH JEHOVAH OF HOSTS . . .

Have you not wondered why things are as they are? It is because you have not "put first things first." *"Go up into the mountain, and bring wood and build the house . . . my house lieth waste while ye run every man to his own house."*

"Therefore" for your sake . . . to teach you a lesson . . . I withhold the moisture and the earth withholds its fruit.

"I CALLED FOR A DROUGHT."

How many Christians do you know today who are living dull monotonous lives, who are not really rejoicing in the Lord, whose life

1:11-14   HAGGAI

is seemingly blessed little more than their pagan neighbors? Such people are pre-occupied with their own affairs. They have not learned that God's temple, the church, must come first. They do not believe that Jesus spoke the truth for our time when He said if we seek His kingdom first these *things* will be added to us.

It is our own fault if we live a humdrum life of spiritual drought and dissatisfaction.

AND JEHOVAH STIRRED UP THE SPIRIT OF ZERUBBABEL . . . v. 12-15

To the man who obeys the message of God in whose heart the Spirit of God has stirred there is no question of the right *time*. Such a one lives by eternal values. The only time he knows is *now*. The only thing that counts is God's work.

Zerubbabel got the message, and so did Joshua the high priest and so did God's remnant. They were still close enough to the captivity to know God was not playing games. Their fathers had refused to hear Isaiah and Amos and Micah and the rest and they had themselves grown up in exile as a consequence.

That was enough. They obeyed the voice of Jehovah as it had spoken through Haggai.

Then came the reassurance of God.

(Verse 12) Haggai is careful to record that not just the leaders but the people themselves heeded His admonition. The Word of God brought about obedience, from the greatest to the least. The lack of wisdom manifest in their failure to fear God is in contrast to the response of the remnant. The fathers had refused to hear the pre-exilic prophets because they did not fear God. Fearing God, their children obeyed the message of the Lord voiced by Haggai.

I AM WITH YOU . . . v. 13

The very first sign of obedience was siezed upon by God. He, at once, declares because of their fear and obedience that He is with them.

GOD STIRRED UP THE SPIRIT . . . v. 14

The Spirit stirred in both Zerubbabel and Joshua and the people. Through the preaching of His word through Haggai, God's Spirit stirred in the hearts of His covenant nation.

It is ever so. When His Word is heeded and obeyed, His presence through the Spirit is with His people.

EXPOSITION OF HAGGAI 1:14—2:8

And the result is inevitable. The people in whom the Spirit stirred rose up and built the house of God.

And the God Who lived in Haggai's day is just the same today. When God's covenant people, both leaders and others, fear the Lord, heed and obey His Word, the Spirit *always* moves in their hearts and His house is built. We who are, as Christians, concerned with the building of the real temple, the church, will do well to learn this eternal lesson. We do not need to agonize and grovel and beg for His Spirit. We need rather to *fear* Him, even in this sophisticated age when a misunderstanding of His love often causes us to be overly familiar and without fear. We need to obey Him as He tells us through inspired writers what He would have us do. When this is done, His Spirit will move in us and His house will be built.

By the same token, we need to recognize it is His Spirit who must motivate us if what we do is to be *His* work. Our American overemphasis on methods and techniques for church growth often seems to deny this. As Don Atkin put it recently, "We need to stop trying to get Him into our programs and become concerned for getting ourselves into His." It is one thing to know the doctrine of the Holy Spirit. It is quite another to know the Spirit Himself. It is not enough to know the Word of God. We must know the God of the Word!

IN THE FOUR AND TWENTIETH DAY . . . v. 15

It was just twenty three days from the beginning of Haggai's preaching to the beginning of building. Surely God must always be pleased when His people are so responsive to His Word.

THE SECOND MESSAGE . . . Haggai 2:1-9

RV . . . In the seventh month, in the one and twentieth day of the month, came the word of Jehovah by Haggai the prophet, saying, Speak now to Zerubbabel the son of Shealtiel, governor of Judah, and to Joshua the son of Jehozadak, the high priest, and to the remnant of the people, saying, Who is left among you that saw this house in its former glory? and how do ye see it now? is it not in your eyes as nothing? Yet, now be strong, O Zerubbabel, saith Jehovah; and be strong, O Joshua, son of Jehozadak, the high priest; and be strong, all ye people of the land, saith Jehovah, and work; for I am with you, saith Jehovah of hosts, according to the word that I covenanted with you when ye came out of Egypt, and my Spirit abode among you: fear ye not. For thus saith Jehovah of hosts, Yet once, it is a little while, and I will shake the heavens, and the earth, and the sea, and the dry land; and I will shake all nations; and the precious things of all nations shall come; and I will fill this house with glory, saith Jehovah of hosts. The silver is mine, and the gold is mine, saith Jehovah of hosts. The latter glory of this house shall be greater than the former, saith Jehovah of hosts; and in this place will I give peace, saith Jehovah of hosts.

LXX . . . In the seventh month, on the twenty-first day of the month, the Lord spoke by Aggaeus the prophet, saying, Speak now to Zorobabel the son Salathiel, of the tribe of Juda, and to Jesus the son of Josedec, the high priest, and to all the remnant of the people, saying, Who is there of you that saw this house in her former glory? and how do ye now look upon it, as it were nothing before your eyes? Yet now be strong, O Zorobabel, saith the Lord; and strengthen thyself, I Jesus the high priest, the son of Josedec; and let all the people of the land strengthen themselves, saith the Lord, and work, for I am with you, saith the Lord Almighty; and my Spirit remains in the midst of you; be of good courage. For thus saith the Lord Almighty; Yet once I will shake the heaven, and the earth, and the sea, and the dry land; and I will shake all nations, and the choice portions of all the nations shall come: and I will fill this house with glory, saith the Lord Almighty. Mine is the silver, and mine the gold, saith the Lord Almighty. For the glory of this house shall be great, the latter more than the former, saith the Lord Almighty: and in this place will I give peace, saith the Lord Almighty, even peace of soul for a possession to every one that builds, to raise up this temple.

COMMENTS

THE WORD OF JEHOVAH . . . v. 1-2

Claiming again the inspiration of God for his message, Haggai, a month after rebuilding was resumed, addressed himself again to the civil and spiritual leaders and the people.

THE FORMER GLORY . . . v. 3

There were a few who had returned from captivity who longed for the "good old days." The modest dimensions and decor of the second temple could not compare with the splendor of the first. (*I Kings 6:22, 28, 30, 32, & 7:48-50*)

"*How do you see it?*" asks the prophet. The temple they were building was nothing compared to their memory of the one erected by Solomon.

Traditionally, several things were absent from the second temple by which it could not compare to the first:

(1) The Ark of the Covenant was gone. Its fate still remains a mystery. The idea that it was taken directly into heaven has been held by some on the strength of *Revelation 11:19*. The apocalyptic nature of Revelation, however, makes a literal interpretation very unreliable.

(2) The Shekinah glory . . . the pillar of cloud and of fire was absent . . . proof that the full glory of God was not yet come.

(3) Following Malachi, the Spirit of prophecy was apparently silent and the inspired prophet was replaced by the professional scribe.

(4) The sacred fire, kindled by God upon the altar was extinguished, and God no longer smote the priests for replacing it with strange fire. (cf. *Leviticus 10:1-ff*)

(5) The Urim and Thummim were also gone. (cp. *Exodus 28:30*) The literal meanings of these words are *lights* and *perfections*, respectively. The exact nature of them is problematical. They may have been some divine manifestation or they may have been an appendage on the breastplate of the priests. (cp. *Deuteronomy 33:8* and *I Samuel 28:6*) It has been suggested that the Urim and Thummim were jewels set in the breast plate of the high priest. (cp. *Exodus 28:29, Exodus 39:8* and *Leviticus 8:8*)

No doubt much else was lacking. The first temple had been erected by a wise ruler of a wealthy nation in collaboration with building experts. The second was built by a vassal state, with no king and no real wealth.

This actual inferiority was exaggerated in the memory of those in whose minds sixty-six years had no doubt added even to the real glory of Solomon's temple.

The key to Haggai's message to those who were depressed and disappointed in the inferiority of their handiwork, is the question *"how do ye see it?"* They were overly concerned with material embellishments.

I AM WITH YOU . . . v. 4-5

The important thing in regard to the rebuilding of the temple, as as God saw it, was that His people were back in their land, and He was with them. And His presence is according to the everlasting covenant.

Here is the heart of the prophetic message. This is the reason the remnant had been returned. This is the reason the temple must be rebuilt. His promise to bless all the nations of the earth in the seed of Abraham was the reason they became a nation in the beginning. (cf. *Exodus 2:34, 19:5-6*) It is equally the reason for the restoration of their national identity.

In their national pride and religious exclusiveness, they were about to forget again the reason for their existence. It was vital that, upon this restoration as in their beginnings as a people *(Genesis 1:1-3)* and as a nation *(Exodus 19:5-6)*, that the people be once more made aware of their covenant purpose. Here is the real purpose of the preaching of Haggai, for in the reconstruction of the temple was the symbolic re-affirmation of the covenant.

THE LATTER GLORY OF THIS HOUSE SHALL BE GREATER THAN THE FORMER ... v. 6-9

Through the restored remnant the Christ would come. Never again would Baal be worshipped among His people. They would forget the covenant purpose as a nation. Their religion would become a hollow form, but with it all, the faithful few would remain true and the Messiah would come in fulfillment of the covenant promise. (cp. *Matthew 1:1, Luke 1:33, 55, 72-73)*

"Thus saith the Lord" in verse six is dependant upon the covenant mentioned in verse five.

The phrase "in a little while" has been rendered variously, "it is as yet a little while," and "one period more—a brief one it is." The Septuagint has "yet once." The sense is that of repetition.

Just as the power of the Lord had shaken Sinai *(Hebrews 12:26)* as God manifest His moral power to Israel, so again He will demonstrate His power in the shaking of "the heavens and the earth and the sea and the dry land and ... all nations, and the precious things of all nations." (v. 7)

The Hebrew writer sees the fulfillment of this in the coming of the new covenant. *(Hebrews 12:18-29)* The coming of the church, the new temple *(Hebrews 8:1-ff)* and ultimate fulfillment of the Abrahamic covenant *(Galatians 3:29)* shook and put an end to the nations of the pre-Christian world.

The shaking began during the "silent years" between the Testaments. The Persian Empire crumbled before Alexander. Alexander's kingdom, divided after his youthful death, in turn gave way to Rome, and the west began its current domination of the east which heretofore had set the culture of the world.

"*The desire of all nations*" (KJV) in verse seven is unmistakably Messianic. There could hardly be a more vivid expression of the covenant promise, "in thy seed shall all the nations of the earth be blessed." Even the rabbis saw in it the coming of the Messiah. The true riches of God, the "silver" and "gold" of verse eight will make the glory of the house of God outshine the glory of Solomon's temple.

And so the prophet comforts the people in such a way as to turn their minds from their ambitions of national grandeur to the glorious hope of covenant fulfillment.

The statement in verse nine, "*the latter glory of this house shall be greater than the former,*" is deserving of special attention. The argument of the book of Hebrews for the superiority of the new covenant over the old is a glorious re-statement of this truth.

It is patently obvious that Haggai cannot be saying that when the second temple is complete it will be more splendid than the first. This simply could not be true in the nation's post-exilic circumstances. Historically it was not true, even with Herod's embellishments during the Roman era. Haggai is looking to something far more meaningful than stone and mortar.

Lump Solomon's temple, Zerubbabel's temple, and Herod's temple all together and their glory cannot surpass that of the real temple, the church. That the Jews identified the material temple with their ambitions for national glory was a grave error for them. Ultimately, it brought about their rejection of Jesus. But it did not alter the spiritual facts. (cp. *Daniel 2:36-45, 4:19-27, Ezekiel 40-48, Zechariah 2:3-13, 6:9-15, 8:13, 18-23, 9:9-10, 14:16-21, Psalm 145:6, 9-13, 21*)

The true tabernacle, or temple is superior to the old because it is based on a superior revelation by a superior Revelator (*Hebrews, chapters 1-3*) and because it is ministered by a superior priesthood. (*Hebrews 4:14—10:18*) It is more glorious than "the former" because it is related to God by a better covenant and accomplishes better services. The scene, conditions and results of its ministry are ideal whereas those of the old temple were symbolic, shadowy types of the real temple. The former temple was passing away, the latter temple is eternal. The sacrifices offered in the former were dead animals. Those in the new are living men. (*Romans 12:1-2*)

The promise of peace is also related to the new temple rather than the old. The peace which God gives to those who are the new temple, the spiritual house *(I Peter 2:5),* is beyond the comprehension of those who think of material glory. *(Philippians 4:7)*

The world seeks peace in terms of silent guns and rusted swords. The world seeks peace in terms of easy going tolerance in all human relationships. The world seeks peace through positive thinking, tranquilizers and electro-therapy.

But the peace which prevails in the true and more glorious temple of God is not "as the world gives." *(John 14:27)* Such peace comes only from complete surrender to and complete trust in Him Who is the meaning of the old temple and the High Priest of the new.

It is related to the reality of the Holy Spirit, not as a doctrine but as a present Person. *(John 14:26-27)* Haggai knew about this. In verse 5, he says *"My Spirit abideth among you, fear not."*

THE THIRD MESSAGE . . . Haggai 2:10-19

RV . . . In the four and twentieth day of the ninth month, in the second year of Darius, came the word of Jehovah by Haggai the prophet, saying, Thus saith Jehovah of hosts: Ask now the priests concerning the law, saying, If one bear holy flesh in the skirt of his garment, and with his skirt do touch bread, or pottage, or wine, or oil, or any food, shall it become holy? And the priests answered and said, No. Then said Haggai, If one that is unclean by reason of a dead body touch any of these, shall it be unclean? And the priests answered and said, It shall be unclean. Then answered Haggai and said, So is this people, and so is this nation before me, saith Jehovah; and so is every work of their hands; and that which they offer there is unclean. And now, I pray you, consider from this day and backward, before a stone was laid upon a stone in the temple of Jehovah. Through all that time, when one came to a heap of twenty measures, there were but ten; when one came to the winevat to draw out fifty vessels, there were but twenty. I smote you with blasting and with mildew and with hail in all the work of your hands; yet ye turned not to me, saith Jehovah. Consider, I pray you, from this day and backward, from the four and twentieth day of the ninth month, since the day that the foundation of Jehovah's temple was laid, consider it. Is the seed yet in the barn? Yea, the vine, and the fig-tree, and the pomgranate, and the olive-tree have not brought forth; from this day will I bless you.

LXX . . . On the four and twentieth day of the ninth month, in the second year of Darius, the word of the Lord came to Aggaeus the prophet, saying, Thus saith the Lord Almighty; Inquire now of the

EXPOSITION OF HAGGAI 2:10-19

priests concerning the law, saying, If a man should take holy flesh in the skirt of his garment, and the skirt of his garment should touch bread, or pottage, or wine, or oil, or any meat, shall it be holy? And the priests answered and said, No. And Aggaeus said, If a defiled person is unclean by reason of a dead body, touch any of these, shall it be defiled? And the priests answered and said, It shall be defiled. And Aggaeus answered and said, So is this people, and so is this nation before me, saith the Lord; and so are all the works of their hands: and whosoever shall approach them, shall be defiled (because of their early burdens: they shall be pained because of their toils; and ye have hated him that reproved in the gates.) And now consider, I pray you, from this day and beforetime, before they laid a stone on a stone in the temple of the Lord, what manner of men ye were. When ye cast into the cornbin twenty measures of barley, and there were only ten measures of barley: and ye went to the vat to draw out fifty measures, and there were but twenty. I smote you with barrenness, and with blasting, and all the works of your hands with hail; yet ye returned not to me, saith the Lord. Set your hearts now to think from this day and upward, from the four and twentieth day of the ninth month, even from the day when the foundation of the temple of the Lord was laid; consider in your hearts, whether this shall be known on the corn-floor, and whether yet the vine, and the fig-tree, and the pomegranate, and the olive-trees that bear no fruit are with you: from this day will I bless you.

COMMENTS
THE FOUR AND TWENTIETH DAY OF THE NINTH MONTH . . . v. 10

The third message came from Jehovah to the prophet Haggai exactly three months after the favorable response of the people to the first message. As the first message cautions against false contentment and the second cautions against false discontentment, the third exhorts them not to build from false motives.

THUS SAITH THE LORD . . . v. 11

As in the previous messages, so here, Haggai is careful to let his hearers know the message is not his but the Lord's.

ASK NOW THE PRIESTS CONCERNING THE LAW . . .

This admonition is followed by two questions. The questions are, in essence, can the *holy* make the *unholy holy* and can the *unholy* make the *holy unholy?* The priests' answers are accurate. To the first they answer no. To the second yes.

A basic principle is revealed here. The influence of holiness is not as far reaching as unholiness. A rotten apple will corrupt a barrel of good apples, but a good apple will not make a barrel of bad ones good.

"So is this people." The construction of a holy temple will not automatically sanctify the land or its inhabitants any more than the flesh of a sacrifice will make holy a garment in which it is carried.

When the first temple stood, the people could not believe God would allow evil to come upon them. They made a fetish of the building. It must not happen again by assuming the work of re-building can sanctify an unclean people.

Here is a warning to today's Christian who assumes he is "right with God" because he associates with an active church, regardless of his personal commitment to God or trust in Jesus.

CONSIDER ... BACKWARD ... v. 15-17

Haggai challenges his people to consider what has happened since they returned from captivity, prior to the beginning of the reconstruction. Conditions have not changed since they began to build. Prosperity did not immediately result from their work on the temple. The reason was the far-reaching result of past neglect. It could not be erased by three months of obedience.

In verse 17 Haggai indicates that, although the people have resumed building, they have not really returned to the Lord. If they have, it is only recently. Here, just following their return from Babylon, is the beginning of the strange malady confronted by Jesus. "This people honoreth me with their lips: but their heart is far from me." *(Matthew 15:8)* Isaiah had confronted this same spiritual failure in the people prior to the captivity. *(Isaiah 29:13)*

A building program such as that in which Haggai's readers were engaged, or a full program of activity in the building, such as that in which Jesus' hearers participated, can neither one substitute for genuine commitment to God and concern for His covenant purpose.

CONSIDER ... BACKWARD ... v. 18-19

Again Haggai calls upon the people to remember. A new era is about to begin, as indicated in verse fifteen by the transitional phrase "and now." This seems to be the reason for Haggai's repeated emphasis on dates.

The term in Hebrew does not mean "backward" exactly, as our versions render it (v. 15 and 18). It is used rather to call attention from the past to the future. Past calamities are contrasted with the beginning of the new period of Jewish history.

The plea seems to be for patience. Since the laying of the first stones there has not been enough time for Jehovah to relieve the wants of the people short of a miracle. The fig and pomegranate and olive harvests are yet on the trees. Their present obedience will yet be rewarded.

THE FOURTH MESSAGE . . . Haggai 2:20-23

RV . . . And the word of Jehovah came the second time unto Haggai in the four and twentieth day of the month, saying, Speak to Zerubbabel, governor of Judah, saying, I will shake the heavens and the earth; and I will overthrow the throne of kingdoms; and I will destroy the strength of the kingdoms of the nations; and I will overthrow the chariots, and those that ride in them; and the horses and their riders shall come down, every one by the sword of his brother. In that day, saith Jehovah of hosts, will I take thee, O Zerubbabel, my servant, the son of Shealtiel, saith Jehovah, and will make thee as a signet; for I have chosen thee, saith Jehovah of hosts.

LXX . . . And the word of the Lord came the second time to Aggaeus the prophet, on the four and twentieth day of the month, saying, Speak to Zorobabel the son of Salathiel, of the tribe of Juda, saying, I shake the heaven, and the earth, and the sea, and the dry land; and I will overthrow the thrones of kings, and I will destroy the power of the kings of the nations; and I will overthrow chariots and riders; and the horses and their riders shall come down, every one by the sword striving against his brother. In that day, saith the Lord Almighty, I will take thee, O Zorobabel, the son of Salathiel, my servant, saith the Lord, and will make thee as a seal: for I have chosen thee, saith the Lord Almighty.

COMMENTS

Twice on the twenty-fourth day of the month the word of Jehovah came to Haggai. How it came we do not know. That the prophet considers his message as the Lord's rather than his own is unmistakeable. The second time the word of Jehovah came it resulted in Haggai's fourth message.

Again the prophet addresses Zerubbabel, the governor of Judah. This fourth message is concerned with the time of fulfillment of the promises recorded in *2:6-9*. (See comment above on Haggai's second message.)

The shaking of the heavens and earth here (v. 21) and in *2:6* cannot mean the chaos which threatened the Persian empire during and just prior to the accession of Darius in 521 B.C. Haggai's message was delivered in 520 B.C. when this threat had been largely abated by the decisive action of Darius.

God's promise to Zerubbabel has to do with the reversal of human values rather than political agitation. It occured, according to the understanding of the Hebrew writer, with the establishment of the church. (cp. *Hebrews 12:25-29*) Verse 22 finds a parallel in *Ezekiel 38:19-21*. We shall find Zechariah confirming this idea in *Zechariah 4:13*.

As Richard Wolfe says, "Self destructive and mutually destructive wars shall rage on the earth and the power of the heathen shall be overthrown . . . by God." The Prince of Peace shall rule at last. (cf. *Psalm 20:7*)

The ultimate fulfillment of this oft repeated predictive prophecy is to be seen in the final great struggle *(Revelation 20:7-10)* ushering in the new heaven and new earth.

There is no reason to assume that Haggai mistakenly identifies Zerubbabel as the Messiah. His crowning, albeit secretly according to tradition lest it bring down the wrath of Persia upon Judah, could easily be seen as prophetic of Messiah's coming. In his time the nations did not flock to the temple for instruction, the world's kingdoms were not overthrown, the age of Messiah did not begin, and Zerubbabel himself did not live to participate in it.

Nevertheless, with the restoration of the remnant and the rebuilding of the symbolic temple, Zerubbabel can easily be seen as a type of Christ, just as David himself is frequently referred to in the same light. (eg. *Psalm 16:8-11, 110:1*)

This typology of Christ in Zerubbabel is seen in that he led the people out of the Babylonian bondage as Christ would lead His people from the bondage of sin. Zerubbabel built a temple to God, as Jesus is building the church. (cp. *Ephesians 2:19-22*)

May we, as Haggai's readers, be encouraged in our faithfulness to God to the building of the real temple by our hope of the coming great "Day of Jehovah."

EXPOSITION OF HAGGAI

Chapter XXIV—*Questions*

Exposition of Haggai

1. Write an outline of Haggai.
2. Haggai's first message is concerned with?
3. What were the results of the first message?
4. Discuss the ancestry of Zerubbabel in light of *Haggai 1:1, I Chronicles 3:17-19,* and *Luke 3:27.*
5. The message Haggai was _____ message.
6. Haggai's first message attacks _____.
7. How does the message apply to us who would build the church?
8. How does Haggai account for the drought and austere conditions which had beset the people?
9. Discuss "Jehovah stirred up the spirit of Zerubbabel."
10. What is the gist of Haggai's second message? To whom is it addressed?
11. What was missing from the second temple?
12. What is meant by "the latter glory of the house?"
13. Discuss Haggai 2:7 in light of *Hebrews 8:1-ff* and *Galatians 3:29.*
14. What is meant by "desire of all nations?"
15. What is the gist of Haggai's third message?
16. What false motives might have been involved in rebuilding the temple?
17. What malady confronting Haggai was also addressed by Jesus?
18. Show evidence that Haggai considered his message to be God's rather than his own.
19. Discuss the shaking of the heavens and earth *(Haggai 2:21* cp. *Haggai 2:6)*
20. Why could not this shaking have referred to the chaotic conditions of Darius' early reign?
21. Where in the Bible do we find the ultimate fulfillment of this prophecy?
22. Discuss Zerubbabel as a type of Christ. Show parallels between them.

PART VII
ZECHARIAH

ZECHARIAH

OUTLINE OF ZECHARIAH

SECTION I ... Chapters 1-8

A. Introduction 1:1-6
B. Symbolic visions 1:7—6:15
   1. Horses 1:7-17
   2. Horns and smiths 1:18-21
   3. Measuring line, chapter 2
   4. High priest, chapter 3
   5. Menorah and olive trees, chapter 4
   6. Flying scroll 5:1-4
   7. Flying basket 5:5-10
   8. War chariots 6:1-8
C. Coronation of Joshua 6:9-15
D. Teaching about worship, chapters 7-8
   1. Meaning of fasting
   2. Questions concerning worship
   3. Divine requirements for worship
   4. Response of Jews to requirements
   5. God's response to refusal
   6. God's love revealed in power
   7. God's pattern for living
   8. God's mission program

SECTION II ... Chapters 9-14

A. Alexander, Ptolomies, Selucids
B. God's protection; Greek and Maccabee
C. Advent and reign of Messiah
D. Destruction of Jerusalem by Rome
E. Dissolution of Jewish polity
F. Conversion and restoration
G. Overthrow of the confederacy
H. Gentiles join Jehovah worship

CHAPTER XXV

PREFACE TO ZECHARIAH

Zechariah was contemporary with Haggai. With him he shared the task of encouraging the returned remnant to rebuild the temple.

PREFACE TO ZECHARIAH

(The reader is urged to re-read Chapter 23, "The Preface to Haggai," by way of reviewing the historic setting of both of these prophets.)

In contrast to Haggai, who was a "layman," Zechariah was a Levitical priest, and a member of one of the outstanding priestly families. His grandfather, Iddo, had been among the first to return from Babylon under Zerubbabel. The prophet himself may well have been born in Babylon. *(2:4)*

There is no difficulty in specifically dating the beginning of Zechariah's prophetic work. He places it in the second year of Darius and the eighth month. This would make it, on our calendar, November of 520 B.C. just two months after the beginning of the work of Haggai.

Zechariah's second messages, a series of visions, began three months later on February 24, 519 B.C. The final message, another series of visions, was delivered on December 4, 518 B.C.

As was Haggi's, so was Zechariah's purpose the motivation of the people to build the themple. His approach is strikingly different. Whereas Haggai's message was simple and plainly written, the younger prophet, Zechariah, writes poetically and with flights of fancy which sometimes make his writing almost indecipherable to the twentieth century reader. He goes even beyond Isaiah in the use of symbolic and figurative language, establishing his book as distinctly apocalyptic.

Zechariah thus takes his place with Daniel and Ezekiel among Old Testament apocalypse. Only four Biblical books, including Revelation are written in this way.

Perhaps a word should be said here concerning apocalyptic writing. While it is no less inspired, and so no less important than other Biblical literature, it is extremely difficult of exegesis and therefore does not lend itself to dogmatic certainty. Many, failing to recognize this limitation, attempt to prove their pet systems, particularly systems of eschatology, by quoting passages from these books out of both historical and grammatical context. These proof texts are usually organized into printed charts, thus forming a supposedly irrefutable proof of the chartmaker's peculiar position and prophetic views. This is, to say the very least, dangerous procedure if not downright dishonest.

The figures and symbols used in apocalyptic writings are figures common to the day in which the writer and his first readers lived. The difficulty of the modern student in understanding these symbols lies largely in the fact that centuries have passed, and with them, the common usage of the symbols.

Generally speaking, there are three keys to the understanding of apocalyptic figures and symbolism: (1) Often the figure or symbol suggests its own meaning. With such there is little difficulty, if one will "do his homework" and place himself in the historic climate of the writer. (2) The context of the symbolic passage often contains the necessary key to the meaning of the symbol. This type of symbol is not so easily understood as the first, but it is less difficult than the third. (3) The third key is the historical allusion. Here one must be thoroughly conversant with the historic setting of the book in question. Often this requires years of disciplined study of ancient and Biblical history. Most dogmatic chart-makers are not inclined to this sort of discipline and so read into such symbols their own ideas which would be completely unrecognizable by the prophet.

Unfortunately, there are many passages of apocalypsis in which none of the three keys is apparent. Further, the symbols are not always used with the same meaning from book to book, or even within the same book. Many times a particular author, as for instance Zechariah, uses symbols that are found in no other Biblical work. These of course require special attention indeed.

The difficult nature of apocalyptic writing does not make these books any less the Word of God. In fact, such symbols frequently are used because God is attempting to communicate an idea for which human language has no literal terminology. Obviously any literal interpretation of such language cannot be accurate.

Whatever else may be said about the study of apocalyptic prophecy, one must never allow himself to become closed-minded in his understanding of it. It certainly ought never become the basis of division among God's people.

To come back specifically to Zechariah; his message may be summed up simply as God's appeal to Judah to "Return to me and I will return to you." (1:3)

This is a recurring theme of the prophets, particularly the minor prophets. It is stated repeatedly in terms of unfaithfulness, punishment, exile, restoration, remnant. Sometimes it applies to historic return from captivity. Other times it refers to a more long-ranged return.

Zechariah re-opens a series of prophecy which, in a sense, had been closed by Ezekiel. Ezekiel had been told to lie for 390 days on his left side and then lie 40 days on his right side. The 390 days represented the punishment of the northern kingdom and the 40 days represented the punishment of the southern kingdom. At the close of that time (390 plus 40 days) during which he was silent, Ezekiel forecast that there would be a period of prophetic silence. The vision would be removed from Judah.

PREFACE TO ZECHARIAH

Zechariah re-opens the prophetic contact. This work is to bridge the silence gap, to bring the people back to the land from which they had been taken and to look ahead to the coming of the Messiah. They were within the borders, but they would not be completely returned until they re-built the temple of Jehovah.

Zechariah does not refer to the Messiah by inference or allusion. He's the most specific of all the minor prophets in his Messianic forecasts. Only Isaiah is more graphic and realistically recognizable in his prepicturing of the life of Christ. For this reason, Zechariah ranks with Isaiah, some have even said above Isaiah, in his influence on the Christology of the New Testament, particularly the Gospels.

An outline of Zechariah shows the book divided quite naturally into two sections. The first begins with a series of eight symbolic visions (1:-6:15) which were designed to remove from the people, step by step, the obstacles which stood in the way of Messiah's coming. They are followed by the coronation of Joshua in a symbolic merger of the functions of priest and king.

Following the coronation, Zechariah presents a rather lengthy passage (chapters 7-8) in which he teaches concerning worship. This he also relates to the coming of Christ.

The second major section of the prophecy begins with chapter nine and concludes the book. Here Zechariah foretells the coming of the Messianic age and the glorious future of God's people. The present (520 B.C.) returnees are only a token of those who will return. A time will come when false shepherds will betray the people, but at least God's Israel will be vindicated. Then will come the universal reign of God over all men.

Chapter XXV—*Questions*
Preface to Zechariah

1. Zechariah was contemporary with_____.
2. These two prophets shared what common task?
3. Contrast Haggai with Zechariah.
4. What is the date of Zechariah?
5. Zechariah's writing is apocalyptic. What is apocalyptic writing?
6. Why is apocalyptic writing especially difficult to understand today?
7. What are three keys to understanding apocalyptic symbols and figures?

8. What verse in chapter one sums up Zechariah's message?
9. Zechariah re-opens a series of prophecy which in effect had been closed by _____.
10. Does Zechariah refer to the Messiah by allusion or directly?
11. How does the second section of Zechariah differ from the first?
12. Outline Zechariah.

CHAPTER XXVI
INTRODUCTION TO SECTION I
ZECHARIAH 1:1-6

RV . . . In the eighth month, in the second year of Darius, came the word of Jehovah unto Zechariah the son of Berechiah, the son of Iddo, the prophet, saying, Jehovah was sore displeased with your fathers. Therefore say thou unto them, Thus saith Jehovah of hosts: Return unto me, saith Jehovah of hosts, and I will return unto you, saith Jehovah of hosts. Be ye not as your fathers unto whom the former prophets cried, saying, Thus saith Jehovah of hosts, Return ye now from your evil ways, and from your evil doings: but they did not hear, nor hearken unto me, saith Jehovah. Your fathers, where are they? and the prophets, do they live for ever? But my words and my statutes, which I commanded my servants the prophets, did they not overtake your fathers? and they turned and said, Like as Jehovah of hosts thought to do unto us, according to our ways, and according to our doings, so hath he dealt with us.

LXX . . . In the eighth month, in the second year of the reign of Darius, the word of the Lord came to Zacharias, the son of Barachias, the son of Addo, the prophet, saying, The Lord has been very angry with your fathers. And thou shalt say to them, Thus saith the Lord Almighty; Turn to me, saith the Lord of hosts, and I will turn to you, saith the Lord of hosts. And be ye not as your fathers, whom the prophets before charged, saying, Thus saith the Lord Almighty; Turn ye from your evil ways, and from your evil pratices: but they hearkened not, and attended not to hearken to me, saith the Lord. Where are your fathers, and the prophets? Will they live for ever? But do ye receive my words and mine ordinances, all that I command by my spirit to my servants the prophets, who lived in the days of your fathers; and they answered and said, As the Lord Almighty determined to do to us,

INTRODUCTION TO SECTION I 1:1-6

according to our ways, and according to our practices, so has he done to us.

COMMENTS

(Verse 1) As was indicated in the previous chapter, Zechariah's date is easily determined. The first decree permiting the Jews to return to Judah from Babylon was issued by Cyrus in 538 B.C. Cyrus died in 529 B.C. whereupon Campbsus became ruler in Persia. Following his death in 522 B.C. a period of anarchy was finally brought to an end by the ascension to the throne of Darius in 521 B.C.

Zechariah 1:1 states that the word of Jehovah came to the prophet in the second year of Darius, which of course is 520 B.C. The eighth month would be our month of November.

Zechariah identifies himself as the son of Barachiah, the son Iddo, the prophet. We know of one prophet of a former day named Iddo. (cf. *II Chronicles 12:15*) It is possible Zechariah is identifying himself as a progeny of that Iddo. The terminology certainly allows this conclusion, though it by no means demands it.

Some have thought that Zechariah, the son Barachiah, is the same individual to whom Jesus refers as having been slain between the sanctuary and the altar. (cf. *Matthew 23:35*) Possibly, since Jesus is reckoning up the innocent blood shed by the Jews, beginning with Abel, He ends with this last of the prophets to so die. This seems a rather unlikely argument, however, since no Jewish history or tradition, including Josephus, makes any mention of Zechariah as having been martyred. It seems more probable that the Zechariah mentioned by Jesus is another person altogether.

(Verse 2) Here the prophet reminds his readers of the pre-exilic sin of their ancestors and alludes to the punishment from which they have themselves only recently returned. Obviously, his intent is to warn them that such punishment is again possible unless those who have physically returned to the land shall also spiritually return to the Lord. (Modern Israel please take note!)

(Verse 3) This verse is the key-note of the entire book. Its tone is that of all the minor prophets, both before and after the captivity. *"Return unto me . . . and I will return to you."* was the plea of Jehovah through all His Old Testament prophets. (eg. *Malachi 3:7*)

(Verse 4-6) Observe that Zechariah has now three times referred to God as *"Jehovah of hosts."* The readers are thus reminded of His sovereign power and universal dominion. It is a subtle appeal to the elementary fear of punishment; certainly not the loftiest, but nevertheless a very real motive for turning to God. It is very desirable to have the Lord of hosts as friend. It is a fearful thing to place ourselves in the position of an enemy to Him. (cp. *Hebrews 10:31*)

Their fathers had been similarly warned and had not heeded. Consequently, the punishment of Jehovah had fallen. Zechariah's plea is *"Be ye not as your fathers."*

"Where are your fathers?" asks the prophet. It is a rhetorical question. A whole generation had been swept away. The prophets who warned them were also gone. These, their children, knew very well that that the warnings of God were not hollow threats. The sentences of Jehovah are executed. Whoever runs is overtaken by them and there are none who escape.

The justice of God is so well defined that even those against whom it comes must agree that He deals with them according to their ways.

Chapter XXVI—*Questions*

Introduction to Section I

1. Identify Zechariah the prophet.
2. Why does Zechariah remind the returnees of the pre-exilic sin of their fathers?
3. Which verse is the key note of the entire book of Zechariah?
4. Discuss the term "Jehovah of hosts."
5. What does Zechariah mean by "Be not as your fathers?"

CHAPTER XXVII

A VISION OF HORSES

ZECHARIAH 1:7-17

RV . . . Upon the four and twentieth day of the eleventh month, which is the month Shebat, in the second year of Darius, came the word of Jehovah unto Zechariah the son of Berechiah, the son of Iddo, the prophet, saying, I saw in the night, and behold, a man riding upon a red horse, and he stood among the myrtle-trees that were in the bottom; and behind him there were horses, red, sorrel, and white. Then said I, O my lord, what are these? And the angel that talked with me said unto me, I will show thee what these are. And the man that stood among the myrtle-trees answered and said, These are they whom

A VISION OF HORSES 1:7-17

Jehovah hath sent to walk to and fro through the earth, and, behold, all the earth sitteth still, and is at rest. Then the angel of Jehovah answered and said, O Jehovah of hosts, how long wilt thou not have mercy on Jerusalem and on the cities of Judah, against which thou hast had indignation these threescore and ten years? And Jehovah answered the angel that talked with me with good words, even comfortable words. So the angel that talked with me said unto me, Cry thou, saying, Thus saith Jehovah of hosts: I am jealous for Jerusalem and for Zion with a great jealously. And I am very sore displeased with the nations that are at ease; for I was but a little displeased, and they helped forward the affliction. Therefore thus saith Jehovah: I am returned to Jerusalem with mercies; my house shall be built in it, saith Jehovah of hosts, and a line shall be stretched forth over Jerusalem. Cry yet again, saying, Thus saith Jehovah of hosts: My cities shall yet overflow with prosperity; and Jehovah shall yet comfort Zion, and shall yet choose Jerusalem.

LXX . . . On the twenty-fourth day in the eleventh month, this is the month Sabat, in the second year of the reign of Darius, the word of the Lord came to Zacharias, the son of Barachias, the son of Addo, the prophet, saying, I saw by night, and behold a man mounted on a red horse, and he stood between the shady mountains; and behind him were red horses, and grey, and piebald, and white. And I said, What are these, my lord? And the angel that spoke with me said to me, I will shew thee what these things are. And the man that stood between the mountains answered, and said to me, These are they whom the Lord has sent forth to go round the earth. And they answered the angel of the Lord that stood between the mountains, and said, We have gone round all the earth, and, behold, all the earth is inhabited, and is at rest. Then the angel of the Lord answered and said, O Lord Almighty, how long wilt thou have no mercy on Jerusalem, and the cities of Juda, which thou hast disregarded these seventy years? And the Lord Almighty answered the angel that spoke with me good words and consolatory sayings. And the angel that spoke with me said to me, Cry out and say, Thus saith the Lord Almighty; I have been jealous for Jerusalem and Sion with great jealousy. And I am very angry with the heathen that combine to attack her: forasmuch as I indeed was a little angry, but they combined to attack her for evil. Therefore thus saith the Lord: I will return to Jerusalem with compassion; and my house shall be rebuilt in her, saith the Lord Almighty, and a measuring line shall yet be stretched out over Jerusalem. And the angel that spoke with me said to me, Cry yet, and say, Thus saith the Lord Almighty;

1:7-14   ZECHARIAH

Yet shall cities be spread abroad through prosperity; and the Lord shall yet have mercy upon Sion, and shall choose Jerusalem.

COMMENTS

In verse 7, Zechariah begins the first of the series of eight visions which are resigned to remove the obstacles to Messiah's coming. He first records the vision and then the angelic interpretation of it.

WHAT THE PROPHET SAW . . . v. 8-11

In the night, the prophet saw a man riding on a red horse. He was riding among a grove of myrtle trees in a bottom, *ie.* a shady place. With him were other horsemen, some on red, some on sorrel, and some on white horses.

Seeing this dark and solitary scene, the prophet asked of the angel through whom the visions were given, what these things were and was immediately granted an answer.

These horsemen were they whom Jehovah had sent to walk to and fro in the earth. The angel who stood among the myrtle trees, probably the first horseman, reported that the horsemen have ridden to and fro through the earth, and that the entire earth was at rest.

WHAT THE VISION MEANT . . . v. 12-17

To clarify to the prophet the meaning of his vision, the angel of whom he had asked the meaning (v. 9) addresses Jehovah directly. His question is *"how long will you not have mercy on Jerusalem and on the cities of Judah?"* It has been seventy years since God's mercy was removed from them.

Jehovah's answer was not harsh, so the angel addresses Zechariah with the answer to his question.

The prophet is to pass along, to cry aloud, to the people the answer of Jehovah. God is very much concerned for both Jerusalem, the city, and for Zion, the city as capital of the covenant people.

Not only so, but He is displeased with the nations of the earth who are at ease while Israel suffers the humiliation of a vassal state. Even while these nations had helped with God's chastizing of His people, He had been "a little displeased" with them.

Therefore, Jehovah is returned to Jerusalem with mercies. The temple is to be rebuilt and the city itself will know the measuring line of the builder.

Not only so, His cities shall flow with prosperity, and God will comfort His people. Jerusalem shall yet be His.

Jehovah's message here might well have been made in answer to the objections raised in *Haggai 1:2-4*. There the people were complaining that it was not yet time to rebuild the temple. They had not been home long enough, there was drought in the land and other concerns must take precedent over the construction of God's house.

In fact, Haggai and Zechariah spoke to the same audience. The answer was directed to the objections. God recognizes the length of the punishment they have endured and re-assures them that His mercies are now returned. It is indeed time to build. Both the temple and the city will prosper, as will the outlying cities of Judea.

Seeing this entire passage as a unit, as well as verse by verse, will help us comprehend its meaning. Some have identified the rider of the red horse (v. 7) as the Messiah Himself. Others have said he is the angel of *Joshua 5:13-14* who in turn they see as the Messiah also. In each case, he is supposed to be standing ready to wreak swift bloodshed against the foes of Israel.

Neither of these seem to me to answer the historic context of Zechariah. Rather, it would seem the horsemen are symbolic of Darius and his hosts under whose iron rule the world languished "at ease" in a sort of *Pax Romana*.

The red color of the leader's horse does indeed represent bloodshed. The white implies death, as the pale horse of Revelation. The sorrel, (literally speckled) a combination of red and white, implies a condition in which some prosper and some do not.

This is a picture of the Persian empire under Darius. The enforcement of peace through military power and the inequity in which some prosper and some are in want has aroused to sore displeasure that which was formerly a "little displeasure." (*v. 15*)

The myrtle grove, among whom the horsemen are stationed is symbolic of the returned remnant who, far from being free are a humbled vassal state paying tribute to Darius.

It is the pointed reference to this historic situation which caused Zechariah's message to be couched in the hidden language of apocalypse. To have openly predicted the rising prosperity of the vassal state of Israel would have brought dire consequences indeed.

The first vision means simply that God is aware of the harsh occupation of the world and especially of Israel by Persian forces. Despite the apparent peace, the world was actually languishing under the stern discipline of military might.

In the midst of these circumstances, God wants His people to know that, if they will return with their hearts to Him, Jerusalem will once again be the city of His choice and the neighboring cities of Judea will also prosper. The enforced peace of Persia assures the opportunity to build without molestation. Just as God had raised up the Chaldeans to punish His people, so He has raised up Persia to protect them during the period of reconstruction. Thus the time is ripe for the rebuilding of the temple and the city.

Chapter XXVII—*Questions*
A Vision of Horses

1. The eight visions which begin with 1:7 are designed to _____.
2. Describe the first vision.
3. What was Zechariah's immediate response to this vision?
4. Who were the horsemen of the first vision?
5. What was the question of the angel to Jehovah?
6. Was Jehovah's answer harsh?
7. What was Zechariah instructed to do?
8. Why was Jehovah displeased with the nations?
9. God had returned to Jerusalem with_____.
10. How does Jehovah's answer here relate to *Haggai 1:2-4?*
11. The horsemen are symbolic of_____.
12. What do the various colors of the horses represent?
13. What, in this first vision, is directly related to Zechariah's reason for writing in apocalyptic style?

CHAPTER XXVIII
A VISION OF FOUR HORNS AND SMITHS
ZECHARIAH 1:18-21

RV . . . And I lifted up mine eyes, and saw, and, behold, four horns. And I said unto the angel that talked with me, What are these? And he answered me, These are the horns which have scattered Judah, Israel, and Jerusalem. And Jehovah showed me four smiths. Then said I, What come these to do? And he spake, saying, These are the horns which scattered Judah, so that no man did lift up his head; but these are

A VISION OF FOUR HORNS AND SMITHS   1:18-21

come to terrify them to cast down the horns of the nations, which lifted up their horn against the land of Judah to scatter it.

LXX . . . And I lifted up mine eyes and looked, and behold four horns. And I said to the angel that spoke to me, What are these things, my lord? And he said to me, These are the horns that have scattered Juda, and Israel, and Jerusalem. And the Lord shewed me four artificers. And I said, What are these coming to do? And he said, These are the horns that scattered Juda, and they broke Israel in pieces, and none of them lifted up his head: and these are come forth to sharpen them for their hands, even the four horns, the nations that lifted up the horn against the land of the Lord to scatter it.

COMMENTS

Zechariah's second vision is also a vision of restoration. What the four horns have scattered, the four smiths will re-unite.

The horn is a frequently used symbol for the military might of a nation or a ruler. To a pastoral people, the horn of the lead ram lends itself quite naturally to such symbolism. In this case, the four horns refer to the four powers who had had a hand in the scattering of both the northern and southern kingdoms.

Assyria, of course, as the destroyer of the northern kingdom, answers to the first of these horns. Babylon, who actually smote Judah, and Egypt, upon whom the Jews had depended for protection from Babylon, are easily seen as the second and third powers involved in their scattering.

It is a bit more difficult to account for the fourth horn. Traditionally the commentators have divided into three schools of thought on the matter. Some have said that the four horns are Assyria, Egypt, Babylon, and the Medo-Persians. Assyria and Babylon are obvious. Egypt is understandable since their failure to provide the protection for which Judah had entered into an alliance with her contributed to the scattering of the people.

The difficulty lies with the Medo-Persians. It was this empire which overthrew the Babylonians and opened the way for the return from exile. It was first Cyrus and later Darius, rulers of the Medo-Persian kingdom, who issued the edicts permitting the return and allowing the rebuilding. It seems highly unlikely, therefore, that this power should be included among those who scattered Judah.

The second school of thought among the commentators indicates that the number four is figurative of the four points of the compass.

1:18, 19   ZECHARIAH

The powers therefore would be: to the north the Assyrians, Chaldeans and Samaritans; to the south Egypt and Arabia; to the east Ammon and Moab, and to the west Philistia. To see this interpretation of the four horns requires the ignoring of the historic relationships among the powers indicated.

The third hypothesis presented is that the first two horns were Babylon and the Medo-Persians. The third and fourth powers had at the time of Zechariah not yet risen. These would be the Graeco-Macedonians under Alexander and the Roman Empire. This interpretation results from an attempt to force Zechariah into the mold of Daniel, chapters two and seven, where four powers are predicted prior to the coming of the Messianic kingdom.

This view presents many difficulties, not the least of which is the previously mentioned fact that the Medo-Persians are historically cast in the role of deliverer and protector of the remnant rather than among the scatterers of Judah and Jerusalem.

If we will examine the pre-exilic history of Judah's neighbors, we will discover a fourth, almost forgotten power. Prior to the rather confusing shift of alliances which finally produced the Medo-Persian empire, the Medes had themselves been a power to be reckoned with in the middle east. It was they who warred against Assyria, finally destroying the capital city of Nineveh and swept across western Asia to the gates of Sardis.

Within a generation after having destroyed Nineveh, the Median empire came to an end. Its tenure was short, so short in fact that it contributed little to the rise of civilization as we know it. The exploits of Tiglath-Pileser and later of Sargon write a brief but bloody chapter in ancient history.

It was Sargon who placed several Israelites in the cities of Media (cf. *II Kings 17:6,24*), thus contributing to the scattering of God's people.

It was under Cyaxares that the Median confederation reached the zenith of its brief power. Nobopalassar, the satrap of Chaldea joined Cyaxares in an alliance against Assyria and his daughter was given as wife to Nebuchadnezzar, the Babylonian king who "scattered Judah and Jerusalem."

The Medes later, under the corrupt influence of Cyaxares' successor son, became weakened to the point that they were easy prey for the rising power of Cyrus the Persian who annexed Media to form the Medo-Persian empire.

A VISION OF FOUR HORNS AND SMITHS 1:19-21

The horns of Zechariah are then, in my opinion, Assyria, Egypt, Media and Babylon. The four pre-exilic powers who contributed to the scattering of both Israel and Judah.

(Verses 20-21) The Septuagint has artificers where our text (the Revised Version) has smiths. The King James translators render the word "carpenters." The idea in the word itself seems to be those who are "skilled in demolition."

In Zechariah's second vision he is perplexed and asks *"what come these to do?"* The answer indicates that these four skillful workers are come to destroy the four powers who had scattered Judah and conquered the holy land.

In a figure the Lord promises the prophet that the world powers would be broken, indeed the Assyrians, Egyptians, Medes and Babylonians were already broken. The Medo-Persians, Greeks and Romans each fell in turn. God is ruler over human history. The nations He raises up He has also the power to pull down.

One reason the returned Jews were so hesitant to begin rebuilding was that they feared their neighbors. Rehum and Shimshai and other Samaritans opposed the building of the temple *(Ezra 4:8)*. Sanballat and Tobiah and the Ammonites and Arabians opposed the building of the wall *(Nehemiah 4:7)*. The prophet must reassure the people that God will pull down any power *"which lifted up their horn over the land of Judah to scatter it."* The time has come to build and Jehovah will brook no interferences.

Chapter XXVIII—*Questions*

A Vision of Four Horns and Smiths

1. Describe Zechariah's second vision.
2. The horn is frequently used to symbolize ―――――.
3. Who are the horns?
4. Why is the fourth horn harder to identify?
5. Why would the Medo-Persian empire not likely be included among those who scattered Judah?
6. To see the horns as representing the four points of the compass requires one to ignore ―――――.
7. Discuss the difficulties in the third hypothesis listed above, in which the commentators attempt to force the four horns into the mold of Daniel.

2:1-13   ZECHARIAH

8. Who is the fourth, almost forgotten, power involved in the pre-exilic history of Judah?
9. Discuss the term smiths in 1:20-21.
10. Why did the returning Jews hesitate to attempt the building of the temple?

CHAPTER XXIX
A VISION OF A MEASURING LINE
ZECHARIAH, CHAPTER 2:1-13

RV . . . And I lifted up mine eyes, and saw, and, behold, a man with a measuring line in his hand. Then said, I, Whither goest thou? And he said unto me, To measure Jerusalem, to see what is the breadth thereof, and what is the length thereof. And, behold, the angel that talked with me went forth, and another angel went out to meet him, and said unto him, Run, speak to this young man, saying, Jerusalem shall be inhabited as villages without walls, by reason of the multitude of men and cattle therein. For I, saith Jehovah, will be unto her a wall of fire round about, and I will be the glory in the midst of her. Ho, ho, flee from the land of the north, saith Jehovah; for I have spread you abroad as the four winds of the heavens, saith Jehovah. Ho Zion, escape, thou that dwellest with the daughter of Babylon. For thus saith Jehovah of hosts: After glory hath he sent me unto the nations which plundered you; for he that toucheth you toucheth the apple of his eye. For, behold, I will shake my hand over them, and they shall be a spoil to those that served them; and ye shall know that Jehovah of hosts hath sent me. Sing and rejoice, o daughter of Zion; for lo, I come, and I will dwell in the midst of thee, saith Jehovah. And many nations shall join themselves to Jehovah in that day, and shall be my people; and I will dwell in the midst of thee, and thou shalt know that Jehovah of hosts hath sent me unto thee. And Jehovah shall inherit Judah as his portion in the holy land, and shall yet choose Jerusalem. Be silent, all flesh, before Jehovah; for he is waked up out of his holy habitation.

LXX . . . And I lifted up mine eyes, and looked, and behold a man, and in his hand a measuring line. And I said to him, Whither goest thou? And he said to me, To measure Jerusalem, to see what is the breadth of it, and what is the length of it. And, behold, the angel that spoke with me stood by, and another angel went forth to meet

A VISION OF A MEASURING LINE 2:1-13

him, and spoke to him, saying, Run and speak to that young man, saying, Jerusalem shall be fully inhabited by reason of the abundance of men and cattle in the midst of her. And I will be to her, saith the Lord, a wall of fire round about, and I will be for a glory in the midst of her. Ho, ho, flee from the land of the north, saith the Lord: for I will gather you from the four winds of heaven, saith the Lord, even to Sion: deliver yourselves ye that dwell with the daughter of Babylon. For thus saith the Lord Almighty; After the glory has he sent me to the nations that spoiled you: for he that touches you is as one that touches the apple of his eye. For, behold, I bring my hand upon them, and they shall be a spoil to them that serve them: and ye shall know that the Lord Almighty has sent me. Rejoice and be glad, O daughter of Sion: for, behold, I come, and will dwell in the midst of thee, saith the Lord. And many nations shall flee for refuge to the Lord in that day, and they shall be for a people to him, and they shall dwell in the midst of thee: and thou shalt know that the Lord Almighty has sent me to thee. And the Lord shall inherit Juda his portion in the holy land, and he will yet choose Jerusalem. Let all flesh fear before the Lord: for he has risen up from his holy clouds.

COMMENTS

The first two of Zechariah's visions were intended to reassure the people that their security was guaranteed during the time they would be pre-occupied with building the temple and the city of Jerusalem. In the vision of the horses the prophet was reminded of the patrolling power of Persia which held the world in an enforced peace. In the vision of the horns and smiths he was assured that God's power was equal to any threat which might be directed upon them.

Now, to motivate them to apply themselves to the task, God shows Zechariah a vision of the future glories of Jerusalem.

(Verse 1-2) The prophet sees a man with a measuring line. This is a figure used elsewhere in prophetic Scripture. It first appears in *Ezekiel 40:3-4.*

There Ezekiel sees a vision of a man holding a line and a measuring rod standing at the gate. His purpose is to give specifications for the rebuilding of the city and particularly of the temple. Ezekiel's temple roughly follows the general design of the original built by Solomon, though with significant variations.

The measuring rod is twice mentioned again in the apocalypes of

2:1-6

John. *(Revelation 11:1, 21:15-17)* John is given a measuring rod and told to go measure the temple of God and the worshippers.

The final reference to such measurement is found in *Revelation 21:15-17*. This time the measuring rod is in the hand of the angel who uses it to measure the New Jerusalem.

In every reference using this figure, that which is to be measured is either the temple *(Ezekiel 40:3-4)*, the city *(Revelation 21:15-17* or both *(Zechariah 2:1-ff)*. In each case the purpose of the measurement is to call attention to the special glory of that which is measured.

(Verses 3-5) The first angel who is interpreting the vision to Zechariah, and who holds the measuring line, is met by a second angel who instructs him to run and say to "that young man" *(ie.* Zechariah) that Jerusalem shall be a city without walls because of the multitude of people and animals that inhabit it.

The city is to spread out far beyond its previous location. Judea is hereafter to be marked by unwalled villages (cp. *Ezekiel 38:11).* The Lord Himself will be a "wall of fire" around His people.

The people had been more concerned for their security than for God's work. As the man in the vision, they had been ready to measure for the walls which would circumscribe the holy city. It was a normal approach to city building in that day. An unwalled city was unheard of and the walls must be built before it would be safe to build ought else.

The tragedy of a wall about a city is that it not only protects, it also confines and limits. God will have none of it. His ideal is inclusion rather than exclusion, expansion rather than restriction. His great designs for His people are not to be restricted by a tape line. He will Himself be their protecting wall.

Not only so, He would be the glory within her. Haggai saw the glory of the restored people in terms of tributary silver and gold *(Haggai 2:8-ff).* Zechariah sees their glory in the Divine Presence.

(Verses 6-9) The overwhelming vision of an unlimited, unwalled city with God's presence as its glory and protection gives rise to two lyrical epilogues in which Zechariah looks beyond the immediate restoration to the Messianic fulfillment of its purpose. *(v. 6-9* and *10-13)* God had not chastened His people and delivered them from the chastisement simply for their own sakes. What they would restrict with a measuring line He would make available to all men.

In verse 6, He calls to those of the northern kingdom who have been scattered to the four winds to return . . . flee back to Him.

A VISION OF A MEASURING LINE 2:7-11

In verse 7, He calls to those of Judah who have remained in Babylon to escape to Zion.

(Verse 8) God has not forgotten His covenant purpose, the people are still "the apple of His eye." (cp. *Deuteronomy 32:10, Psalms 17:8, Proverbs 7:2*)

(Verse 9) Having already assured those who have returned of His presence and protection, He follows His plea to the others with the same reassurances. A simple wave of God's hand can defeat any foe of His people and cause their enemies to be plunder to those who have been slaves.

(Verses 10-13) In the second epilogue the prophet moves from concern with the immediate task of rebuilding which confronted the returnees from Babylon to the future glory of the Messianic kingdom in which many races would come to the Lord.

In verse 8, the word *"After glory He hath sent me into the nations,"* and in verse 9, *"Ye shall know that Jehovah of hosts hath sent me"* can only be Messianic in intent.

Now, in verse 10, the Lord promises to dwell personally in the midst of His people. Here is "the promise of the Father" which was fulfilled in the coming of the Holy Spirit to live in the church. Elsewhere God had promised to pour out His Spirit on all flesh. (cp. *Acts 1:4, Joel 2:28-ff, Acts 2:16-ff)*

(Verse 11) Paul would write the Galatians and say the purpose of our redemption was "that upon the Gentiles might come the blessings of Abraham in Jesus Christ" that we might receive the promise of the Spirit through faith. *(Galatians 3:13-14)*

Peter would preach that "to you is the promise and to your children and to all who are afar off, even as many as the Lord our God shall call unto Him." *(Acts 2:39)*

In the first epilogue to the third vision, *(Zechariah 2:6-9)* the Lord calls the dispersed of Israel to return that He may live in and protect them. In the second epilogue *(Zechariah 2:10-12)* these are called to rejoice because of His indwelling. In verse eleven the promise reaches beyond the faithful remnant of Israel. *"Many nations shall join themselves to Jehovah in that day, and shall be my people; and I will dwell in the midst of thee and thou shalt know that Jehovah of hosts hath sent me unto thee."*

It would be difficult to imagine a more vivid or graphic prediction of the universal outreach of God through the church. That which God had promised to Abraham is to become not alone the possession of his physical descendants. Many from everywhere will come and He will also live in and protect them.

Even a cursory reading of the book of Acts will reveal the fulfillment of this promise in the church. Beginning on Pentecost when "devout men from every nation under heaven" heard the gospel and were baptized into Christ, the church in one short generation embraced men and women of every ethnic origin. It began with the receiving into fellowship of Hellenists *(Acts 6:1)*. It grew with the conversion of the Samaritans *(Acts 8:4-ff)*. The outreach broadened with the inclusion of the Ethiopian proselyte *(Acts 8:26-ff)*. It passed the supreme milestone with the reception of the Roman centurian *(Acts 10)*. And the all inclusive nature of the church, God living in men of every race, became the distinguishing mark of God's people in Antioch *(Acts 11: 20-ff)*. As a consequence they received a new name which, more than anything else, calls attention to God's love for all men. *(Acts 11:26,* cp. *Isaiah 62:1-3)*

Immediately following the establishment of universal outreach in the Acts record is the account of Peter's angelic release from prison and the awful death of Herod, both of which demonstrate the truth that the Lord is indeed a wall of fire around His people so long as they are faithful to His purposes.

In the second half of *Zechariah 2:11* is yet another affirmation that the proof of the divine mission of Messiah would be His people. The fulfillment of this "promise of the Father" is the main thrust of the book of Acts as Luke narrates the continuing work of the Christ in His people. That which He began in the days of His flesh, Luke records in the third gospel. In *Acts 1:1* he refers to this as the record of what "Jesus began." Acts is the record of what He continues as through the church, His new body, He fulfills the second half of what the Old Testament had ascribed as His work. In the days of His flesh, according to the law of Moses and the prophets and the Psalms, the Messiah must "suffer, and rise again from the dead . . ." The same Old Covenant Scriptures taught that "repentance and remission of sins should be preached in His name unto all the nations, beginning at Jerusalem." *(Luke 24:45-47)*

Zechariah is one of those prophetic books in which this is stated. By this, wrote Zechariah, *"thou shalt know that Jehovah of hosts sent me unto thee."*

(Verses 12-13) The beginning of Messiah's dwelling in the midst of His people was Jerusalem *(Luke 24:47 (b))*. The heavenly Jerusalem (cp. *Hebrews 12:22*) had its beginning in the earthly city to be rebuilt

A VISION OF A MEASURING LINE   2:1-13

by Zechariah's people. The real temple (*Hebrews 9:8-9*), of which the rebuilt temple was a type, a fore-shadowing, was established in the shadow of its material counterpart. (*Acts 2*)

So in Messiah's people God would "yet choose Jerusalem" when men from every nation "are come to Mount Zion, and into the city of the living God, the heavenly Jerusalem . . . to the general assembly and church of the firstborn who are enrolled in heaven . . ." (*Hebrews 12:22-23*)

The waking of Jehovah out of His habitation is a statement of His fulfillment of His promised purpose.

Chapter XXIX—*Questions*

A Vision of a Measuring Line

1. What was the purpose of Zechariah's first two visions?
2. What is the purpose of the third vision?
3. Describe what Zechariah saw in the third vision.
4. Where else is the measuring rod mentioned in Biblical apocalypse?
5. What is the message of the second angel to Zechariah?
6. The people had been more concerned for_____ than for God's Word.
7. What is the tragedy of a wall about a city?
8. Without a wall, how is Jerusalem to be protected?
9. In response to the third vision Zechariah writes two lyrical epilogues which look beyond the rebuilding to_____.
10. What is the significance of "the apple of His eye?"
11. What is the promise of Jehovah in 2:10?
12. Discuss 2:11 in connection with Galatians, chapter 3.
13. Discuss 2:11 in light of the spreading of the church as recorded in Acts.
14. What proof of the divine mission of the Messiah is given in 2:11?
15. The beginning of Messiah's dwelling in the midst of His people was in_____.

CHAPTER XXX

A VISION OF THE HIGH PRIEST

ZECHARIAH, CHAPTER 3:1-10

RV . . . And he showed me Joshua the high priest standing before the angel of Jehovah, and Satan standing at his right hand to be his adversary. And Jehovah said unto Satan, Jehovah rebuke thee, O Satan; yea, Jehovah that hath chosen Jerusalem rebuke thee: as a brand plucked out of the fire? Now Joshua was clothed with filthy garments, and was standing before the angel. And he answered and spake unto those that stood before him, saying, Take the filthy garments from off him. And unto him he said, Behold, I have caused thine iniquity to pass from thee, and I will clothe thee with rich apparel. And I said, Let them set a clean mitre upon his head. So they set a clean mitre upon his head, and clothed him with garments; and the angel of Jehovah was standing by. And the angel of Jehovah protested unto Joshua, saying, Thus saith Jehovah of hosts: If thou wilt walk in my ways, and if thou wilt keep my charge, then thou also shalt judge my house, and shalt also keep my courts, and I will give thee a place of access among these that stand by. Hear now, I Joshua the high priest, thou and thy fellows that sit before thee; for they are men that are a sign: for, behold, I will bring forth my servant the Branch. For, behold, the stone that I have set before Joshua; upon one stone are seven eyes; behold, I will engrave the graving thereof, saith Jehovah of hosts, and I will remove the iniquity of that land in one day. In that day, saith Jehovah of hosts, shall ye invite every man his neighbor under the vine and under the fig-tree.

LXX . . . And the Lord shewed me Jesus the high priest standing before the angel of the Lord, and the Devil stood on his right hand to resist him. And the Lord said to the Devil, The Lord rebuke thee, O Devil, even the Lord that has chosen Jerusalem rebuke thee: behold! is not this as a brand plucked from the fire? Now Jesus was clothed in filthy raiment, and stood before the angel. And the Lord answered and spoke to those who stood before him, saying, Take away the filthy raiment from him: and he said to him, Behold, I have taken away thine iniquities: and clothe ye him with a long robe, and place a pure mitre upon his head. So they placed a pure mitre upon his head, and clothed him with garments: and the angel of the Lord stood by. And the angel of the Lord testified to Jesus, saying, Thus saith the Lord

A VISION OF THE HIGH PRIEST 3:1-5

Almighty; If thou wilt walk in my ways, and take heed to my charges, then shalt thou judge my house: and if thou wilt diligently keep my court, then will I give thee men to walk in the midst of these that stand here. Hear now, Jesus the high priest, thou, and thy neighbours that are sitting before thee; for they are diviners, for, behold, I bring forth my servant The Branch. For as for the stone which I have set before the face of Jesus, on the one stone are seven eyes: behold, I am digging a trench, saith the Lord Almighty, and I will search out all the iniquity of that land in one day. In that day, saith the Lord Almighty, ye shall call together every man his neighbour under the vine and under the fig-tree.

COMMENTS

Zechariah's fourth vision continues the growing Messianic crescendo of his prophecy. Here the attention shifts from the city and temple to the high priest. Both the high priest and his fellow priests are presented as a sign to be revealed in the coming of The Branch.

(Verses 1-3) Joshua the high priest (the Septuagint calls him Jesus) stands before the angel of the Lord as representative of his people. Satan stands in the position of accuser. This is the first time in the Bible that the Devil is mentioned by this name.

The filthy garments with which Joshua is clothed are symbolic of the sins of the people. They are still contaminated by the idolatry of their fathers to which is added their own present rebellion against rebuilding the temple. Satan may rightly charge that they are not fit to be God's people or to do God's work.

Jehovah's answer to Satan's accusation is that these are His people not by their merit but by His choice. He has brought them back from near extinction.

The ten northern tribes are gone. The generation which went into Babylon is dead. Those who have returned are but a handful compared to the numbers who elected to remain in Babylon. Unless God had plucked them as a brand from the fire they would no longer be a people.

(Verses 4-5) At this point in the vision the angel commands that the filthy garments be removed from Joshua and that they be replaced with rich apparel. A clean mitre, or turban, is to be placed on his head so that he will stand clean before both the angel and Satan.

The intent is to show that God is not going to hold the

guilt of past sins against His redeemed remnant. Their sin will be forgiven in order that they may get on with His work.

(Verses 6-7) Having cleansed the high priest, symbolic of the forgiveness of the people, the angel now addresses him directly. What he says to Joshua is intended to be heard and heeded by the people. He makes two emphatic points.

First, their forgiveness was conditional. *If* Joshua will walk in His ways and *if* he will keep His charge, *then* as high priest he will judge God's house and keep His courts.

The instrumental relationship which the Israelites held to God as His people was always conditional. (cf. *Exodus 19:5-6*)

(Verse 8) *Second,* Jehovah's angel makes it quite clear that His willingness to forgive His people is related to the fulfillment of a larger purpose and is therefore not arbitrary.

The entire priesthood, both the high priest and those who sit with him are a sign. The justification of the sins of the people and the ultimate meaning of the priesthood are to be found in the coming Branch.

The Branch is identified as the servant of Jehovah. This is a significant title given the Messiah by both Isaiah and Ezekiel. (cp. *Isaiah 42:1, 49:3, 50:10, 52:13, 53:11* and *Ezekiel 34:23, 24*) It was primarily the failure of the Jews to see the Messiah in this light that caused their rejection of the Messiah when He came.

The term Branch also has prior establishment as a Messianic term. It refers to the Messiah as a tender shoot of the almost extinct royal Davidic line. (cf. *Isaiah 4:2, 11:1* and *Jeremiah 23:5, 33:15*) Luke's term "day spring" refers to this term (*Luke 9:78*)

(Verses 9-10) To encourage the people toward the building of God's house, the vision now identifies the Messiah as the chief corner stone of the temple. Upon the stone in the prophet's vision are seven eyes. It is to be engraven by the Master Architect Himself.

The stone which is the chief corner stone of the true temple is not a lifeless, senseless stone. It has seven eyes. It is living and has intelligence illuminated by perfect vision. (The figure seven is the apocalyptic symbol for completeness or perfection.)

I Peter 2:4-5 speaks of Jesus much as Zechariah's vision describes Him. He is the living stone chosen of God upon which God's people are built as a spiritual house.

Peter also alludes to the ideal priesthood typified in Zechariah's vision by Joshua and his attendant priests. The living stone is also the high priest of the real priesthood. The people of God are at once the temple of His dwelling and the priests of His service.

Is is in that day, *ie.* the day of the coming of the living stone and the true priest, that God will actually remove the sins of His people. In that day also the people of God will invite their neighbors to share in the bounties of the Messianic kingdom.

The language here is reminiscent of *Micah 4:4* in which the Messianic age is presented in terms of spiritual idealism.

Two characteristic of Messiah's day stand out in this passage. It is the day of cleansing from iniquity and it is the day of inviting others to share the blessings of God. Surely Jesus must have had this passage and others like it in mind when He said that the entire message of the Old Testament is summed up in His death and resurrection on the one hand and the preaching of repentance and remission of sins in every nation on the other. (*Luke 24:44-49*)

Chapter XXX—*Questions*
A Vision of the High Priest

1. In the fourth vision, the attention shifts to_____.
2. Describe the fourth vision.
3. The forgiveness of the Jews was conditional upon their_____ _____.
4. Jehovah's willingness to forgive His people is related to what larger purpose?
5. Discuss the Biblical significance of the term "The Branch."
6. Who is identified as the chief corner stone in the temple?
7. Discuss Zechariah's fourth vision in relation to I Peter 2:4-5.
8. What two characteristics of Messiah's day stand out in Zechariah, chapter three?

CHAPTER XXXI
A VISION OF A MENORAH AND OLIVE TREES
ZECHARIAH, CHAPTER 4:1-14

RX . . . And the angel that talked with me came again, and waked me, as a man that is wakened out of his sleep. And he said unto me,

4:1-14 ZECHARIAH

What seest thou? And I said, I have seen, and, behold, a candlestick all of gold, with its bowl upon the top of it, and its seven lamps thereon; there are seven pipes to each of the lamps, which are upon the top thereof; and two olive-trees by it, one upon the right side of the bowl, and the other upon the left side thereof. And I answered and spake to the angel that talked with me, saying, What are these, my lord? Then the angel that talked with me answered and said unto me, Knowest thou not what these are? And I said, No, my lord. Then he answered and spake unto me, saying, This is the word of Jehovah unto Zerubbabel, saying, Not by might, nor by power, but by my Spirit, saith Jehovah of hosts. Who art thou, O great mountain? before Zerubbabel thou shalt become a plain; and he shall bring forth the top stone with shouting of Grace unto it. Moreover the word of Jehovah came unto me, saying, The hands of Zerubbabel have laid the foundation of this house; his hands shall also finish it; and thou shalt know that Jehovah of hosts hath sent me unto you. For who hath despised the day of small things? for these seven shall rejoice, and shall see the plummet in the hand of Zerubbabel; these are the eyes of Jehovah, which run to and fro through the whole earth. Then answered I, and said unto him, What are these two olive-trees upon the right side of the candlestick and upon the left side thereof? And I answered the second time, and said, unto him, What are these two olive-branches, which are beside the two golden spouts, that empty the golden oil out of themselves? And he answered me and said, Knowest thou not what these are? And I said, No, my lord. Then said he, These are the two anointed ones, that stand by the Lord of the whole earth.

LXX . . . And the angel that talked with me returned, and awakened me, as when a man is awakened out of his sleep. And he said to me, What seest thou? And I said, I have seen, and behold a candlestick all of gold, and its bowl upon it, and seven lamps upon it, and seven oil funnels to the lamps upon it: and two olive-trees above it, one on the right of the bowl, and one on the left. And I inquired, and spoke to the angel that talked with me, saying, What are these things, my lord? And the angel that talked with me answered, and spoke to me, saying, Knowest thou not what these things are? And I said, no, my lord. And he answered and spoke to me, saying, This is the word of the Lord of Zorobabel, saying, Not by mighty power, nor by strength, but by my Spirit, saith the Lord Almighty. Who art thou, the great mountain before Zorobabel, that thou shouldest prosper? whereas I will bring out the stone of the inheritance, the grace of it the equal of my grace. And

A VISION OF A MENORAH AND OLIVE TREES 4:1-3

the word of the Lord came to me, saying, The hands of Zorobabel have laid the foundation of this house, and his hands shall finish it: and thou shalt know that the Lord Almighty has sent me to thee. For who has despised the small days? surely they shall rejoice, and shall see the plummet of tin in the hand of Zorobabel: these are the seven eyes that look upon all the earth. And I answered, and said to him, What are these two olive-trees, which are on the right and left hand of the candlestick? And I asked the second time, and said to him, What are the two branches of the olive-trees that are by the side of the two golden pipes that pour into and communicate with the golden oil funnels? And he said to me, Knowest thou not what these are? and I said, No, my lord. And he said, These are the two anointed ones that stand by the Lord of the whole earth.

COMMENTS

Zechariah's fifth vision presents the rebuilding of the temple against the backdrop of two traditional symbols of Israel, the menorah, or seven branched candlestick, and the olive trees.

Again, as in the first vision especially, the record divides itself naturally along the lines of the prophet's questions and the angel's answers. In this case, the angel seems somewhat surprised that the prophet could not answer his own question.

(Verse 1) The angel rouses Zechariah from the ecstacy of the previous vision to show him the present one.

WHAT THE PROPHET SAW . . . v. 2-3

The seven branched lampstand or menorah became the symbol of Israel at the time of the building of the tabernacle. Moses was instructed by God to place the menorah as the only source of light in the tent of worship. *(Exodus 25:31-40)* Made of fine gold, it consisted of a shaft five feet tall. At three points on the shaft, two branches at each point curved out and upward from the central shaft. The branches so formed, rose to the level of the central shaft, thus forming, with the shaft, a cluster of seven candlesticks. The cluster measured three feet six inches across at the top. Its seven wicks were fed from a bowl of oil which formed its base.

The menorah provided the sole source of light in the tabernacle, the fact which gave it its symbolic significance. As it stood in the south of the Holy Place, directly opposite the table of showbread, it illuminated both the table and the altar of incense which stood on the west side of the Holy Place just outside the veil which separated this first sanctuary from the Holy of Holies.

The menorah had occupied a similar station in the original temple where ten such lights illuminated the sanctuary. Along with the other sacred implements these menorahs had been returned by Cyrus at the end of the Babylonian exile. The lampstand would take its place in the new temple when the re-construction was finally completed.

In Zechariah's vision the form of the Menorah is changed. Rather than a single shaft with its branches forming a single seven branched lampstand, the symbolic menorah of the vision is constructed in such a way that each branch of the main shaft forms the center shaft of a smaller menorah. The effect is seven smaller menorahs branching off from the main menorah. The intent is obviously seven times seven, which is an emphatic statement of absolute perfection, God's perfect word to Israel.

WHAT THE MENORAH IN THE VISION MEANT . . . v. 4-10

(Verses 4-5) These verses form the bridge between the vision and its meaning as interpreted by the angel. First the prophet asks the meaning of the vision. Then the angel asks him if he doesn't know the answer to his own question. The prophet answers in the negative. The next verse marks the beginning of the angel's answer.

(Verse 6) The multiple menorah of the vision represents the word of God to Zerubbabel and through him to the people. The multiplied perfection symbolized by the forty-nine lamps springing from a central shaft emphasize the correctness of that word.

In the vision attention is called to the bowl of the central shaft out of which the lamps originated. *(v. 2-3)* The bowl was a container for the oil which fueled the lamps. In the original menorah of the tabernacle, specific instructions were given concerning this oil container.

The oil contained in this bowl symbolized the Spirit of God which was in reality the source of divine illumination just as the oil was the ultimate source of the light of the menorah.

It is to this that the angel directs the prophet in verse six. *"Not by might, nor by power, but by my Spirit saith Jehovah of hosts."*

This message is addressed specifically to Zerubbabel as chief civil authority. He is to rebuild the temple not by the use of an army (might) or by (human) power but by the Spirit of God. *Haggai* has pointed out that the work was to be done by the Spirit *(Haggai 2:5)*. Therefore Zerubbabel is not to be discouraged by the human weaknesses with which he must contend.

A VISION OF A MENORAH AND OLIVE TREES 4:6-10

As we have seen, these weaknesses largely manifested themselves as fear. There was a desire on the part of the people to build a wall before the temple, lest they be attacked by their neighbors. There was a desire to tend first to business and farming lest their physical needs not be met during the building. God will have them know that military protection and the supplying of their own needs through their own efforts are not necessary. If they will apply themselves, His Spirit will supply every protection and need.

It is appropriate that this message be addressed to Zerubbabel. Zerubbabel was governor of Judah, appointed by Darius. He is mentioned in Ezra, Nehemiah, and Haggai, as well as Zechariah. From these books we know that it was he who, with Joshua the high priest, led the little band of released captives from Babylon and began rebuilding the temple in the second year of Darius.

According to Josephus and the apocraphal book of *I Ezdras,* he was a personal friend of Darius, having won the king's friendship by winning in his presence a contest to determine what was strongest in all the world . . . wine, kings, women, or truth. Zerubbabel demonstrated that truth was strongest of all and so won the king's admiration. With it he won permission to go up to Jerusalem and build the temple, the center for the spreading of truth.

Along with the permission to rebuild the temple, Zerubbabel was given the office of governor, with the stipulation that he also serve as *tirshatha,* or tax collector, sending Judean tribute to the Medo-Persian king.

With all his "connections" in high places, along with his own dynamic personality and wisdom, there is no doubt the governor needed Zechariah's reminder that God's work does not depend upon such things but upon His Spirit.

Having made Joshua fit to serve as religious authority in the preceding vision, God now prepares Zerubbabel to serve as civil authority. In the eighth and final vision these two offices will be symbolically united as one to be filled ultimately by the Messiah.

(Verses 7-10) Trusting the divine power of the Spirit of God, Zerubbabel is to find the great mountain of difficulty in rebuilding suddenly become a level plain. He would have the honor of completing the temple which he had begun and of placing the final coping stones to the accompaniment of the cheers and praises of the people.

Recognizing that the work has been completed in the power of the Spirit rather than human might and power, the people will shout, "grace, grace," when the chisled top stone is brought forth and put in place as the final act of building.

Those who have "despised small things" *(v. 10), ie.* who have looked with contempt on the beginning of reconstruction, will be silenced when the final stone is placed. *"Thou shalt know that Jehovah of hosts hath sent me unto you."* There can be no doubt of the divine origin of prophecy when it is fulfilled before their eyes. Isaiah, prior to the captivity, had predicted ". . . saying to Jerusalem, thou shalt be built." *(Isaiah 44:26)*

In the beginning of the reconstruction, some had despised the footers of the second temple because it seemed the end product would be inferior to that of Solomon *(Ezra 3:1-2)*. These shall be won to optimism when they see the governor himself at work with the plummet in his hand. They will recognize in the plumbing of the work by Zerubbabel the all seeing eyes of Jehovah *(v. 10(b))*. He whose eyes "run to and fro through the whole earth," *ie.* who is in constant command of all things everywhere, will also be watching this work.

WHAT THE OLIVE TREES MEANT . . . v. 11-14

The explanation of the two olive trees *(v. 3)*, as well as that of the menorah, begins with a question. This time the question is directed to the angel by Zechariah. The trees stood on either side of the menorah and the prophet did not grasp their significance.

(Verses 12-13) Before the angel answers, Zechariah repeats the question, *this* time noting that the two olive trees are pouring oil into the menorah.

Once more the angel indicates surprise, or at least concern, that the prophet cannot answer his own question. One is reminded of Jesus' response to Nicodemus, "Art thou a teacher of Israel and understandest not these things." *(John 3:10)*

In verse fourteen we come to the angel's answer. The two olive trees are "the two anointed ones, that stand by the Lord of the whole earth." The two anointed ones are Joshua the high priest and Zerubbabel the governor. These have been set apart by God to the task of re-establishing His people in the holy land. Through them the power of God's Spirit will complete the task of reconstruction. This is apparent from the fact almost overlooked by Zechariah in asking for an explanation, namely that the oil which supplied the menorah was being poured out by the two olive trees.

A word must be said here in regard to the Spirit of God in this text. One of the objections of the Jews through the ages to the Chris-

A VISION OF A MENORAH AND OLIVE TREES 4:14

tian faith has been their inability to accept the so-called doctrine of the trinity. They have the impression that Christians worship three gods.

If we are to take our understanding of the Father, Son, Holy Spirit from the traditional creeds of Romanism and Protestantism, the charge certainly seems a valid one. Such credal statements, however, are not Scripture.

In Zechariah are references to God from the view of three manifestations. These in effect amount not to three gods, but to one God in three relationships to His people. None would question that the frequent references to Jehovah in Zechariah answer to the manifestation of deity commonly called "the Father."

In *Zechariah 2:10(b)*, Jehovah speaks. The conclusion of His statement in *2:11(b)* is *"and thou shalt know that Jehovah of hosts hath sent me unto thee."* Jehovah presents Himself as both sent and sender! This is precisely the relationship expressed by Isaiah and repeated by Matthew, "Behold, a virgin shall be with child, and shall bring forth a son, and they shall call His name, Emmanuel, which being interpreted is, God with us."

In Zechariah, the Spirit is added to these relationships of God to His people. Chapter four, verse six, indicates that the rebuilding of the temple is to be done by the Spirit of Jehovah. In the symbolism of Zechariah's vision this Spirit is poured into the work through His two anointed servants. There is no essential difference between the Spirit of God here and the Spirit of God promised to His people as a presence under the New Covenant.

The Spirit Who directed the re-building of the second temple through Joshua and Zerubbabel, today directs the building of the church through Jesus in Whom the civil and priestly offices are combined as the Anointed One. (cp. *Ephesians 3:14-ff)*

Chapter XXXI—*Questions*

A Vision of a Menorah and Olive Trees

1. What is the backdrop against which Zechariah's fifth vision is presented?
2. Describe Zechariah's fifth vision?
3. Describe the menorah used in the tabernacle.
4. Describe the menorah of Zechariah's vision.
5. What is symbolized by the multiple menorah of the vision?

6. The oil contained in the bowl of the menorah symbolized _____ as the source of God's light to His people.
7. The human weaknesses of those to whom Zechariah spoke were manifest largely as _____.
8. Show the appropriateness of this part of Zechariah's message being addressed to Zerubbabel.
9. What was Zerubbabel's relationship to Darius?
10. Along with permission to build the temple, Zerubbabel was charged by Darius to _____.
11. Who are "those who have despised small things?"
12. What is the meaning of the two olive trees in Zechariah's vision?
13. How does the vision of the Menorah and the olive trees relate to the Jewish objection to the doctrine of the trinity?
14. In the symbolism of this vision, the Spirit is poured into the work through _____.
15. The Spirit who directed the rebuilding of the temple by Zerubbabel also directs us today in the building of _____.

CHAPTER XXXII

A VISION OF A FLYING SCROLL

ZECHARIAH 5:1-4

RV . . . Then again I lifted up mine eyes, and saw, and, behold, a flying roll. And he said unto me, What seest thou? And I answered, I see a flying roll; the length thereof is twenty cubits, and the breadth thereof ten cubits. Then said he unto me, This is the curse that goeth forth over the face of the whole land: for every one that stealeth shall be cut off on the one side according to it; and every one that sweareth shall be cut off on the other side according to it. I will cause it to go forth, saith Jehovah of hosts, and it shall enter into the house of the thief, and into the house of him that sweareth falsely by my name; and it shall abide in the midst of his house, and shall consume it with the timber thereof and the stones thereof.

LXX . . . And I turned, and lifted up mine eyes, and looked and behold a flying sickle. And he said to me. What seest thou? And I said, I see a flying sickle, of the length of twenty cubits, and of the breadth of ten cubits. And he said to me, This is the curse that goes forth over the face of the whole earth: for every thief shall be punished with death on this side, and every false swearer shall be punished

A VISION OF A FLYING SCROLL 5:1-4

on that side. And I will bring it forth, saith the Lord Almighty, and it shall enter into the house of the thief, and into the house of him that swears falsely by my name; and it shall rest in the midst of his house, and shall consume it, and the timber of it, and the stones of it.

COMMENTS

WHAT THE PROPHET SAW . . . v. 1-2

Zechariah lifted up his eyes. This is the phrase which introduces four of the prophet's eight visions. In the present vision what is seen is described as a flying scroll measuring thirty feet long by fifteen feet wide.

The angel again asks what the prophet sees to which the prophet answers very literally by describing the flying scroll. Unlike the previous visions, the angel makes no attempt to get Zechariah to interpret this one. Whether this be because of the prophet's inability to understand the others, or because of the extremely onerous nature of the meaning of the flying scroll we cannot be sure.

WHAT THE VISION MEANT . . . v. 3-4

At least in this instance Zechariah seems justified in not being able to understand. Here, for the first time, the Law is depicted as a curse.

The overwhelming significance of this truth and of its appearance in the Old Testament Scriptures cannot be overstated. For centuries both Jews, in attempting to justify their rejection of the Christian faith, and liberal theologians in their attempt to discredit the New Testament, have held that the evaluation of the law as a curse is the peculiar theology of Paul. (cf. *Galatians 3:13*) That Paul is not the originator of this thought becomes apparent here!

The curse of the law is that it makes no allowance for human infirmity. By it comes the accurate knowledge of sin, but by it comes no remedy for sin. By it comes the just wrath of God upon the sinner, but by it comes no forgiveness of sin. (cf. *Romans 7:7-24*)

The curse of the law is not limited to the Jew alone. The scroll goes forth over the whole earth.

Paul will make this universal indictment of God against all men crystal clear. In *Romans 2:14-15,* the apostle shows that all men are in fact under the law, aside from Christ. The Jew because he has the written oracle of God. The Gentile because, while not having the written law, he became a law unto himself. This is because every person has in his conscience the awareness of right and wrong. True, the Gentile without the revealed Law of God does not *know* what is, *in fact,* right or wrong. Nevertheless, he is aware that there is right and that there is wrong. He stands guilty because he does not live up to what he believes is right and wrong and in this failure violates the fundamental principle upon which the Law rests.

This is seen in the modern sociological fad called the New Morality. Based upon a philosophy called existentialism, the New Morality is the practical expression of situation ethics.

In simple terms, this amounts to the denial of *established* right and wrong as written in the Ten Commandments. It is at its root the denial of the authority if not the very existence of God. *But the New Morality does not deny the basic principles of right and wrong.* It simply says there is no *pre-determined* right and wrong. Right and wrong must be determined subjectively within the framework of the existing situation.

Paul would say that the situationist stands guilty of breaking the law in that, having become a law unto himself, he proceeds to violate even his own understanding of right and wrong.

No individual, whether he accepts the written law or becomes a law unto himself, consistently does in every situation of life what he believes is right. Thus the curse of the law covers the whole earth.

In Zechariah's vision, two particular commandment violations become the target of God's wrath expressed in the curse of the law symbolized by the flying scroll. They are the infraction of the eighth commandment, *"Thou shalt not steal,"* and the ninth commandment, *"Thou shalt not bear false witness against thy neighbor."* (cf. *Exodus 20:15-16)*

The latter, swearing falsely in the name of God, is an affront to the majesty of God. The former, entering a neighbor's house to steal his personal property, is a violation of the dignity of the neighbor's humanity! Jesus will teach that the very foundation of the law is the recognition of these two sacred truths.

According to Him, the whole law hangs on the first and second commandments, ie. *"Thou shalt love the Lord thy God and thy neighbor as thyself."* *(Matthew 22:34-ff)* To swear falsely in God's name or to steal another's personal possessions is to strike at the very foundation of morality as it is revealed by God in the Law.

The effect of this curse is deadly. The sinner himself will be "cut off," and his household will be destroyed. The phrase "cut off" is a covenant term. (cp. *Exodus 17:14, 12:15,19, Leviticus 7:20,21,27, 17:4,9,14,* etc.)

To violate the commandments of God is to be cut off from the covenant relationship with Him. A Jew in this condition was no different from a Gentile who was completely ignorant of the covenant. (cf. *Ephesians 2:11-12*) Hence . . . "there is no distinction." *(Romans 3:22)*

Not only does the sinner suffer as a result of his own disregard for God's majesty and human dignity, his family suffers also. Zechariah pictures the curse of the law as entering and abiding in the sinner's home, even to the consuming of the wood and masonry.

The same principle is stated in *Exodus 34:6-7*. "And the Lord passed by before him, and proclaimed, The Lord, the Lord God, merciful and gracious, long-suffering, and abundant in goodness and truth. Keeping mercy for thousands, forgiving iniquity and transgression and sin, and that will by no means clear the guilty; visiting the iniquity of the fathers upon the children, and upon the children's children, unto the third and to the fourth generation."

If we consider this in terms of the family being held accountable for the father's sins, we shall miss the point altogether. What is intended is the self-evident truth that what effects a man effects his family also, and nothing effects a man more adversely than his own sin.

We deceive ourselves if we believe that the effects of our sinning are confined to ourselves. *Deuteronomy 8:15-18* spells this out in great detail. "But it shall come to pass, if thou wilt not hearken unto the voice of the Lord thy God, to observe to do all his commandments and his statutes which I command thee this day; that all these curses shall come upon thee, and overtake thee; Cursed shalt thou be in the city, and cursed shalt thou be in the field. Cursed shall be thy basket and thy store. Cursed shall be the fruit of thy body, and the fruit of thy land, the increase of thy kine, and the flocks of thy sheep."

Conversely, obedience to God brings blessings on others than ourselves. *Proverbs 3:33 says,* "The curse of the Lord is in the house of the wicked: but he blesseth the habitation of the just."

The man who deliberately, habitually blasphemes God's name and/or disregards the human dignity of his neighbor through the violation of his property rights brings the curse of God not only upon himself but those with whom he lives.

Chapter XXXII—*Questions*

A Vision of a Flying Scroll

1. Describe Zechariah's sixth vision.
2. How is Zechariah justified in not being able to understand this vision?
3. What is the significance of the depicting of the law as a curse in this particular passage?
4. Discuss this in relation to Romans 2:14-15.
5. How is the universal acknowledgement of the fact of right and wrong demonstrated in "the New Morality?"
6. How do such people "break the law" of God?
7. What two commandment violations are the target of God's wrath in the vision of the flying scroll?
8. What is the effect of the curse symbolized in this vision?
9. Compare Zechariah 5:1-4 and Exodus 34:6-7.
10. Are the effects of our sins confined to ourselves?

CHAPTER XXXIII

A VISION OF A WOMAN IN A FLYING BASKET

ZECHARIAH 5:5-11

RV . . . Then the angel that talked with me went forth, and said unto me, Lift up now thine eyes, and see what is this that goeth forth. And I said, What is it? And he said, This is the ephah that goeth forth. He said moreover, This is their appearance in all the land (and, behold, there was lifted up a talent of lead); and this is a woman sitting in the midst of the ephah. And he said, This is Wickedness: and he cast her down into the midst of the ephah; and he cast the weight of lead upon the mouth thereof. Then lifted I up mine eyes, and saw, and, behold, there came forth two women, and the wind was in their wings; now they had wings like the wings of a stork; and they lifted up the ephah between earth and heaven. Then said I to the angel that talked with me, Whither do these bear the ephah? And he said unto me, To build her a house in the land of Shinar: and when it is prepared, she shall be set there in her own place.

A VISION OF A WOMAN IN A FLYING BASKET 5:5-11

LXX . . . And the angel that talked with me went forth, and said to me, Lift up thine eyes, and see this that goes forth. And he said, This is their iniquity in all the earth. And behold a talent of lead lifted up: and behold a woman sat in the midst of the measure. And he said, This is iniquity. And he cast it into the midst of the measure, and cast the weight of lead on the mouth of it. And I lifted up mine eyes, and saw, and behold, two women coming forth, and the wind was in their wings; and they had stork's wings: and they lifted up the measure between the earth and the sky. And I said to the angel that spoke with me, Whither do these carry away the measure? And he said to me, To build it a house in the land of Babylon, and to prepare a place for it; and they shall set it there on its own base.

COMMENTS

WHAT THE PROPHET SAW

The angel commands Zechariah to lift his eyes to receive the seventh in the series of visions. It, like the one just previous, will be seen in the sky.

In preceding visions the prophet occasionally had difficulty grasping the meaning of what appeared. This time he cannot believe his eyes! "What is it . . . ?" is his exclamation. There in the sky is a flying basket and in it sits a woman! Pressing upon her is a talent of lead weight. (An ephah is a basket of approximately 3¼ pecks. A talent weighs approximately 118 lbs. troy.)

The angel informs the prophet that this is the appearance of the ephah and the woman as they go forth over all the land.

So saying, he declares the woman to be Wickedness and, forcing her into the basket, he casts the lead weight in on top of her. Whereupon two winged women appear and lift the basket up into the sky.

In answer to the prophet's inquiry, the angel says that they are bearing her away to build her a house in Shinar where she will set up her own place.

WHAT THE VISION MEANT!

Unlike the previous visions of Zechariah, the angel gives us very little explanation of the meaning of this vision, other than to say that the woman is wickedness (v. 8) and that the ephah bearing her is going forth over the whole land. We must therefore proceed with caution in our attempt to explain its meaning.

It has been suggested that we have here a picture of Judah sending her sin to Babylon *(Shinar . . . cp. Genesis 10:10, Daniel 1:2)* where the ephah will be worshipped. This latter is based upon the assumption that "house" in verse eleven means temple. The ephah, whose liquid capacity is about six gallons, is taken to mean the base of an image upon which the woman will stand as a goddess.

Another interpretation sees the ephah as a small barrel with a leaden disk as a lid. The woman is trying to escape, which is why the angel pushes her into the ephah and casts the lead on top of her. The two flying females are considered demonic. Shinar, or Babylon, becomes the site of a temple where the woman will be worshipped as personified evil.

Yet another interpretation has the ephah alluding to the previous vision of theft and falsification. "This is their appearance" (v. 6) is thus seen as representing what the Jews have done and what they shall suffer.

Shinar is here seen, not as Babylon, but as the total Gentile world into which the Jews are to be totally dispersed.

In all this is seen the total removal of sin from the holy land. The house is seen as the capital of the world of wickedness as opposed to the kingdom of God and the woman is somehow identified as "the man of sin." *(II Thessalonians 2:3)*

What such interpretations show, more than anything else, is the ludicrous extremes to which men's theological systems take them in the study of apocalyptic Scriptures.

The angel does give us some insight into this vision, and it is here we must begin to understand it. In verse six he said, "This is the ephah that goeth forth."

The ephah, as previously indicated, was a basket with the capacity of 3¼ pecks, just less than our standard bushel. The law made strict provision for its use, giving interpretation regarding just measure in trade. *(Leviticus 19:36)* The "ephah that goeth forth" is the measure used in the trading or selling of such commodities as are sold at a certain price per ephah.

The angel indicates that the ephah is "their appearance in all the land." The word appearance in the original is literally "eye."

There was then lifted up a talent (literally a disc) of lead.

Concerning the woman, the angel said, "This is wickedness." So saying he put her in the basket and placed the lead upon it. Notice, the woman is wickedness as an abstract principle, not wicked people.

A VISION OF A WOMAN IN A FLYING BASKET   5:5-11

So we have a legal measure filled with wickedness and upon it a heavy (118 lb.) lid. Obviously, the reason for such a lid is to prevent the escape of the basket's content, which is evil. This much is plain.

The angel gives no explanation as to the identity of the two women with stork's wings. He does say they are bearing the full measure of evil to the land of Shinar where a house (or temple) is to be built in which the woman (evil) will be set in her own place (literally on her own base).

There is Scriptural evidence that Shinar is synonmous with Babylon. (cp. *Genesis 10:10*) The term Shinar is used for obvious reasons. Babylon was now in the hands of Darius, ruler of the Medo-Persian empire. To have used the common name would have been to incur, unnecessarily, the wrath of the emperor whose good offices had permitted the return of the exiles and who was encouraging the reconstruction of the temple. For our purposes, it is important only to know that Shinar is Babylon.

Babylon is used throughout the apocalyptic literature of the Bible to depict the false religion which is inevitably the source of evil and therefore the enemy of God and His people. She is associated with enforced evil and idolatry.

In *Revelation 17:5* she is called mother of harlots, dressed in haughty splendor and drunken with the blood of the martyrs. The evils which have come out of her idol worship and opposition to God's people are called the wine of her fornication. Her name there is "Mystery, Babylon, the Great, Mother of Harlots and of the abominations of the Earth."

Mystery alludes to the mystery religions which originated in Babylon. (See Chapter 4, *Baal Worship*) *Babylon the Great* to her temporal power (which in Revelation becomes symbolic of Rome), *Mother of Harlots* to the fact that she had spawned the false religions of the world, and *the abominations of the earth* to the overall offensiveness of Babylon before God.

So the full measure of the wickedness which spread across the land of Judah was to be sent back to its source where it would be set up on a pedestal and worshipped, as indeed it had always been, wickedness and immorality being the soul and expression of the idolatry throughout the ancient world.

Keeping in mind that the writing of the book of Zechariah was intended to move the people to the rebuilding of the temple, the force of this vision is obvious. The wickedness which the people have brought with them from Babylon must be recognized for what it is. It must be sent on the wings of the wind back, full measure, where it came from. In Babylon, wickedness is the object of worship. In God's land among God's people it has no place at all. It must therefore be removed.

Chapter XXXIII—*Questions*
A Vision of a Woman in a Flying Basket

1. Describe Zechariah's seventh vision.
2. What is an ephah?
3. What is the weight of the talent?
4. Where did the woman in the flying ephah go?
5. The woman in the ephah is declared by the angel to be _____.
6. What is the significant difference between this and the other visions as recorded by Zechariah?
7. Discuss several possible interpretations of this vision as suggested above.
8. What is shown by such interpretations?
9. What is the significance of the fact that the ephah was a *legal* measure?
10. Shinar is Scripturally synonmous with _____.
11. Babylon, throughout the Bible, especially in apocalyptic literature, is used to depict _____.
12. *Mystery* alludes to _____.
13. The full measure of wickedness was to be sent _____.
14. What was the force of this vision to those who had the task of rebuilding the temple?

CHAPTER XXXIV
A VISION OF WAR CHARIOTS
ZECHARIAH 6:1-8

RV . . . And again I lifted up mine eyes, and saw, and, behold, there came four chariots out from between two mountains; and the mountains were mountains of brass. In the first chariot were red horses; and in the second chariot black horses; and in the third chariot white horses; and in the fourth chariot grizzled strong horses. Then I answered and said unto the angel that talked with me, What are these, my lord?

A VISION OF WAR CHARIOTS 6:1-8

And the angel answered and said unto me, These are the four winds of heaven, which go forth from standing before the Lord of all the earth. The chariot wherein are the black horses goeth forth toward the north country; and the white went forth after them; and the grizzled went forth toward the south country. And the strong went forth, and sought to go that they might walk to and fro through the earth: and he said, Get you hence, walk to and fro through the earth. So they walked to and fro through the earth. Then cried he to me, and spake unto me, saying, Behold, they that go toward the north country have quieted my spirit in the north country.

LXX . . . And I turned and lifted up mine eyes, and looked, and, behold, four chariots coming out from between two mountains; and the mountains were brazen mountains. In the first chariot were red horses; and in the second chariot black horses; and in the third chariot white horses; and in the fourth chariot piebald and ash-coloured horses. And I answered and said to the angel that talked with me, What are these, my lord? And the angel that talked with me answered and said, These are the four winds of heaven, and they are going forth to stand before the Lord of all the earth. As for the chariot in which were the black horses, they went out to the land of the north; and the white went out after them; and the piebald went out to the land of the south. And the ash-coloured went out, and looked to go and compass the earth: and he said, Go, and compass the earth. And they compassed the earth. And he cried out and spoke to me, saying, Behold, these go out to the land of the north, and they have quieted mine anger in the land of the north.

COMMENTS
WHAT THE PROPHET SAW . . . v. 1-4

This is the final in the series of eight visions. It comes full circle, back to the universal concerns expressed in the first two. Visions three through seven have focused our primary attention on the recently returned Jews in Judah. The truths revealed have had to do primarily with the moral and spiritual qualities which must characterize them in order that God's purpose in them may be accomplished.

On occasion we have seen that the same moral and spiritual obstacles which beset Judah are common to all mankind. The first two visions were concerned with their relationship to their neighbors as these affected their security while rebuilding. In this final vision we again look outward from Judah.

From between two mountains come four chariots drawn by different colored horses. They are red, black, white and dappled (grizzled). The last are particularly noted for their strength.

Having presented themselves before the Lord, the chariots are commanded to go out through all the earth; north, south, east and west. All are impatient to start, but particular attention is drawn to the north.

WHAT THE VISION MEANT . . . v. 5-8

Upon Zechariah's inquiry as to the meaning of the vision, particularly as to the identity of the four chariots, the angel explains that these are four winds or spirits which go forth from before the Lord of all the earth. The marginal reading *"spirit"* is preferred here rather than winds. They walk to and fro through the earth.

The end result is that the Lord's Spirit is quieted in the north. Verse 8 (b) thus becomes the key to understanding the final vision.

If we are correct in asserting that these visions represent God's dealing with the obstacles which stood in the way of Messiah's coming, particularly as they prevented the rebuilding of the temple in which the symbolic priestly-sacrificial system must foreshadow His advent, this final vision may well be intended to mark the beginning of the Messianic age. The details are unclear to us, largely because they been blurred by time, but the next following paragraph depicts the coronation of the high priest which symbolizes the merging of the two offices of priest and king in the Messiah.

The two mountains of verse one are probably Mount Moriah on which sat the temple and Mount Zion to the south of Moriah. Since the temple is the symbolic dwelling place of God, it is fitting that, in the vision, the chariots representing His Spirit going out to all the earth should be sent from this place.

In Bible times the valley of the cheese merchants divided Moriah and Zion. It has since been filled and the two today appear as a single mountain.

In the vision these mountains are of brass, more accurately bronze. At the time of Zechariah the bronze age in Persia and Egypt had given way to iron in the making of weapons. Nevertheless, bronze remained one of the strongest, and possibly the single most enduring metal of the ancient world. No doubt the symbolism here is a statement of the enduring presence of God and His eternal concern for all men.

The colors of the horses are similar to those of the first vision. Red represents bloodshed as in the first. The second, the white horse, as in the first vision also, represents death. The black horse, a color not mentioned in the first vision, represents famine and sorrow (cp *Revelation 6:5-6*). The grizzled or dappled, as in the first vision, represents a mixture of prosperity and adversity. The "strong horses" is more accurately translated "swift."

Rather than become entangled in a vain attempt to find a specific in the colors of the horses as related to the direction each went, it is best to consider them as an overall representation of the universal judgement of God.

Special attention is called to the north, toward which the chariot with black horses is directed. Any invader which came upon Jerusalem must come from either the south or north. To the south lay Egypt, now subjected to Persian dominance in world affairs and unlikely to engage in any war of conquest. To the north lay the route along which Babylon must march if she is again to threaten the rebuilders of the temple. Along this northern route also the Medo-Persians must come if they are to harrass Judah. From the north the Assyrians had come to wipe out the northern kingdom.

To the north is directed the chariot pulled by black horses. The chariot drawn by white horses follows the first. This has been variously understood to be desolation visited on Babylon three after Zechariah's prophecy was written, and the subduing of Darius' kingdom itself by Alexander in the fourth century B.C. In any case, Judah was never again seriously threatened by Babylon or Persia.

The war chariots are similar in purpose to the wall of fire seen in the third vision. Judah will remain secure so long as she is dedicated to the accomplishment of God's purpose which at this time was primarily concerned for the rebuilding of the temple. It is a recurrance of the theme stated in *1:3,* "Therefore say thou unto them, Thus saith Jehovah of hosts: Return unto me, saith Jehovah of hosts, and I will return unto you, saith Jehovah of hosts."

Chapter XXXIV—*Questions*

A Vision of War Chariots

1. Describe the eighth vision of Zechariah.
2. The eighth vision comes full circle back to_____.
3. Who were the four chariots?

4. What verse is the key to the understanding of this vision?
5. What are the two mountains?
6. In Bible times _____ divided Moriah and Zion.
7. What is the significance of the colors of the horses?
8. Why does Zechariah's vision call special attention to the north?
9. How are the war chariots similar to the wall of fire in the third vision?
10. In this vision is a recurrence of _____ .

CHAPTER XXXV
THE PROCLAMATION OF THE MESSIAH
ZECHARIAH 6:9-15

RV . . . And the word of Jehovah came unto me, saying, Take of them of the captivity, even of Heldai, of Tobijah, and of Jedaiah; and come thou the same day, and go into the house of Josiah the son of Zephaniah, whither they are come from Babylon; yea, take of them silver and gold, and make crowns, and set them upon the head of Joshua the son of Jehozadak, the high priest; and speak unto him, saying, Thus speaketh Jehovah of hosts, saying, Behold, the man whose name is the Branch: and he shall grow up out of his place; and he shall build the temple of Jehovah; even he shall build the temple of Jehovah; and he shall bear the glory, and shall sit and rule upon his throne; and he shall be a priest upon his throne; and the counsel of peace shall be between them both. And the crowns shall be to Helem, and to Tobijah, and to Jedaiah, and to Hen the son of Zephaniah, for a memorial in the temple of Jehovah. And they that are far off shall come and build in the temple of Jehovah; and ye shall know that Jehovah of hosts hath sent me unto you. And this shall come to pass, if ye will diligently obey the voice of Jehovah your God.

LXX . . . And the word of the Lord came to me, saying, Take the things of the captivity from the chief men, and from the useful men of it, and from them that have understood it; and thou shalt enter in that day into the house of Josias the son Sophonias that came out of Babylon. And thou shalt take silver and gold, and make crowns, and thou shalt put them upon the head of Jesus the son of Josedec the high priest; and thou shalt say to him, Thus saith the Lord Almighty: Behold the man whose name is The Branch; and he shall spring up

PROCLAMATION OF THE MESSIAH   6:9-11

from his stem, and build the house of the Lord. And he shall receive power, and shall sit and rule upon his throne; and there shall be a priest on his right hand, and a peaceable counsel shall be between them both. And the crown shall be to them that wait patiently, and to the useful men of the captivity, and to them that have known it, and for the favour of the son of Sophonias, and for a psalm in the house of the Lord. And they that are far from them shall come and build in the house of the Lord, and ye shall know that the Lord Almighty has sent me to you: and this shall come to pass, if ye will diligently hearken to the voice of the Lord your God.

COMMENTS

Zechariah's first eight visions, as we have seen, have to do with removing the obstacles to the coming of the Messiah. The second and concluding section of the book, beginning with chapter nine, deals with His coming. The present passage describing the coronation of Joshua and the subsequent passages which teach about worship form a bridge between these two main divisions of the book.

There are some textual difficulties in the passage immediately before us. However, the scope and purpose of this book will not permit our dealing with them. We shall simply take the text as it presently stands and comment on it.

(Verses 9-11) Rather than a vision, Zechariah receives "the word of Jehovah" instructing him to take from three recent returnees from Babylon, Heldai, Tobijah and Jedaiah, who are residing with one Josiah, the gold and silver necessary to make crowns. The marginal reading here is "a crown" and is probably the preferred reading.

We do not know anything of these men beyond Zechariah's identification of them as having recently returned from the captivity. Possibly they were successful merchants, as many Jews had become in Babylon. If so, they may have volunteered the gift to mark their arrival in the holy land.

It has been suggested that the gold and silver were sent by Darius and that Heldai, Tobijah and Jedaiah were simply delivering it for the king. The former seems more likely in view of verse fourteen. There the name of Hen is added to the threesome mentioned in verse ten and the crown (or crowns) is to be left in the temple as a memorial to them.

(Verses 12-15) These verses, the first two of which are the message of Jehovah through Zechariah to Joshua the high priest, form a very definite Messianic prophecy. In the coronation Joshua became *symbolically* the Messiah.

The term Branch was previously applied to Joshua in *3:8-9* during the prophet's third vision. (See comments) In *3:8*, it is stated that Joshua in particular and the accompanying priests in general were together a *sign* or symbol of *"my servant The Branch."*

Isaiah 11:1-ff establishes The Branch as a term referring to the Messiah as the promised Seed of David. *Isaiah 4:2-ff*, where the term is used with Messianic meaning for the first time by Isaiah, connects the Branch with the return of the remnant from the captivity.

Jeremiah 23:5 predicts the coming of Branch in these words, *"Behold the days come, saith the Lord, that I will raise unto David a Branch, and a King shall reign and prosper and execute Judgement and Justice in the earth."* (KJV) A similar passage is found in *Jeremiah 33:15*.

The Branch is thus seen as a term long established as referring to the kingly Messiah. In the symbolism of Joshua's coronation, His kingly office is merged with that of high priest. *Zechariah 4:6-9* had alluded to this when the prophet saw the two olive trees pouring their oil simultaneously into the bowl at the base of the multiple menorah.

The menorah was the established symbol of Israel. Zechariah's multiple menorah was the seven branched lampstand multiplied by seven. The meaning is apparent: Israel perfected. Israel perfected is Messianic Israel. Her Spirit, symbolized by the oil in the menorah comes to her from the Messiah who is both priest and king.

In Zechariah, chapter nine, we shall find a detailed prophetic presentation of the Messianic king. For an expose of the high priestly function of the Messiah we have only to read the New Testament book of Hebrews. In *Hebrews 5:1-10* the writer establishes that Jesus fulfills the qualifications of this office. He must offer gifts and sacrifices for sins (v.1). He must have compassion on the ignorant and the wayward (v. 2). He must be called of God. (v. 4).

Jesus fulfilled these qualifications. He offered prayers and supplications (v. 7). He was called of God (v. 10). His priesthood is superior to the Levitical priesthood which was only a symbol of His (*7:1-28*). The high priestly office of the Christ manifests a new covenant, and the true tabernacle of which the former tabernacle was only a shadow (*9:15-28*). His high priestly sacrifice is final, as opposed to the symbolic sacrifices of the Law (*10:1-10*). This finality is established by the comparison of it to the oft-repeated sacrifices of the Levitical priesthood (*10:11-14*). The finality of His sacrifice establishes the new covenant as final in that it brings absolute remission of sin (*10:15-18*).

In verse twelve Jehovah says concerning Joshua as symbolic of the Branch what Pilate would one day say concerning the Branch Himself, "Behold the man." (cp. *John 19:5*) As Joshua now stood with the mitre of the high priest capped by the crown of the king, so Jesus would stand offering Himself as the high priestly sacrifice and crowned with a crown of thorns. And above the head of this high priest as He offered Himself in sacrifice for His people, Pilate would write, "Behold the King of the Jews."

Joshua's coronation could not be more than symbolic, since he could never be king, not being of David's lineage. The temple which Joshua would build, would be also symbolic of the true temple to be built by the Christ.

Actually Joshua did not build the second temple. It was built under the direction of Zerubbabel, who governed Judah by appointment of Darius. This is one of the textual problems of *Zechariah 6:9:15*. It has been suggested that the name Zerubbabel actually appeared in the original rather than Joshua. This seems unlikely since the term Branch applied here is previously applied to Joshua. (cp. *Zechariah 3:8*)

It seems more likely that the prophet here credits Joshua with building the temple in order to carry forward the symbolic merger of the two offices of king and priest. In fact Judah, at this time, had no king. The civil authority resided in Zerubbabel and that by Persian appointment.

(Verse 13) When the true Branch came, of whom Joshua was only a symbol, He would build the true temple, of which the present temple would only be a symbol. (cp. *Ephesians 2:19-22* and *Hebrews 8:1-2*)

Further, The Branch shall bear the glory. The Hebrew *hod,* here rendered "glory," means literally "honor, beauty, majesty." *Hebrews 1:3* will say He is the effulgence (or brightness) of God's glory. Certainly this could only be said symbolically of Joshua.

The prophet makes three additional assertions concerning The Branch. He shall sit and rule upon His throne, He shall be a priest upon His throne, and the counsel of peace shall be between them, *ie.* between His functions as King and priest.

Men have died, the Christ has been crucified, denominations have been formed and countless souls have been lost eternally over the seeming inability of men to agree as to what is meant by the Christ sitting on a throne and ruling.

6:13-15 ZECHARIAH

Had Jesus been willing to yield to the pressures of first century Jewry and lead an armed revolt for the purpose of establishing Himself upon a materialistic throne to rule an earthly kingdom, those who forced His crucifixion would have been among His most ardent supporters. He refused this kind of throne. He asserted His kingdom was not of this world. Yet thousands of His followers today insist that when He returns, He will do precisely what He refused to do in the first century.

Those who do not accept this materialistic view of Christ's reign are called everything from liberal to spiritualizers. It is assumed that to take the Bible literally is to take it materialistically.

And so the argument over Christ's kingly rule goes on. Surely, whatever the truth is, it is not to be found in such vindictiveness!

Of one thing we may be certain in this verse. It could not be said of Joshua that he would sit and rule upon his throne. Historically this simply is not true. The statement applies to Him of whom Joshua was merely a "sign." (3:8)

Zechariah further informs us that He shall sit as a priest on His throne. Here is the ultimate statement of the merger of the kingly and priestly offices in the Christ. In no other way did a high priest ever sit upon a throne in Israel.

And lastly, the counsel of peace shall be between these two Messianic functions. The co-working of civil and spiritual authority are never in conflict with one another. The majesty of the King never overshadows the self-effacing self-sacrifice of the priest. Nor does the loving compassion ever over-rule the just judgements and ultimate authority of the King.

The Jews would have had Jesus as King to rule over them and subjugate the Gentiles, but they could not accept His priestly offering of Himself as the ultimate sacrifice for the sins of His people.

The modern American Protestant is willing for Him to be the merciful and compassionate self-effacing priest but is not willing to accept His Kingly authority.

(Verse 14) The crowns, following the symbolic coronation of Joshua were to be kept in the temple as a memorial to those who had provided the gold and silver from which they were made.

(Verse 15) Here, in conjunction with the symbolic merging of the King and high priest, is a very important statement of the nature of the Messianic Temple. It is to be built not just by the Jews but by *"those that are afar off."* Here is a term pregnant indeed with Messianic meaning.

At the preaching of the Gospel on the first Pentecost, Peter assured his listeners that the promise was not alone to them, who were all Jews, but to *"all that are afar off, even as many as the Lord our God shall call unto Himself."*

In *Ephesians 2:17* Paul informs us that Christ Jesus came and *"preached peace to them that were afar off,"* as well as *"to them that were nigh."* This the apostle sees, as did Zechariah, as included in the building of the real temple for, "So then ye (Gentiles) are no more strangers and sojourners, but ye are fellow-citizens with the saints, and of the household of God, being built upon the foundation of the apostles and prophets, Christ Jesus Himself being the chief cornerstone: in whom each several building, fitly framed together groweth into a holy temple in the Lord; in whom ye also are builded together for a habitation of God in the Spirit."

Please note, the ultimate temple, built by the King-priest and those who are afar off is a habitation for God in the Spirit.

Zechariah, chapter six, closes with another recurrance of the theme stated in *1:3*. All that has been here promised is conditional. The remnant must do what their fathers seldom had done, namely diligently obey the voice of Jehovah God.

Chapter XXXV—*Questions*

The Proclamation of the Messiah

1. The eight visions deal with the removal of obstacles to Messiah's coming. The present "word of Jehovah" deals with _____.
2. Rather than a vision in *6:9-15*, Zechariah receives_____ ___.
3. Who were the donors of the gold and silver for the crowns?
4. The gold and silver may have been a gift from_____.
5. In the coronation_____became, symbolically, the Messiah.
6. Discuss "The Branch" in *9:12* in relationship to the same term in *3:8-9*.
7. Isaiah establishes "The Branch" as_____ _____.
8. Jeremiah predicts The Branch in what terms?
9. Israel perfected is_____Israel.
10. What does Joshua's coronation symbolize?
11. When the true Branch came He would build the true_____.
12. How will The Branch "bear the glory?"

13. What three additional assertion does Zechariah make concerning The Branch?
14. How could Jesus have won the allegiance of those who brought about His crucifixion?
15. Distinguish between taking the Bible "literally," and taking it "materialistically."
16. Show how the counsel of peace is between the kingly and priestly functions of the Messiah.
17. What was to be done with the two crowns following Joshua's coronation?
18. Discuss "Those that are afar off." (v. 15) in connection with *Acts 2:39* and *Ephesians 2:17*.
19. The ultimate temple built by our King-Priest is a habitation for God _____ _____ _____.
20. What recurrs another time in the close of this section?

CHAPTER XXXVI
TEACHING ABOUT WORSHIP

Chapter seven has been called *"A Call to Civic Duty."* We cannot subscribe to this summary of the prophetic message contained in this chapter, but we mention it to underscore a truth which shines through both chapters seven and eight, namely that outward formal religious observances unrelated to present life are an affront to God. His promises are to those whose relationship to Him makes a real difference in their relationship to their fellowmen.

QUESTIONS ABOUT FASTING . . . Zechariah 7:1-3

RV . . . And it came to pass in the fourth year of king Darius, that the word of Jehovah came unto Zechariah in the fourth day of the ninth month, even in Chislev. Now they of Beth-el had sent Sharezer and Regem-melech, and their men, to entreat the favor of Jehovah, and to speak unto the priests of the house of Jehovah of hosts, and to the prophets, saying, Should I weep in the fifth month, separating myself, as I have done these many years?

LXX . . . And it came to pass in the fourth year of Darius the king, that the word of the Lord came to Zacharias on the fourth day of the ninth month, which is Chaseleu. And Sarasar and Arbeseer the king and his men sent to Baethel, and that to propitiate the Lord, speaking to

TEACHING ABOUT WORSHIP 7:1-3

to the priests that were in the house of the Lord Almighty, and to the prophets, saying, The holy offering has come in hither in the fifth month, as it has done already many years.

COMMENTS

On December 4, 518 B.C., just over two years after the beginning of Zechariah's prophetic ministry, the Jews who lived in Beth-el sent two envoys, Sharezer and Regem-melech, to inquire of the priests of Jehovah concerning the continuation of the fasts which for seventy years had commemorated the destruction of Jerusalem and the temple.

Beth-el is located east of an imaginary line running north from Jerusalem to Nablus.

Beth-el's ruins were discovered by Robinson and are now identified with the village of Betin. Formerly inhabited by Canaanite kings, it became home to a number of Jews following the captivity. In Zechariah's day, as in the time of the pre-exilic divided kingdom, Beth-el lay just south of the border that divided Judea and Israel. In New Testament days the boundary between Judea and Samaria ran south of the village. This has led some to the erroneous conclusion that Zechariah's visitors were Samaritans, while in point of fact they were Jews returned from Babylon. They had settled in the northernmost part of what was originally the land of Benjamin and they had come to Jerusalem for instruction concerning the requirements of worship on the part of the returnees.

(Verse 3) The question asked is, *"Should I weep in the fifth month, separating myself as I have these so many years?"* The concern is for the facts which related to the captivity.

In the fifth month, on the seventh day of the month, which marked the nineteenth anniversary of Nebuchadnezzar's ascending the throne of Babylon, he sent his servant to Jerusalem to burn the temple and main buildings of the city.

In the seventh month, apparently of the same year, a member of the Babylonian royal family had assassinated the Jewish governor, Gedaliah, of Judah, and the Jews who were with him.

In memory of those two tragic events the Jews had fasted twice a year on the days marking their occurance. It had been a burdensome experience for a people in captivity. The people of Beth-el now want to know if it is required to continue the practice.

7:4-7 ZECHARIAH

THE FIRST ANSWERING STATEMENT ... Zechariah 7:4-7

RV ... Then came the word of Jehovah of hosts unto me, saying, Speak unto all the people of the land, and to the priests, saying, When ye fasted and mourned in the fifth and in the seventh month, even these seventy years, did ye at all fast unto me, even to me? And when ye eat for yourselves, and drink for yourselves? Should ye not hear the words which Jehovah cried by the former prophets, when Jerusalem was inhabited and in prosperity, and the cities thereof round about her, and the South and the lowland were inhabited?

LXX ... And the word of the Lord of hosts came to me, saying, Speak to the whole people of the land, and to the priests, saying, Though ye fasted or lamented in the fifth or seventh months (yea, behold, these seventy years) have ye at all fasted to me? And if ye eat or drink, do ye not eat and drink for yourselves? Are not these words which the Lord spoke by the former prophets, when Jerusalem was inhabited and in prosperity, and her cities round about her, and the hill country and the low country was inhabited?

COMMENTS

(Verses 4-7) Zechariah's answer to the question from Beth-el is made in six statements. Each statement is introduced with exact statements which indicate the prophet's words were actually those of Jehovah.

The *first* of these statements begins with 7:4 and continues through 7:7. The *second* begins with 7:8 and concludes the chapter. The *third* begins at 8:1 and runs through 8:7. The *fourth* statement begins with 8:9 and continues through 8:13. The *fifth* statement begins at 8:14 and ends with 8:17. The *sixth* and final statement in answer to the question from Beth-el begins with 8:18 and closes the chapter. It also forms the final paragraph of the first section of Zechariah's writing.

Jehovah's *first* answering statement (7:4-7) begins by reminding the questioners that the fasts in question had not been instituted by any divine directive. The reminder is in the form of three questions. *"Did ye at all fast unto me, even unto me?"* *"And when ye eat and when ye drink, do not ye eat for yourselves, and drink for yourselves?"*

To paraphrase these first two questions we might say *"When you began fasting in memory of the destruction and death, did you ask me?"*

The obvious conclusion is stated in the third question, *"Should ye not hear* (more accurately *have heard*) *the words which Jehovah cried by the former prophets ... ?"* It would have been better for them to have heard and heeded the former prophets than to have invented fasts for themselves with no divine directive.

The former prophets were those who had preached in the times before the captivity. The practice of what they taught would have been the appropriate response to the captivity rather than self-appointed fasts of mourning. Rather than mourn over what God had brought upon them, they should have corrected the circumstances which caused Him to punish them.

THE SECOND ANSWERING STATEMENT . . . Zechariah 7:8-14

RV . . . And the word of Jehovah came unto Zechariah, saying, Thus hath Jehovah of hosts spoken, saying, Execute true judgement, and show kindness and compassion every man to his brother; and oppress not the widow, nor the fatherless, the sojourner, nor the poor; and let none of you devise evil against his brother in your heart. But they refused to hearken, and pulled away the shoulder, and stopped their ears, that they might not hear. Yea, they made their hearts as an adamant stone, lest they should hear the law, and the words which Jehovah of hosts had sent by his Spirit by the former prophets: therefore there came great wrath from Jehovah of hosts. And it is come to pass that, as he cried, and they would not hear, so they shall cry, and I will not hear, said Jehovah of hosts; but I will scatter them with a whirlwind among all the nations which they have not known. Thus the land was desolate after them, so that no man passed through nor returned: for they laid the pleasant land desolate.

LXX . . . And the word of the Lord came to Zacharias, saying, Thus saith the Lord Almighty; Judge righteous judgement, and deal mercifully and compassionately every one with his brother: and oppress not the widow, or the fatherless, or the stranger, or the poor; and let not one of you remember in his heart the injury of his brother. But they refused to attend, and madly turned their back, and made their ears heavy, so that they should not hear. And they made their heart disobedient, so as not to hearken to my law, and the words which the Lord Almighty sent forth by his Spirit by the former prophets: so there was great wrath from the Lord Almighty. And it shall come to pass, that as he spoke, and they hearkened not, so they shall cry, and I will not hearken, saith the Lord Almighty. And I will cast them out among all the nations, whom they know not; and the land behind them shall be made utterly destitute of any going through or returning: yea they have made the choice land a desolation.

COMMENTS

The second answering statement to the questioners from Beth-el is a summary of what was taught by the former prophets. (It would be helpful here to review at least one of the pre-exilic prophets, possibly Micah.)

(Verses 8-10) The demands of God which, if heeded, would have averted the necessity of the Babylonian exile can by no means be called unreasonable. He asked that the courts execute "true judgement." Yet, as we saw in our study of Micah, the courts were in the hands of evil men who used them for their own gain in extorting land and money from the poor and the defenseless.

It seems, looking back across centuries at the iniquities of the courts of another people, that justice for all would have been a matter of simple decency. Yet one cannot but wonder at our own judicial system. Heavy charges have been alleged against our courts to the effect that justice in America is a rich man's commodity. If this be so, we may be assured that the God Who executes judgement over all nations will not allow it to go unnoticed. This is the sort of thing that destroys nations. Whatever else we learn from the captivity of the Jews by Babylon, this is obvious.

The questioners are further reminded that God had, through the former prophets, commanded their fathers to *"show kindness and compassion, every man to his brother; and oppress not the widow, nor the fatherless, the sojourner, nor the poor; and let none devise evil against his brother in your heart."*

Again these things seem, when viewed objectively, the common customs of any civilized people, particularly a people who claim to be God's people. Yet, as we saw, Micah described in detail the cruel and often violent violation of each of these practices and he had warned their fathers of the consequences.

As in the case of the other evils which brought about Judah's exile to Babylon, American culture today seems fairly riddled with such cruelty. Most any daily newspaper will supply ample illustrations of the truth of this charge.

(Verses 11-14) In these verses Zechariah reviews the response of the pre-exilic nation to the warnings of the prophets, and the consequences of that response. They had hardened their hearts, turned away and refused to listen.

Therefore God's wrath had come, and the people had been driven from the land as chaff is driven before a whirlwind. It was part of this wrath that had brought about the burning and death which they commemorated by their annual fasts of mourning.

God's first answer to the questions about fasting may be summarized like this: the fasts in question were not ordained of God. The events remembered in the fasts were part of God's just punishment of the wickedness of the people. The people had not only deserved the punishment because of their evil ways, they deserved it doubly because they had refused to hear God's prophets who were sent to call them to repentance and to warn them of what would happen if they failed to repent. Therefore, those who mourned the just punishment of God upon their fathers had best leave off such meaningless ceremonies and themselves heed the teaching of the former prophets.

As James would have it "pure religion and undefiled before our God and father is this, to visit the fatherless and widows in their affliction, and to keep oneself unspotted from the world." *(James 1:27)*

THE THIRD ANSWERING STATEMENT . . . Zechariah 8:1-8

RV . . . And the word of Jehovah of hosts came to me, saying, Thus saith Jehovah of hosts: I am jealous for Zion with great jealousy, and I am jealous for her with great wrath. Thus saith Jehovah: I am returned unto Zion, and will dwell in the midst of Jerusalem: and Jerusalem shall be called The city of truth; and the mountain of Jehovah of hosts. The holy mountain. Thus saith Jehovah of hosts: There shall yet old men and old women dwell in the streets of Jerusalem, every man with his staff in his hand for every age. And the streets of the city shall be full of boys and girls playing in the streets thereof. Thus saith Jehovah of hosts: If it be marvellous in the eyes of the remnant of this people in those days, should it also be marvellous in mine eyes? saith Jehovah of hosts. Thus saith Jehovah of hosts: Behold, I will save my people from the east country, and from the west country; and I will bring them, and they shall dwell in the midst of Jerusalem; and they shall be my people, and I will be their God, in truth and in righteousness.

LXX . . . And the word of the Lord Almighty came, saying, Thus saith the Lord Almighty; I have been jealous for Jerusalem and for Sion with great jealousy, and I have been jealous for her with great fury. Thus saith the Lord; I will return to Sion, and dwell in the midst of Jerusalem: and Jerusalem shall be called a true city, and the mountain of the Lord Almighty a holy mountain. Thus saith the Lord Almighty; There shall yet dwell old men and old women in the streets of Jerusalem, every one holding his staff in his hand for age. And the broad places of the city shall be filled with boys and girls playing in the streets thereof. Thus saith the Lord Almighty; If it shall be impossible in the sight of the remnant of this people in those days, shall it also be impossible in my sight? saith the Lord Almighty. Thus saith the Lord Almighty; Behold, I will save my people from the east country, and the west country; and I will bring them in, and cause them to dwell in the midst of Jerusalem: and they shall be to me a people, and I will be to them a God, in truth and in righteousness.

COMMENTS

The *third* statement made by God through Zechariah to the questioners from Beth-el is a statement of His love for His people and a desire that they be happy in the knowledge that He is with them in the land. Such a joyous relationship has no room for fasts, especially not for fasts of human origin.

(Verses 1-2) This is not the only passage of Scripture in which God is said to be jealous. (cp. *Exodus 20:5, 34:14, Deuteronomy 4:24, 5:9, 6:15, Joshua 24:19, Nahum 1:2*) In every one of these passages, God's jealousy is set against the background either of the covenant or the violation of the covenant in the worship of false gods.

Zechariah's statement of Jehovah's jealousy is likewise in the context of the covenant. It is Zion over which He is jealous. It is the restored remnant who marvel at the joys of His return to Jerusalem *(v. 6)*. It is Jehovah of hosts who speaks *(v. 4)*. The mountain (Zion) of Jehovah is the holy mountain. These are covenant terms.

God's jealousy is the jealousy of a righteous husband for His bride. In more than one passage in the pre-exilic prophets, Israel is presented as Jehovah's bride. (eg. *Isaiah 49:18, 61:10, 62:5, Jeremiah 2:32, 7:34, 16:9, 25:10, 33:11, Joel 2:16*).

Nor is the idea strange to the New Testament. (eg. *John 3:29, Revelation 18:23, 21:2,9, 22:17*) Israel, as presented in the New Testament, is the covenant people consisting of all who by obedient faith are God's people.

In both the Old and New Testaments, idolatry in particular and false worship in general are called harlotry or spiritual adultry. In turning from God to the worship of false gods, Israel played the role of the unfaithful wife. This, as we have previously seen, was the ultimate cause of the evil in the pre-exilic kingdoms of Israel and Judah, and so the ultimate reason for the destruction of Israel and the captivity of Judah.

(Verses 3-5) Now the punishment of the faithless bride by her jealous husband is over. He has returned her to the homeland. In building the temple she has at last returned in her heart to Him. He will therefore return to live in the house Israel has built for Him. The twin hills, Zion and Moriah upon which Jerusalem and the temple sit are to be known as the holy mountain.

Bear in mind, that which is holy is that which is set apart to the accomplishment of God's purpose. The ultimate fulfillment of God's covenant promise would come when, on this very mountain, God's message of repentance and remission of sins began its call to all the nations of the earth. (cp. *Luke 24:44-ff, Acts, chapter 2*)

The happiness of the restored people in their land with their God is pictured by the prophet in figures of happy homelife. Old men and old women sit in the streets. Those who, because of age must lean upon a staff, go about the city. The streets are full of children at play. It is a picture of happy contented safety on the part of those who trust and obey the Lord and who thereby are aware of His presence in their midst. Long life and many children was, among the Jews, the epitome of the "good life."

(Verse 6) The remnant, having returned to a desolate forsaken land with its buildings all in ruins, would look with amazement upon the restoration.

"Should it also be," Jehovah asks rhetorically, *"marvellous in mine eyes?"* Those who had failed to heed his warnings before the captivity, had also failed to hear His promises of deliverance. Therefore they were astounded that it should come so completely to pass. But to Jehovah, Who from the beginning had planned it so, it was no cause for marvel at all.

(Verses 7-8) The joy of the returnees, and their amazement at what God has wrought through them blends quite normally into a glimpse of the final fulfillment in Messianic Israel. In that day, Jehovah will save His people, not only from Babylon and from among the Jews. His people will come from the east and the west. The presence of God among them will not be symbolic, as in the temple, but in truth and righteousness. Jesus saw this in His own coming. At the Samaritan well He said that the hour was now that true worship would be in spirit and truth rather than in the temple made with hands. (cf. *John 4:23-24*)

8:9-13

THE FOURTH STATEMENT . . . Zechariah 8:9-13

RV . . . Thus saith Jehovah of hosts: Let your hands be strong, ye that hear in these days these words from the mouth of the prophets that were in the day that the foundation of the house of Jehovah of hosts was laid, even the temple, that it might be built. For before those days there was no hire for man, nor any hire for beast; neither was there any peace to him that went out or came in, because of the adversary: for I set all men every one against his neighbor. But now I will not be unto the remnant of this people as in the former days, saith Jehovah of hosts. For there shall be the seed of peace; the vine shall give its fruit, and the ground shall give its increase, and the heavens shall give their dew; and I will cause the remnant of this people to inherit all these things. And it shall come to pass that, as ye were a curse among the nations, O house of Judah and house of Israel, so will I save you, and ye shall be a blessing. Fear not, but let your hands be strong.

LXX . . . Thus saith the Lord Almighty; Let your hands be strong, ye that hear in these days these words out of the mouth of the prophets, from the day that the house of the Lord Almighty was founded, and from the time that the temple was built. For before those days the wages of men could not be profitable, and there could be no hire of cattle, and there could be no peace by reason of the affliction to him that went out or to him that came in: for I would have let loose all men, every one against his neighbour. But now I will not do to the remnant of this people according to the former days, saith the Lord Almighty. But I will shew peace: the vine shall yield her fruit, and the land shall yield her produce, and the heaven shall give its dew: and I will give as an inheritance all these things to the remnant of my people. And it shall come to pass, as ye were a curse among the nations, O house of Juda, and house of Israel; so will I save you, and ye shall be a blessing: be of good courage, and strengthen your hands.

COMMENTS

(Verses 9-10) Before the blessed state described in the third statement can become reality the people must get to work with their hands and build the temple. There will be little prosperity in the land until this is accomplished. Their labour will be all in vain and they will be constantly at odds with one another until they have finished the task the Lord, through His prophets, has set before them. (cp. *Haggai 1: 6-11*)

(Verses 11-12) Once the temple has been rebuilt the promised blessed conditions will be forthcoming. God's relationship to the restored remnant will then be different than it is now in their hesitancy to rebuild, different than it has been during the centuries of their rebellion and punishment. Rather than chastisement, He will heap upon them the blessings of the land.

(Verse 13) Again the ecstacy of blessing blends forward into a Messianic prediction. Israel, who have been a curse among the nations shall be saved and become a blessing.

Here, in capsule form, is a statement of God's covenant purpose in the Jewish people. The term "house of Judah" is that from which we derive the term Jew. The term Israel is the term which stresses the covenant relationship of the Jews to Jehovah.

The remnant of the Jewish race has returned to the land promised by God in the establishment of the covenant. As the remainder of the race they have been saved (or will be upon completion of the temple).

The remnant was also the remainder of the covenant people. As such they would be saved in a much greater way with the coming of the Messiah. At that point they would be a blessing.

Here, at the beginning of their restored national life, is the same covenant terminology which has marked every other beginning in the history of this people. In the call of Abraham, when the covenant was voiced for the first time, God had made the promise to him in words identical to these *(Genesis 12:2)*. In the same statement, God had made it clear to Abraham that the blessing was intended for the whole human race. *(Genesis 12:3)*

In the soliloquy recorded in *Genesis 18:17-ff,* God reaffirms this covenant purpose in very similar language. *(v. 18)*

To Isaac God spoke similarly, as the covenant passed from the first to the second generation. *(Genesis 26:4)*

When the covenant was reaffirmed to Jacob, the language was the same. *(Genesis 28:14)*

It was this promise that God remembered when He was about to lead Jacob's progeny out of Egypt. *(Exodus 2:24)* The progeny accepted this covenant as the condition upon which they would become a peculiar treasure to Jehovah, and a nation of priests. *(Exodus 19:5-6)*

Now the remnant, upon taking up residence in the land once more, once more becoming a nation of priests in the restored temple, are reminded very pointedly that the reason for their existence has to

8:13-17   ZECHARIAH

do with their relationship to God's purpose in all the nations of the earth.

They had, in time past, become a curse rather than a blessing upon the nations. They had assumed they were special before God merely for their own sakes, and so believed the rest of the world inferior. They had proved unfaithful to God themselves and so thwarted the fulfillment of His purpose to bless all nations through them.

Consequently, ten of the twelve tribes had been wiped out and the remaining people led captive.

Now, returned from exile and re-established with the symbolic presence of Jehovah in their midst they are not to forget why He has spent all these patient centuries with them. The purpose for which they had been called into being in the beginning is exactly the purpose of their present restoration.

Therefore, because God has more at stake in their work than do they, they are once more called upon to *"fear not, but let your hands be strong."* To understand God's purpose in building is to fearlessly build in the strength of the Lord.

THE FIFTH STATEMENT . . . Zechariah 8:14-17

RV . . . For thus saith Jehovah of hosts: As I thought to do evil unto you, when your fathers provoked me to wrath, saith Jehovah of hosts, and I repented not; so again have I thought in these days to do good unto Jerusalem and to the house of Judah: fear ye not. These are the things that ye shall do: Speak ye every man the truth with his neighbor; execute the judgement of truth and peace in your gates; and let none of you devise evil in your hearts against his neighbor; and love no false oath: for all these are things that I hate, saith Jehovah.

LXX . . . For thus saith the Lord Almighty; As I took counsel to afflict you when your fathers provoked me, saith the Lord Almighty, and I repented not: so have I prepared and taken counsel in these days to do good to Jerusalem and to the house of Juda: be ye of good courage. These are the things which ye shall do; speak truth every one with his neighbour; judge truth and peaceable judgement in your gates: and let none of you devise evil in his heart against his neighbour; and love not a false oath: for all these things I hate, saith the Lord Almighty.

COMMENTS

(Verses 14-15) The *fifth* statement is, in effect, a brief reaffirmation of the first. The fathers, *ie.* those who lived on the other side of the exile, had provoked Jehovah's wrath. He had determined to punish them and would not be disuaded.

Now He is equally determined to "start all over again" with the remnant. Just as originally He had intended a blessed and peaceful relationship with Israel in the land of promise while leading them toward the fulfillment of His purpose, so now in the restoration it is His desire to bless the remnant toward the same end.

(Verses 15(c)-17) For this reason they are not to live in fear. God's wrath is neither petulant nor arbitrary. So long as they are faithful and live as He desires they have no reason to fear it.

There can be no doubt as to what will please Him. They must, as the former prophets had entreated their fathers, be honest with each other. They must be just in their judicial proceedings. They must not scheme to take advantage of the weak and poor. They must not go to court with false oaths to accomplish selfish purposes.

The reason is plain. He hates all these things. A righteous God could scarcely do otherwise.

THE SIXTH STATEMENT . . . Zechariah 8:18-23

RV . . . And the word of Jehovah of hosts came unto me, saying, Thus saith Jehovah of hosts; The fast of the fourth month, and the fast of the fifth, and the fast of the seventh, and the fast of the tenth, shall be to the house of Judah joy and gladness, and cheerful feasts; there love truth and peace. Thus saith Jehovah of hosts: It shall yet come to pass, that there shall come peoples, and the inhabitants of many cities; and the inhabitants of one city shall go to another, saying, Let us go speedily to entreat the favor of Jehovah, and go to seek Jehovah of hosts: I will go also. Yea, many peoples and strong nations shall come to seek Jehovah of hosts in Jerusalem, and to entreat the favor of Jehovah. Thus saith Jehovah of hosts: In those days it shall come to pass, that ten men shall take hold, out of all the languages of the nations, they shall take hold of the skirt of him that is a Jew, saying, We will go with you, for we have heard that God is with you.

LXX . . . And the word of the Lord Almighty came to me, saying, Thus saith the Lord Almighty, The fourth fast, and the fifth fast, and the seventh fast, and the tenth fast, shall be to the house of Juda for joy and gladness, and for good feasts; and ye shall rejoice; and love ye the truth and peace. Thus saith the Lord Almighty; Yet shall many peoples come, and the inhabitants of many cities; and the inhabitants of five cities shall come together to one city, saying, Let us go to make

8:18-23   ZECHARIAH

supplication to the Lord, and to seek the face of the Lord Almighty; I will go also. And many peoples and many nations shall come to seek earnestly the face of the Lord Almighty in Jerusalem, and to obtain favour of the Lord. Thus saith the Lord Almighty; In those days my word shall be fulfilled if ten men of all the languages of the nations should take hold—even take hold of the hem of a Jew, saying, We will go with thee; for we have heard that God is with you.

COMMENTS

The *final* statement in answer to the questioners from Beth-el is also the final entreaty of God to the people to build the temple. It begins with a promise of joy in the stead of fasting and closes with a Messianic promise that through His people all the people of earth will come to share His blessings.

(Verses 18-19) The fasts occasioned, albeit without divine sanction, by the punishment of Judah through Babylon will give way to joy and gladness. The fast days themselves will become feast days.

Jewish history provides an ironic footnote concerning these fasts which God promised would become feasts. The fast of the fourth month observed on the 17th of the Hebrew month of *Tammuz,* is now observed in connection with four incidents: (1) the building of the golden calf, (2) Moses' breaking of the tablets of the law, (3) the ceasation of daily sacrifices prior to the actual Babylonian conquest of Jerusalem and (4) the actual occupation of Jerusalem by Nebuchadnezzar.

The fast of the fifth month, is held on the 9th day of *Abh* by modern Jewry, in connection with the destruction of Solomon's temple by Nebuchadnezzar and of the second temple on the same day of the year by Titus in 70 A.D. Connected with the modern observance of this fast also is the memory of the day God turned the Israelites back from entering the promised land a year and a half after they left Egypt, and the capture of the city of Bether by Hadrian c. 135 A.D.

The fast of the seventh month, now observed on the third day of *Tishri* remembers the murder of Gedaliah at Mizpah, just as during the captivity.

The tenth month fast remembers, on the tenth day of *Tibheth,* as it did in Babylon, the beginning of the siege of Jerusalem by Nebuchadnezzar.

From this it would seem that the Jews have missed the joy of their deliverance from captivity, just as in rejecting Jesus they have missed the joy of their deliverance from sin.

On is constrained to believe that Zechariah's picture of joy in this passage, as others, is symbolic of the joy of salvation in Christ rather than of any joy on the part of those who seem forever blind to the blessings of Jehovah.

(Verses 20-2) The Messianic age will come. People of many nations will join the faithful of Israel in the enjoyment of God's blessings. The passage is a perfect picture of what is happening as the influence of the church, beginning in Jerusalem, has brought to the world the Jehovah once known only to the Jews.

These verses are very reminiscent of *Isaiah 2:-4,* and of *Joel 2:28-ff.* If by them we are to understand material promises, then history fails to record their fulfillment. If, on the other hand, these verses, and other such prophetic passages are symbolic of the real blessings of Jehovah for His people in the Messianic age, we have but to count our blessings as Christians to know the real meaning of these verses. Personally, I believe the latter to be the intent of the passage.

What God began in the Spirit will not be perfected in the flesh (cp. *Galatians 3:3*). God's purpose has always been to bless the peoples of the whole earth. When the temple is completed and the symbolic priesthood and sacrifices restored, the final barrier to Messiah's coming will have been removed. When He comes, men from every nation under heaven will seek the God of Israel. The faithful remnant would become the nucleus of the Messiah's true Israel, and as they went everywhere from Jerusalem preaching the Gospel, men of every nation would turn to them for knowledge of the one true God.

Chapter XXXVI—*Questions*

Teaching About Worship

1. Outward formal religious observances unrelated to present life are an_____to_____.
2. God's promises are to those whose relationship to Him makes a real difference in_____.
3. On December 4, _____ B.C. those who lived in Beth-el sent messengers to Jehovah with a question.
4. What was that question?
5. Where is Beth-el?

ZECHARIAH

6. Show that those who lived in Beth-el were not Samaritans but Jews.
7. The fast on the seventh day of the fifth month marked the _____anniversary of_____.
8. The fast of the seventh Month remembered_____.
9. Zechariah's answer to the question from Beth-el was in _____statements.
10. Give the references for each of these statements.
11. What was the first answer?
12. Who were "the former prophets?"
13. What was the second answer?
14. The questioners are further reminded that God, through the former prophets, had commanded their fathers to "_____ _____.

18. The happiness of the restored people is presented in figures of happy_____.
19. The joy and amazement of the returnees blends quite normally into a glimpse of_____.
20. What is Zechariah's fourth answering statement?
21. Again the ecstasy of blessing blends forward into_____ prediction.
22. At the beginning of their restored national life is the same _____ terminology which had marked the beginning of_____.
23. The returned remnant is once more to be a nation of_____ _____.
24. How had the Jews become a curse upon the nations rather than a blessing?
25. Discuss the idea that "God has more at stake in this work than do they."
26. What was the fifth statement in answer to the questioners from Beth-el?
27. How does it relate to the first statement?
28. So; long as the people are_____and_____they have no reason to fear God's wrath.
29. What was the sixth statement?
30. This statement is also an entreaty to God's people to_____ _____.
31. It begins with a promise of_____instead of_____ and closes with a_____promise.

32. Modern Jews observe the fast of the fourth month in connection with _____, _____, _____, and _____.
33. The fast of the fifth month is held in connection with _____, and _____. It also remembers _____ and _____.
34. The fast of the seventh month is now observed in rememberance of _____.
35. The tenth month fast recalls _____.
36. What do you conclude from the fact that these fasts are still observed by the Jews?
37. Verses 20-23 are a perfect picture of what is happening as the influence of the _____, beginning at _____ has brought the world the _____ once known only to the Jews.

CHAPTER XXXVII
PREFACE TO SECTION II

The opening verse of Zechariah, chapter nine, marks the beginning of the truly apocalyptic section of the prophet's work. As has been previously indicated, the probable reason for the shift to this style of writing is to avoid a confrontation with the Medo-Persian authorities. We shall see that, in this last six chapters, Zechariah makes predictions which, if written literally, would have brought the wrath of an otherwise benevolent Darius down upon Judah perhaps to her permanent destruction. Daniel, written during the Babylonian captivity, and Revelation, written during the heat of Roman persecution are two further examples among others in the Bible of the use of apocalypsis in writing predictive prophecy for the purpose of protecting the readers.

Because of the sudden shift in style of writing between this and the first section of the book, the form critics of the Bible have had a field day with Zechariah. Their attacks have centered largely upon the date of writing and the identity of the author.

It is not within the scope of this work to answer these critics, except to say that there is no solid evidence, either internal or external to deny its place as part of the message of Zechariah. The sudden change in style is brought about by the content of the predictions. The change in subject matter is occasioned by the fact that, unlike the

ZECHARIAH

first eight chapters, this section is not written to motivate the people to build. It deals with that which is to come after the building of the temple.

Having said this in defense of the second section of Zechariah, we must, for the sake of our own study, recognize that, in all probability, the second section of Zechariah was written much later in the life of the prophet than the first section. There are in it no problems relating to the building of the temple The author does not use the first person singular, as he did in the first section, and most important, the historical viewpoint is entirely changed from the first part of the book.

A broad outline of the section will divide it into three major divisions: (1) the triumph of Zion through her Messiah (9:1-10:12), (2) the good and foolish shepherds (11:1-17) and (3) final events (chapters 12-14).

The third of these major divisions may be subdivided into (a) Judah's victory over the attackers and (b) the approaching Day of the Lord.

The final section of Zechariah is easier to follow if one keeps in mind (1) the prophet is concerned primarily with the final consummation of God's dealing with the Jews as a race and nation and (2) in the foretelling of this he interrupts himself frequently to deal with historic events which will intervene between his own time and the end time.

The coming of the Messiah must await the rebuilding of the temple, the invasion of the Greeks, and the Maccabean revolt. The final restoration of the Jewish nation must await the coming of the Good Shepherd, His rejection by the Jews, and the consequent dissolution of the covenant relationship with the Jews as a race. This will be followed by a break up of the nation and its dispersion throughout the world. Only then will the nation be re-established, and wail at the sight of Him Whom they have pierced and become the instrument of establishing the universal reign of Jehovah.

We must digress here to call attention again to Zechariah's influence on the New Testament. Most of this influence comes from the second section of the book.

In the first section we saw the recurrent references to the Branch. These are not directly quoted in the New Testament, but the concept of the Messiah as priest and King expressed in this figure plays a prominent role in the New Testament understanding of Jesus as Lord and Christ.

PREFACE TO SECTION II

The emphasis which we find in thhe second section of Zechariah are directly quoted in the New Testament as applying specifically to the events and the person of Jesus. The king riding on the ass *(Zechariah 9:9)* is seen as fulfilled literally in Jesus' triumphal entry into Jerusalem (cf. *Matthew 21:4-ff, John 12:15).*

The betrayal of Jesus by Judas for thirty pieces of silver is seen as the fulfillment of *Zechariah 11:12-f.* (cp. *Matthew 26:15, 27:9-ff)*

When the Jews who insisted to Pilate that Jesus be executed looked upon the dying Savior, the Gospel writers saw it as the fulfillment of *Zechariah 12:10.* (cp. *John 19:37, Revelation 1:7)*

The smitten shepherd of *Zechariah 13:7* is seen fulfilled in the crucifixion also. (cp. *Matthew 26:31, Mark 14:27*)

Jesus is also seen as the King who reigns from sea to sea *(Zechariah 9:10)* and the fountain for cleansing *(Zechariah 13:1).*

Other influences of Zechariah on the New Testament include the prophet's insistence upon honesty of God's people one with another *(Zechariah 8:16* cp. *Ephesians 4:25),* as well as some of John's word pictures in Revelation, as for example the four horsemen *(Zechariah 6:1-8* cp. *Revelation 6:2-ff),* the two olive trees *(Zechariah 4:3-ff* cp. *Revelation 11:4),* and the lampstand and seven eyes *(Zechariah 4:2-10* cp. *Revelation 1:12-f).*

Chapter XXXVII—*Questions*

Preface to Section II

1. The opening verse of chapter nine marks the beginning of the truly _____ section of the prophetic work of Zechariah.
2. What is the probable reason for the shift to this style?
3. How have the critics attacked Zechariah at this point?
4. Suggest some answers to this criticism.
5. When was Zechariah 9-14 written in relationship to the opening chapters?
6. Give a brief outline of Zechariah, chapters 9-14.
7. The first half of the final section of Zechariah is concerned with _____.
8. The final half of this section is concerned with _____.
9. Discuss Zechariah's influence on the New Testament.
10. What are other Biblical examples of apocalyptic writing?

CHAPTER XXXVIII

THE TRIUMPH OF ZION THROUGH HER MESSIAH

JUDGEMENT AGAINST ISRAEL'S ENEMIES . . . Zechariah 9:1-8

RV . . . The burden of the word of Jehovah upon the land of Hadrach, and Damascus shall be its resting place (for the eye of man and of all the tribes of Israel is toward Jehovah); and Hamath, also, which bordereth thereon; Tyre and Sidon, because they are very wise. And Tyre did build herself a stronghold, and heaped up silver as the dust, and fine gold as the mire of the streets. Behold, the Lord will dispossess her, and he will smite her power in the sea; and she shall be devoured with fire. Ashkelon shall see it, and fear; Gaza also, and shall be sore pained; and Ekron, for her expectation shall be put to shame; and the king shall perish from Gaza, and Ashkelon shall not be inhabited. And a bastard shall dwell in Ashdod, and I will cut off the pride of the Philistines. And I will take away his blood out of his mouth, and his abominations from between his teeth; and he also shall be a remnant for our God; and he shall be as a chieftain in Judah, and Ekron as a Jebusite. And I will encamp about my house against the army, that none pass through or return; and no oppressor shall pass through them any more: for now have I seen with mine eyes.

LXX . . . The burden of the word of the Lord in the land of Sedrach, and his sacrifice shall be in Damascus; for the Lord looks upon men, and upon all the tribes of Israel. And in Emath, even in her coasts, are Tyre and Sidon, because they were very wise. And Tyrus built strongholds for herself, and heaped up silver as dust, and gathered gold as the mire of the ways. And therefore the Lord will take them for a possession, and will smite her power in the sea; and she shall be consumed with fire. Ascalon shall see, and fear; Gaza also, and shall be greatly pained, and Accaron; for she is ashamed at her trespass; and the king shall perish from Gaza, and Ascalon shall not be inhabited. And aliens shall dwell in Azotus, and I will bring down the pride of the Philistines. And I will take their blood out of their mouth, and their abominations from between their teeth; and these also shall be left to our God, and they shall be as a captain of a thousand in Juda, and Accaron as a Jebusite. And I will set up a defence for my house, that they may not pass through, nor turn back, neither shall there any

THE TRIUMPH OF ZION THROUGH HER MESSIAH 9:1

more come upon them one to drive them away: for now have I seen with mine eyes.

COMMENTS

The theme of chapter nine is struck in verse nine. It is the coming of the Messianic King *(vs. 9-17)*. The judgement of God against Israel's traditional enemies set forth in these opening verses are to be seen as preparation for that event. Not only God's dealing with these nations as the enemies of His people, but all his dealings in history prior to Messiah's coming were in preparation for it.

(Verse 1) The term *"burden* (more accurately "oracle") *of the word of Jehovah"* is reminiscent of Malachi. It is calculated to place the stamp of divine origin on the second section of the book. The method of inspiration seems to differ from that of the first section in that the prophet does not claim here to have seen a vision. Nevertheless, what he is about to say is not a matter of his own subjective understanding of historic events. He is speaking from God as one moved by the Holy Spirit. (cp. *II Peter 1:19-21, Hebrews 1:1*)

The first part of this oracle is concerned with the land of Hadrach, and its focal point is Damascus. (cp. *Isaiah 21:13*) Hadrach is a symbolic name for Syria. The name itself was a little used one applying to a region of Syria also called Bikathanen. It is the western interior part of the country surrounded by hills. Hadrach takes its name from this surrounding. The word means literally "enclosed."

The burden of Jehovah would focus on Damascus until that ancient enemy of Israel was utterly brought to its knees. History records the fulfillment of this prediction when Alexander the Great took the city, c. 344 B.C. It subsequently became Hellenized and is listed as the first of ten such cities which formed the Decapolis.

The parenthetical statement by which Zechariah explains this must not be overlooked if one would begin to understand the hand of Providence in the ebb and flow of history. The English text is misleading when it states, *"the eye of man and of all the tribes of Israel is toward Jehovah."* The marginal rendering in the Standard Edition is more to the point, *"Jehovah hath an eye upon men and upon the tribes of Israel."* The point being that God's covenant purpose to bless all the nations of the earth in Israel's Seed is the all determining factor in every historic development, even the defeat of one pagan nation by another.

(Verses 2-4) In rapid succession Zechariah deals with the future of the other enemies of Israel immediately adjacent to her. Tyre and Sidon were next in Alexander's plan to conquest. Sidon, as Damascus, surrendered peaceably, but Tyre was subdued only after a siege.

The city harbored a large squadron of mercenaries in the pay of the Persians. The resistance was so bitter that, when Tyre finally fell, Alexander departed from his usual policy of benevolence toward conquered cities and allowed his Macedonians to slaughter eight thousand Tyrians and sell thirty thousand into slavery.

(Verse 5) Ashkelon, seeing the fate of Tyre, surrendered without resistance. Thus the ancient seaport of the Philistines became, in turn, a Greek city to plague Israel no more.

Gaza, on the other hand, chose to resist the Macedonian conqueror. Durant records, "Gaza fought till every man in the city was dead and every woman raped."

Ekron, the southernmost of the Philistine cities, had hoped in vain that Alexander would be stopped by Tyre in his march through Palestine to Egypt. The hope was turned to disappointment as the Macedonian phalanx swept down the Mediterranean coast engulfing by either peaceful surrender or siege all who stood in its path.

The king of Gaza comes in for special attention by the prophet, as well he might, considering what lay in store for him. When Gaza fell, following a two month siege, and ten thousand of its inhabitants were killed while the rest were sold to the slave merchants who followed in the wake of Alexander's armies, special treatment was waiting Betis, the Persian satrap. This puppet "king" found himself tied to Alexander's chariot by two thongs through the soles of his feet and dragged through the city in one of the young conqueror's characteristic fits of revenge against one who resisted his forward march.

(Verses 6-7) Ashdod shall be ruled by an alien race. (The rendering "bastard" here is misleading.) (The Septuagint is more accurate.) It is a clear prediction of the reign of the Greeks and Romans, beginning with Alexander.

The pride of the Philistines has to do with the peculiar form of idolatry practiced in Philistia which included the drinking of the blood of sacrificed animals. Hence, when the Philistines are conquered by Alexander, Hellenized by the Ptolemaic dynasty of Egypt, and subsequently converted to Jehovah, the blood was taken "out of his mouth."

The law made the drinking of blood an abomination (cf. *Genesis 9:4, Leviticus 7:26*). When in Philistia "the son of the stranger joined himself to the Lord" *(Isaiah 56:3)* the abomination would be taken

THE TRIUMPH OF ZION THROUGH HER MESSIAH 9:8-17

"from between his teeth," and the Philistine also became part of Jehovah's faithful remnant! Just as the Jebusites, the original inhabitants of Jerusalem had been incorporated into the people of Judah *(II Samuel 24:16,* etc.) in a subordinate position *(I Kings 9:20,21),* so the Philistines, traditional enemies of Israel are to ultimately be assimilated as proselytes. Again history vindicates prophecy.

(Verse 8) The prophet reassures his readers, who have worked to rebuild the temple, that when all this is taking place around them, they, and their work will be protected by the Lord. History records that Alexander's conquest of Jerusalem was by invitation. He did not oppress them, but rather afforded them privileges. No Jew was injured.

THE COMING OF THE MESSIAH KING . . . Zechariah 9:9-17

RV . . . Rejoice greatly, O daughter of Zion; shout, O daughter of Jerusalem; behold, thy king cometh unto thee; he is just, and having salvation; lowly, and riding upon an ass, even upon a colt the foal of an ass. And I will cut off the chariot from Ephraim, and the horse from Jerusalem; and the battle bow shall be cut off; and he shall speak peace unto the nations; and his dominion shall be from sea to sea, and from the River to the ends of the earth. As for thee also, because of the blood of thy covenant I have set free thy prisoners from the pit wherein is no water. Turn you to the stronghold, ye prisoners of hope: even today do I declare that I will render double unto thee. For I have bent Judah for me, I have filled the bow with Ephraim; and I will stir up thy sons, O Zion, against the sons of Greece, and will make thee as the sword of a mighty man. And Jehovah shall be seen over them; and his arrow shall go forth as the lightning; and the Lord Jehovah will blow the trumpet, and will go with whirlwinds of the south. Jehovah of hosts will defend them; and they shall devour, and shall tread down the sling-stones; and they shall drink, and make a noise as through wine; and they shall be filled like bowls, like the corners of the altar. And Jehovah their God will save them in that day as the flock of his people; for they shall be as the stones of a crown, lifted on high over his land. For how great is his goodness, and how great is his beauty! grain shall make the young men flourish, and new wine the virgins.

LXX . . . Rejoice greatly, O daughter of Sion; proclaim it aloud, O daughter of Jerusalem; behold, the King is coming to thee, just, and a Saviour; he is meek and riding on an ass, and a young foal. And he shall destroy the chariots out of Ephraim, and the horse out of Jerusalem, and the bow of war shall be utterly destroyed; and there shall be abundance and peace out of the nations; and he shall rule over the waters as far as the sea, and the rivers to the ends of the earth. And thou by the blood of thy covenant hast sent forth thy prisoners out of the pit that has no water. Ye shall dwell in strongholds, ye prisoners of the congregation: and for one day of thy captivity I will recompense thee double. For I have bent thee, O Juda, for myself as a bow, I have filled Ephraim; and I will raise up thy children, O Sion, against the children of the Greeks, and I will handle thee as the sword of a warrior. And the Lord shall be over them, and his arrow shall go forth as lightning: and the Lord Almighty shall blow with the trumpet; and shall proceed with the tumult of his threatening. The Lord Almighty shall protect them, and overwhelm them with sling-stones; and they shall swallow them down as wine, and fill the bowls as the altar. And the Lord their God shall save them in that day, even his people as a flock; for holy stones are rolled upon his land. For if he has anything good, and if he has anything fair, the young men shall have corn, and there shall be fragrant wine to the virgins.

COMMENTS

The predictions of this section find their immediate meaning in the Maccabean revolt and their ultimate fulfillment in the coming of Jesus. The victory of Judas Maccabee over Antiochus Epiphanes led the prophet quite naturally to exultation over God's final victory through the Messiah.

For the sake of clarity we shall deal with the two aspects of this section separately, first as it applies to the Maccabean revolt, and afterward as it applies to the coming of Jesus Christ.

In order to understand the prophecies concerning the Maccabean war with the Seleucid Emperor Antiochus IV, it is helpful to review the history of Hellenism in the near east immediately following the death of Alexander the Great.

After nine years in Asia, Alexander began to doubt the wisdom of Aristotle's instruction to him to treat the "barbarians" as slaves. He found in the aristocratic elements of Persia a refinement seldom seen among the temperamental and warring Greeks. He doubted that his uncouth Macedonians could replace these Persian nobles in successful administration of the conquered peoples of the orient.

He began to think of himself not as a Macedonian emperor ruling a conquered Persian empire but as a Graeco-Persian emperior ruling over Greeks and Persians as equals.

Pursuant to this policy Alexander married a Bactrian princess and encouraged his officers to follow his example. He opened the Persian land to Greek colonists and gave large doweries to his soldiers who would marry middle eastern women.

All this marked the beginning of the Hellenization of that part of the world which included the holy land and which was vital to the development of events in the Seleucid empire following the death of Alexander.

Another factor in Alexander's reign was to greatly influence the subsequent history of the holy land. He did not choose a successor. When he was dying in Babylon following a drinking bout at the age of thirty three (323 B.C.) he was asked to whom he would leave his empire. He answered simply, "To the strongest."

Alexander's empire had no solid root. He was a Macedonian attempting to be Greek and he became almost a Persian. His attempt to Hellenize the orient resulted in no strong bond designed to hold the empire together. It was consequently no strange thing that it came apart, so to speak, shortly after his death.

The division came in five parts. Antipater took Macedonia and Greece; Lysimachus ruled Thrace; Antigonus, Asia Minor; Ptolemy, Egypt; and most significant for our purposes, Seleucus took Babylon, including Palestine as far south as the southern border of Samaria.

A struggle insued between Seleucid Asia and Ptolemaic Egypt for control of what the Romans would later call Palestine. The original division gave Palestine south of Samaria to Ptolemy and it became part of Egypt. The Seleucids never agreed to this division, desiring full control of the trade route which passed through Damascus and Jerusalem.

From 312-198 B.C. the Ptolemies were able to resist the Seleucid attempts to wrest Judea from them by force. The Jews were allowed a large measure of local self-government. The ruling elements were the hereditary high priest and the gerousia or Council of Elders which had been established by Ezra and Nehemiah. The pattern of Orthodox Judaism from that time to now was set by the regulations passed by this body of seventy and called Dibre Soferim.

In effect this regulation simply attempted to prevent the Jews from succumbing to the Hellenistic pressures with which they were surrounded. Art, music, dress, customs, and most of all religion were over-shadowed by the synagogue chant of the rabbis, "Shammai Israel, Adonai eleenu, Adonai echod," "Hear O Israel: the Lord is our God, the Lord is One."

A concerted effort was made by the Hellenists to break down this resistance. Judea was ringed with a series of Greek settlements in league with the trans-Jordanian Decapolis. Each of these tantilized the Judeans with temples to Greek gods and goddesses, Academies, schools, gymnasiums and nude games.

The extent to which the Hellenizing efforts succeeded is seen in the fact that several young Jews submitted to surgery to remove the sign of the covenant so they would not be ridiculed when participating in the games.

Historians believe three factors prevented the complete overwhelming of the Jews by Hellenism. The persecution of Antiochus IV which drove the Orthodox underground and polarized public sympathy in their favor, the protection of the Romans which came at the request of the Maccabees, and the power and prestige of the Law of Moses which even the most Hellenistic Jews agreed came from God.

The persecution began in 198 B.C. when Antiochus III finally defeated the Ptolemys and Judea became part of the Seleucid Empire. Antiochus III was received by the Jews as a liberator, but their joy was short-lived. His successor Antiochus IV proved to be a veritable despot. He appointed as high priest one Jason who was a leader of Hellenistic sympathizers in Jerusalem. An order came from Antiochus at Jason's request for the establishing of Greek institutions like those of the Decapolis in Jerusalem itself.

Unhappy with Jason for the slowness with which the Hellenizing of Judea was proceeding, Antiochus replaced him with Menelous. Menelous proceeded to get to the core of the matter. Jehovah was made one with the Greek Zeus and sacrifices were offered to them according to the Greek practice rather than the Jewish law.

Such shocking practice brought predictable consequences. The majority of the Jews swung to the Chasidim, or anti-Hellenist party. Antiochus IV declared himself Epiphanes or "God made manifest."

In 168 B.C. Antiochus was defeated by the Ptolemaic Pharaoh Popilius, and Jerusalem received the mistaken report that he had been killed. Their celebration was cut short by Antiochus himself appearing on the scene.

Convinced that the Jews had been responsible for his failure in Egypt, he slaughtered thousands of them, robbed the temple, restored Menelaus whom the Jews had deposed and rededicated the temple to

Zeus. He ordered the destruction of the altar, replaced it with a Greek altar and then committed the ultimate blasphemy by sacrificing a pig on it! Jews were forced on pain of death to eat pork so sacrificed. Jerusalem was razed by flames and the Jewish population was sold into slavery.

The entire reign of Antiochus Epiphanes was, and still is, known as "the abomination of desolation," in Jewish historical writings.

During all this, the Chasidim preached guerilla resistance. Among those who went underground was one Mattathias of the house of Hasonai of the tribe of Aaron, and his five sons Judas, Simon, Eleazor, Jonathan and Johannan Caddis.

Mattathias began the active revolt by killing a Jew who was approaching the altar to offer a swine, and shouting, "Whoever is zealous for the Law, and wishes to support the covenant, let him follow me." He had set the stage for every Jewish Zealot from then until now.

Upon Mattathais' death, leadership of the revolt passed to Judas who was called Maccabee, "the hammer." Judas was a saint in prayer and a terror in battle. Against great odds he defeated the Greek mercenaries at Emmaus. The victory was complete, yet Antiochus was not convinced. He sent an even larger force to wipe out the rebels.

These were in turn wiped out at Mizpah. In 164 B.C. Judas cleansed and rededicated the temple and restored the priestly services.

Upon the death of Antiochus Epiphanes in 163 B.C., his successor, Lysias, offered the Jews full religious freedom if they would disarm. The Chasidim consented. Judas refused, asserting that to be really religiously free the Jews must be politically free. This difference was the beginning of civil strife which produced the party of the Pharisees, who agreed with the Chasidim and the Sadducees whose political ambitions matched those of Judas.

Civil war ensued with the Maccabeans now persecuting those of the Hellenistic faction. Israel was engulfed in civil strife.

Judas was slain in 161 B.C. His successor, brother Jonathan, was killed in 143. The only surviving brother curried the favor of Rome and with the help of that growing power established Jewish independence in 142 B.C. Thus establishing the Hasmonian dynasty.

This period of independence prevailed, although torn by internal strife, until the coming of the Roman Legions seventy nine years later.

In *Zechariah 9:9-10* the prophet begins to rejoice. Now that the temple is built and the land has returned to Jehovah, the appearance of the Messianic King seems imminent. We will have more to say shortly about this King and His appearance.

9:9-17   ZECHARIAH

In *9:11-f* the joyous coming of the Messiah is postponed by the stark reality of the present grim situation. The struggle with Greece must first be won. The disbursed are encouraged to return to their home land and join in the struggle. They have the promise that they will prevail *(v. 13)*. Jehovah Himself will fight for them *(v. 14-15)*. He will save them as His people *(v. 16)*. The sling-stones of the Maccabees will eat the flesh of the Seleucids. The victorious rebels would be drenched with blood like the horns of the altar *(v. 15)* and in their victories they would shine like the glittering jewels of a crown *(v. 16)*.

The fierce description of the struggle for independence from the Hellenizing Seleucid Greek empire ends on a note of praise to God for His goodness.

THE MESSIANIC ASPECT OF ZECHARIAH . . . 9:9-17

It is indeed not strange that Zechariah should mingle his prophecy of Maccabean independence with that of the coming of Christ. The defeat of the Seleucids marked the last foreign presence in the holy land prior to that historic period in which Christ finally came. The excited rejoicing of the prophet is indeed understandable.

On the other hand, it is equally easy to see how the Jews of later times reading such intermingled predictions could cast their longed for Messiah in the mold of Judas Maccabee. The desire for political independence as a base for religious freedom would be as strong under Caesar as under Antiochus Epiphanes.

Nevertheless, when the Messiah did come, He scorned such a militarily attained and supported political kingdom to fulfill God's ultimate purpose in blessing all the nations of the earth. It required His own resurrection from the dead to establish His Messianic identity in view of His renunciation of this worldly power and ambition.

(Verse 9) Zechariah calls upon the theocratic people, "Daughter of Zion . . . Daughter of Jerusalem" to rejoice at the coming of her king. (cp. *Psalm 2:11*) He is not at all what she expected, but He is Messiah.

He is just, a characteristic attributed by the prophets to the Messiah in connection with salvation (cp. *Isaiah 45:21, 53:11, Jeremiah 23:5,6*).

In contrast with Antiochus, whom the Jews mistakenly welcomed as a savior from Egyptian oppression but who came to destroy, the Messiah King will come to save.

He is lowly and He comes riding on an ass; not the symbol of humiliation as some have supposed but the symbol of peace, as the horse was a symbol of war. Messiah will lead no armed revolt. He will not receive His kingly dominion from Satan (cp. *Luke 4:6-7*) but by going the way of the suffering servant.

This verse finds its literal fulfillment in Jesus' final entry into Jerusalem. *(cp. Matthew 21:4-5)*

(Verse 10) Ephraim, symbolic of the northern tribes, and Jerusalem, symbolic of the southern are to be restored at Messiah's coming. The people will be restored to their full promised dominion *(Genesis 15:18)* from the Red Sea to the Mediterranean.

And beyond, He shall speak peace to all nations, His dominion shall be to the ends of the earth.

The Jews understood such passages to indicate that the Messiah would conquer the world, as had Alexander. Jesus showed the true sense when He commissioned His apostles to preach the gospel to the uttermost part of the earth.

(Verses 11-17) With the words, "as for thee also," Zechariah turns to the coming deliverance from Greek oppression. It will be because of the covenant that the people will be rescued from the threat of complete extinction by Hellenization.

Chapter XXXVIII—*Questions*

The Triumph of Zion Through Her Messiah

1. The theme of chapter nine is struck in verse _____.
2. This theme is the coming of the _____.
3. The term "burden of the word of Jehovah" is calculated to _____.
4. The first part of the oracle is concerned with the land of _____.
5. Hadrach is the symbolic name for _____.
6. This prediction was fulfilled c. 344 B.C. by the invasion of _____ by _____.
7. God's purpose to _____ is the all-determining factor in every historic development.
8. List the traditional enemies of Israel mentioned in chapter nine, and give the symbolic name of each as given by Zechariah.
9. _____ was the southern-most of the Philistine cities mentioned here.
10. What world conqueror fulfilled this predictive passage? *(9:1-8)*
11. The predictions of this section find their immediate fulfillment in what historic event?

12. The ultimate fulfillment of this passage is found in the coming of _____.
13. Describe the events leading to the Maccabean revolt.
14. To what three factors do historians attribute the failure of the Greeks to completely Hellenize the Jews?
15. Following the death of Alexander, the land of Palestine became at first part of what empire?
16. Antiochus IV was called Epiphanes meaning _____.
17. Who were the Chasidim?
18. Whom did Antiochus Epiphanes blame for his defeat at the hand of the Egyptian Ptolemies?
19. What, in Jewish history, is referred to as "the abomination of desolation?"
20. Who was Mattathias?
21. Who was called "the hammer?"
22. Upon the death of Antiochus IV, Lysias offered the Jews complete religious freedom if they would lay down their arms. Why did they refuse?
23. What caused the Jewish civil war following their victory under Judas Maccabee?
24. What was the origin of the party of the Pharisees?
25. What was the origin of the Sadducees?
26. What finally ended the internal strife which followed the Maccabean revolt?
27. In 9:11-f the joyous coming of the Messiah is postponed by_____.
28. Why does Zechariah mingle the prediction of the coming of Christ with that of the Maccabean revolt?
29. Show how the Jews in later times confused these two predictions.
30. What was Jesus' attitude toward the desire of the Jews for a military independence and a political kingdom?
31. Contrast Antiochus IV with the Messiah King.
32. What is the symbolism of the ass upon which the Messiah would ride?
33. What New Testament event fulfills this prediction?
34. Beyond the traditional boundaries of Israel, the Messiah will speak peace to _____.
35. The Jews understood such passages to indicate that _____.

CHAPTER XXXIX
ISRAEL RESTORED
ZECHARIAH, CHAPTER 10:1-12

RV . . . Ask ye of Jehovah rain in the time of the latter rain, even of Jehovah that maketh lightnings; and he will give them showers of rain, to every one grass in the field. For the teraphim have spoken vanity, and the diviners have seen a lie; and they have told false dreams, they comfort in vain; therefore they go their way like sheep, they are afflicted, because there is no shepherd. Mine anger is kindled against the shepherds, and I will punish the he-goats, for Jehovah of hosts hath visited his flock, the house of Judah, and will make them as his goodly horse in the battle. From him shall come forth the corner-stone, from him the nail, from him the battle bow, from him every ruler together. And they shall be as mighty men, treading down their enemies in the mire of the streets in the battle; and they shall fight, because Jehovah is with them; and the riders on horses shall be confounded. And I will strengthen the house of Judah, and I will save the house of Joseph, and I will bring them back; for I have mercy upon them; and they shall be as though I had not cast them off: for I am Jehovah their God, and I will hear them. And they of Ephraim shall be like a mighty man, and their heart shall rejoice as through wine; yea, their children shall see it, and rejoice; their hearts shall be glad in Jehovah. I will hiss for them, and gather them; for I have redeemed them; and they shall increase as they have increased. And I will sow them among peoples; and they shall remember me in far countries; and they shall live with their children, and shall return. I will bring them again also out of the land of Egypt, and gather them out of Assyria; and I will bring them into the land of Gilead and Lebanon; the place shall not be found for them. And he will pass through the sea of affliction, and will smite the waves in the sea, and all the depths of the Nile shall dry up; and the pride of Assyria shall be brought down, and the sceptre of Egypt shall depart. And I will strengthen them in Jehovah; and they shall walk up and down in his name, saith Jehovah.

LXX . . . Ask ye of the Lord rain in season, the early and the latter; the Lord has given bright signs, and will give them abundant rain, to every one grass in the field. For the speakers have uttered grievous things, and the diviners have seen false visions, and they have spoken

10:1-12   ZECHARIAH

false dreams, they have given vain comfort: therefore have they fallen away like sheep, and been afflicted, because there was no healing. Mine anger was kindled against the shepherds, and I will visit the lambs; and the Lord God Almighty shall visit his flock, the house of Juda, and he shall make them as his goodly horse in war. And from him he looked, and from him he set the battle in order, and from him came the bow in anger, and from him shall come forth every oppressor together. And they shall be as warriors treading clay in the ways in war; and they shall set the battle in array, because the Lord is with them, and the riders on horses shall be put to shame. And I will strengthen the house of Juda, and save the house of Joseph, and I will settle them; because I have loved them; and they shall be as if I had not cast them off: for I am the Lord their God, and I will hear them. And they shall be as the warriors of Ephraim, and their heart shall rejoice as with wine: and their children also shall see it, and be glad; and their heart shall rejoice in the Lord. I will make a sign to them, and gather them in; for I will redeem them, and they shall be multiplied according to their number before. And I will sow them among the people; and they that are afar off shall remember me: they shall nourish their children, and they shall return. And I will bring them again from the land of Egypt, and I will gather them in from among the Assyrians; and I will bring them into the land of Galaad and to Libanus; and there shall not even one of them be left behind. And they shall pass through a narrow sea, they shall smite the waves in the sea, and all the deep places of the rivers shall be dried up: and all the pride of the Assyrians shall be taken away, and the sceptre of Egypt shall be removed. And I will strengthen them in the Lord their God; and they shall boast in his name, saith the Lord.

COMMENTS

In chapter nine, verses nine through ten, Zechariah exalted at the coming of Messiah. In *9:11-17,* he interrupted his rejoicing to predict the victorious struggle with the Greeks which would precede His actual coming. In chapter ten, he returns to the theme of Zion triumphant through the Messiah.

(Verse 1) The key to this chapter seems to be "in the time of the latter rain."

To understand the symbolism here, we must know something of the climate of the holy land. During summer it almost literally never rains. From May first through October fifteenth, one can almost guarantee no rain will fall.

The rainy season, from October to May, comes in three parts. They are known as the first or former rains, the winter rains, and the latter rains. The former are the light rains of October and the early days of November. These moisten the soil after the summer drought and allow the planting of winter grain.

The heaviest rains are the winter rains, which fall during December, January and February. The bulk of the water in the land comes from these rains.

Most vital to the completion of the harvest are the *latter rains*. These perfect the fruit and grain just prior to harvest, and so are most welcome and celebrated of all. (cf. *Joel 2:21-24*)

In a land where water is always in such critical supply as in Palestine, it is not surprising that rain should become a favorite symbol of divine blessing. (eg. *Isaiah 44:3-4, Hosea 6:3, Psalms 72:6*)

It is essential that the rains come, it is equally essential that they come at the proper time. Lack of rain at the right time results in complete crop failure. The *latter rains* are essential to the *final* perfection of the crop. Without the *latter rain* all that has developed through the former and winter rains will be lost.

By "rain in the time of the latter rain," Zechariah means God's blessing at the critical point in the history of His people when the fruit of His purpose was nearly ripe for harvest. The coming of the Messiah would usher in the fulfillment of God's purpose in Israel. Now that the people are back in the land and the temple is restored, the harvest season is rapidly drawing near.

God had planted the seed in the call of Abraham. His blessings upon the patriarchs were the "former rains." His continued blessings upon them through the centuries since Moses had nourished them as the winter rain. Now they must ask for the rain in the time of the latter rain in order that God's harvest may be realized in the coming of the long-awaited Christ.

(Verse 2) The prophet is concerned that prayer for the latter rains be made to Jehovah. Previous to the captivity their ancestors had asked the blessing of other gods.

The *teraphim* were household idols or images. (cp. *Genesis 31: 19,30, Judges 7:5*) In light of *I Samuel 19:13* it seems they bore the likeness of some human figure. They also took the form of the signs of the Zodiac and other instruments of astrology. Hosea had used the word to describe the idolatrous state of the people prior to the captivity. *(Hosea 3:4)*

Zechariah's use of the term here indicates his desire that the returned people not repeat the error of their fathers. The blessings required for the realization of Jehovah's purpose must come from Him. All else is vanity.

The *diviners* have had false visions. In the mystery religions associated with Baal various absurd methods were used to conjure up supernatural information concerning future events. Hallucigens were drunk as potions and the mind-expanding "trips" of the diviners were considered as divinely directed visions.

Other devices included the shooting of arrows to predict the direction of a person whose name was engraved thereon. *(eg. Ezekiel 21: 21)* The declaring staff, or divining rod, employed by some present-day superstitions finds its origin in these practices.

The result of such ridiculous superstitions is to cause those who follow them to go their way like stray sheep. Isaiah had said of the pre-exilic people whose religion was shot through with Baal worship, "All we like sheep have gone astray." *(Isaiah 53:6)* Jesus would look with compassion on His contemporaries when He saw them "as sheep having no shepherd." *(Matthew 9:36)*

(Verse 3) The *shepherds* are the spiritual leaders of the people, the *he-goats* the civil leaders. Previously those who held these positions had led the people after false gods. God's anger is kindled against such leadership. He will not allow it to go unpunished.

Jehovah has personally visited His flock. They are no longer to be victimized by such leadership. Here we again see Zechariah's Messianic insight. In the coming of the Messiah, Jehovah visited His flock, the house of Judah.

The Hebrew *Yaweh* (Jehovah) literally means "the one who is." He is ultimate reality understood as a Person. The Septuagint uses the Greek *Kurios* (Lord) to translate *Yaweh*. This word is applied to Jesus by those who were familiar with its Old Testament meaning. The conclusion of the apostles was that He is "both *Lord (Kurios)* and Christ." *(Acts 2:36)* Jesus is Jehovah, Emanuel, God with us.

He visited Judah, the Jews, and the result was the setting aside of the shepherds (*ie.* spiritual leaders, priesthood) and the rejection of the he-goats when the political system which was national Israel was wiped out by the Romans.

The sense of Zechariah's statement here is the declaration of Jehovah's intention to accomplish the ultimate deliverance of His people.

(Verse 4) The Jews were no longer to be subject to foreign rule. "From him," *ie.* from Judah, shall come its ruler. The Maccabean deliverers from Antiochus Epiphanes fulfilled the primary meaning of this prophetic promise, but it looks forward to the Messiah.

The figure of the corner-stone is one of the best known of those applied to the Christ in the New Testament. Jesus applied it to Himself. *(Matthew 21:42, Mark 12:10, Luke 20:17)* Peter applied it to Him *(Acts 4:11, I Peter 2:7)* as did Paul *(Ephesians 2:20).*

The *nail* was in reality a large peg in the center of the tent upon which were hung most of the valuables of the nomadic shepherd. In prophetic type the glories of the people hung on Juda Maccabee. In point of factual fulfillment, they hang on the Messiah.

God's people will not need to depend upon any worldly alliance. He will Himself be their battle bow. (cp. *Psalm 45:4-5, Revelation 6:2)*

(Verses 5-12) This section must look beyond the Maccabean period as well as beyond the post-Babylonian restoration for its fulfillment. To see its real meaning we must bear in mind several significant terms used here by Zechariah, and we must keep in mind that he deliberately does *not* use certain other terms.

First, in this entire chapter the term Judah is used consistently, *never Israel.* Judah signifies the Jews as a political-ethnic group, whereas Israel, which does not appear here, is the covenant name for those whose relationship to God is based on faith rather than national or racial origin.

Second, the house of Judah is joined by the house of Joseph. Judah is, technically, the southern kingdom while Joseph is the ten northern tribes.

Third, the Hebrew verb here translated "I will bring (them) back" is a compound word which includes also "I will place them." (cp. *Jeremiah 32:37)*

Fourth, the reason for the restoration here is not merit on the part of the Jews, but "I have mercy upon them."

Fifth, "they shall be as though I had not cast them off, for I am Jehovah their God, and I will hear them."

We are dealing with God's ultimate intention for the Jewish people. *Jew* and *Israel* are now two separate concepts. Jew means the nation, the race. Israel means God's covenant people. In the Messianic age, especially in the writings of Paul, this distinction becomes very sharp. The church, composed of obedient believers from every race, is now God's Israel.

10:5-12 ZECHARIAH

But what of the Jews?

(Verse 5) One cannot be dogmatic when dealing with apocalyptic prophecy. On the other hand, one cannot afford to be blind to what is taking place presently in the middle east. In four wars fought since the birth of the present state of Israel, not only those who warred against them, but the entire world has been confounded by the repeated victories of the Israelis against overwhelming odds.

(Verse 6-7) The term "Israel," applied to the modern state of the Jews is a misnomer, because the present state is Jewish. It ought more accurately be called Judah, meaning covenant people. The Christian church is Israel.

In this modern Jewish state the house of Judah (the ancient southern kingdom) and the house of Joseph (the people of the ancient northern kingdom) are indistinguishable. Few modern Jews, excepting those named Cohen (priest) or Levi, know their tribal origins.

The Jews, as a race and as a national entity, were cast off *per se* upon their rejection of Jesus. There is no other historic fulfillment of this threat to cast them off. Today they are as though they had not been cast off. Again there is no historic fulfillment of Zechariah's prophetic promise to bring back and place them until the establishment of the modern state of Israel.

Today's Jewish Israeli does indeed rejoice. Their hearts are glad in Jehovah. Specifically they rejoice because they believe (both Orthodox and Reformed) that the recent history of the Jewish state marks the beginning of the Messianic age. The irony of their rejoicing is not in their recognizing of the coming of the Messianic age, but in their misinterpreting the preparation for His *return* as preparation for His *first* appearing.

(Verses 8-12) In western Jerusalem today there is a grotesquely beautiful memorial to the Nazi holocaust in which six million Jews were exterminated. The building is built in the form of the gas chambers of the concentration camps. The stones in the walls are symbolic of the corpses piled high in their desperate attempts to escape the unexpected gas. An eternal flame burns in a wrought iron brazier to symbolize the cremation room, and on the black marble floor in gold letters are the names of Auschwitz, Buchanwald, and all the other horror chambers in which helpless men, women and children died for being Jews.

In the basement room are larger-than-life reproductions of Nazi anti-Jewish propaganda, and pictures of the concentration camp barracks: a record of utter nauseating barbarism.

To visit this shrine, in the midst of the modern miracle that is today's Jewish nation, is to know the meaning of *"I will hiss for them, and gather them; for I have redeemed them; they shall increase as they have increased."* The word "hiss" should more accurately be translated "whistle." The Lord will call the Jews as the shepherd whistles for his sheep. Those who were sown among the peoples because of their rejection of the Christ, have indeed remembered Jehovah in far countries. True, they are plagued with their share of self-acclaimed atheists, as are all nations, but throughout the world and in the concentration camps of Europe they have paid dearly for remembering their God. It was their attempts to keep His law which stamped them as peculiar enough to foster the kind of racism and bigotry to which Nazi Germany subjected them.

It is true, the Jews stood outside Pilate's judgement hall and cried for the blood of God's Son to be upon their heads and the heads of their children. *(Matthew 27:25)* But enough is enough. *"Except the Lord of Sabbaoth had left us a seed, we had become Sodom and Gomorrah."* *(Isaiah 1:9,* cp. *Romans 11:29)*

No time in history, since Zechariah, has seen a mass return of Jews to the ancient homeland until the years just following the second world war. It seems He has "brought them back" and "placed them." The reason is not merit, but mercy for the sake of the fathers.

Paul tells us "I would not, brethren, have you ignorant of this mystery, lest ye be wise in your own conceits, (we Gentile believers) that a hardening in part hath befallen Israel, until the fullness of the Gentiles be come in . . ." *(Romans 11:25)* Modern historians are describing the age since World War II as the "post-Christian era." The term is a misnomer, but it is evidence of a significant historic phenomenon. The time when most Gentiles were willing at least to admit the influence of Christ on their culture, if not actually to accept Him personally, is past. In my opinion we are witnessing the end of Paul's "time of the Gentiles," as the primary participants in the program of God.

It is too soon to evaluate this in terms of eschatology, but there can be little doubt we are witnessing some very significant events in today's state of Israel.

Zechariah 10:10 predicts God's bringing of Jews from Egypt, Assyria, Gilead (modern Jordan) and Lebanon at a time when ". . . *place shall not be found for them."* One hears much today about a million and a half Arab refugees who were driven from their homes in the establishment of the modern Jewish state. There is no way to morally justify this, and no reason to assume it was God's will. But, it is not so commonly known that the United Nations' partitioning of Palestine also displaced some 700,000 Jews in the surrounding Arab lands. These have been assimilated into Israel, but "a place was not found for them" in the lands named here by Zechariah.

The exact meaning of *Zechariah 10:11* in the present middle eastern situation is difficult to ascertain. Egypt's much touted Aswan dam, which was supposed to be the means of a great economic revival in that nation has proven to be something less than an unmixed blessing. Marshes which once bred an abundance of game are now dried up. The death-dealing microscopic parasites which have always been a danger to those who would stick their feet in the Nile have reached near epidemic proportions. The Delta is receding since the river is no longer rushing into the Mediterranean, and the fishing grounds off the mouth of the Nile have been all but abandoned. Can this be what is described here by the prophet in connection with the restoration of the Jewish state?

The pride of Assyria has indeed been brought down in the Israeli defeat and occupation of the Golan heights overlooking the Galilee.

(Verse 12) If we are correct, if what we are seeing in the middle east is a fulfillment of Zechariah's prophecy, there is a more and greater development yet to come. The world would indeed be confounded if the Israeli's should fully realize that it is God Who has wrought in and for them . . . if they did actually begin to "walk up and down in His name."

Chapter XXXIX—*Questions*

Israel Restored

1. In this chapter Zechariah returns to the theme _____.
2. The key to the chapter seems to be "in the time of the latter rain." Explain the climatic circumstances in the holy land which give rise to this term.
3. What is peculiarly essential about the *latter* rains as opposed to the former and winter rains?
4. What event in the Old Testament history of the Jewish people answers to the "former rain?"
5. What to the "winter rain?"
6. What were the teraphim?
7. What is Zechariah's desire concerning the prayers of the people?

8. What was the result of praying for protection to false gods?
9. Who are the shepherds of verse three? the he-goats?
10. What is the literal meaning of Yaweh (Jehovah)?
11. Show the relationship of this meaning of Jehovah to the term Lord applied to God in the Septuagint and to Jesus in the New Testament.
12. What was the result, in relation to the spiritual leaders, of Jesus' visit to Israel?
13. Discuss the "corner stone" in verse four.
14. Discuss the "nail" in verse four.
15. Verses five through twelve must look beyond _____ as well as _____ for its fulfillment.
16. In Zechariah 10, _____ and never _____ signifies the Jews.
17. The uniting of Joseph and Judah represents the uniting of the old _____ and _____ kingdoms.
18. The Hebrew word translated "I will bring them back" is a compound word which also includes _____.
19. The reason for the Jewish restoration described in chapter ten is not merit but _____.
20. In this chapter we are dealing with God's ultimate _____.
21. Jew and _____ are two separate concepts.
22. Jew means _____.
23. Israel means _____.
24. The _____ composed of obedient believers from every race is now God's _____.
25. The Jews as a race were cast off upon _____.
26. The modern Israeli Jew believes that the present Jewish state marks the beginning of the _____.
27. The word "hiss" really means _____. (10:8)
28. What is meant by "Except the Lord of Sabbaoth had left us a seed, we had become as Sodom and Gomorrah?"
29. Discuss this chapter in light of the current developments in the middle east, particularly the holy land.
30. In your opinion, what would be the effect upon the world if modern Israel were to openly declare that their victories have been wrought by God in fulfillment of prophecy?

CHAPTER XL
A PARABLE OF SHEPHERDS

RUIN OF HOSTILE POWERS . . . Zechariah 11:1-3

RV . . . Open thy doors, O Lebanon, that the fire may devour thy cedars. Wail, O fir-tree, for the cedar is fallen, because the goodly ones are destroyed: wail, O ye oaks of Bashan, for the strong forest is come down. A voice of the wailing of the shepherds! for their glory is destroyed: a voice of the roaring of young lions! for the pride of the Jordan is laid waste.

LXX . . . Open thy doors, O Libanus, and let the fire devour thy cedars. Let the pine howl, because the cedar has fallen; for the mighty men have been greatly afflicted: howl, ye oaks of the land of Basan; for the thickly planted forest has been torn down. There is a voice of the shepherds mourning; for their greatness is brought low: a voice of roaring lions; for the pride of Jordan is brought down.

COMMENTS

It has been suggested that these verses alluding to Bashan and Lebanon describe an invasion of Israel. Bearing in mind the context (uninterrupted in the original text by a chapter heading or number) this seems very unlikely. It is more likely a threat of destruction against the enemies of Judah, particularly since great forests are used occasionally to symbolize military power (cp. *Isaiah 10:34*). The *shepherds* of verse three are the leaders of these hostile powers. *Devouring fire (v. 1)*, symbol of irremediable destruction, is to come swiftly upon those powers whose rulers would then *howl* in despair like the lions driven out of the jungle along the Jordan.

The entire passage *(10:3-11:3)* is designed to point up the difference between the Jewish nation and its Gentile neighbors, especially those who have historically oppressed the Jews. It looks forward to the day when the shoe will be on the other foot. This could only happen when the Jews, both northern and southern, were returned to their homelands and established as an independent state.

FAITHFUL AND FOOLISH SHEPHERDS . . . Zechariah 11:4-17

RV . . . Thus said Jehovah my God: Feed the flock of slaughter; whose possessors slay them, and hold themselves not guilty; and they that sell them say, Blessed be Jehovah, for I am rich; and their own

A PARABLE OF SHEPHERDS 11:4-17

shepherds pity them not. For I will no more pity the inhabitants of the land, saith Jehovah; but, lo, I will deliver the men every one into his neighbor's hand, and into the hand of his king; and they shall smite the land, and out of their hand I will not deliver them. So I fed the flock of slaughter, verily the poor of the flock. And I took unto me two staves; the one I called Beauty, and the other I called Bands; and I fed the flock. And I cut off the three shepherds in one month; for my soul was weary of them, and their soul also loathed me. Then said I, I will not feed you: that which dieth, let it die; and that which is to be cut off, let it be cut off; and let them that are left eat every one the flesh of another. And I took my staff Beauty, and cut it asunder, that I might break my covenant which I had made with all the peoples. And it was broken in that day; and thus the poor of the flock that gave heed unto me knew that it was the word of Jehovah. And I said unto them, If ye think good, give me my hire; and if not, forbear. So they weighed for my hire thirty pieces of silver. And Jehovah said unto me, Cast it unto the potter, the goodly price that I was prized at by them. And I took the thirty pieces of silver, and cast them unto the potter, in the house of Jehovah. Then I cut asunder mine other staff, even Bands, that I might break the brotherhood between Judah and Israel. And Jehovah said unto me, Take unto thee yet again the instruments of a foolish shepherd. For, lo, I will raise up a shepherd in the land, who will not visit those that are cut off, neither will seek those that are scattered, nor heal that which is broken, nor feed that which is sound; but he will eat the flesh of the fat sheep, and will tear their hoofs in pieces. Woe to the worthless shepherd that leaveth the flock! the sword shall be upon his arm, and upon his right eye: his arm shall be clean dried up, and his right eye shall be utterly darkened.

LXX . . . Thus saith the Lord Almighty, Feed the sheep of the slaughter; which their possessors have slain, and have not repented; and they that sold them said, Blessed be the Lord; for we have become rich; and their shepherds have suffered no sorrow for them. Therefore I will no longer have mercy upon the inhabitants of the land, saith the Lord: but, behold, I will deliver up the men every one into the hand of his neighbour, and into the hand of his king; and they shall destroy the land, and I will not rescue out of their hand. And I will tend the flock of slaughter in the land of Chanaan: and I will take for myself two rods; the one I called Beauty, and the other I called Line; and I will tend the flock. And I will cut off three shepherds in one month; and my soul shall grieve over them, for their souls cried out against me. And I said, I will not tend you: that which dies, let it die; and that which falls off, let it fall off; and let the rest eat every one the flesh of his neighbor. And I will take my beautiful staff, and cast it away, that I may break my covenant which I made with all the people. And it shall be broken in that day; and the Chananites, the sheep that are kept for me, shall know that it is the word of the Lord. And I will say to them, If it be good in your eyes, give me my price, or refuse it. And they weighed for my price thirty pieces of silver. And the Lord said to me, Drop them into the furnace, and I will see if it is good metal, as I was proved for their sakes. And I took the thirty pieces of silver, and cast them into the furnace in the house of the Lord. And I cast away my second rod, even Line, that I might break the possession between Juda and Israel. And the Lord said to me, Take yet to thee shepherd's implements belonging to an unskilful shepherd. For, behold, I will raise up a shepherd against the land: he shall not visit that which is perishing, and he shall not seek that which is scattered, and he shall not heal that which is bruised, nor guide that which is whole: but he shall devour the flesh of the choice ones, and shall dislocate the joints of their necks. Alas for the vain shepherds that have forsaken the sheep! the sword shall be upon the arms of such a one, and upon his right eye: his arm shall be completely withered, and his right eye shall be utterly darkened.

COMMENTS

Between the time Zechariah and the establishment of the Jewish people as described in the last section, there was to be another period during which they will feel the wrath of Jehovah. The time of the fulfillment of this prediction is fixed beyond question by the verses twelve and thirteen. The verses are applied very literally to the betrayal of Jesus in *Matthew 26:5, 27:9-10*. Therefore, the prediction of the passage must have to do with the "hardening in part" *(Romans 11:25)* which caused Him to take the kingdom from the Jews and give it to the church. "A nation bringing forth the fruits thereof." *(Matthew 21:33-43)*

The prediction is presented allegorically. The nation is the flock, the Messiah is the faithful Shepherd. Because of their stubbornness, the Shepherd turns from them as they sell Him for thirty pieces of silver. The key is verse ten in which Jehovah severs His covenant relationship with the nation.

A PARABLE OF SHEPHERDS 11:4, 5

(Verses 4-5) As we turn to a detailed examination of the passage, we are immediately confronted with a strange command given by Jehovah to the prophet, "Feed the flock of slaughter." The term "flock of slaughter" is what gives the command a strange ring. We will find it again in verse seven.

The Jews, during the Roman period, were like sheep, bought and sold by their *shepherds, ie.* rulers who not only used the people for their own aggrandizement, but actually thanked God for their evily procured riches and power. They felt no guilt for using the people to accomplish their own ends.

It would be difficult to imagine a more vivid description of the Herods, and the temple priests who served in their puppet government of the Jews.

With the people at the mercy of such leadership, the prophet is called upon to feed the flock as one exposed for slaughter.

(Verse 6) The consequence of the leadership of the Herods and the self-seeking priests of his day was that described here. It became a time for riots, for the guerilla warfare of the Zealots, for false Messiahs and finally anarchy which brought the legions of Rome down upon them in a fury. God delivered them into the hand of the king (emperor) who did indeed smite the land. And, as He warns here, God did not intervene.

When the armies of Titus marched against Jerusalem in a campaign which ended on September 7, 70 A.D., it was the last of a chain of events which included a call by the Sanhedrin to the Roman procurator, Florus, and the puppet king, Herod Agrippa II, for military aid. The tumult in Judea grew into anarchy as a result of the Jews' refusal to accept Roman occupation. Conditions worsened, despite frequent changes of procurators by emperial appointment.

The Jews broke up into factions at all social, religious and economic levels. Even the appointment of high priests brought riot.

Rome's answer to such conditions in occupied lands was unchanging . . . the swift decisive use of the *Makaira* . . . the short sword.

The death of Festus in 62 A.D. left the power of Judean government in the hands of Annas the high priest. His calling of a clandestine session of the Sanhedrin at which James, the just, and other leading Christians were condemned, alienated whatever Gentile sympathy may have survived to this point.

At the same time, Herod's temple, which had been under construction for decades was completed, throwing hundreds of workers into unemployment.

11:6

Shortly thereafter, Albinus arrived to succeed Festus as procurator. Unable to control the Zealots, he was replaced in 64 A.D. by Gessius Florus.

Gessius was a true Roman, relying on brute force. He was greeted by riots in Caesarea of such proportion that hundreds of Jews fled the land never to return.

In 66 A.D. Gessius raided the temple treasury to make up a 40 talent deficit in the tribute demanded annually by Rome. The result was near revolution, averted only by a speech in which Agrippa convinced the Jews that such action would bring about the final utter destruction of the Jewish nation by Rome. *(Acts 12:21-23)*

Shortly thereafter, Agrippa left Jerusalem. During his absence the revolutionary forces again threatened war. Realizing the inevitable consequences of this threatened action, the Sanhedrin sent for military assistance.

In late summer of 66 A.D. Galles left Antioch for Jerusalem with 44,000 battle-hardened legioneers. He arrived in September, having been delayed by a revolt in Galilee, long a breeding ground for the Zealot Sicari.

By this time, the revolutionaries controlled Jerusalem and Galles was unable to breach the walls.

The rebels not only stood firm, but routed the Romans, killing 6,000 of them as they retreated to Caesarea.

In response to this defeat of Roman force, Nero reacted by sending his greatest general Titus Flavius Vespasian to restore order in Palestine.

Titus arrived in Galilee, re-establishing Roman control there, and went into winter quarters with fifty thousand troops.

Meanwhile, the Jews who had succeeded in holding Jerusalem against Galles, began to fight among themselves and anarchy again gripped the city. Such was the state of affairs when Titus lay seige from Mount Scopus in the summer of 68 A.D.

A brief respite came to the Jews upon the death of Nero in June of 68 A.D. and the period of turmoil in which three emperors in quick succession were overthrown in Rome. This led the army of Hitus Vespasian to decide to place their general on the emperial throne. To accomplish this it was necessary to settle matters quickly in Jerusalem.

Titus gave Jerusalem a chance to surrender. When his offer was refused, the bloodbath began. By July 5 the tower of Antonia, in the northwest corner of the temple area, was occupied by Legioneers. The carnage in the temple itself, where the revolutionaries fought to the last man, was the worst to that time in Jewish history. Over a million Jews died in the siege by the time the last Sicari committed suicide at Massada.

As emperor, Titus Vespasian, issued a decree that the Jewish religion should be ended for all time. The priesthood and Sanhedrin were abolished, the temple tax was now paid to the shrine of Jupiter. A colony of Roman veterans was settled near the ruins of the demolished capital of Judaism.

But it was not finally over. In 131 A.D., one Bar Cocheba, with the endorsement of the leading rabbi, Akiba, was accepted by the Jews as Messiah. The result was a desperate religious war which ended when Vespasian's successor, Hadrian, utterly flattened the city of Jerusalem and caused it to be ploughed as a field.

Upon the sight Hadrian erected Colonia Aelia Capitolina, a colony dedicated to Jupiter capitolinus. It was the end of the Jewish state until 1948. It was the last time the Jews would control the temple site until June, 1967.

(Verse 7) In response to Jehovah's command, the prophet fed the flock destined for slaughter. *"The poor of the flock"* here is more accurately *"the most miserable of sheep."* (Re: marginal rendering in the Standard Edition)

In this verse the prophet's role blends forward into that of the Messiah. As was done by real shepherds, he took two staffs. They are named *grace* and *binders,* or unity. (*Beauty* here in the English version expresses graciousness rather than physical beauty. *Bands* is an attempt to render for smooth reading a word which means binders.)

The first of the staffs, grace, represents the divine favor of Jehovah in guaranteeing to protect the Jews against outside forces. The second symbolizes the unity which was to prevail between the tribes of Joseph and Judah following the return from exile.

(Verse 8) The response to the shepherding of the post-exilic prophets on the part of the Jews was such that *"their soul loathed me."* It was seen ultimately in the rejection of Him Who presented Himself to them as "the Good Shepherd." (cp. *John 10:11*) There can be little doubt that Jesus had these verses in mind when He called Himself the Good Shepherd.

Verse nine, in which the prophet states his intention not to feed the flock, but rather to let it die, brings to mind two key New Testament passages. One in which Jesus wept over Jerusalem because of her historic failure to heed the prophets (*Luke 13:33-35*) and the other one in which He predicted the destruction of the city (*Luke 21:5-6*).

The cannibalism described here was fulfilled literally when, during the final days of the siege of Titus, those who held out in the temple area ate the bodies of their fallen comrades.

(Verses 10-11) The symbolic breaking of the staff of grace (beauty) has significance which cannot be overstated. It is cut asunder *"That I might break my covenant."* The Jews came into being as a people because of the covenant. Their national identity was established in the Law given upon their agreement to keep the covenant. (cf. *Exodus 19:5-9*) Generation after generation, century upon century, they had failed to do so.

God's patience was mistaken as slackness by this stiffnecked people. We saw how they refused to believe the warnings of the pre-exilic prophets on the ground that Jehovah would not so treat His people. Punished by the destruction of the northern kingdom and the captivity of the southern, they refused to rebuild His temple after their release.

In the intervening years, between the return from Babylon and the coming of Jesus, their concern turned completely from the covenant intended to bless all races of people to fanatic nationalism. The promised Seed of Abraham became, to them, a warrior . . . a revolutionist who would make them masters of the world. When He refused such a kingdom, they convicted Him of trumped-up charges and nailed Him, by the hands of lawless men, (*Acts 2:23*) to a cross. *From this time forward the fulfillment of the covenant and the fate of the Jew per se are two entirely separate matters.*

A covenant is always conditional. The failure of one party frees the other from the terms of the covenant. In all justice, God could have terminated His relationship to the Jews many times in the Old Testament period. When the time finally came that He did take the kingdom from them, only the remnant saw the justice of it.

The poor of the flock, the remnant *that gave heed* to the prophets knew the termination of the covenant with the Jews was according to the word of Jehovah.

(Verses 12-14) The final act of unfaithfulness came when the Good Shepherd appealed to the Jews for His hire, *ie.* for that which was rightly His in payment for all He had done for them. Even without the covenant, indeed if it had never existed in the first place, His care, protection and even His chastisement of the Jewish people above the other races of the world should have entitled Him to their immediate acceptance and undying allegiance.

A PARABLE OF SHEPHERDS 11:12-14

Instead they betrayed Him, and sold Him for the price of an injured slave. Thirty pieces of silver (about $25) was the amount fixed by the law in compensation for the injury of another's slave. (cf. *Exodus 21:32*)

It is no coincidence that this prophecy was fulfilled by one whose chief concern was the establishment of Israel as the ruling world empire. Judas had followed Jesus for three years in the full expectation that He would indeed prove to be another Judas Maccabee, that He would not only free the Jews from Roman rule but establish them as the greatest and final world power. When he saw Jesus riding into Jerusalem on an ass instead of a war horse to the shouts of children instead of the cheers of an army, when he heard Jesus foretell the destruction of the city which, in Jewish ambition, was to become the capital of the Messianic world, it was too much. He bartered his revenge for the price of an injured slave. (cf. *Matthew 26:5, 27:9-10*)

The accuracy of Zechariah's prophecy is seen in the minute fulfillment of it in the detailed disposal of the money paid Judas. Verse thirteen says it was *"cast unto the potter."* *Matthew 27:9* quotes the prophecy of *Jeremiah 18:2, 19:2,11, 32:6-9* in recording that the money returned by Judas prior to his suicide was used to purchase a potters field. *Acts 1:18-19* mentions this fact also.

Following the crucifixion, and the consequent destruction of Jerusalem by Titus and Hadrian, (see above on verse six), the Jews were scattered throughout the world. The unity which had prevailed following their return from exile was thus broken, an historic event predicted symbolically in verse fourteen by the breaking of the second staff called Bands or unity. The result was a nearly nineteen century postponement of the fulfillment of the promises made in Zechariah, chapter ten.

(Verses 15-17) G. A. Smith is quoted by Professor J. E. McFadyen as saying, concerning the crucifixion of Jesus, "The guilty sacrifice the innocent, but in this execute their own doom. That is the summary of the history of Israel." The message of *Zechariah 11:15-17* could scarcely be better paraphrased.

Following the crucifixion, as we have seen (see above on *11:6*) the nation of the Jews became a political football in the hands of the Herods and a series of inept Roman procurators. These, personified here as the foolish shepherd, presided over the final dissolution of the nation into anarchy and final obliteration.

The foolish shepherd may well have been personified in Bar Cocheba and his ill-fated attempt at revolt against Hadrian. The futility of his military activity is well described here in verse seventeen.

11:1-14   ZECHARIAH

Chapter XL—*Questions*

A Parable of Shepherds

1. Discuss the symbolism of the forests in *11:1-3*.
2. Of what is fire symbolic in verse one?
3. The entire passage (*10:3-11:3*) is designed to point up the difference between_____ and_____.
4. Between the time of Zechariah and the establishment of the Jewish people as described in chapter ten, there was to be _____.
5. *Zechariah 11:12-13* is applied literally to_____ in *Matthew 26:5, 27:9-10*.
6. Explain the allegory of the flock and the shepherd in this passage.
7. Why does God promise to sever His covenant relationship to the Jews?
8. What is meant by "flock of slaughter?"
9. What is described in verse six?
10. Review the events leading to the destruction of Jerusalem in 70 A.D. and 135 A.C.
11. Who was Bar Cocheba?
12. What is the symbolism of the two staffs?
13. Who fulfills the picture of the good shepherd in this passage? (Compare *John 10:11*)
14. Why, in verse nine, does the shepherd decide to let the flock die rather than feed it?
15. What was symbolized in the breaking of the two staffs?
16. God's patience was mistaken by the Jews as_____.
17. In the intervening years between the Babylonian exile and the coming of Jesus, the concern of the Jews turned completely from_____ to_____.
18. A covenant is always _____.
19. The final act of unfaithfulness came when_____.
20. Instead of paying him his due, the people_____ him and sold him.
21. What is the significance of the thirty pieces of silver?
22. How does the disposal of the blood money by Judas demonstrate the accuracy of Zechariah's prediction?
23. What happened to the Jewish people immediately following the destruction of Jerusalem in 135 A.D.?

CHAPTER XLI
IN THE FIRST DAY

The future glory of the restored nation of the Jews, predicted in chapter ten (see comments), was to be delayed in its accomplishment by their rejection of the Good Shepherd, the dissolving of the covenant between the nation and Jehovah, and the prolonged dispersion following the defeat of Bar Cocheba, the self-acclaimed Messiah in 135 A.D.

Chapters 12, 13, and 14 actually compose a single unit of thought which climaxes Zechariah's prophecy in a blaze of apocalyptic eschatology, some of which is nearly impossible to understand clearly.

The key to these final chapters is found in the phrase *"in the day"* which is repeated no less than sixteen times throughout the passage.

This unit of thought is expressed in regard to two "days," which from Zechariah's point of view remained in the future. The first day and its happenings comprise *12:3-13:7* and prefigures the Messianic age. The final day of the Lord is described in the final chapter, *14:1-21*.

It will be helpful here to go back and read the comment on *yom YHWH* (the day of Jehovah) in the Introduction to Zechariah, Chapter XIX. We noted there four characteristics of "that day:" (1) the judgement of Israel, Judah and the nations of the pre-Christian world, (2) the deliverance and preservation of the remnant during and after the captivity, (3) the first coming of the Messiah and (4) the second coming of the Messiah and His final judgement of all men and nations.

To understand Zechariah's "in that day," we must be alert to all four elements.

The term first appears in Zechariah in chapter three, verse 10. There it refers to the time when Jehovah will bring forth His Servant, The Branch. *In that day,* everyone will invite his neighbor under the vine and under the fig tree. The intention is obviously to describe a time of peace and plenty. The significant aspect here is the sending of the Branch and the removal of the iniquity of the land in one day. (*Zechariah 3:8-10*)

As we saw in our study of that passage (see comment) *in that day* here referred to the coming of the living stone and true priest in whom God will remove the sins of His people and invite their neighbors to share the fruits of the Messianic Presence.

THE BURDEN OF THE LORD . . . Zechariah 12:1-2

RV . . . The burden of the word of Jehovah concerning Israel. Thus saith Jehovah, who stretcheth forth the heavens, and layeth the founda-

12:1, 2   ZECHARIAH

tion of the earth, and formeth the spirit of man within him; Behold, I will make Jerusalem a cup of reeling unto all the peoples round about, and upon Judah also shall it be in the siege against Jerusalem.

LXX . . . The burden of the word of the Lord for Israel; saith the Lord, that stretches out the sky, and lays the foundation of the earth, and forms the spirit of man within him. Behold, I will make Jerusalem as trembling door-posts to all the nations round about, and in Judea there shall be a siege against Jerusalem.

COMMENTS

The lengthy section (chapters 12, 13, 14) in which the term *"in that day"* is used repeatedly, is introduced as *"the burden of the word of Jehovah concerning Israel."* Israel as we have seen, is in the minor prophets a term designating the covenant people. The time would come (*11:10*) when the relationship would be broken off with the Jewish race, but as Zechariah wrote this had not yet occurred. What he is about to write has to do with the fulfillment of God's covenant purpose.

Jehovah is here referred to as the creator of the heavens, the earth, and the spirit of man. These are words calculated to remind the prophet's readers that the purpose which is to be fulfilled is the eternal purpose in the mind of God before creation. It is the reason man was created. It is the reason the covenant was established and a covenant people developed. It is the purpose behind all God's activity in history, both of the Jews and of the nations of the earth. This purpose is the reason God will bring to pass those things which Zechariah is about to describe.

The purpose is stated many times in many ways throughout the Bible, but never more succinctly than the Pauline statement of *Ephesians 1:3-10*. There the apostle informs us that, before the foundation of the earth, God chose in Christ to have a people holy and pure and adopted to Himself as children. That purpose and its accomplishment in Christ is the meaning of the entire Bible.

The days referred to by "in that day" in these chapters are two different periods. The first is addressed to Israel, the covenant people (*v. 1*) and has to do with the first coming of the Messiah who will be looked upon as pierced (*12:10*).

The second period referred to by "in that day" is designated by "Behold, a *yom YHWH* (day of Jehovah) cometh" (*14:1*). It has to do with the final consummation and the second coming of the Messiah.

IN THAT DAY (1) . . . Zechariah 12:3

RV . . . And it shall come to pass in that day, that I will make Jerusalem a burdensome stone for all the peoples; all that burden themselves with it shall be sore wounded; and all the nations of the earth shall be gathered together against it.

LXX . . . And it shall come to pass in that day that I will make Jerusalem a trodden stone to all the nations: every one that tramples on it shall utterly mock at it, and all the nations of the earth shall be gathered together against it.

COMMENTS

The first statement of what will happen "in that day" is made briefly in *Zechariah 12:3*. It introduces the time of Messiah's first coming, and is addressed to Israel (*v. 1*). Israel at the time of this writing could be none other than the faithful remnant among those Jews who had returned from exile.

In the time of Messiah's first coming, Jerusalem will be made a burdensome stone for all the peoples. This statement sets the stage for the struggle described in the next three verses.

IN THAT DAY (2) (3) . . . Zechariah 12:4-6

RV . . . In that day, saith Jehovah, I will smite every horse with terror, and his rider with madness; and I will open mine eyes upon the house of Judah, and will smite every horse of the peoples with blindness. And the chieftains of Judah shall say in their hearts, The inhabitants of Jerusalem are my strength in Jehovah of hosts their God. In that day will I make the chieftains of Judah like a pan of fire among wood, and like a flaming torch among sheaves; and they shall devour all the peoples round about, on the right hand and on the left; and they of Jerusalem shall yet again dwell in their own place, even in Jerusalem.

LXX . . . In that day, saith the Lord Almighty, I will smite every horse with amazement, and his rider with madness; but I will open mine eyes upon the house of Juda, and I will smite all the horses of the nations with blindness. And the captains of thousands of Juda shall say in their hearts, We shall find for ourselves the inhabitants of Jerusalem in the Lord Almighty their God. In that day I will make the captains of thousands of Juda as a firebrand among wood, and as a torch of fire in stubble; and they shall devour on the right hand and on the left all the nations round about; and Jerusalem shall dwell again by herself, even in Jerusalem.

COMMENTS

During the time of the Messiah the Jews would struggle with all nations. Jehovah will sustain them in the struggle and they shall "yet again dwell in their own place." (see comment above on *10:6*)

Please note this is to be during the time of the Messiah, *ie.* in the Messianic age.

IN THAT DAY (2) . . . verses 4-5

Historically, that form of attack against which the Jewish defense had proved least effective was a cavalry charge. It was this from which Jehovah had miraculously delivered them in the exodus. (cf. *Exodus 15:19-21*) God promises symbolically to protect the Jews in their weakness. He will "open His eyes" and watch over them.

At the same time He will smite the horse of the peoples with blindness. Those who seek to destroy the Jews will plunge blindly to their own destruction. We have seen a classic example of this in our day in Nazi Germany.

The strength of the Jews over the centuries of the Christian era has been their regard for Jehovah worship, here symbolized by the name of Jerusalem, the center of monotheism.

IN THAT DAY (3) . . . verse 6-7

In the day of Judah's restoration to her homeland, though small, she will consume the enemies that surround her.

They of Jerusalem, *ie.* the Jews who are true to the worship of Jerusalem, "shall again dwell in their own place, even Jerusalem." It is interesting to note that in the establishment of the Jewish state at present, the Orthodox Jews are virtually all gathered in a selfimposed ghetto in the city of Jerusalem.

IN THAT DAY (4) . . . Zechariah 12:8

RV . . . In that day shall Jehovah defend the inhabitants of Jerusalem; and he that is feeble among them at that day shall be as David; and the house of David shall be as God, as the angel of Jehovah before them.

LXX . . . And it shall come to pass in that day, that the Lord shall defend the inhabitants of Jerusalem; and the weak one among them in that day shall be as David, and the house of David as the house of God, as the angel of the Lord before them.

IN THE FIRST DAY 12:9-14

COMMENTS

Ask any modern Israeli to explain the fantastic success of his little country against impossible odds in the four wars they have fought and he will reply, "*We* know why we are fighting." Zechariah foresees the weakest of them as strong as David, inspired by the knowledge that God is "on their side." (cp. *v.* 5)

IN THAT DAY (5) (6) . . . Zechariah 12:9-14

RV . . . And it shall come to pass in that day, that I will seek to destroy all the nations that come against Jerusalem. And I will pour upon the house of David, and upon the inhabitants of Jerusalem, the spirit of grace and of supplication; and they shall look unto me whom they have pierced; and they shall mourn for him, as one mourneth for his only son, and shall be in bitterness for him, as one that is in bitterness for his first-born. In that day shall there be a great mourning in Jerusalem, as the mourning of Hadadrimmon in the valley of Megiddon. And the land shall mourn, every family apart; the family of the house of David apart, and their wives apart; the family of the house of Nathan apart, and their wives apart; the family of the house of Levi apart, and their wives apart; the family of the Shimeites apart, and their wives apart; all the families that remain, every family apart, and their wives apart.

LX . . . And it shall come to pass in that day, that I will seek to destroy all the nations that come against Jerusalem. And I will pour upon the house of David, and upon the inhabitants of Jerusalem, the spirit of grace and compassion: and they shall look upon me, because they have mocked me, and they shall make lamentation for him, as for a beloved friend, and they shall grieve intensely, as for a first-born son. In that day the lamentation in Jerusalem shall be very great, as the mourning for the pomegranate grove cut down in the plain. And the land shall lament in separate families, the family of the house of David by itself, and their wives by themselves; the family of the house of Nathan by itself, and their wives by themselves; the family of the house of Levi by itself, and their wives by themselves; the family of Symeon by itself, and their wives by themselves; all the families that are left, each family by itself, and their wives by themselves.

12:9-14   ZECHARIAH

COMMENTS

IN THAT DAY (5) . . . v. 9

Jehovah Himself will seek to destroy all the nations that come against Jerusalem. Since God does what He attempts to do, it will be a black day for anyone who attacks the city He defends.

This is a significant verse, in as much as every attacker of Jerusalem to the present day has been successful in overthrowing it. If it means symbolically that God will defend His worshippers against the attacks of skepticism, as some have suggested, this has been done repeatedly in all ages.

If, on the other hand, this verse describes the defense of Jerusalem literally in the days of the present restoration of the Jewish nation, one may rest assured that any nation will be defeated who attempts the overthrow of that city.

(Verse 10) It is this verse which fixes "in that day" in this section as the Messianic age. It would be difficult to imagine a clearer prediction of the detail of Christ's crucifixion. As Halley points out, "this description is in nowise applicable to any other known person."

IN THAT DAY (6) . . . v. 11-14

The apostle John sees in Jesus' death the fulfillment of this verse. (cp. *John 19:34-37*) John also recalls this verse in connection with the second coming. (cp. *Revelation 1:7*)

Some have seen in the mourning for Him Whom they have pierce a prediction that the Jews will be converted to Christ. This cannot, of course, be ruled out. Paul speaks of the possibility that the Jews who rejected Jesus may be grafted into God's true Israel. This, however, is definitely conditioned upon ". . . *if they continue not in their unbelief.*" (*Romans 11:17-24*)

In view of the nature of conversion, which is *always* an individual experience, it seems unlikely that the whole Jewish nation could be said to be converted. It seems more likely that this mourning came to pass at the preaching on Pentecost, when those who stood accused of murdering their Messiah, were cut to the heart so deeply that three thousand of them accepted Him as "both Lord and Christ." (cp. *Acts 2:22-41*)

The mourning over the pierced one is compared to "the mourning of Hadad-Rimmon in the valley of Megiddo." This was probably the village in the plain of Megiddo where king Josiah was killed in the battle against the Egyptians. (cp. *II Chronicles 35:22-25*) There had been great mourning at his death because it marked the end of his great religious reform.

The mourning is from the highest (David) to the lowest (Nathan) of the royal house, and from the highest (Levi) to the lowest (Shemei) of the priestly order. All the families that remain, *ie.* those who are of neither the kingly or priestly houses, shall also mourn.

Each family shall mourn alone, and the women separately from the men. (cp. *Exodus 15:1,20*)

IN THAT DAY (7) ... Zechariah 13:1

RV ... In that day there shall be a fountain opened to the house of David and to the inhabitants of Jerusalem, for sin and for uncleanness.

LXX ... In that day every place shall be opened to the house of David and to the inhabitants of Jerusalem for removal and for separation.

COMMENTS

In connection with the mourning over Him Whom they pierced, a fountain is to be opened for sin and uncleanness. Sin is transgression against the law of God. Uncleanness is that condition of one's soul which makes him unfit for the presence of God. The death of David's Branch (cp. *3:8* and *6:12*) Who is seen here in the hour of His death (pierced) provides the fountain for sin and uncleanness.

Jesus' understanding of the Old Testament was that the Christ should suffer, and rise again the third day. When this has been done, repentance and remission of sins is to be preached in His name. (cf. *Luke 24:44-47*)

The death and resurrection opened the fountain. The preaching of repentance, which is a deliberate decision for the will of God by one who has stood against it, relates the fountain to sin which is a transgression of the Law. Remission of sins, which is God's answer to the moral impurity resulting from sin, relates the fountain to uncleanness.

An entire volume could be written showing, from Scripture, that this fountain is the blood of Jesus.

13:2-6 ZECHARIAH

IN THAT DAY (8) . . . Zechariah 13:2-3

RV . . . And it shall come to pass in that day, saith Jehovah of hosts, that I will cut off the names of the idols out of the land, and they shall no more be remembered; and also I will cause the prophets and the unclean spirit to pass out of the land. And it shall come to pass that, when any shall yet prophesy, then his father and his mother that begat him shall say unto him, Thou shalt not live; for thou speakest lies in the name of Jehovah; and his father and his mother that begat him shall thrust him through when he prophesieth.

LXX . . . And it shall come to pass in that day, saith the Lord of hosts, that I will utterly destroy the names of the idols from off the land, and there shall be no longer any remembrance of them: and I will cut off the false prophets and the evil spirit from the land. And it shall come to pass, if a man will yet prophesy, that his father and his mother which gave birth to him shall say to him, Thou shalt not live; for thou hast spoken lies in the name of the Lord: and his father and his mother who gave him birth shall bind him as he is prophesying.

COMMENTS

Still referring to the Messianic age, Jehovah promises that the names of idols will be cut out of the land and forgotten. Idolatry is frequently associated with uncleanness. (eg. *Ezekiel 36:25* cp. *Romans 1:18-ff*)

The preaching of the Christian gospel is generally credited with ministering the *coup de grace* to the classic idolatry which had been a constant blight on the Jews throughout their pre-Christian history. Excepting for the shrines of Catholicism, one will search the holy land in vain for such practices today.

The prophecy condemned here is false prophecy. The passage is a sort of paraphrase of *Deuteronomy 13:6-10, 18:20* which roundly condemns false prophets. Should any utter such prophecies he would incur the wrath of his own parents. The loyalty of Messiah's people to Him will exceed the tenderest natural affections. (cp. *Matthew 10:37* and *Luke 14:26*)

IN THAT DAY (9) . . . Zechariah 13:4-6

RV . . . And it shall come to pass in that day, that the prophets shall be ashamed every one of his vision, when he prophesieth; neither shall they wear a hairy mantle to deceive: but he shall say, I am no prophet, I am a tiller of the ground; for I have been made a bondman from my youth. And one shall say unto him, What are these wounds between thine arms? Then he shall answer, Those with which I was wounded in the house of my friends.

LXX . . . And it shall come to pass in that day, that the prophets shall be ashamed every one of his vision when he prophesies; and they shall clothe themselves with a garment of hair, because they have lied. And one shall say, I am not a prophet, for I am a tiller of the ground, for a man brought me up thus from my youth. And I will say to him What are these wounds between thine hands? and he shall say, Those with which I was wounded in my beloved house.

COMMENTS

The false prophet shall himself be ashamed of his calling and his vision. In *Acts 19:13-20*, Luke records a detailed description of one incident when this became literally true. Following their conversion at the preaching of Paul, certain false prophets, whom Luke describes as practicing magical arts, repented of their false teaching and burned their own books.

(Verse 6) Here is another clear prediction of the crucified Messiah. Its presence in this particular context, just following the reference to false prophets could be misleading. *Him* in this verse refers not to the false prophet, but to Him Whom they have pierced. *(12: 10)*

The wounds "between thine arms" are a vivid description of the scourging suffered by Jesus. The word is *makkah* and means a wound made by a stroke or blow.

We are reminded of *Isaiah 53:5*, *"He was wounded (chalal— pierced) for our transgression and by His stripes we are healed."*

He was wounded in the house of His friends. To quote a cliche, with friends like that, He needed no enemies!

EPILOGUE TO THE FIRST DAY . . . Zechariah 12:7-9

RV . . . Awake, O sword, against my shepherd, and against the man that is my fellow, saith Jehovah of hosts: smite the shepherd, and the sheep shall be scattered; and I will turn my hand upon the little ones. And it shall come to pass, that in all the land, saith Jehovah, two parts therein shall be cut off and die; but the third shall be left therein. And I will bring the third part into the fire, and will refine them as silver is refined, and will try them as gold is tried. They shall call on my name, and I will hear them: I will say, It is my People; and they shall say, Jehovah is my God.

LXX . . . Awake, O sword, against my shepherds, and against the man who is my citizen, saith the Lord Almighty: smite the shepherds, and draw out the sheep: and I will bring mine hand upon the little ones. And it shall come to pass, that in all the land, saith the Lord, two parts thereof shall be cut off and perish; but the third shall be left therein. And I will bring the third part through the fire, and I will try them as silver is tried, and I will prove them as gold is proved: they shall call upon my name, and I will hear them, and say, This is my people: and they shall say, The Lord is my God.

COMMENTS

(Verse 7) When Peter preached the first recorded sermon following the resurrection, he pointed out that the suffering of Jesus had been by "the determinate counsel and foreknowledge of God." *(Acts 2:23)* Here is evidence to support that claim.

Jehovah of hosts, *ie.* the God of the covenant, gives specific orders that the sword awake against the shepherd. We have seen that the good shepherd of Zechariah is indeed the Christ (see on *11:10-ff*). That this Christ is Jesus, Who was crucified by the Romans is evidenced by the particular weapon named to symbolize those who were to smite Him. Many ancient powers were symbolized by their most characteristic weapon, *eg.* Persia by the bow, Egypt by the chariot, Greece by the lance and phalanx, etc. Rome is characterized by the short sword. Because of prevailing circumstances at the time of Jesus' trial, He could be legally executed only by Rome, since the Jews were denied the right of capital punishment. (There is much question concerning the legality of Jesus' trials, but there is no doubt His execution was performed by Romans.)

Jesus Himself applied this verse to His own death. *(Matthew 26:31, Mark 14:27)*. At His arrest, His disciples fled or followed afar off. During and after His crucifixion all but John were in hiding, and John apparently joined the others just following His death. The sheep were indeed scattered when the Shepherd was smitten.

Here is further evidence that "in that day" in this section applies to the day of the Messiah rather than to the time of the end.

(Verse 8) After the death and resurrection of Jesus, the number of his followers was greatly reduced. Apparently there were five hundred who could be counted as disciples (cf. *I Corinthians 15:6*). One hundred twenty were present when the church was born on Pentecost (cf. *Acts 1:15*). If one adds the three thousand baptized that day, the number totals some three thousand, six hundred. It was a small group indeed, compared to the six hundred thousand Jewish males who formed the original flock. *(Exodus 12:37)*.

(Verse 9) The few followers of Jesus in the early days of the church soon found themselves the object of the most savage religious persecution ever, to that time, raised against a people. Peter described this persecution in words borrowed from *Zechariah 13:9*. "Wherein ye greatly rejoice, though now for a little while, if need be, ye have been put to grief in manifold trials, that the proof of your faith, being more precious than gold that perisheth though it is proved by fire, may be found unto praise and glory and honor at the revelation of Jesus Christ. *(I Peter 1:6-7)*

There is no doubt the early church interpreted these verses in reference first to Jesus and then to themselves.

To those who endured persecution, Jehovah gives recognition that they are His people. They acknowledge Jehovah as their God. Both terms, people and Jehovah, are covenant terms. The church is God's new Israel!

Chapter XLI—*Questions*

In the First Day

1. The future glory of the restored Jewish nation was delayed by their_____.
2. The key to the final chapters of Zechariah is found in the phrase _____.
3. This term describes two days which from Zechariah's point of view were both in_____ _____.
4. The first of these days describes_____.
5. The second "day" describes_____.
6. Review the four characteristics of the day of Jehovah. (See introduction of Zechariah.)
7. Zechariah's first use of "in the day" *(3:8-10)* refers to_____.
8. What is the significance of the term *Israel* in *Zechariah 12:1?*

13:1-9 ZECHARIAH

9. Why does Zechariah here refer to Jehovah as the creator of the heavens and the earth and the spirit of man?
10. The first period referred to by "in that day" is addressed to _____ and has to do with _____.
11. The second period referred to as "in that day" has to do with _____.
12. Several things are said to be going to happen in the Messianic age. Each is introduced by "in that day." They are:
    a. In that day (1)
    b. In that day (2)
    c. In that day (3)
    d. In that day (4)
12. e. In that day (5)
    f. In that day (6)
    g. In that day (7)
    h. In that day (8)
    i. In that day (9)
13. *Israel* at the time of Zechariah could be none other than _____.
14. What of Jerusalem in the time of Messiah's first coming?
15. What was to be the relationship of the Jews to all nations during the Messianic age?
16. Historically the military action against which the Jews were least effective was the _____.
17. What is meant by Jehovah smiting the peoples and horses with blindness?
18. Who are "they of Jerusalem?" *(12:7)*
19. How does *Zechariah 12:10* fix this section as being fulfilled in the Messianic age?
20. Compare *Zechariah 12:10-14* with *John 19:34-37*.
21. What is the condition upon which Jews may again become part of God's true Israel? (cf. *Romans 11:17-24*)
22. Conversion is always an _____ experience.
23. How was the mourning over Him who they had pierced fulfilled on Pentecost?
24. Who are "all the families that remain?"
25. In connection with the mourning over Him whom they pierced a _____ was to be opened for _____ and _____.
26. The _____ opened the fountain.
27. _____ relates the fountain to sin.
28. _____ relates the fountain to moral impurity or _____.
29. _____ is frequently associated with uncleanness.

364

30. The _____ is generally credited with ministering the *coup de grace* to classic idolatry.
31. What prophecy is condemned during the Messianic age?
32. How does *Zechariah 13:6* relate to Him whom they pierced?
33. What is meant by the wounds "between thine arms?"
34. Discuss *Zechariah 12:7* in light of *Acts 2:23*.
35. What nation is symbolized historically by the sword?
36. Jesus could be legally executed by _____.
37. Compare *Zechariah 13:7* to *Matthew 26:31* and *Mark 14:27*.
38. Following the death of Jesus the number of His followers was about _____.
39. Compare *Zechariah 13:9* and *I Peter 1:6-7*.
40. To those who endured persecution, Jehovah gives _____, and they acknowledge _____. Both are _____.
41. The _____ is God's new Israel.

CHAPTER XLII

IN THE SECOND DAY

If our overall understanding of Zechariah to this point is correct, chapter fourteen, deals almost exclusively with eschatology. Eschatology may be defined simply as the study of the last things, or last times.

Most commentators agree that this is the subject matter of the present chapter. However, unanimity of opinion concerning Zechariah's last chapter ends with this agreement. Rabid pre-millenialists have a field day here, as they do with the other apocalyptic writings of the Bible, because of the apocalyptic nature of the work itself. They see here the proof of their contention that Jesus plans, upon His second coming, to establish an earthly kingdom which will stand for a thousand years, and in which the Jews, with Him as king, will rule the world, and in general do what Jesus refused to do the first time He came to earth. They also claim the Jews will do what the church has failed to do, namely convert the world to Jehovah and Christ. These conclusions are arrived at by ignoring the symbolic nature of apocalypsis almost entirely.

The post-millenialists on the other hand, shift from the literal to the symbolic and back with surprising ease and assure us the last chapter of Zechariah describes the bringing of the world to the worship of God during our present Messianic age. When this is done, Messiah, they claim, will return and reign over a perfect world. The fact that

14:1-3   ZECHARIAH

the developments of history during the past nineteen hundred years, and especially in our own century, are obviously not moving toward any such Utopian world does not phase the post-millenialist in the least.

As we mentioned previously, one can never be intellectually honest and be dogmatic about the interpretation of eschatology, particularly that which the Bible writers couch in apocalypsis. The very fact that the events of eschatology, by their nature, have yet to occur deprives us of what, in the understanding of other prophecy, is a very useful tool; namely the events of history. With other predictive prophecy one can, with some accuracy, say—this was foretold, and here in such a place it has happened. Not so with those events which are yet to come.

Deprived of historic fulfillment, and faced with the elusive figures, often indecipherable, of apocalyptic writing, we can only suggest the possible, at most the probable, meaning of such predictions. With this limitation firmly fixed in our consciousness, we shall now attempt to understand at least the gist of Zechariah fourteen.

A DAY OF JEHOVAH COMETH . . . Zechariah 14:1-3

RV . . . Behold a day of Jehovah cometh, when thy spoil shall be divided in the midst of thee. For I will gather all nations against Jerusalem to battle; and the city shall be taken, and the houses rifled, and the women ravished; and half of the city shall go forth into captivity, and the residue of the people shall not be cut off from the city. Then shall Jehovah go forth, and fight against those nations, as when he fought in the day of battle.

LXX . . . Behold, the days of the Lord come, and thy spoils shall be divided in thee. And I will gather all the Gentiles to Jerusalem to war, and the city shall be taken, and the houses plundered, and the women ravished; and half of the city shall go forth into captivity, but the rest of my people shall not be utterly cut off from the city. And the Lord shall go forth, and fight with those Gentiles as when he fought in the day of war.

COMMENTS

(Verse 1) For an understanding of the term "a Day of Jehovah," please review the comments in the Introduction to Zechariah and in the beginning of Chapter XLI.

"A Day of Jehovah" is always a closing of one historic era and the beginning of another. It is upon this premise that we postulated the belief that the term "in that day" in chapter thirteen and chapter fourteen refers to two different times. (See comment.) The first day, referred to in chapter thirteen, is the Messianic age in which we live. The second day, referred to in chapter fourteen, is the last time.

(Verse 1(b)-3) In the coming day of Jehovah the spoil of Jerusalem is to be divided in her midst. The occasion for this pillage will be the gathering of the nations against Jerusalem for battle. The treatment of the city's inhabitants is to be barbaric with half the population being taken into slavery. Those not taken into captivity are to remain in the city.

Those who see the subsequent verses symbolically fulfilled in the church, take this verse to refer to the Roman conquest of Jerusalem. This raises grave questions. For example, if we are to take this verse literally of the invasion by Rome, why are we to assume the subsequent verses are figurative? And, how can we identify Rome as "all nations?"

The Roman occupation of Palestine was by invitation, initially, and so does not fit the description here at all. The final destruction of Jerusalem by Rome, as the result of the failure of the Jews to accept Roman rule, more closely resembles the picture presented by Zechariah, but to explain these verses solely on this basis requires a sudden unexplainable shifting from the literal to the figurative in the verses immediately following.

For example, those who take "Jerusalem" as meaning the city literally, in verses one through three, insist that the term is metaphorically used in following verses concerning the Mount of Olives. Such inconsistency is a gross violation of the rules of sound exegesis. It is more honest to simply say we do not know exactly what is being described here.

It seems quite likely that we are dealing with events of the end time and the last rebellion of man against God. Perhaps we must leave the explanation of the prophet's language to Him in Whose hands such things rest. Perhaps we, as the twelve, must reluctantly accept the fact that there are certain matters which it is not our prerogative to know as completely as we might like. (cp. *Acts 1:6-7*)

IN THAT DAY (10) . . . Zechariah 14:4-5

RV . . . And his feet shall stand in that day upon the mount of Olives, which is before Jerusalem on the east; and the mount of Olives shall be cleft in the midst thereof toward the east and toward the west, and there shall be a very great valley; and half of the mountain shall

14:4, 5   ZECHARIAH

remove toward the north, and half of it toward the south. And ye shall flee by the valley of my mountains; for the valley of the mountains shall reach unto Azel; yea, ye shall flee, like as ye fled from before the earthquake in the days of Uzziah king of Judah; and Jehovah my God shall come, and all the holy ones with thee.

LXX . . . And his feet shall stand in that day on the mount of Olives, which is before Jerusalem on the east, and the mount of Olives shall cleave asunder, half of it toward the east and the west, a very great division; and half the mountain shall lean to the north, and half of it to the south. And the valley of my mountains shall be closed up, and the valley of the mountains shall be joined on to Jasod, and shall be blocked up as it was blocked up in the days of the earthquake, in the days of Ozias king of Juda; and the Lord my God shall come, and all the saints with him.

COMMENTS

    This is one of the most difficult of all prophetic predictions. It has called forth some of the most ludicrous explanations ever offered as interpretation of Scripture. A nationally known television evangelist tells a wild story in which a large motel chain, investigating the possibility of building on the Mount of Olives, found a fault in the mountain of such extent that it could not support such a building. Just how preposterous this is is obvious to anyone who has visited the holy land and has seen the huge buildings which do stand on Olivet! Near the summit is the church of the *Pater Noster.* Just to the south a few hundred yards is the luxurious Intercontinental Hotel. South of the Intercontinental is another hotel, the Panorama, and not far away a mosque has recently been erected.

    If the Mount of Olives is to literally split at the coming of Jesus, it will not be because of any fault in the earth, but because of the power of God!

    The Mount of Olives is the predominant peak of a line of hills which begins just less than a mile east of Jerusalem and ranges north and south about a mile. Between the Mount of Olives, on the slopes of which the Garden of Gethsemane, a sabbath day's journey (7/8 of a mile) from the city. The mountain is separated from Jerusalem by the Kidron Valley. It stands some 295 feet higher than Mount Moriah, the site of the temple.

    To the east of the Mount of Olives lies the Judean wilderness. On a clear day one can stand on the mountain's top and view the Dead

Sea in the distance. The road to Bethany winds round the north, beyond which lies Mount Scopus.

It seems likely that Jesus ascended to Heaven from the slopes of Olivet, *(Acts 1:11)*, though such is not specifically stated. (Others believe He ascended from a hill in Galilee. (cp. *Mark 16:19*, etc.) Upon this assumption, some have seen *Zechariah 14:4* as a prediction that He will return to the very spot from which He departed.

The statement that the Mount of Olives will cleave when the Lord stands upon it has given rise, as we have seen, to all sorts of speculations. What is described is the division, east and west, of the mountain resulting in the formation of "a very great valley." If such were to happen literally, the city of Jerusalem would be much more accessible from the east.

(Verse 5) Such a valley would also form a way of easy escape from the city. Zechariah pictures the inhabitants of Jerusalem fleeing down the newly-formed valley between the northern and southern extremities of the then divided Mount of Olives. In verse three he has said that Jehovah will fight "as in the day of battle." As He separated the Red Sea to allow the Jews to escape from Pharaoh's chariots, He will then separate the mountain to allow those in Jerusalem to escape from the assembled nations.

Azel has not been identified by archeologists. Many have speculated as to its location, but none have offered any real help.

Two hundred years before Zechariah, in the days of king Uzziah, a severe earthquake had caused many to flee Jerusalem. The prophet sees the exodus following the division of the Mount of Olives as similar to that historic event.

The Lord is next pictured as coming in company with all the saints. This prediction is reminiscent of one made in *Jude 14*. "And to these also Enoch, the seventh from Adam, prophesied, saying, Behold, the Lord came with ten thousands of his holy ones . . ." It is also quite similar to John's description of Christ's coming in *Revelation 1:7*, "Behold, he cometh with the clouds; and every eye shall see him, and they that pierced him; and all the tribes of the earth shall mourn over him." Jesus Himself predicted in *Matthew 24:30*, ". . . and then shall appear the sign of the Son of man in heaven; and then shall all the tribes of the earth mourn, and they shall see the Son of man coming on the clouds of heaven with power and great glory."

Such descriptions of the Lord in Scripture are always in association with Christ's second coming. It is therefore unlikely that what Zechariah is presenting here is, as some have suggested, a metaphorical

14:6, 7 ZECHARIAH

description of the preaching of the gospel and the escape of some Jews by accepting it in 30 A.D.

IN THAT DAY (11) . . . Zechariah 14:6-7

RV . . . And it shall come to pass in that day, that there shall not be light; the bright ones shall withdraw themselves: but it shall be one day which is known unto Jehovah; not day, and not night; but it shall come to pass, that at evening time there shall be light.

LXX . . . And it shall come to pass in that day that there shall be no light, and there shall be for one day cold and frost, and that day shall be known to the Lord, and it shall not be day nor night: but towards evening it shall be light.

COMMENTS

The description is typical of many in which the day of Jehovah is pictured in the prophets. Isaiah said "Then the moon shall be confounded, and the sun ashamed, when the Lord of hosts shall reign in mount Zion, and in Jerusalem, and before his ancients gloriously," *(Isaiah 24:23)* and "Behold, the day of the Lord cometh, cruel both with wrath and fierce anger, to lay the land desolate: and he shall destroy the sinners thereof out of it. For the stars of heaven and the constellations thereof shall not give their light: the sun shall be darkened in his going forth, and the moon shall not cause her light to shine." *(Isaiah 13:9-10)* Joel stated "The sun and the moon shall be darkened, and the stars shall withdraw their shining." *(Joel 3:15)* Jesus' own description was "Immediately after the tribulation of those days shall the sun be darkened, and the moon shall not give her light, and the stars shall fall from heaven, and the powers of the heavens shall be shaken: And then shall appear the sign of the Son of man in heaven: and then shall all the tribes of the earth mourn, and they shall see the Son of man coming in the clouds of heaven with power and glory. And he shall send his angels with a great sound of a trumpet, and they shall gather together his elect from the four winds, from one end of heaven to the other." *(Matthew 24:29-31)*

On Pentecost Peter saw at least the beginning of this prediction being fulfilled in the coming of the Holy Spirit. Nothing that happened on Pentecost, however, answers to the last two verses of Joel's prediction, as quoted by Peter (cf. *Acts 2:17-20*). Perhaps here is a clue to the events described by Zechariah. The coming of the Holy

Spirit marked the beginning of the day of Jehovah *(Acts 2:17-18)*. The happenings pictured by Isaiah, Joel, Jesus, and John marked its end. *(Acts 2:19-20)*

IN THAT DAY (12) . . . Zechariah 14:8-12

RV . . . And it shall come to pass in that day, that living waters shall go out from Jerusalem; half of them toward the eastern sea, and half of them toward the western sea; in summer and in winter shall it be. And Jehovah shall be King over all the earth: in that day shall Jehovah be one, and his name one. All the land shall be made like the Arabah, from Geba to Rimmon south of Jerusalem; and she shall be lifted up, and shall dwell in her place, from Benjamin's gate unto the place of the first gate, unto the corner gate, and from the tower of Hananel unto the king's winepresses. And men shall dwell therein, and there shall be no more curse; but Jerusalem shall dwell safely. And this shall be the plague wherewith Jehovah will smite all the peoples that have warred against Jerusalem: their flesh shall consume away while they stand upon their feet, and their eyes shall consume away in their sockets, and their tongue shall consume away in their mouth.

LXX . . . And in that day living water shall come forth out of Jerusalem; half of it toward the former sea, and half of it toward the latter sea; and so shall it be in summer and spring. And the Lord shall be king over all the earth: in that day there shall be one Lord, and his name one, compassing all the earth, and the wilderness from Gabe unto Remmon south of Jerusalem. And Rama shall remain in its place. From the gate of Benjamin to the place of the first gate, to the gate of the corners, and to the tower of Anameel, as far as the kin's winepresses, they shall dwell in the city; and there shall be no more any curse, and Jerusalem shall dwell securely. And this shall be the overthrow with which the Lord will smite all the nations, as many as have fought against Jerusalem; their flesh shall consume away while they are standing upon their feet, and their eyes shall melt out of their holes, and their tongue shall consume away in their mouth.

COMMENTS

(Verses 8-9) If the Day of Jehovah *(verse 1)* did begin on Pentecost (see above on *Zechariah 14:6-7*) and the violence described in *14:4-7* are to occur at the end of it, the present verse is easily identifiable with Jesus' statement to the Samaritan woman in John chapter four. "Jesus answered and said unto her, Every one that drinketh of this water shall thirst again: but whosoever drinketh of the water that I shall give him shall never thirst; but the water that I shall give him shall become in him a well of water springing up unto eternal life." This living water did indeed flow east and west from Jerusalem as repentance and remission of sin began to be preached in the whole world, beginning from Jerusalem.

In the end of the day in which the living water began to flow, the Lord shall be king over the whole earth.

God has always been king over the whole earth. In the end He will be universally recognized as what He has always been. Evidence of His universal reign is to be the abolishing of false gods. Zechariah has already informed us that this would happen in the holy land. In the end it will happen throughout the earth. That it has by no means happened yet proves further that Zechariah's prediction remains to be completely fulfilled.

(Verses 10-11) *Geba* . . . the name literally means a *hill*__ was located on the northern border of the land of Benjamin. (cf. *Joshua 31:17*, cp. *I Kings 15:22*) *Rimmon*, meaning pomegranate, was situated south of Jerusalem, in Judah. It was rebuilt following the Babylonian exile. (cf. *Joshua 15:32, 19:7*)

It seems that the phenomenon which is to split the Mount of Olives, opening a new valley, will also cause other topographical changes in the vicinity of Jerusalem. Geba and Rimmon marked the northern and southern limits of post-exilic Judah. The mountain ridge thus occupied is pictured here as sinking to form a plain above which Jerusalem is lifted up or exalted.

Zechariah speaks of Jerusalem as it appeared in his own day. The gate of Benjamin was on the north and is probably to be identified with the gate of Ephriam (cp. *II Chronicles 25:23, Nehemiah 8:16, 22:39*) The tower of Hananeel still stood while the first gate seems to have been destroyed, since he speaks of its "place" rather than the gate itself.

(Verse 11) During this cataclysmic upheaval, the city itself will be untouched. Those in it will be safe.

(Verse 12) Those who are arrayed against Jerusalem at the time of the upheaval will shortly thereafter be smitten by a plague. The description of those struck by it is appalling. The only thing like it so far seen on earth was seen at Hiroshima and Nagasaki! If what we are reading here is the symbolic description of a final war on earth, the weapons for it are already in the arsenals.

IN THAT DAY (14) . . . Zechariah 14:13-19

RV . . . And it shall come to pass in that day, that a great tumult from Jehovah shall be among them; and they shall lay hold every one on the hand of his neighbor, and his hand shall rise up against the hand of his neighbor. And Judah also shall fight at Jerusalem; and the wealth of all the nations round about shall be gathered together, gold, and silver, and apparel, in great abundance. And so shall be the plague of the horse, of the mule, of the camel, and of the ass, and of the beasts that shall be in those camps, as that plague. And it shall come to pass, that every one that is left of all the nations that came against Jerusalem shall go up from year to year to worship the King, Jehovah of hosts, and to keep the feast of tabernacles. And it shall be, that whoso of all the families of the earth goeth not up unto Jerusalem to worship the King, Jehovah of hosts, upon them there shall be no rain. And if the family of Egypt go not up, and come not, neither shall it be upon them; there shall be the plague wherewith Jehovah will smite the nations that go not up to keep the feast of tabernacles. This shall be the punishment of Egypt, and the punishment of all the nations that go not up to keep the feast of tabernacles.

LXX . . . And there shall be in that day a great panic from the Lord upon them; and they shall lay hold every man of the hand of his neighbour, and his hand shall be clasped with the hand of his neighbour. Juda also shall fight in Jerusalem; and God shall gather the strength of all the nations round about, gold, and silver, and apparel, in great abundance. And this shall be the overthrow of the horses, and mules, and camels, and asses, and all the beasts that are in those camps, according to this overthrow. And it shall come to pass, that whosoever shall be left of all the nations that came against Jerusalem, shall even come up every year to worship the king, the Lord Almighty, and to keep the feast of tabernacles. And it shall come to pass, that whosoever of all the families of the earth shall not come up to Jerusalem to worship the king, the Lord Almighty, even these shall be added to the others. And if the family of Egypt shall not go up, nor come; then upon them shall be the overthrow with which the Lord shall smite all the nations, whichever of them shall not come up to keep the feast of tabernacles. This shall be the sin of Egypt, and the sin of all the nations, whosoever shall not come up to keep the feast of tabernacles.

14:13-19   ZECHARIAH

COMMENTS

(Verse 13) The result of the previously described cataclysm and plague is consternation. Mutual lack of trust seems to run amuck. Each one lays hold of the hand of his neighbor and raises up his own hand against him.

(Verse 14) Judah (the Jews) shall also fight at Jerusalem in that day. Whatever has been taken in the pillage described in *Zechariah 14.1-2* will be returned, and more beside.

(Verse 15) The plague which strikes the nations gathered against Jerusalem shall also smite the animals. The law said that, if an entire city became polluted by idolatry, not only the people but their animals were to be destroyed (cf. *Deuteronomy 8:15*). Here the justice of God fulfills His law against the pagan people who have attacked His holy city.

(Verse 16) The result of God's judgement is to be repentance. Those left of those who warred against Jerusalem now turn and worship her King.

The feast of the tabernacles commemorated the pilgrim life of the Jews during their years between the Red Sea and the Jordan. It celebrated not only entrance into the promised land, but the lessons learned through forty years of desert wandering during which an entire rebellious generation died. The nations who have at last learned, as Israel of old, the consequence of rebellion against God will keep the feast which commemorates that learning experience.

(Verse 17) If any nation fails to keep the feast of tabernacles, the result will be drought. Lack of rain soon turns the richest land to waste. The withholding of water as a means of chastisement has a long history in the Old Testament. (cf. *Amos 4:7, I Kings 18:9-16, 28:5*.)

(Verses 18-19) Egypt is singled out for special treatment should she refuse to keep the feast. This nation, whose history in ancient times was as interwoven with that of the Jewish nation as it is today, has had more first-hand experience of the power of God at work in His people than anyone else.

Drought was no threat to Egypt through the withholding of rain. It virtually never rains in Egypt anyway. Therefore, should Egypt fail to repent and keep the feast, she will suffer a special plague. Just what that plague will be is not stated.

Ultimately the plague visited upon unrepentant Egypt is to be shared by all nations which refuse to keep the feast.

IN THAT DAY (15) (16) . . . Zechariah 14:20-21

RV . . . In that day shall there be upon the bells of the horses, HOLY UNTO JEHOVAH; and the pots in Jehovah's house shall be like the bowls before the altar. Yea, every pot in Jerusalem and in Judah shall be holy unto Jehovah of hosts; and all they that sacrifice shall come and take of them, and boil therein; and in that day there shall be no more a Canaanite in the house of Jehovah of hosts.

LXX . . . In that day there shall be upon the bridle of every horse Holiness to the Lord Almighty; and the caldrons in the house of the Lord shall be as bowls before the altar. And every pot in Jerusalem, and in Juda shall be holy to the Lord Almighty: and all that sacrifice shall come and take of them, and shall seethe meat in them: and in that day there shall be no more Chanaanite in the house of the Lord Almighty.

COMMENTS

Finally, everything in Jerusalem is inscribed with HOLINESS UNTO THE LORD, from the bells on the horses of the trade caravans to the pots in the temple. The utensils in the houses will share this inscription. The artificial distinction between the scared and the secular will be broken down and everything, even the most commonplace things, such as kitchen utensils will be recognized as sacred because all of life is sacred.

There will be no more Canaanite in the land. Those who were the first enemies of God's people in His land, whose heathen gods were the first to turn Israel from Jehovah are no more.

Chapter XLII—*Questions*

In the Second Day

1. Chapter fourteen deals almost exclusively with _____.
2. Eschatology may be defined simply as _____.
3. Do scholars generally agree on the meaning of this chapter?
4. Discuss the two extreme views of pre and post millenialists in regard to Zechariah fourteen.
5. One can never be _____ and be dogmatic about eschatology, especially when it is written in apocalyptic form.

14:1-21   ZECHARIAH

6. In the study of eschatology we are deprived of a very useful tool in the interpretation of prophecy in general. What is that tool?
7. Review the meaning of "a day of Jehovah" in chapter forty-one.
8. In the day of Jehovah described in Zechariah fourteen the _____ of Jerusalem is to be divided in her midst.
9. Half the population of Jerusalem is to be _____.
10. Why does the Roman occupation of Jerusalem not fit the description here?
11. List the events of Zechariah
    a. In that day (10)
    b. In that day (11)
    c. In that day (12)
    d. In that day (13)
    e. In that day (14)
    f. In that day (15)
    g. In that day (16)
12. Describe the present setting of the Mount of Olives.
13. The division of the Mount of Olives would provide an easy _____.
14. The events here are compared to an historic earthquake in the days of _____.
15. The description of the Lord in company with all the saints always refers to _____.
16. What other prophets described the day of the Lord in terms similar to those used here by Zechariah?
17. Peter saw at least the beginning of the fulfillment of a similar prediction by Joel in _____.
18. God has always been king over the whole earth. In the end He will be _____.
19. Locate Geba and Rimmon.
20. What other topographical alterations accompany the splitting of the Mount of Olives?
21. Who will be safe during these catclysmic events?
22. Describe the plague which is to come upon those arrayed against Jerusalem.
23. What is the result of this plague?
24. What Jewish feast is to be celebrated by all the nations? What is its significance?

IN THE SECOND DAY

25. What is to be the consequence if any nation fails to keep the feast?
26. Why is Egypt here singled out for special punishment should she fail to keep the feast?
27. Finally the inscription _____ is to be seen on everything in Jerusalem.
28. Explain the significance of this inscription appearing on such diverse items as altar utensils and cook pots in the home.
29. Who were the Canaanites?

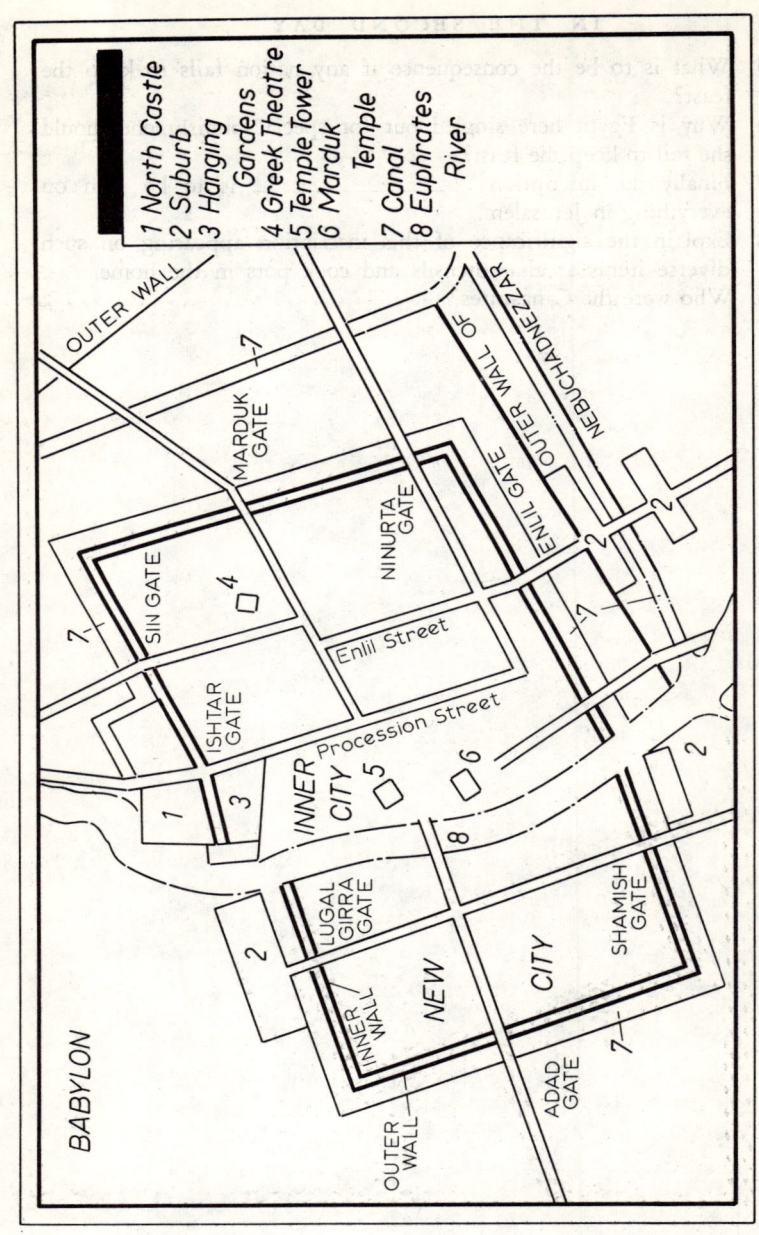

PART VIII
MALACHI

MALACHI

OUTLINE OF MALACHI

Superscription . . . 1:1
I. Denunciation of unfaithfulness . . . 1:2—2:16
  A. God loves Israel . . . 1:2-5
  B. The unfaithful priesthood . . . 1:6-2:9
  C. God despises infidelity . . . 2:10-16
II. The coming day of the Lord . . . 2:17—4:3
  A. The Lord will send His messenger to prepare for His day . . . 2:17-3:6
  B. If the people will return in devotion to God, He will yet bless them . . . 3:7-12
  C. When the day comes, true worshipers will be spared . . . 3:13—4:3
Conclusion
  Remember . . . 4:4-6

CHAPTER XLIII

INTRODUCTION

Jewish tradition says that prophecy continued forty years under the second temple, and this prophet (Malachi) they call the *seal of prophecy,* because in him the series or succession of prophets broke off.

The traditional Christian view is that Malachi is the link between the Old and New Covenants. Tertullian called him "the shirt and boundary of Christianity."

The authenticity of this writing is established by references to it in the New Testament. (eg. *Matthew 11:10, 17:12, Mark 1:2, 9:11, 12, Luke 1:17, Romans 9:13*)

Malachi's exact date we do not know, but it is probably about 460 B.C. Some have placed it as late as 424 B.C.

The remnant had returned from Babylon in 538 B.C. Haggai and Zechariah had succeeded in getting them to rebuild the temple in 520-516 B.C. In 457 Ezra had lent his assistance to Jewish national restoration. Fifteen years later in 444 B.C., Nehemiah had rebuilt the walls of Jerusalem.

In all, about a century had lapsed since the return from captivity. There was no resurgence of the idolatry which had driven their fathers into such punishment, but indifference and lack of real commitment were the order of the day. The laxity of the priests in teaching and enforcing the law was evidenced in the people's lack of support of the temple services. Unacceptable sacrifice of the worst rather than the first of their flocks were brought to God. Tithes went unpaid and the practice of intermarrying with Gentile women again reared its ugly head. (cp. *Ezra 9*)

In this state the coming of the Messiah for Whom they waited was in reality a threat rather than a promise.

We do not know the name of the author of this last Old Testament writing. The word Malachi means *"my messenger"* and is the name of the writer's function. It is suggested that he is called Malachi because of his emphatic prediction of a personal Messiah. The term "Malachi" is actually translated "my messenger" in *3:1*.

This primary prediction of the book (*3:1*) is applied to John the Baptist, also the Messiah's messenger. (cp. *Matthew 11:10, Mark 1:2, Luke 7:17, Matthew 17:10-12, Mark 9:11-12, Luke 1:16-17*)

Most commentators point out that Malachi's prophecy coincided with the first period of Daniel's seventy weeks (cf. *Daniel 9:24*). Thus the emphasis upon him as the Messiah's messenger seems fitting.

MALACHI'S MESSAGE . . .

Malachi's central concern is for fidelity to the covenant. (See the Covenant Theme in the Prophets, chapter III.) The priests have corrupted the worship which was designed to perpetuate covenant consciousness among the people. The men are marrying foreign women and so opening the door to idolatry as had Solomon of old.

In refuting this evil, Malachi rises to one of the heights of Old Testament prophecy in describing the purpose of the covenant in the ultimate worship of God among the Gentiles. His references to God as Father, the ideal priest, and the blessings of true obedience are equally striking in their Messianic overtones. He further clarifies, "the Day of the Lord," and points to the forerunner of the Messiah.

It is no doubt for these reasons that Malachi immediately precedes the New Testament in our English versions of the Bible.

The next word from Jehovah to His people is John's preaching.

CHAPTER XLIV
DENUNCIATION OF UNFAITHFULNESS

SUPERSCRIPTION . . . Malachi 1:1

RV . . . The burden of the word of Jehovah to Israel by Malachi.

1:1-5   MALACHI

LXX . . . The burden of the word of the Lord to Israel by the hand of his messenger. Lay it, I pray you, to heart.

COMMENTS

Malachi begins with the prophet's usual claim to inspiration, "the burden of the word of Jehovah." The message is to Israel.

The term "Israel" appears four times in Malachi. (*1:1, 1:5, 2:16, and 4:4*) There can be little doubt that its use in this context is designed to underscore the covenant relationship of the people to Jehovah. (See review of the use of "Israel" in Chapter IV, comments on *Micah 1:5*)

The message will first convince, then comfort; first discover sin, then reprove it. It will reach its climax in the promise of Him Who is to take away sin.

GOD LOVES ISRAEL . . . Malachi 1:2-5

RV . . . I have loved you, saith Jehovah. Yet ye say, Wherein hast thou loved us? Was not Esau Jacob's brother? saith Jehovah: yet I loved Jacob; but Esau I hated, and made his mountains a desolation, and gave his heritage to the jackals of the wilderness. Whereas Edom saith, We are beaten down but we will return and build the waste places; thus saith Jehovah of hosts, They shall build, but I will throw down; and men shall call them The border of wickedness, and The people against whom Jehovah hath indignation for ever. And your eyes shall see, and ye shall say, Jehovah be magnified beyond the border of Israel.

LXX . . I have loved you, saith the Lord. And ye said, Wherein hast thou loved us? Was not Esau Jacob's brother? saith the Lord: yet I loved Jacob, and hated Esau, and laid waste his borders, and made his heritage as dwellings of the wilderness? Because one will say, Idumea has been overthrown, but let us return and rebuild the desolate places; thus saith the Lord Almighty, They shall build, but I will throw down; and they shall be called The borders of wickedness, and, The people against whom the Lord has set himself for ever. And your eyes shall see, and ye shall say, The Lord has been magnified upon the borders of Israel.

COMMENTS

In these verses Israel is charged with being insensible to God's love. To overcome this insensitivity, He says emphatically, "I have loved you."

DENUNCIATION OF UNFAITHFULNESS 1:2-5

It is not the first time He has declared His love. (cp. *Jeremiah 31:3-4*) All of His dealings, from the initial establishment of the covenant, have been the result of this love.

In answer to the anticipated question "Wherein hast thou loved us?" Jehovah answers specifically in terms of His preference for Jacob over Esau.

The Jews were prone to think of themselves as superior to other races. Here God reminds them He has shown His love to them, not just in preference to other races, but in preference over those of their own race. Jacob and Esau were twin brothers, yet God established His covenant with Jacob, father of all Israelites, rather than with Esau, father of the Edomites. "I loved Jacob . . . I hated Esau."

God does not, of course, unequivocally, hate any man or race of men. (cf. *Acts 10:34, 35*) This statement must be kept in context. It is in contrast to His great love for His covenant people that His love for others seems hatred by comparison. Much in the same vein, Jesus demands that we "hate" father, mother, brother, sister, wife and even self. (*Luke 14:26*) We know He does not want us to literally hate anyone. (cp. *Matthew 5:43-48*) Neither does He hate anyone, excepting in comparison to His love for His chosen people.

The evidence of His preferential love for Israel over Edom is pictured in contrast of Edom's homeland to the "land flowing with milk and honey" into which He led His people. Edom lies southeast of the Dead Sea in the Arabian desert. Its capital, Petra, was cut out of solid red limestone cliffs. The surrounding area is desolate and barren.

Paul set upon the contrast between Jacob and Esau in establishing God's love for His covenant people. (*Romans 9:13*) The apostle points out the contrast is not between two nations *per se,* for "they are not all Israel that are of Israel." (*Romans 9:6*) The real contrast is between the covenant people and the noncovenant people for "this is a word of promise, At this time will I come, and Sarah shall have a son. And not only this; but when Rebecca also had conceived by one, even by our father Isaac; (For the children being not yet born, neither having done any good or evil, that the purpose of God according to election might stand, not of works, but of him that calleth;) It was said unto her, The elder shall serve the younger. As it is written, Jacob have I loved, but Esau have I hated." (*Romans 9:9-13*)

Since it was His promise to redeem all mankind that was the heart of His covenant, His preferential treatment of Israel is ultimately evidence of His love even for Edom!

Nevertheless, in the years before Christ, He could point with justification to His treatment of His people in comparison to others as evidence of His love.

ISRAEL IS UNFAITHFUL . . . Malachi 1:6-2:9

RV . . . A son honoreth his father, and a servant his master; if then I am a father, whereis mine honor? and if I am a master, where is my fear? saith Jehovah of hosts unto you, O priests, that despise my name. And ye say, Wherein have we despised thy name? Ye offer polluted bread upon mine altar. And ye say, Wherein have we polluted thee? In that ye say, The table of Jehovah is contemptible. And when ye offer the blind for sacrifice, it is no evil! and when ye offer the lame and sick, it is no evil! Present it now unto thy governor; will he be pleased with thee? or will he accept thy person? saith Jehovah of hosts. And now, I pray you, entreat the favor of God, that he may be gracious unto us; this hath been by your means: will he accept any of your persons? saith Jehovah of hosts. Oh that there were one among you that would shut the doors, that ye might not kindle fire on mine altar in vain! I have no pleasure in you, saith Jehovah of hosts, neither will I accept an offering at your hand. For from the rising of the sun even unto the going down of the same my name shall be great among the Gentiles; and in every place incense shall be offered unto my name, and a pure offering: for my name shall be great among the Gentiles, saith Jehovah of hosts. But ye profane it, in that ye say, The table of Jehovah is polluted, and the fruit thereof, even its food, is contemptible. Ye say also, Behold what a weariness is it! and ye have snuffed at it, saith Jehovah of hosts; and ye have brought that which was taken by violence, and the lame, and the sick; thus ye bring the offering; should I accept this at your hand? saith Jehovah. But cursed be the deceiver, who hath in his flock a male, and voweth, and sacarificeth unto the Lord a blemished thing; for I am a great King, saith Jehovah of hosts, and my name is terrible among the Gentiles. And now, O ye priests, this commandment is for you. If ye will not hear, and if ye will not lay it to heart, to give glory unto my name, saith Jehovah of hosts, then will I send the curse upon you, and I will curse your blessings; yea, I have cursed them already, because ye do not lay it to heart. Behold, I will rebuke your seed, and will spread dung upon your faces, even the dung of your feasts; and ye shall be taken away with it. And ye shall know that I have sent this commandment unto you, that my covenant may be with Levi, saith Jehovah of hosts. My covenant was with him of life and peace; and I gave them to him that he might fear; and he feared me, and stood in awe of my name. The law of truth was in his mouth, and unrighteousness was not found in his lips; he walked with me in peace and uprightness, and turned many away from iniquity. For the priest's lips should keep knowledge, and they should seek the law at his mouth; for he is the messenger of Jehovah of hosts. But ye are turned aside out of the way; ye have caused many to stumble in the law; ye have corrupted the covenant of Levi, saith Jehovah of hosts. Therefore have I also made you contemptible and base before all the people, according as ye have not kept my ways, but have had respect of persons in the law.

LXX . . . A son honours his father, and a servant his master: if then I am a father, where is mine honour? and if I am a master, where is my fear? saith the Lord Almighty. Yet the priests are they that despise my name: yet ye said, Wherein have we despised thy name? In that ye bring to mine altar polluted bread; and ye said, Wherein have ye polluted it? In that ye say, The table of the Lord is polluted, and that which was set thereon ye have despised. For if ye bring a blind victim for sacrifices, is it not evil? and if ye bring the lame or the sick, is it not evil? offer it now to thy ruler, and see if he will receive thee, if he will accept thy person, saith the Lord Almighty. And now intreat the face of your God, and make supplication to him. These things have been done by your hands; shall I accept you? saith the Lord Almighty. Because even among you the doors shall be shut, and one will not kindle the fire of mine altar for nothing, I have no pleasure in you, saith the Lord Almighty, and I will not accept a sacrifice at your hands. For from the rising of the sun even to the going down thereof my name has been glorified among the Gentiles; and in every place incense is offered to my name, and a pure offering: for my name is great among the Gentiles, saith the Lord Almighty. But ye profane it, in that ye say, The table of the Lord is polluted, and his meats set thereon are despised. And ye said, These services are troublesome: therefore I have utterly rejected them with scorn, saith the Lord Almighty: and ye brought in torn victims, and lame, and sick: if then ye should bring an offering, shall I accept them at your hands? saith the Lord Almighty. And cursed is the man who had the power, and possessed a male in his flock, and whose vow is upon him, and who sacrifices a corrupt thing to the Lord; for I am a great King, saith the Lord Almighty, and my name is glorious among the nations. And now, O priests, this commandment is to you. If ye will not hearken, and if ye will not lay it to heart, to give glory to my name, saith the Lord Almighty, then I will send forth the curse upon you, and I will bring a curse upon your blessing; yea, I will curse it, and I will scatter your blessing, and it shall not exist among you, because ye lay not this to heart. Behold, I turn my back upon you, and I will scatter dung upon your faces, the dung of your feasts, and I will carry you away at the same time. And ye shall know that I have sent this commandment to you, that my covenant might be with the sons of Levi, saith the Lord Almighty. My covenant of life and peace was with him, and I gave it him that he might reverently fear me, and that he might be awe-struck at my name. The law of truth was in his mouth, and iniquity was not found in his lips: he walked before me directing his way in peace, and he turned many from unrighteousness. For the priest's lips should keep knowledge, and they should seek the law at his mouth: for he is the messenger of the Lord Almighty. But ye have turned aside from the way, and caused many to fail in following the law; ye have corrupted the covenant of Levi, saith the Lord Almighty. And I have made you despised and cast out among all the people, because ye have not kept my ways, but have been partial in the law.

COMMENTS

God's love and faithfulness to His covenant people stands in stark contrast to their unfaithfulness to Him. They neither fear Him as a master nor honor Him as a father . . . and their priests are the chief offenders.

The severe reproof of the priests is a just one. They have profaned the holy things of God with which they were intrusted. It was their sin that was leading the people to be unfaithful.

They took His name in vain, not by pronouncing it in profanity, but by offering unacceptable sacrifices to him. They are accused of polluting the altar.

When they deny the charge, saying, "Wherein have we polluted thee?", Jehovah's answer is "In that ye say the table of Jehovah is contemptible."

The term "bread of God" is synonymous with "sacrifices to God" *(Leviticus 21:8)*, so we should not think here of the table of shewbread, but of the sacrificial flesh offered upon the altar.

The priests have declared the table of God contemptible by sanctioning the offering of skimpy and blemished sacrifices. The sacrificial animals Darius, and no doubt his successors had provided Israel as a vassal state were kept to replenish their own flocks and only the culls were brought to God.

Such cheap religion is less than worthless, it is an affront to God.

The law said such animals were not to be offered as sacrifice (cp. *Leviticus 22:17-25, Deuteronomy 15:21*) yet the priests addressed here saw no harm in it.

The governor appointed by the Gentile emperor would not eat the meat they offered to God, yet they presented it as an act of worship and said, "it is not evil."

Their real error in offering blemished sacrifices lies in the fact that such animals could not do what the sacrifices were designed to do, namely, typlify the ultimate Sacrifice, without spot or blemish. (*I Peter 1:19*) It was to keep this prophetic object lesson before the people that the temple had been rebuilt. It was to maintain this constant covenant reminder in the eyes of the people that the sacrifices *must* be made according to divine directive. A blemished animal could not possibly portend the coming Lamb of God, and without that portent the entire sacrificial system was meaningless.

The scathing irony of verse nine underscores this truth. Malachi challenges the unfaithful priests to try it, if they think such unacceptable sacrifices will win them the favor of God.

The entire passage draws a vivid contrast between man's religion and God's sacrificial scheme of redemption. Men, in their religious efforts to curry God's favor, always think of themselves as bringing *Him* something. The advent of the Christ, toward which the sacrificial system pointed, is the exact opposite. God was bringing the Real Sacrifice to man.

From the beginning God has not been served by men's hands as though *He* needed anything. (cp. *Psalm 10:1-12, Acts 17:25*) In demanding the presentation of the very best of Israel's flocks to be slain upon the altar, God intended that they learn something of the price He would pay for our redemption when He offered the "Choice Jewel of Heaven" on Calvary. If He were to tolerate a lesser offering, the whole point of the sacrifices would be missed.

GOD DESPISES INFIDELITY . . .

(Verse 10) Calvin points out that, in the temple, one priest was stationed at the doors of the court of burnt offerings for the express purpose of keeping out animals unfit for sacrifice. In this verse, God cries out in anguish for just one priest whose concern for God's law would cause him to shut the door against such blemished sacrifices as were being offered daily. It would be better to let the fires go unkindled than to continue to desecrate the altar and mar the meaning of God's covenant by offering animals unfit to depict the coming Real Sacrifice. Better none at all than these. (cp. *Isaiah 1:11-15*)

Since no such priest stood at the door, God would Himself refuse to accept their sacrifices.

(Verse 11) This verse is reminiscent of Paul's attitude toward those Jews who rejected the preaching of the Gospel. (*Acts 13:46*) God, Who lives in eternity and so is much less pre-occupied with time than we, treats the acceptance of His Sacrifice by the Gentiles as an already accomplished fact. He Who knows the end from the beginning is able of the very stones to raise up children to Abraham (*Matthew 3:9*). Other sheep He has which are not of this fold (*John 10:16*). "For when the Gentiles which have not the law, do by nature the things contained in the law, these, having not the law, are a law unto themselves . . . " (*Romans 2:14*) and God is glorified. His name is, in fact, great among the nations. (cp. *Isaiah 1:11-15*)

"Sacrifice," in verse 11, is used figuratively as in *Psalm 51:17, Hebrews 13:10,15,16* and *I Peter 2:5,12,* but the truth is that "in every nation he that feareth Him, and worketh righteousness, is accepted with Him." (*Acts 10:35*)

(Verses 12-13) Whereas the ineffable name of God is thus glorified among the nations who have not the law and are thus separated from the Messianic hope, foreigners in the commonwealth of Israel, oblivious of the promises of God and unaware of any hope as yet (*Ephesians 2:12*), that same name is made a mockery among those who have for centuries been His covenant people.

They offer to God what they would not eat themselves, and even this is "a drag," irksome service! Isaiah had informed their fathers that it was God Who is wearied by such service and not they. (*Isaiah 43:22-f*)

Meat taken by violence, *ie.* torn by animals, was not even lawful for human consumption, yet they offered it to God. (cp. *Exodus 22:31*)

(Verse 14) For "deceiver" here, read hypocrite. It was not poverty, as some pretended, which caused such niggardly sacrifices. It was greed which placed personal gain above God's required service. They possessed "a male," *ie.* such as required by law sacrifice, yet they offered God blemished animals. (cp. *Leviticus 1:3-10*) Even the Gentiles would be too fearful of God to do such things.

DENUNCIATION OF UNFAITHFULNESS 2:1-9
ESPECIALLY FOR PRIESTS . . .

(*2:1-2*) Here begins a special decree for the priests of Israel who are the cause of Israel's infidelity. "Ministers," Moore points out, "cannot sin or suffer alone. They drag down others if they fall." Thus does God, for the sake of His people, pronounce a curse on their unfaithful spiritual leaders. That which had been their special blessing as priests would become a curse.

(Verse 3) The maw of the sacrificial victims was, on feast days, the special food of the priests. (*Deuteronomy 18:3*) The stomach, or maw, was regarded as one of the choice delicacies. Instead of receiving this, God threatens to fling dung in their faces because of the defiled offerings from which it came.

By law, the dung of the sacrifices was to be carried outside the gate and disposed of. Because of the awful way the priests insulted God in the offering of blemished animals, they were to be carried with it.

Whether the threat to fling dung in their faces and to carry themselves to the dung heap is to be understood literally or not, it leaves little doubt as to how much God despises those who make a sham of His services. They are to be banished from His presence.

(Verse 4) The reason for God's rebuke of the priests is that the special priestly covenant which He had made with Levi, the priestly tribe, must be maintained.

(Verses 5-9) Here Malachi describes the promises and conditions of the Levitical covenant, Levi's former observance of this covenant, and the rewards of such observance. Over against these he sets the consequences of violating this covenant as these priests were doing.

Formerly, God had bestowed life and prosperity upon Levi (the priestly tribe). On him God laid the duty of reverence. In return the priests had revered God and respected His name. They had given true instructions to the people and had spoken no injustice. They had lived in accord with Him and in so doing had turned many people from sin to God. Men then stood in respect of the priests and sought to learn from them because they recognized in them God's messengers.

The unfaithful priests of Malachi's time, in contrast, have left off the righteous practices of their predecessors. Instead of leading many from sin to God, they have caused many to fall into sin. Whereas the former priests of Levi had taken their special relationship to God very much to heart, these have treated it as of no consequence.

As a result, God will make them despicable in the eyes of the people. Because of their sinful lives and unjust application of the law

2:9-16

for favor (cp. *Leviticus 19:15*) the people would no longer respect them as a special class and their special privileges would cease.

The principles underlying God's denunciation of the priests through Malachi merit our attention. We, as Christians, are all priests of God (*I Peter 2:9*). As such, we enjoy blessings those outside of Christ never dream of. We, too, are charged to offer sacrifices to God, holy and acceptable (*Romans 12:1-2*). To do less is to make a mockery of His name before the world.

If we do not offer ourselves as holy and acceptable sacrifices to God, we may be assured that our relationship to Him will become a curse rather than a blessing. Un-Christian men will be able to point at us and say they have more fear of God than do we. We shall then be stumbling blocks, leading them deeper into sin rather than teaching them God's truth, for they will not heed the words of priests whose lives do not match their doctrines.

GOD DESPISES INFIDELITY . . . Malachi 2:10-16

RV . . . Have we not all one father? hath not one God created us? why do we deal treacherously every man against his brother, profaning the covenant of our fathers? Judah hath dealt treacherously, and an abomination is committed in Israel and in Jerusalem; for Judah hath profaned the holiness of Jehovah which he loveth, and hath married the daughter of a foreign god. Jehovah will cut off, to the man that doeth this, him that waketh and him that answereth, out of the tents of Jacob, and him that offereth an offering unto Jehovah of hosts. And this again ye do: ye cover the altar of Jehovah with tears, with weeping, and with sighing, insomuch that he regardeth not the offering any more, neither receiveth it with good will at your hand. Yet ye say, Wherefore? Because Jehovah hath been witness between thee and the wife of thy youth, against whom thou hast dealt treacherously, though she is thy companion, and the wife of thy covenant. And did he not make one, although he had the residue of the Spirit? And wherefore one? He sought a godly seed. Therefore take heed to your spirit, and let none deal treacherously against the wife of his youth. For I hate putting away, saith Jehovah the God of Israel, and him that covereth his garment with violence, saith Jehovah of hosts; therefore take heed to your spirit, that ye deal not treacherously.

LXX . . . Have ye not all one father? Did not one God create you? why have ye forsaken every man his brother, to profane the covenant of your fathers? Juda has been forsaken, and an abomination has been committed in Israel and in Jerusalem; for Juda has profaned the holy things of the Lord, which he delighted in, and has gone after other gods. The Lord will utterly destroy the man that does these things, until he be even cast down from out of the tabernacles of Jacob, and from among them that offer sacrifice to the Lord Almighty. And these things which I hated, ye did: ye covered with tears the altar of the Lord, and with weeping and groaning because of troubles: is it meet for me to have respect to your sacrifice, or to receive anything from your hands as welcome? Yet ye said, Wherefore? Because the Lord has borne witness between thee and the wife of thy youth, whom thou hast forsaken, and yet she was thy partner, and the wife of thy covenant. And did he not do well? and there was the residue of his spirit. But ye said, What does God seek but a seed? But take ye heed to your spirit, and forsake not the wife of thy youth. But if thou shouldest hate thy wife and put her away, saith the Lord God of Israel, then ungodliness shall cover thy thoughts, saith the Lord Almighty: therefore take ye heed to your spirit, and forsake them not.

COMMENTS

(Verses 10-12) The special covenant which made priests of the tribe of Levi was not unrelated to the everlasting covenant which is the prophet's primary concern. The common father here *(v. 10)* is not God as some have said, but Jacob. The Levites as well as the people were the children of Israel (*i.e.* Jacob)

Of all the nations on earth, they alone worshipped but one God. In any other nation the people professed varied loyalties to various household deities.

Because all Israel, priests and people alike, stood under one covenant before one God, unfaithfulness to one another constituted unfaithfulness to the covenant. And such abominable practices were present, the prophet assures his readers, in all Judah and even in the holy city in the shadow of the temple. The holy relationship of the covenant was being violated in loving and marrying pagan women.

(Verse 12) The words of verse twelve are not idle threat. The practice of inter-marriage with foreign women had brought Baal worship among the people and it was this which brought about the destruction of the northern tribes as well as the captivity of the southern tribes. If it again gained ascendance among the returned remnant, God's covenant purpose would indeed be in jeopardy.

To avoid this, God here threatens to cut off to the man, *ie.* on an individual basis, all who indulge in such practice. "Out of the tents of Jacob" signifies separation from the people of the covenant.

(Verse 13-a) This sin had once, since the return, been checked by Ezra *(Ezra 9:10)*. Malachi here addresses a relapse. "This again ye do."

(Verse 13(b)-14) The covering of the altar with tears is symbolic of the weeping of wives who were being deserted for foreign women. These were Israelite women who were of the covenant people. Their abuse covered the altar *ie.* the covenant with tears.

It was customary for such marriages, *ie.* "the wife of thy youth," to be contracted when the parties were very young. Many were only thirteen or fourteen and their wives even younger. (cf. *Proverbs 5:8, Isaiah 54:6*) The couple was bound not only by the covenant of marriage, but by the even deeper relationship they shared as children of God's covenant. Those who, at later age, abandoned the wives of their youth to marry foreign women were not only breaking their own marriage vows, they were violating God's everlasting covenant with Israel.

(Verse 15) "Did He not make one . . . " Malachi's argument here in reference to this abandonment is similar to that of Jesus concerning divorce. (cp. *Matthew 19:3-ff*) God, in the beginning, made one male and one female, although He had unlimited spiritual resources and could have made more of either. These two, male and female, are called *one man* (humankind). (cf. *Genesis 1:27*) Malachi, as Jesus, understands this to indicate God's intent that there be one wife for each man.

The prophet says the reason God established this unity is that He "sought a godly seed." The modern concern of the sociologist for the effect of broken marriages upon the children (seed) of those marriages is well-founded. Eternity alone will reveal the number of children who have turned from God because their fathers abandoned their mothers to marry pagan women!

Every Christian father stands in covenant relationship to God, as did those in Israel who were addressed by Malachi. Such a father always jeopardizes his children's relationship to God when he leaves the "wife of his youth" for another woman.

"Therefore," says Malachi, "take heed to your spirit, and let none deal treacherously against the wife of his youth."

(Verse 16) "I hate putting away . . . " Whatever doubt may linger concerning God's attitude toward divorce is certainly dispelled by this verse. The statement of His hatred of the practice is accompanied by His name *Jehovah* as God of the covenant people. It could not be more emphatic.

"*Him that covereth his garments with violence.*" A better translation would be "*Him that covereth his violence with a garment.*" One commentator has suggested "their *violence* is the putting away of their wives; the *garment* with which they try to cover it is the plea of Moses permission."

The terminology of *Genesis 20:16, Deuteronomy 22:30, Ruth 3:9,* and *Ezekiel 16:8* in which husbands and wives are each described as a covering for the eyes of the other would tend to indicate that the *garment* here is the wife and the *violence* with which the garment is covered is the divorce. The thought in these passages is that one's love for and marriage to one's wife should cover his eyes against the attraction of other women.

Whatever the meaning of this idiomatic expression, it is obvious that Malachi is denouncing, in God's name, the practice of leaving a wife who is of the faith for another who is not of the faith, and denouncing divorce in general.

Chapter XLIV—*Questions*

Denunciation of Unfaithfulness

1. The prophet _____ is considered by Jewish tradition as the *seal of prophecy.*
2. The traditional Christian view is that Malachi is the bridge between the _____ and the _____.
3. Malachi probably wrote about _____ B.C.
4. Malachi means _____.
5. Malachi's prophecy coincides with the _____ period of Daniel's seventy weeks.
6. Malachi's central concern is _____.
7. Discuss the corruption of the priesthood as addressed by Malachi and show its effect upon the people.
8. Why does Malachi immediately precede the New Testament in our English versions of the Bible?
9. Outline the book of Malachi.
10. The next word from Jehovah to His people after Malachi would be spoken by _____.

CHAPTER XLV

THE COMING DAY OF THE LORD

THE LORD WILL SEND A MESSENGER TO PREPARE FOR HIS DAY . . . Malachi 2:17—3:6.

RV . . . Ye have wearied Jehovah with your words. Yet ye say, Wherein have we wearied him? In that ye say, Every one that doeth evil is good in the sight of Jehovah, and he delighteth in them; or where is the God of justice? Behold, I send my messenger, and he shall prepare the way before me; and the Lord, whom ye seek, will suddenly come to his temple; and the messenger of the covenant, whom ye desire, behold, he cometh, saith Jehovah of hosts. But who can abide the day of his coming? and who shall stand when he appeareth? for he is like a refiner's fire, and like fullers' soap: and he will sit as a refiner and purifier of silver, and he will purify the sons of Levi, and refine them as gold and silver; and they shall offer unto Jehovah offerings in righteousness. Then shall the offering of Judah and Jerusalem be pleasant unto Jehovah, as in the days of old, and as in ancient years. And I will come near to you to judgement; and I will be a swift witness against the sorcerers, and against the adulterers, and against the false swearers, and against those that oppress the hireling in his wages, the widow, and the fatherless, and that turn aside the sojourner from his right, and fear not me, saith Jehovah of hosts. For I, Jehovah, change not; therefore ye, O sons of Jacob, are not consumed.

LXX . . . ye that have provoked God with your words. But ye said, Wherein have we provoked him? In that ye say, Every one that does evil is a pleasing object in the sight of the Lord, and he takes pleasure in such; and where is the God of justice? Behold, I send forth my messenger, and he shall survey the way before me; and the Lord, whom ye seek, shall suddenly come into his temple, even the angel of the covenant, whom ye take pleasure in: behold, he is coming, saith the Lord Almighty. And who will abide the day of his coming? or who will withstand at his appearing? for he is coming in as the fire of a furnace and as the herb of fullers. He shall sit to melt and purify as it were silver, and as it were gold: and he shall purify the sons of Levi, and refine them as gold and silver, and they shall offer to the Lord an offering in righteousness. And the sacrifice of Judah and Jerusalem shall be pleasing to the Lord, according to the former days, and according to the former years. And I will draw near to you in judgement;

and I will be a swift witness against the witches, and against the adulteresses, and against them that swear falsely by my name, and against them that keep back the hireling's wages, and them that oppress the widow, and afflict orphans, and that wrest the judgement of the stranger, and fear not me, saith the Lord Almighty. For I am the Lord your God, and I am not changed:

COMMENTS

WHERE IS THE GOD OF JUSTICE ... v. 17

Two things in the arguments of the priests wearied Jehovah. *First,* they considered evil to be good, so they declared it good "in the sight of Jehovah."

Second, they said "where is the God of justice." They looked at the drought, crop failures and generally unprosperous conditions of Judah on the one hand, and on the other, the fact that the forms of the ceremonial law were being observed and concluded that God was slack in His justice. As we have seen, the *quality* of the sacrifices and the *spirit* in which they were offered put the lie to their arguments.

BEHOLD, I SEND MY MESSENGER ... v. 1

Here is God's answer to their question, "where is the God of justice." Suddenly the Lord will appear in the temple heralded by His forerunner.

Isaiah had made a similar prediction. *(Isaiah 40:3-5).*

The New Testament applies Malachi's prophecy to John the Baptist. (eg. *Matthew 3:3, 11:10, Mark 1:2-3, Luke 1:76, 3:4, 7:26-27, John 1:23)* The obvious fulfillment of this promise in the baptist's ministry would be difficult for any open-minded Bible student to overlook.

The sudden appearance of the Lord mentioned here was interpreted by the Rabbis as a dramatic explosive visitation by which the Messiah would announce His presence. It was this popular expectation which the devil exploited in tempting Jesus to cast Himself from the pinnacle of the temple. *(Luke 4:9)* To have done so would have won for Him instant acceptance as the Messiah on the basis of popular though erroneous expectation.

"The messenger of the covenant ... " What more apt description could there be of Him Whose coming formed the heart of God's covenant promise? How fitting that the writer of Hebrews should intro-

duce his comparison of the Old and New Covenants with the argument for the superiority of the New based on the superiority of the Son over the prophets, angels and Moses, who were the messengers of the Old. (cp. *Hebrews 1:1-2:4*)

(Verses 2-6) *"Who can abide the day of His coming?"* The Messiah was coming but not to confirm the racial arrogance or religious exclusiveness of these false Israelites. John will speak of Him as one "whose fan is in His hand, and He will thoroughly cleanse His threshing-floor; and He will gather His wheat into the garner but the chaff He will burn up with unquenchable fire." *(Matthew 3:12).*

Malachi here makes a like prediction. By a change of metaphors he describes the Messiah's judgement first as fuller's soap then as refiners fire.

In this sense, soap and fire have one thing in common, both remove impurity. The entire ministry of the Messiah, including His first coming, the intervening age and His second coming, will purge the impurities from the people of God. Those whose profession is false, whose hope is based on false ambition and nationalistic exclusiveness will be removed from Israel. The remnant will be saved.

This refining process is described by Zechariah as removing all but a third of those who call themselves Israel. (cp. *Isaiah 1:25*)

(Verses 3-4) Since Malachi's primary concern is with false priests (see above on *1:10-ff),* he pictures the Messiah, in verse three, as a refiner sitting before the crucible in which the sons of Levi are purged of those who are unfaithful so that they will offer to Jehovah offerings in righteousness.

The offerings to the Christ are not the blemished animals of Malachi's day. Rather they are to be "holy and acceptable unto God," (cf. *Romans 12:1, Hebrews 13:5, I Peter 2:5)* as were those offered in the beginning by Aaron.

(Verses 5-6) They have asked "where is the God of justice." *(2:17)* When Messiah comes they will have their answer. He will testify against the sorcerers *(Acts 8:1, 13:6, Galatians 5:20),* against adulterers *(Matthew 5:28),* against false swearers *(Matthew 5:34,36),* against those that oppress the hireling, the widows, the fatherless, and they that turn aside the sojourners *(Matthew 25:31-46),* and that fear not me *(Matthew 10:26-28).*

Special notice should be taken of the inclusion in this list of priestly sins of "those that turn aside the sojourner." A sojourner was one of another land who was not a Jew. God's concern for all men, rather than just for the Jew, as stated in the covenant is apparent throughout

His dealings with the people through whom He purposed to bless all men.

(Verse 6) It is a tragic error to assume that, because God has not smitten the wicked, He has changed from a God of justice to one of easy-going tolerance. Malachi points out to his readers that God's unchanging nature is the only reason they were not themselves long since wiped out!

Paul points out in Romans eleven (cf. *v. 29*) that God's mercy toward even the covenant people finds its source in His unfailing faithfulness to His own covenant.

Peter speaks to the same fatal fallacy when he writes, "But forget not this one thing beloved, that one day is with the Lord as a thousand years, and a thousand years as one day. The Lord is not slack concerning His promise, as some count slackness; but is longsuffering to you-ward, not wishing that any should perish, but that all should come to repentance." *(II Peter 3:8-9)*

IF THE PEOPLE WILL RETURN IN DEVOTION TO GOD HE WILL YET BLESS THEM . . . Malachi 3:7-12

RV . . . From the days of your fathers ye have turned aside from mine ordinances, and have not kept them. Return unto me, and I will return unto you, saith Jehovah of hosts. But ye say, Wherein shall we return? Will a man rob God? yet ye rob me. But ye say, Wherein have we robbed thee? In tithes and offerings. Ye are cursed with the curse; for ye rob me, even this whole nation. Bring ye the whole tithe into the store-house, that there may be food in my house, and prove me now herewith, saith Jehovah of hosts, if I will not open you the windows of heaven, and pour you out a blessing, that there shall not be room enough to receive it. And I will rebuke the devourer for your sakes, and he shall not destroy the fruits of your ground; neither shall your vine cast its fruit before the time in the field, saith Jehovah of hosts. And all nations shall call you happy; for ye shall be a delightsome land, saith Jehovah of hosts.

LXX . . . but ye, the sons of Jacob, have not refrained from the iniquities of your fathers: ye have perverted my statutes, and have not kept them. Return to me, and I will return to you, saith the Lord Almighty. But ye said, Wherein shall we return? Will a man insult God? for ye insult me. But ye say, Wherein have we insulted thee? In that the tithes and first-fruits are with you still. And ye do surely look off from me, and ye insult me. The year is completed, and ye have brought all the produce into the store-houses; but there shall be the plunder thereof in its house: return now on this behalf, saith the Lord Almighty, see if I will not open to you the torrents of heaven, and pour out my blessings upon you, until ye are satisfied. And I will appoint food for you, and I will not destroy the fruit of your land; and your vine in the field shall not fail, saith the Lord Almighty. And all nations shall call you blessed; for ye shall be a desirable land, saith the Lord Almighty.

COMMENTS

FROM THE DAYS OF YOUR FATHERS . . . v. 7

When Stephen stood before the council and accused them with, "Ye stiffnecked and uncircumcised in heart and ears . . . as your fathers did, so do ye," *(Acts 7:51)* he was in good company. Malachi here levels the same charge against his readers.

Just as their ancestors had turned aside from God's ordinances to worship Baal, these were turning aside in making a mockery of the same ordinances. The withholding of tithes, the offering of blemished animals, the indulging in sorcery and adultery and false swearing while showing unconcern for human need by oppressing wage-earners, widows, orphans and non-Jews indicated theirs was a religion of form rather than sincerity. The prophet sees no advantage in this over the false religion which had brought on the Babylonian captivity.

There is an eternal principle presented here which the modern church member cannot afford to ignore. The observance of outward form and the passive abstention from false religion are a sham if done as these did them. The cheapening of the ordinances of God as they did in offering unacceptable sacrifices, or as is often done in present day churches by penny-wise and niggardly church budgets are no more advantageous than false doctrine. The lack of any real concern for the poor, the abandoned, the downtrodden, that is frequently hidden under an annual Christmas basket, does not deceive Him Who knows the hearts of His people.

The entreaty of God to such people to return to Him is frequently met today as in Malachi's time (*v. 7*) with a blank faced and feigned innocence expressed in "wherein shall we return?"

(Verse 8-13) Malachi's answer to this sham is "will a man rob God?" When their response was again an assumed innocence expressed in, "wherein have we robbed thee," the prophet goes directly to the heart of the matter . . . *"in tithes and offerings."*

THE COMING DAY OF THE LORD 3:8-10

That they could answer in such false righteousness after what the prophet has written in the preceding chapters about their unholy sacrifices, is amazing. It is no more so than the assumed correctness of the "New Testament Christian" today whose sacrifices of himself is an hour or two on Sunday and whose giving of "tithes and offerings" consists of less than he spends for soft drinks and tobacco.

"Ye are cursed with a curse because ye rob me" declares Malachi *(v. 9).* Our own consciences may accept a cut-rate allegiance to God, but He will not. The country parson who said, "Salvation is free but it ain't cheap," spoke the truth!

There is a significant distinction drawn here between tithes and offerings. The law defined the first tithe as a tenth of all that was left *after* the first fruits were paid. This tenth went directly to the Levites for their support. *(Leviticus 27:30-33)* A tenth was to be paid in turn to the priests. *(Numbers 18:26-28)*

A second tithe was to be paid for the entertainment of the Levites and their own families at the temple. *(Deuteronomy 12:18)*

A third tithe was to be paid every third year for the welfare of the poor, etc. *(Deuteronomy 14:28)* It has been estimated that the total tithes amounted annually to approximately 27% of one's gross income.

The offerings were in addition to the tithes. These consisted of not less than 1/60 of one's corn, wine, and oil *(Deuteronomy 18:4, Nehemiah 13:10-12).*

So the Israelite under the Old Covenant gave in three categories. (1) He sacrificed the first fruits of his fields and flocks (2) he tithed three times, first of all remaining after the sacrifices, second for the entertainment (expenses) of the Levites and thirdly for the sake of supporting the poor, and (3) he then gave an offering of at least 1/60 of all his grain, wine and oil.

It was common, during the lean years, such as those which prevailed at the time of this writing, to neglect the tithes and offerings. Malachi, as we have seen, accuses his readers of also bringing much less than the first fruits for sacrifice.

Jehovah's challenge *(v. 10)* is to bring all the tithes (he whole tithe) into the storehouse and see if times do not change. Jesus would say, "seek ye first His kingdom and His righteousness, and all these things shall be added unto you." (cp. *Matthew 6:19-34)*

Here is the eternal principle of giving which continues from covenant to covenant. The support of the Lord's work must come *first* in the economic lives of His covenant people. He who gives only what he can afford has not given at all!

This passage, especially verses nine and ten, are frequently used to prove that one who does not give ten per cent of his income to the church is robbing God. Conversely, on the basis of these same verses, promises are frequently extended that "God will open the windows of Heaven" to those who practice "store-house tithing."

Before one makes such accusations or promises from these verses it would be wise to keep in mind several pertinent points concerning Mosaic tithing; (1) The tithes spoken of here had to do with the tithes of the fruit of the land, not wages *per se*. (2) These words are directed specifically to Judah because of the neglect of the ordinances of the law. (3) No *money* was involved. The tithe was a portion of the produce of an agrarian society. (4) The promise to "open the windows of heaven" has to do with rain which would end a drought and cause the land to again become productive when the people met the requirements of giving.

The principle taught, which must be learned by Christians, is stated by Jesus, not as a command to count one dollar of every ten into the offering, but to put the kingdom of God before the material necessities of life. (cf. *Matthew 6:33*) When this principle is applied to the giving of money, ten per cent seems a frightfully immature and inadequate amount, especially when those who "had witness borne to them through their faith, (even though they) received not the promise . . ." (*Hebrews 11:39*) were *required* to give 27% of all they produced on the land.

(Verses 11-12) Upon their return to faithfulness in tithes and offerings, God promised to remove the blight from the land. Whatever was organically wrong with the crops would be corrected. They had robbed God *(v. 8)* from the very first *(v. 7)*. They were now cursed *(v. 9)* with drought *(v. 10)*. The curse brought about by their dishonesty had taken two forms, drought and locusts *(v. 11)*. Their repentance would be the occasion of unmeasured blessing, blessing so great they would be the envy of surrounding nations. *(v. 12)*

God's provisions are always more than adequate to those who are honest in their dealings with Him.

WHEN THE DAY COMES, TRUE WORSHIPPERS WILL BE SPARED . . . Malachi 3:13—4:3

RV . . . Your words have been stout against me, saith Jehovah. Yet ye say, What have we spoken against thee? Ye have said, It is vain to serve God; and what profit is it that we have kept his charge, and that we have walked mournfully before Jehovah of hosts? and now we call the proud happy; yea, they that work wickedness are built up; yea, they tempt God, and escape. Then they that feared Jehovah spake one with another; and Jehovah hearkened, and heard, and a book of remembrance was written before him, for them that feared Jehovah, and that thought upon his name. And they shall be mine, saith Jehovah of hosts, even mine own possession, in the day that I make; and I will spare them, as a man spareth his own son that serveth him. Then shall ye return and discern between the righteous and the wicked between him that serveth God and him that serveth him not. For, behold, the day cometh, it burneth as a furnace; and all the proud, and all that work wickedness shall be stubble; and the day that cometh shall burn them up, saith Jehovah of hosts, that it shall leave them neither root nor branch. But unto you that fear my name shall the sun or righteousness arise with healing in its wings; and ye shall go forth, and gambol as calves of the stall. And ye shall tread down the wicked, for they shall be ashes under the soles of your feet in the day that I make, saith Jehovah of hosts.

LXX . . . Ye have spoken grievous words against me, saith the Lord. Yet he said, Wherein have we spoken against thee? Ye said, He that serves God labours in vain: and what have we gained in that we have kept his ordinances, and in that we have walked as suppliants before the face of the Lord Almighty? And now we pronounce strangers blessed; and all they who act unlawfully are built up; and they have resisted God, and yet have been delivered. Thus spoke they that feared the Lord, every one to his neighbour; and the Lord gave heed, and hearkened, and he wrote a book of remembrance before him for them that feared the Lord and reverenced his name. And they shall be mine, saith the Lord Almighty, in the day which I appoint for a peculiar possession; and I will make choice of them, as a man makes choice of his son that serves him. Then shall ye return, and discern between the righteous and the wicked, and between him that serves God, and him that serves him not. For, behold, a day comes burning as an oven, and it shall consume them; and all the aliens, and all that do wickedly, shall be stubble; and the day that is coming shall set them on fire, saith the Lord Almighty, and there shall not be left of them root or branch. But to you that fear my name shall the Sun of righteousness arise, and healing shall be in his wings: and ye shall go forth, and bound as young calves let loose from bonds. And ye shall trample

3:13-15   MALACHI

the wicked; for they shall be ashes underneath your feet in the day which I appoint, saith the Lord Almighty.

COMMENTS

(Verses 13-15) Malachi continues to list Jehovah's grievances against the people. They needed to return and they feigned unawareness of any such need (*v. 7*). They robbed God, yet pretended not to be aware of the robbing (*v. 8*). They have spoken against God, and again pretended innocence (*v. 13* cp. *2:17*).

The prophet continues to speak frankly, as he answers this latest question, "Ye have said, It is vain to serve God; and what profit is it that we keep his charge?"

Such complaining is not uncommon among those who cannot understand the spiritual nature of God's covenant. Those who see the covenant as a mercenary bargain, attend to outward observance in the hope of receiving material blessings. When such are not forthcoming, because they are at most incidental to God's purpose in His people, such worshippers are always disappointed and prone to despair.

God has never promised wealth to the faithful or poverty to the unjust. We manifest a gross ignorance of His nature and His love when we judge the worth of service to Him on such basis.

The evidence of this misunderstanding on the part of Malachi's readers is seen in the last part of verses fourteen and fifteen. They equate their sacrifice of blemished animals and the withholding of tithes and offerings out of concern for material necessities with "keeping His charge." They equate piety with walking "mournfully." They mistake pride for real happiness and complain that the wicked are better off than the rest. They accuse God, very subtly, of injustice because the wicked "tempt God and escape."

(Verses 16-18) Rather than continuing to rebuke their lack of perception, Malachi turns to words of comfort. He assures them the faithful will not be forgotten. They will be spared who are Godfearers, and ultimately made to understand the real difference between the righteous and the wicked.

A book of remembrance is being written he assures them, in which the names of the faithful were being recorded (cp. *Esther 6*). In the day when Jehovah acts, they will be spared His judgment and beyond this, they will be revealed as Jehovah's peculiar treasure. (cp. *John 3:18, I Peter 2:9*)

THE COMING DAY OF THE LORD 3:16—4:1

Even in dark times there are those few who fear Him and so "speak," *i.e.* converse with one another about Him.

THEY THAT FEARED JEHOVAH ... v. 16

Malachi foresees the repentance of some, though not all the people. They would speak with one another. No doubt their speaking would concern the need for repentance, for genuine worship. As always, the fear of Jehovah would prove the beginning of wisdom for Jehovah would hear and remember.

THEY SHALL BE MINE ... v. 17-18

Malachi's covenant consciousness is evident here. It is those who fear Jehovah and think on His name who are His people. No reference is made to religious ritual or racial origin.

Peter voiced this same conviction. Following the thrice repeated vision which convinced him to go to a non-Jewish home with the gospel, and the resultant demonstration of God's overwhelming approval of his action in the outpouring of the Holy Spirit, Peter exclaimed, "of a truth I perceive that God is no respecter of persons, but in every nation he that feareth Him and worketh righteousness, is acceptable to Him." *(Acts 11:34-35)* Paul confirms this same truth in *Romans 2:13,* "For not the hearers of the law are just before God, but the doers of the law shall be justified."

Malachi would have his readers understand this truth. In the days of Jehovah His people will be those who really serve.

BEHOLD, THE DAY COMETH ... 4:1

The association of fire with the final judgement is a theme which runs throughout much of the Scriptures. Daniel describes it vividly. *(Daniel 7:9-10)* The Psalmist sang of it. *(Psalm 1:3)* Peter affirms it at some length. *(II Peter 3:7-10)*

Malachi promises that those who feel this final fire will be without hope of springing again to life. They will be without branch or root. (See *Amos 2:9)*)

(Verse 2) The prophet does not, however, limit his vision of the coming day to that of doom. In contrast, he presents the effects of its coming on God's people. On those who fear His name the sun of righteousness shall rise with healing in its (His) wings..

Here is one of the most picturesque descriptions of the Messiah to be found in the Old Testament. To dissect it is to destroy it. Suffice

4:1-6   MALACHI

it to say, that as the sun is the light and source of life to all the earth, so the Christ is the light and giver of life to the true worshipper.

In the warmth of this sun of righteousness, God's people shall be as carefree as calves playing in the sunlight.

(Verse 3) When this day comes, and the wicked are punished by fire while God's people are freed from all care, the question of *3:15* will finally be answered.

Jesus' rehearsal of the fate of the rich man and Lazarus is a fine illustration of this truth. (cf. *Luke 16:19-ff)* The unrighteous rich who lord it over the righteous poor will, in that day, find their situations completely reversed . . . eternally and completely.

In our present day, when churches have become pre-occupied with alleviating the temporal needs of men, regardless of their spiritual condition, and when making a profit in business has become, to some, immoral regardless of the good that may be done with such wealth, the idea that the iniquities of this life will be rectified in the next is *passe* to some. In the presence of this spiritual blindness, God's people dare not lose sight of our obligation to be concerned for men's temporal needs in Jesus' name. (cf. *Matthew 25:31-46, I John 3:16-18)* But this concern can, by no form of logc, negate the coming day of judgement

Nor can such concern negate the fact that the injustices of wicked men who prey upon the righteous and deprive the weak obviously go unpunished here and now. Honesty, in business, is not always the "best policy" for those whose chief purpose is personal gain.

Just as surely as this is so, so does the justice of God demand a day of reckoning. For those who come to Christ, the day of reckoning was held on Calvary *(Romans 3:25-26)*. For those who do not fear God, the time of reckoning is yet to come and it will.

CONCLUSION . . . MALACHI 4:4-6

Remember ye the law of Moses my servant, which I commanded unto him in Horeb for all Israel, even statutes and ordinances. Behold, I will send you Elijah the prophet before the great and terrible day of Jehovah come. And he shall turn the heart of the fathers to the children, and the heart of the children to their fathers; lest I come and smite the earth with a curse.

LXX . . . And, behold, I will send to you Elias the Thesbite, before the great and glorious day of the Lord comes; who shall turn again the heart of the father to the son, and the heart of a man to his neighbour, lest I come and smite the earth grievously. Remember the law

THE COMING DAY OF THE LORD 4:4-6

of my servant Moses, accordingly as I charged him with it in Choreb for all Israel, even the commandments and ordinances.

COMMENTS

The Old Testament Scriptures close with a prophetic plea to God's people to remember the law of Moses. It would be some four hundred years before Jehovah would speak again. In the interim, if they are to survive as His people, the law must be remembered.

Special attention is called to the statutes, that is those portions of the law dealing with religious ceremony. These ceremonies, as we have seen, were designed to keep visually and tangibly before the people an object lesson of the coming Lamb of God. If they were to fall into disuse before He came, Calvary would indeed be hard to comprehend.

Fortunately, they did not fall into disuse. During the Maccabean period and shortly thereafter (c. 160 B.C.), the party known as the Pharisees came into being for the express purpose of maintaining the literal outward observances of the statutes governing the Mosaic ceremonies in worship. Regrettably the Pharisees became obsessed with the letter to the neglect of the spirit of these observnces, but they did, quite significantly, preserve the form.

In calling for remembrance of the law, Malachi does so in such a way as to provide the people one last term of its covenant meaning. The burden of the last Old Testament writer was delivered to a stiff-necked and rebellious people. They prided themselves on being Jehovah's people, but he bluntly declared, "I have no pleasure in you, saith Jehovah of hosts." *(Malachi 1:10)* They thought they could play fast and loose with God, but Malachi reminded them of the greatness of Him with Whom they had to do. *(Malachi 1:14)* In their faithlessness, Malachi reminds them of the covenant, and told them flatly they were breaking it. *(Malachi 2:1-9)* He despaired of the nation as a whole and of the race as a race. He foresaw the coming of a terrible day in which this proud and wicked people would be utterly consumed.

But the remnant would survive, made up of those who individually feared Jehovah *(Malachi 4:2)* and thought upon His name. That is, those who had come to understand the true character of the eternal God and His purpose for all men. *(Malachi 3:16)* These faithful would be spared *only because they had fulfilled God's covenant conditions* (cf. *Exodus 19:5-6*) laid down on Mount Horeb (Sinai). Those who were so spared would be God's true Israel; all the rest were doomed.

4:5, 6 MALACHI

Before the terrible day of the Lord, Elijah would come to once more call the remnant. His purpose would be the reconciliation of those present at his coming with the covenant faith of their fathers. Elijah, perhaps more than any other prophet of the pre-exilic period, had pled for a return to the pure worship of Jehovah as implemented in the law. The second Elijah would have the same purpose. Unless this be done, there would be not even a remnant in that day and the whole earth, which Jehovah had striven to redeem, would stand under a curse. The word "curse" (Hebrew *cherem*) means literally a *ban*.

Just as those Gentiles who had not the law and were ignorant of the covenant were without God and without hope in the world (cf. *Ephesians 2:12*), so, if the remnant were not finally called in preparation for the day of the Lord, the whole world would stand permanently alienated, banned forever from the presence of God.

The Old Testament is continuous with the New. The Bible is, in this sense, a single book. The coming of Christ did not constitute an abrupt break, but a fulfillment. The method and purpose of Jesus is a continuation and fulfillment of the method and purpose revealed in the call of Abraham. The new factor is the personal presence of the Messiah.

Malachi's promise of Elijah's coming is fulfilled in the ministry of John the Baptist. Jesus began where Malachi left off and *consciously* continued the work of the prophets. His ministry is understood only in light of God's plan to redeem all the world through a people prepared as the instrument of divine worldwide purpose. (cp. *Luke 24:44-47* and *Ephesians 1:23*)

Chapter XLV—*Questions*

The Coming Day of the Lord

1. What were the two arguments of the wicked priests?
2. What was God's answer to the questions, "Where is the God of justice?"
3. The New Testament applies *Malachi 3:1* to _____.
4. Relate the rabbinic interpretation of this verse to Jesus' temptations.
5. What is meant by Malachi's description of the Messiah as fullers' soap and refiner's fire?
6. When Messiah came He would testify against the _____, _____, _____, and against _____.
7. Comment on those "who turn aside the sojourner."

THE COMING DAY OF THE LORD

8. Discuss the proposition that, because God does not immediately smite the wicked, He is no longer a God of justice.
9. Note the similarity of *Malachi 3:7-12* to Stephen's defense *(Acts 7)*.
10. What is the eternal principle presented in these passages?
11. How were Malachi's readers robbing God?
12. What is the distinction between tithes and offerings?
13. What were the first, second and third tithes required by the Law?
14. The offering consisted of not less than _____ of one's corn, wine and oil.
15. The Israelites were commanded to give in thre categories: _____, _____, and _____.
16. How does Jesus express the thought of *Malachi 3:10?*
17. Is this passage a valid proof text for modern "store house tithing?"
18. List four pertinent points concerning Mosaic tithing.
19. When the principles of stewardship presented by Malachi is applied to modern giving, ten per cent seems. _____.
20. What is meant by the promise of Malachi that God would "open the windows of heaven?"
21. God's provisions are always adequate to those who _____.
22. Not only have Malachi's readers robbed God, they have _____ _____.
23. God has never promised _____ to the faithful nor _____ to the unjust.
24. The people equated the sacrifice of blemished animals and withholding of tithes and offerings with _____.
25. A book of _____ is being written.
26. To whom does "they shall be mine" *(Malachi 3:17-18)* refer?
27. Discuss *Malachi 3:17-18* in comparison to *Acts 11:34-35*.
28. Trace the association of fire with judgement.
29. The sun of righteousness shall _____.
30. The wicked are to be punished by fire while God's people are freed from _____.
31. Does the unequal distribution of wealth negate the necessity of righteousness?
32. The justice of God demands a _____.
33. The Old Testament closes with a plea to God's people to _____ _____.
34. Why was it essential that the formal observance of the sacrificial system be preserved?
35. The proud and wicked would be consumed but the _____ _____ would survive.

36. Who is the second Elijah?
37. How is the New Testament continuous with the Old?
38. What is the new factor in the New Testament not present in the Old?
39. The coming of Christ did not constitute an abrupt break but a _____
40. Approximately how much time lapsed between Malachi and Jesus?

BIBLIOGRAPHY

Abingdon Bible Commentary, Abingdon
Alouf, Michel M., *History of Baalbek*, Bouheiry Brothers, Beirut
Alles, Oswald T., *Prophecy and the Church*, Presbyterian and Reformed
Aref, Aref El, *The Dome of the Rock: The Supreme Awaquaf*, Council, Jerusalem
Baramki, D. C., *The Road To Petra*, Anton Nazzal & Sons, Amman, Jordan
Barclay, Wm., *Jesus As They Saw Him*, Harper & Bro.
Barclay, Wm., *Letters of James and Peter*, Westminster
Barclay, Wm., *The King and The Kingdom*, Westminster
Bennett, T. Miles, *The Books of Nahum and Zephaniah*, Baker
Bennett, T. Miles, *The Book of Micah*, Baker
Bright, John, *The Kingdom of God*, Abingdon
Butler, Paul T., *Minor Prophets*, College Press
Carver, W. O., *The Glory of God In The Christian Calling*, Broadman
Carver, W. O., *Missions In The Plan of The Ages*, Broadman
Conner, W. T., *Bible Doctrine*, Broadman
Crawford, C. C., *Genesis, Vol. I*, College Press
Davis, A. Powell, *The Meaning and Message of The Dead Sea Scrolls*, The New American Library
Demont, Max I., *Jews, God and History*, The New American Library
De Hann, M. R., *Coming Events*, Zondervan
Durant, Will, *Our Oriental Heritage*, Simon & Schuster
Durant, Will, *The Life of Greece*, Simon & Schuster
Duty, Guy, *God's Covenants and Our Time*, Bethany Fellowship
Eadie, John, *Eadie's Biblical Cyclopaedia*, Charles Griffin & Company, Ltd., London
Eason, J. Lawrence, *Bible Survey*, Zondervan
Earle, Robert, *The Minor Prophets*, Nazarene Publishing House
Grant, Michael, *Myths of the Greeks and Romans*, The New American Library
Harris, Maurice, *The Story of the Jew*, Bloch Publishing Co.
Halley, *Halley's Bible Handbook*: Zondervan
Henry, Matthew, *Commentary on The Whole Bible*, Vol. IV, Fleming-H. Revell Co.
Hislop, Alexander, *The Two Babylons*, Louizeaux Brothers
Keyes, Nelson Beecher, *Story of The Bible World, The*, Readers Digest Association
Kirkbride, B. B., *New Chain Reference Bible*, B. B. Kirkbride Bible Co. Inc.
Lange, John P., *Commentary on the Holy Scriptures*, Zondervan
Larkin, Clarence, *Dispensational Truth*, Rev. Clarence Larkin Est., Philadelphia
Levin, Meyer and Kuerzband, T. K., *The Story of The Synagogue*, (Jewish Heritage Series) Bekrman House, Inc.

MINOR PROPHETS

Lewis, Jack P., *The Minor Prophets*, Baker
Jamison, Fawsett, & Brown, *Commentary on the Whole Bible*, Zondervan
Maddox, Roy Clark, *The Prophets In Outline*, Baker
Mauro, Phillip, *The Gospel of The Kingdom*, Malloy
May, Herbert G. and Metzger, Bruce, *Oxford Annotated Bible*, Oxford University Press
Morgan, G. Campbell, *Analyzed Bible*, Revell
McGarvey, J. W., *Lands of the Bible*, Standard
Necall, W. Robertson, *The Expositors Greek Testament*, Vol. II, Eerdman
Pentecost, Dwight, J., *Things To Come*, Dunham Pub. Co.
Pfeiffer, Charles F., *The Wycliff Historical Geography of Bible Lands*, Moody Press
Phillips, J. B., *Four Prophets*, MacMillan
Pusey, E. B., *The Minor Prophets, A Commentary*, Vols. I and II, Baker Book House
Redding, M. Wolcott, *Antiquities of the Orient*, Redding & Co.
Robertson, A. T., *Word Pictures In The New Testament*, Vols. 4 and 5, Broadman
Ross, Floyd H. and Hills, Tynette, *The Great Religions*, Fawcett World Library
Smith, Wilbur M., *Israel/Arab Conflict and The Bible*, Regal, G/L
Smith, Wm., *Dictionary of the Bible*, S. S. Scranton
Smith, William, *Old Testament History*, (Revised by W. Fields) College Press
Turnbull, Ralph G., *The Kingdoms of Israel and Judah*, Baker Book House
Wheaton, Wm., *Josephus*, Kregel Publishers
Wolff, Richard, *The Book of Haggai*, Baker
Young, Robert, *Analytical Concordance To The Bible*, Wm. B. Eerdman Publishing Co.
Amplified Bible, Zondervan Publishing House
Encylopaedia Brittanica, Encylopaedia Brittanica Inc.
Everyday Life In Bible Times, National Geographic Society
International Standard Bible Encyclopaedia, Vols. 1-5, Wm. B. Eerdman's Publishing Co.
New English Bible With Apocrypha, Oxford University Press
New Schofield Reference Edition, Oxford University Press
Six Thousand Years of History, Vol. I, E. R. DuMont Publishers
Westminster Study Bible, Collins Clear Type Press

NORTH-EASTERN FACADE AND GRAND ENTRANCE

Careful investigations on the actual site have resulted in this restoration of Sennacherib's palace, from a sketch by J. Fergusson. The building is very different from the heavier structure erected by his father, Sargon II., at Khorsabad and a greater knowledge of the artistic processes which led to this revolution would go far to make the past live for us.